The Empire of the French

*A Chronology of the Revolutionary and
Napoleonic Wars 1792–1815*

THE EMPIRE OF THE FRENCH

A CHRONOLOGY OF THE REVOLUTIONARY AND NAPOLEONIC WARS 1792–1815

by

Brian Taylor

SPELLMOUNT

British Library Cataloguing in Publication Data:
A catalogue record for this book is available
from the British Library

Copyright © Brian Taylor 2006
Maps copyright © Spellmount Ltd 2006

ISBN 1-86227-254-9

First published in the UK in 2006 by
Spellmount Ltd
The Mill, Brimscombe Port
Stroud, Gloucestershire. GL5 2QG

Tel: 01453 883300
Fax: 01453 883233
Website: www.spellmount.com

1 3 5 7 9 8 6 4 2

Printed in Great Britain by
Oaklands Book Services
Stonehouse, Gloucestershire GL10 3RQ

Contents

List of Maps

Preface

Between 1792 and 1815 there raged across Europe the longest period of almost continuous conflict the continent had experienced. The fighting can be divided into two distinct periods: the wars of the French Revolution, which saw the full resources of the French state mobilised into citizen armies to defend their liberty but against a backdrop of terror within France, and the Napoleonic Wars, when Napoleon Bonaparte attempted, successfully until 1812, to impose his will upon the peoples of Europe and expand the borders of France, and French influence, in all possible directions.

The battles that characterised these two periods differed only in so much as Napoleon brought to his wars a professionalism in the commitment of mass armies which the Revolutionary generals had been unable to exert, although through the activities of Lazare Carnot, the French Minister of War, they managed to consolidate the old Royalist army with the new citizen body. Though Napoleon's military ability was unquestionably great, he was not an innovator, he simply perfected the co-ordination of the various arms of the army, together with the efficient functioning of an army staff unit. Faced with the new model French army, her enemies were met with a stark choice: either continue in their old style and face repeated defeat, or copy the French model and bring numbers to bear. The refusal of the Allied powers to learn this lesson quickly was a major factor in the longevity of the conflict, which surged back and forth across Europe for a quarter of a century.

This work is written in a clear chronological style and aims to give the reader an understanding of the sheer scale and breadth of the wars that flowed across Europe during the quarter century following the Revolution. It also aims to give a picture of the constraints placed upon military operations at the turn of the 18th century, from the movement of major formations across territory largely devoid of metalled roads, to the different solutions to supplying the increasingly large armies fielded by the respective combatants. It also demonstrates the clear periods of brilliance shown by Napoleon during his heyday, and the importance of timing and the accidental nature of some of the most influential battles of the period (Marengo being a prime example).

The account is divided into *fronts* for ease of reference, readers being able, if they wish, to concentrate on the actions of a particular campaign or region, or alternatively, to follow the campaigns across all *fronts* simultaneously. The *fronts* are generally titled according to their geographical area of operations. For example, the Allied and French campaigns of 1792–3 were largely conducted in the Austrian Netherlands, so the actions during these campaigns fall within the category *Belgian Front* for the campaigns in the Low Countries but *Prussian Offensive* when referring to Brunswick's reluctant invasion of France which led up to the Battle of Valmy. I have referred to the large campaigns of the Napoleonic period in a similar manner, the long and bloody conflict in Spain and Portugal being covered under *Iberian Front*, while Napoleon's campaigns of 1806 and 1807 come under the aegis of the *German Front* initially, then *Polish Front* as the fighting spread to the east. The various peace treaties and armistices that were agreed and broken throughout this period are found under *International Politics*. This section is placed regularly throughout the text as Napoleon's political ambitions were tied intimately with his military actions. His continual humiliation of defeated enemies meant that the European powers would try time and again to prevent his domination of the continent, and lead Europe into almost continuous conflict.

Throughout the reader will find summaries on the composition of the opposing combatants' armed forces. Where possible, every effort has been made to include the deployment of forces prior to major campaigns and the deployment of armies during major battles. To provide a rounded picture, army strengths and casualties are also recounted when known. During this period the armed forces of the combatants underwent major development, the use of divisional and corps structures developed by Napoleon later being adopted by the Allies. For the most part, the various contingents of respective armies are referred to by their commander's name primarily, and their military designation second. For example, when detailing the actions undertaken by the French III Corps at Auerstadt in 1806, it is by the name of their commander, Marshal Davout, that they are referred to.

The perspective of the text is taken neither from the French nor the Allied angle, but rather seeks to offer factual detail on all combatants during their campaigns. It is difficult not to be awed by the brilliance of such generals as Napoleon or Wellington during the height of their careers, but emotive language has been avoided wherever possible.

As with my other works, this book does not aim to record the many individual soldiers' accounts of the Revolutionary and Napoleonic Wars; these have been covered in excellent detail by many authors. Instead, it aims to provide a commentary, or reference, on the wars as a whole, to put the fighting across Europe into its proper context and in some way, hopefully, to enable the reader to gain an understanding of the impact a quarter century of war had upon Europe.

CHAPTER I

An Introduction to the French Revolution

With massive population growth, rising rates of unemployment, failed harvests bringing about shortages of basic foods and virtual state bankruptcy brought about by French financing of the American Revolutionary Wars, France appeared ripe for Revolution in the closing decades of the 18th century. However, to assess the full reasons behind the Revolution would be a work in its own right. In order to follow the military impact of the Revolution we will look first at the states that fought the Revolutionary wars and then follow the events in France that brought Europe to the brink.

The European States on the Eve of the French Revolution

At the beginning of the Revolutionary period, the population of Europe was around 180,000,000, almost double what it had been just over half a century before. This massive population growth had brought about a new phenomenon, mass unemployment and the movement of large numbers of peasants from the land to the rapidly growing cities. Such a gathering, combined with hunger, proved a breeding ground for civil unrest. However, it was in France that this unrest led to open rebellion, as the old regime struggled to contain the growing voice of the masses.

Before we study the events of the Revolution, and the conflicts that followed, we should first take a brief look at each of the principal nations involved.

Britain, the most protracted protagonist that would face the French, had a population of just over 10,000,000 at the end of the 18th century and was well along the road to industrialisation, leading not only Europe but the world in her technological achievements. Britain and her empire proved to be the bankers for the enemies of Revolutionary France, financing the many coalitions that would be formed during the quarter century of the wars. However, Britain was rent by periodic social disorders, although not on the scale to be experienced by France.

Ireland, Britain's reluctant neighbour, had a population of around 5,000,000. She was ripe for rebellion against British rule and would prove an early target for the export of republicanism from France. However, Irish efforts at independence from the British would during this period remain unfulfilled.

Unlike the continental powers, Britain was governed by a constitutional rather than absolutist monarchy, and real authority rested with her Parliament, albeit without universal manhood suffrage. The British army was small compared to its continental counterparts, being just 50,000 strong. Britain's strength lay in two main areas, her overwhelming financial might and her powerful navy, both of which would inflict crippling blows upon the French in one form or another.

Russia, the most populous nation in Europe with 38,000,000 inhabitants, was ruled by the unpopular Tsar Paul I, son of Catherine the Great. The Russian Kingdom remained essentially a feudal one, her soldiers being raised from uneducated but hardy serfs. Russian soldiers were to prove implacable in the face of battle, but her officer corps, staffed either by the largely incompetent Russian nobility, or not altogether trusted foreigners, was badly organised and lacked flexibility in battle. The army numbered around 400,000 men at the beginning of the Revolutionary period. Western Europe though was only one of the many theatres which the Russian Empire committed itself too. There was an ongoing struggle with the Ottomans for control of the Balkans and Caucasus, and the ever present threat of Austria and Prussia against her western marches. Poland continued to be a focus for Russian interests, the partitions of 1772 and 1793 netting the Russians additional territory.

France, a densely populated state for the time with a citizen body of some 28,000,000, was the largest country in the west of Europe. Her monarchs ruled largely without redress to the Estates, but such a system demanded a strong monarch, which Louis XIV had been but crucially, Louis XVI, who came to the throne in 1774, would prove not to be. The industrial Revolution sweeping Britain had not reached France yet. The French army of 255,000 men was highly developed and her navy, though numerically strong, was in decline. Civil disorder, brought about by poor harvests and a punitive taxation system, was on the increase. Taxation was used in order to try and recoup the massive financial cost of the American Revolution which the French had borne. France had agreed to support the Americans in their fight for independence in 1776, supplying troops, arms and financial support from 1778 onwards, little knowing that their actions would lead to the demise of their own state in no more than two decades. The troubles in France need not necessarily have ended in Revolution had a stronger monarch been on the throne. However, history was to take a different course, changing not just France but all of Europe.

Prussia, the largest and most powerful of the German states, had a population of 9,000,000 and an army of 200,000 which, following the

Seven Years War, was believed to be one of the most highly trained, drilled and disciplined armies in Europe. However, King Frederick William III proved, during the early years of his reign, to be a fairly indecisive and weak monarch. Furthermore, the strict controls placed upon the army prevented it from requisitioning at will, when required, from the civil populace. This meant that during campaigns in their own land, the Prussian troops were poorly supplied due to a lack of produce that could be taken from the land, and when in action in foreign countries, were reliant upon an inadequate supply chain rather than upon forage.

Spain, one of the richest kingdoms of Europe due to the flow of wealth from her American provinces, was racked by factionalism at court, a weak king being dominated by a strong chief minister, Manuel de Godoy. Her zealously religious population stood at 10,500,000. The Spanish army was in a terrible state, her notoriously corrupt officer corps setting a poor example to the rest.

The Austrian Empire had a population of some 27,000,000 and dominated central Europe, proving a bastion between Europe and the Ottoman Turks in the Balkans. Intense rivalries existed between the Austrians, Prussians and Russians, all of whom aimed to gain control of Poland, which had been carved up between them time and again. Austria's greatest weakness was the diversity of her population, dominated by Germans in the north and west, Hungarians in the east and various Balkan nationalities. The Hapsburg monarch was not only Emperor of his own people but also head of the Holy Roman Empire, and as such had great influence upon the German states. Austria also possessed the Netherlands as a major province in the west, although it too was rocked by revolt in 1789, a United States of Belgium being declared by the rebels in January 1790.

The Austrian army was 300,000 strong and fairly well trained. Officer grades were dominated by the nobility, as were those of many other nations at this time, but they led the army to a reasonable degree of professionalism. Austria was to prove to be France's most implacable continental enemy, coming back time and again despite defeat in the field. It was her reluctance to embrace the full breadth of military reforms required that enabled the French to beat them repeatedly, yet her resilience and determination thwarted Napoleonic efforts to dominate central Europe until 1809.

As diverse as Europe was, it was events in France that would lead the continent into war, and it is to these events that we now turn. Much of the following text recounts the political and social events that led to the Revolution and are not strictly within the scope of a military history. However, in order to understand what led the continent into conflict, we must understand the basic reasons why the Revolution occurred, and its impact upon not only the people and armies of France, but also on her neighbours.

* 1786 *

August 1786
FRANCE: POLITICS
Comptroller General Charles Alexandre de Calonne, faced with impending state bankruptcy, proposed a number of reforms to Louis XVI in order to stabilise the civil situation in the face of failed harvests and popular discontent. The proposals included a change in land taxation to include the nobility and clergy, in order to raise additional revenue, a reform of other forms of taxation and the abolition of internal tariffs. Rather than present the reforms to the Paris Parlement, which usually rejected them in the name of historic liberty, Calonne persuaded the king to convoke the Assembly of the Notables.

* 1787 *

22 February 1787
FRANCE: POLITICS
The Assembly of the Notables convened. They were a collection of 144 representatives from all of the Estates from across France. Calonne's proposals to raise taxation were put forward but met with a lack of agreement. Louis agreed to make further concessions but without any great success.

March 1787
FRANCE: CIVIL UNREST
Unrest in Paris grew as the populace protested against rising food prices and the efforts of Calonne to enforce a solution to France's fiscal difficulties.

8 April 1787
FRANCE: POLITICS
Calonne, having fled Paris for London in fear for his life, was dismissed from office. His dismissal was one of the concessions the king had made on 22 February.

30 April 1787
FRANCE: POLITICS
Etienne Charles de Comenie de Brienne joined the government, appointed by Louis XVI to replace Calonne as Comptroller General of Finances. He proposed that Calonne's reforms be enacted.

25 May 1787
FRANCE: POLITICS
Despite having made a number of concessions, the Assembly of the Notables refused to endorse Brienne's reform proposals and demanded that the Estates General be convened. The king therefore dissolved the Assembly.

July 1787
FRANCE: POLITICS
Brienne called for the Parlement of Paris to recognise the tax reforms proposed by Calonne, which had been adopted by his administration. They predictably refused and demanded that the Estates General be convened.

The Church and its clergy, constituting the First Estate, accounted for around 150,000 of France's population and were exempt from most of the taxes levied throughout the country. The nobility, forming the Second Estate, consisted of around 350,000 people and also managed to avoid a large part of the tax burden. By far the heaviest load was borne by the Third Estate, the commons. Constituting some 98% of the population they had limited voting rights due to a system established in favour of the First and Second Estates. This system allowed the Estates to vote as groups, therefore the First and Second Estates, comprising two votes, could outvote the Third Estate's single vote.

14 August 1787
FRANCE: POLITICS
Louis, in response to the refusal of the Parlement of Paris to adopt Brienne's reforms and the demand for the convocation of the Estates General, exiled the Parlement to Troyes.

28 September 1787
FRANCE: POLITICS
Following widespread popular protests after the exile of the Parlement, Brienne modified his proposals, effectively enabling the nobles and clergy to avoid the burden of the new taxation. The Parlement was allowed to return to Paris.

* 1788 *

8 May 1788
FRANCE: POLITICS
Brienne introduced the May Edicts in an effort to push through his reforms without approval. The Parlement protested but was dismissed by Louis. Riots and civil unrest broke out as a result.

June–July 1788
FRANCE: POLITICS
The nobles and clergy revolted against the May Edicts and also began to call upon the king to convoke the Estates General.

7 June 1788
FRANCE: CIVIL UNREST
King Louis' attempts to suppress the Parlement of Grenoble resulted in riots in the city, which became known as the Day of Tiles due to the populace hurling slates at the king's troops as they moved through the streets. Large-scale civil unrest was spreading throughout France as Louis attempted to regain authority, sparking the embers of the Revolution that would eventually sweep the country.

8 August 1788
FRANCE: POLITICS
With the nobility and clergy acting against him, the king finally caved in and agreed to the convocation of the Estates General. The Estates had not met since 1614. The Parlements were attempting to prove that the king's actions constituted despotism and believed the Estates would aid their process. The Estates General was convoked for May 1789.

16 August 1788
FRANCE: ECONOMY
Partial state bankruptcy was declared and payments from the Treasury suspended. France was approaching collapse.

24–26 August 1788
FRANCE: POLITICS
Brienne was forced to resign and the Protestant Swiss banker, Jacques Necker, was appointed Chief Minister and Director of Finances.

25 September 1788
FRANCE: POLITICS
Parlement was restored. The Paris Parlement demanded the 'forms of 1614' for the meeting of the Estates General. This would enable the three Estates to sit separately and each Estate would cast one block vote, allowing the First and Second Estates, which were generally in agreement, to outvote the Third in order to protect their interests. Public reaction was fierce as the commons realised what the first two Estates planned. The demand for voting by head began to be heard.

5 October–12 December 1788
FRANCE: POLITICS
The Second Assembly of the Notables took place to determine the compo-

sition of the Estates General membership. Despite their advice, the king decided to double the size of the members representing the Third Estate but did not clarify upon what grounds voting would take place, by Estate or head.

27 December 1788
FRANCE: POLITICS
Louis clarified that voting in the Estates would be by order, rather than by head, thereby negating the increase in the size of the Third Estate.

* 1789 *

24 January 1789
FRANCE: POLITICS
Regulations for the Estates General were agreed.

February–June 1789
FRANCE: POLITICS
Elections to the Estates General were held.

27–28 April 1789
FRANCE: CIVIL UNREST
There were riots in Paris against the entrepreneurs Reveillon and Henriot.

5 May 1789
FRANCE: POLITICS
The Estates General was convened at Versailles. It was decided that voting would be by order rather than by head, disadvantaging the larger Third Order. To decide their votes, each of the three Estates would meet separately.

6 May 1789
FRANCE: POLITICS
Delegates from the Third Estate refused to meet as a separate group. They began to call themselves 'The Commons'. The Estates General was unable to proceed any further until the issue of separate voting had been decided.

10 June 1789
FRANCE: POLITICS
The Third Estate voted for common verification of credentials, so that all of the Estates could vote as one body rather than separately. Members of the other Estates were invited to join the Third.

13 June 1789
FRANCE: POLITICS
The first parish priests broke ranks with the 'establishment' and joined the Commons.

17 June 1789
FRANCE: POLITICS
A National Assembly was proposed by the Abbé Sieyes and proclaimed by the Third Estate. Following the defection of a number of members of the clergy, it constituted around half of the members of the Estates General. The king failed to act against this alarming development.

20 June 1789
FRANCE: POLITICS
On the orders of the king, the National Assembly was locked out of its meeting area and convened in a disused tennis court. Suspecting a despotic plot to overcome them, the members of the Assembly swore not to disperse until a constitution had been ratified. This declaration became known as the Tennis Court Oath.

23 June 1789
FRANCE: POLITICS
Louis could not decide how to react to the National Assembly, his continued demand for a vote by Order being consistently refused by the Third Estate. After issuing his proposals to the Estates once more, he ordered them to adjourn. The members of the Third refused.

27 June 1789
FRANCE: POLITICS
The Three Estates united, the union being reluctantly accepted by Louis. His continual loss of face and authority gave further strength to the Assembly, which managed to force the monarch to agree to voting by head rather than by Order.

1 July 1789
FRANCE: REVOLUTION
Unnerved by the unrest in the Estates, over the previous week Louis had ordered the concentration of 20,000 troops around Paris.

2 July 1789
FRANCE: REVOLUTION
There were demonstrations at the Palais-Royal against the continuing build up of Royal troops around Paris.

9 July 1789
FRANCE: REVOLUTION
The National Assembly proclaimed itself the Constituent National Assembly, its primary aim being the writing and establishment of a national constitution.

11 July 1789
FRANCE: REVOLUTION
The popular Chief Minister, Jacques Necker, was dismissed from his post and replaced by the reactionary Breteuil. Louis ordered Necker to leave France immediately.

12 July 1789
FRANCE: CIVIL UNREST
Word of Necker's sacking reached Paris. The populace feared that the troops surrounding Paris were about to attack and forcibly disperse the National Assembly. Looting began and the seriously outnumbered police were unable to enforce order. During the afternoon, troops marched to the Tuileries to disperse the crowd but were set upon by the mob and had to withdraw.

13 July 1789
FRANCE: REVOLUTION
There were now 30,000 troops around Paris but chaos reigned in the city. The National Assembly voted for the formation of a militia to restore order. Hundreds volunteered. Mobs began to assault the prisons and set free the inmates, who were generally wrongly believed to be victims of monarchical suppression.

14 July 1789
FRANCE: REVOLUTION
The mob continued to rampage through Paris. People raided the Invalides and seized the arms, some 3,000 muskets and some cannon, watched by troops who had no orders to stop them. Another crowd moved towards the Bastille, believing that it held a huge store of gunpowder. After the Governor, the Marquis de Launey, refused to hand over the fortress to the militia, the crowd stormed it. After a brief struggle, which cost the lives of more than one hundred people, de Launey surrendered and the crowd seized control, freeing the seven prisoners who had been held inside. While marching away the mob murdered the unfortunate Governor.

16 July 1789
FRANCE: REVOLUTION
Reacting to the popular discontent, Louis recalled Necker and withdrew his troops from around Paris.

17 July 1789
FRANCE: REVOLUTION
Despite the continued disturbances in Paris, the king returned from Versailles to the city, where he was received by the newly elected mayor, Jean Sylvian Bailly. Remaining popular with the crowd, which chanted 'Long Live the Nation', Louis donned the blue and red national ribbon on his hat and further increased his popularity by legalising the newly created militia. The militia was the basis of the National Guard. It was to be commanded by the Marquis de Lafayette.

End July 1789
FRANCE: REVOLUTION
The Great Fear spread throughout the countryside as the populace thought the aristocrats would use armed force to regain control of the state.

4–10 August 1789
FRANCE: REVOLUTION
Over the course of a week of fierce proclamations from the Assembly, starting during the night of 4 August, the systems of feudalism, tithes, taxes, compulsory labour on the roads and aristocratic privileges were abolished.

14 August 1789
FRANCE: REVOLUTION
The renunciations of 4 August were codified, although the official tax burden upon the peasantry did not ease significantly. In reality though, many people stopped paying what they felt were unfair taxes. The National Assembly now turned its attentions to providing a written constitution for France.

26 August 1789
FRANCE: REVOLUTION
The Declaration of the Rights of Man and the Citizen were published and adopted by the Assembly. It formed the preamble to the proposed written constitution. King Louis refused to sign the document and the Spanish Inquisition condemned it.

10 September 1789
FRANCE: REVOLUTION
After debate regarding the composition of the legislature, a second chamber was rejected. The National Assembly would be the governing body, supposedly responsible to the king but in reality increasingly independent.

11 September 1789
FRANCE: REVOLUTION
The king's suspensive veto was agreed. This allowed the king to suspend issues for the period of the legislative body.

5–6 October 1789
FRANCE: REVOLUTION
Louis XVI and the Royal family were forced to move from Versailles to the Tuileries Palace in Paris. A crowd of 20,000 people, mainly women, had marched from Paris to Versailles to protest about the economic hardships, such as the lack of food, affecting the populace. The king now effectively became a prisoner of the events happening in Paris. The Assembly also moved from Versailles to a meeting place close to the Tuileries.

24 October 1789
AUSTRIAN NETHERLANDS: REVOLUTION
Belgian patriots rose in revolt against the Austrians. A rebel army quickly formed around Breda under the command of a former officer of the Austrian army, Van der Meersch.

27 October 1789
AUSTRIAN NETHERLANDS: REVOLUTION
Belgian patriot forces under Van der Meersch defeated the Austrians in battle at Tournhout. The Austrians began to withdraw their forces to Luxembourg.

2 November 1789
FRANCE: REVOLUTION
Church property was nationalised and the resulting revenue used in an effort to settle France's national debt. The state took over responsibility for poor relief and public worship. Bishop Talleyrand had advocated the confiscation of church property by the state.

December 1789
FRANCE: ARMED FORCES
The army abolished corporal punishment to maintain discipline. The use of firing squads for capital offences, or transfer to penal units, was still allowed.

9 December 1789
FRANCE: POLITICS
The Assembly began the reorganisation of France into departments.

* 1790 *

January 1790
FRANCE: REVOLUTION
A radical political club began to meet at a former Jacobin monastery in Paris. The organisation took the name 'Jacobins'.

11 January 1790
AUSTRIAN NETHERLANDS: REVOLUTION
Belgian rebels proclaimed independence from Austria, declaring themselves to be the United States of Belgium.

11 June 1790
FRANCE: REVOLUTION
There was a popular Revolutionary uprising in Avignon as the Papal Administration was expelled. The city petitioned for a reunion with France.

19 June 1790
FRANCE: POLITICS
The titles of the hereditary nobility were abolished.

12 July 1790
FRANCE: REVOLUTION
The Civil Constitution of the Clergy was established. The Catholic Church in France was reorganised as a branch of the state, opening a breach with the Papacy. Bishops now had to be elected and all clergy swore an oath to uphold the national constitution.

14 July 1790
FRANCE: REVOLUTION
The Festival of Federation took place on the Champ de Mars to mark the first anniversary of the storming of the Bastille.

10 August 1790
FRANCE: POLITICS
Authority over the French military passed to the National Assembly.

September 1790
PRUSSIA: POLITICS
The Prussians sent an envoy to Austria to seek an alliance. It was proposed that Austria take French Flanders, and Prussia the duchies of Julich and Berg. The rulers of the latter two duchies would be compensated with grants of land in Alsace.

20 November 1790
FRANCE: POLITICS
King Louis began to seek the assistance of other European monarchs to help him regain his Kingship. Louis secretly instructed his ex-foreign minister to ascertain if any other states would be willing to intervene against the Revolutionary government.

3 December 1790
AUSTRIAN NETHERLANDS: REVOLUTION
The Austrians had advanced into Belgium against the rebels and occupied Brussels. The rebellion began to fall apart.

* 1791 *

FRANCE: ARMED FORCES
As the effects of the anti-establishment Revolution spread throughout all levels of French society, the armed forces began to be affected. Aristocratic infantry regiment titles were abolished and numbered regiments created. The composition of regimental units was also formalised. Each battalion within a regiment was set at eight fusilier companies and a grenadier company. Ranks were also renamed, a colonel becoming chef de battalion. The old titles were deemed to have aristocratic connotations. In the spring the Revolutionary regime raised 169 volunteer battalions of National Guards from the existing provincial militias. Their quality was mixed, discipline proving to be a problem.

The infantry of the French army were divided into what became known as the Blues and the Whites. The Whites were regiments of the former Royalist army, who, as the name suggests, wore a white uniform. The Blues were newly created Republican units of National Guards and volunteers. The Whites were the better soldiers, being well disciplined and experienced in combat, while the Blues were at times no better than an unruly mob but were fired by a Revolutionary zeal which was in some cases to prove decisive in battle.

The French navy was in a terrible state, its officer corps having been purged of monarchists. There was also a dire manpower shortage, France having barely enough recruits to man even half of the seventy-six ships of the line in her fleet. Due to the shortages of men, the condition of the French warships deteriorated as essential maintenance was neglected.

11 January 1791
AUSTRIAN NETHERLANDS: REVOLUTION
Austrian forces recaptured Liège as the Belgian revolt was largely quelled. Radical agitation would continue from across the French border.

February 1791
FRANCE: ARMED FORCES
General Kellermann was appointed commander of the Army on the Upper Rhine and later, of the Army on the Lower Rhine.

2 March 1791
FRANCE: REVOLUTION
The Assembly abolished all guilds.

4 March 1791
FRANCE: ARMED FORCES
The provincial militia was officially reformed as the National Guard. It had been acting in this capacity since 1789.

10 March 1791
INTERNATIONAL POLITICS
Pope Pius VI condemned the Civil Constitution of the Clergy in France. French political actions had removed from the Papacy the power to appoint ministers.

April 1791
INTERNATIONAL POLITICS
Pope Pius VI issued a Papal Bull threatening to excommunicate those rebel elements of the French clergy, naming Talleyrand in particular. Over the coming months he became more verbal, calling upon other European monarchs to come to Louis XVI's aid against the Assembly.

14 June 1791
FRANCE: POLITICS
Workers' unions and strikes were prohibited throughout France under the Le Chapelier Law.

20–22 June 1791
FRANCE: REVOLUTION
The French Royal family attempted to flee from Paris in order to organise the forces opposing the National Assembly outside the capital. The Assembly duly issued a warrant throughout France for the apprehension of the Royal family. They were successfully captured at Varennes and, as news of their flight spread, the reputation of the monarchy as protectors of the French people was irreparably damaged, giving rise to a massive surge in republicanism.

5 July 1791
INTERNATIONAL POLITICS
Leopold II of Austria appealed to the monarchs of Europe to restore the

liberty of the French Royal family. The 'Padua Circular' proposed an alliance of Britain, Austria, Prussia, Russia and Spain against the French Revolution and laid down the objective of the Allies' cause, the full restoration of King Louis to his powers.

17 July 1791
FRANCE: CIVIL UNREST
The National Guard, on the orders of Lafayette, fired on a crowd meeting to support the Cordeliers Club demand that the king be placed on trial. The club was also petitioning for a republican government. During the exchanges, fifty civilians were killed. The incident became known as the Champ de Mars Massacre and served to damage the reputation of the hitherto popular Lafayette. From here on he gradually withdrew his support for the Cordeliers.

25 July 1791
INTERNATIONAL POLITICS
A preliminary convention was signed between Austria and Prussia in Vienna.

2 August 1791
INTERNATIONAL POLITICS
The Declaration of Pillnitz was issued. King Frederick William II of Prussia and Emperor Leopold II of Austria and the Holy Roman Empire declared their willingness to co-operate with any European monarchs who aimed to restore the French king to his rightful position. Russia and Sweden half-heartedly agreed to provide armed support but Britain declined, having no wish to help out the king who had acted against them during the American Revolution.

17 August 1791
FRANCE: POLITICS
Frenchmen abroad were summoned by the Assembly to return to their homeland within one month. The Assembly had begun to raise forces on its borders in response to the Declaration of Pillnitz.

5 September 1791
FRANCE: POLITICS
The Assembly finished writing its constitution.

18 September 1791
FRANCE: POLITICS
Louis, completely cowed following his abortive flight to Varennes, promised to uphold the newly written constitution. The National Assembly proclaimed its own abolition for the end of the month and the creation

of the Legislative Assembly as France became a constitutional monarchy. Louis retained the power of veto.

1 October 1791
FRANCE: POLITICS
The new Legislative Assembly came into being. It was divided into distinct, though not rigidly organised, political groups. The first of these groups was the constitutional monarchists who continued to support the role of the king. It included people such as Lafayette and Dumas. The second group comprised the advocates of a republic, these being the Jacobins and Cordeliers. The republicans had the support of an extremist newspaper, run by Maximilien Robespierre. Between the two extremes of monarchists and republicans were the moderate republicans, most of who came from the Gironde region. At first they were known as the Brissotins after their foremost member, Jacques Brissot but were later to become known as the Girondins.

20 October 1791
FRANCE: POLITICS
Brissot made his first speech on foreign affairs, calling for a Revolutionary war. A central theme of the Brissotin, and later Girondin, faction, was their continued demand for foreign war as a means of exporting Revolutionary values throughout Europe. It was a policy that would lead France into almost continuous conflict for much of the Revolutionary period. Robespierre argued against war, believing that France should tackle her internal enemies first.

9 November 1791
FRANCE: POLITICS
A law against émigrés was passed. It demanded that those aristocrats who fled France during the Revolution either return or be declared traitors and forfeit their property.

12 November 1791
FRANCE: POLITICS
The king vetoed the decree against the émigrés.

29 November 1791
FRANCE: POLITICS
The Assembly voted to force Louis XVI to take steps to disperse the émigrés.

14 December 1791
FRANCE: ARMED FORCES
The French armies of the North, Centre and Rhine began to form. Marshal Rochambeau commanded the Army of the North while the Marquis de Lafayette led the Centre. Kellermann commanded the Army of the Rhine.

21 December 1791
INTERNATIONAL POLITICS
Minister Kaunitz, Leopold's head of administration, informed the French ambassador to Austria that General Bender's Austrian forces in Belgium would assist the Elector of Trier if France tried to move to disperse the émigré forces building around Coblenz.

Winter 1791–92
FRANCE: CIVIL UNREST
Shortages of the most basic provisions led to civil unrest and riots throughout France.

* 1792 *

24 January 1792
INTERNATIONAL POLITICS
The Assembly passed a decree accusing the Austrians of breaking the treaty of 1756 and inciting other powers to intervene in France's affairs. France demanded reassurances from Austria by 1 March otherwise a state of war would be declared.

7 February 1792
INTERNATIONAL POLITICS
The Austrians and Prussians came to an agreement and formed a military alliance. They began to move their forces towards the French frontier. Piedmont joined the alliance shortly afterwards.

16 February 1792
INTERNATIONAL POLITICS
King Frederick William II of Prussia met with Austrian officials at Potsdam to decide a plan of attack against France.

1 March 1792
AUSTRIA: SUCCESSION
Following the death of Leopold II, his son Francis became Emperor Francis of the Holy Roman Empire and King of Austria and the Hapsburg Empire.

9 March 1792
FRANCE: POLITICS
Louis dissolved his ministries.

10 March 1792
FRANCE: POLITICS
Moderate Girondin deputies were invited by Louis XVI to form new ministries. The new Ministers included Roland (for the Interior), General Dumouriez, Clavière, Brissot and Vergniaud. The Girondins believed they should go to war against Austria and Prussia. Conversely, the Jacobin faction, led by Robespierre and Marat, believed that war should be avoided, as they did not think France was ready.

15 March 1792
FRANCE: POLITICS
Dumouriez was appointed Foreign Minister. He was military head of the Girondin faction and planned to lead the war effort with an invasion of the Austrian Netherlands.

12 April 1792
NETHERLANDS FRONT
Austria ordered 50,000 troops to reinforce their forces already on the frontier.

20 April 1792
FRANCE: POLITICS
The Legislative Assembly prompted Louis XVI to issue a declaration of war upon Austria. Prussia stood by her alliance with Austria and also entered the conflict. The stated reason for war was the harbouring of émigrés and favouring the return of the French monarchy. Émigré forces had begun to assemble near Coblenz.

Revolutionary France stood on the brink of war, with a coalition of Allied Powers forming against her. Rather than wait to be attacked, and carrying forward a plan to spread the Revolutionary ethos across Europe, France would take the initiative herself. The Revolutionary Wars were about to begin. Europe was about to embark on a conflict that would stretch across the next quarter of a century.

CHAPTER II

The Revolutionary Wars

The Revolution that swept through France in the summer of 1789, and the events that led to the removal from power of the French monarch, were seen as a threat to the stability of the other monarchs of Europe. In order to fully restore Louis to his throne, Austria and Prussia prepared to make war to aid the émigré forces that had assembled on the Rhine frontier. France was about to be assailed upon her borders in a fight for the life or death of the new order. Her armies of Carmognoles, raw recruits fired by Revolutionary zeal, had to prove their worth in battle if the Revolution was to survive.

* 1792 *

28 April 1792
BELGIAN FRONT
The French Army of the North, commanded by Marshal Jean Baptiste de Rochambeau, a veteran of the American War of Independence, invaded the Austrian Netherlands. The French army moved cautiously forward in three columns. This was the first time that the newly created Blues had been committed in action alongside the Whites.

29 April 1792
BELGIAN FRONT
A force of 4,000 men of the Army of the North, commanded by General Dillon, advanced upon Tournai. Despite not even being in contact with the Austrians, the raw French troops panicked and broke, running back towards Lille. The unruly French troops murdered Dillon and a number of his staff during their efforts to get away from the impending scene of battle. Another force of 10,000 under General Biron at least managed to fire off a single volley before it too panicked and fled the field.

1–14 May 1792
BELGIAN FRONT
The Austrians defeated the French in skirmishes around Lille and then proceeded to lay siege to the town. Rochambeau resigned his command in disgust at the behaviour of the undisciplined hordes he had been given to

work with. The Marquis de Lafayette, formerly commander of the Army of the Centre, was appointed to replace him.

15 May 1792
FRANCE: POLITICS
France declared war on the Kingdom of Piedmont & Sardinia.

12 June 1792
FRANCE: POLITICS
Louis dismissed his Jacobin ministers and attempted to replace them with moderates. The Assembly objected to this move, prompting the moderate Lafayette to condemn the Assembly and the Jacobin members.

14 June 1792
FRANCE: POLITICS
Dumouriez resigned his post of Foreign Minister and was appointed Minister of War.

20 June 1792
FRANCE: CIVIL UNREST
Despite the fact the France was at war, popular unrest continued. In Paris, crowds of angry republican supporters invaded the Tuileries Palace to demand that the king give up his right of veto. This move was made in an effort to prevent Louis from dismissing his ministers, as he had instructed on 12 June. The mobs in Paris demanded the return of the Jacobin ministers, further humiliating Louis and undermining his already weak position.

26 June 1792
INTERNATIONAL POLITICS
The Austrians and Prussians formally agreed to the creation of the First Coalition against the French. The hostilities, which had begun in the Austrian Netherlands, and would soon spread along the Rhine, would become known as the War of the First Coalition.

28 June 1792
FRANCE: POLITICS
Lafayette called for the abolition of the Jacobin Club and the punishment of the 20 June demonstrators. The Girondins were gradually losing influence to the Jacobins and Cordeliers. The Jacobins were by this stage advocating the removal of the king and the full declaration of a republican executive.

30 June 1792
BELGIAN FRONT
The French invasion of the Austrian Netherlands ended as the demoralised French army re-crossed the frontier.

11 July 1792
FRANCE: POLITICS
The Legislative Assembly declared 'the Fatherland in danger' (*la Patrie en danger*) and gained emergency powers. This enabled it to ignore the king's veto. The move was propelled more by the Girondins' desire to use the 100,000-strong National Guard to protect it against Jacobin insurgence than against any foreign threat.

RHINE FRONT
Prussian forces under Karl Wilhelm, Duke of Brunswick, began to assemble at Coblenz. Brunswick's force would comprise 42,000 Prussians, 30,000 Austrians plus contingents of Hessians and émigrés. The Allied plan was to strike straight into France through the Ardennes and march, via Chalons-sur-Marne, upon Paris.

Against the Allied forces the French deployed Lafayette's army of 23,000 at Sedan and a force of 20,000 under Kellermann at Metz.

15 July 1792
FRANCE: POLITICS
The Jacobins called for the exile of the king, the election of a new commune for Paris and the arrest of all public enemies.

25 July 1792
INTERNATIONAL POLITICS
The Brunswick Manifesto was issued, the invading forces promising vengeance on Paris if any harm came to the French royal family. Most of Western Europe joined together with a promise to declare war on Revolutionary France, although few carried out their promise immediately. These states promised to exact an exemplary and unforgettable act of vengeance against the French should they repeat any violence similar to that of 20 June, when the mob had invaded the Tuileries.

28 July 1792
FRANCE: POLITICS
The first copies of the Brunswick Manifesto reached Paris. Its full impact of this document would not be realised until it was heard among the Paris mob.

29 July 1792
FRANCE: POLITICS
At a meeting of the Jacobin Club in Paris, Robespierre called for the removal of the king.

30 July 1792
FRANCE: REVOLUTION
Revolutionary troops from Marseille arrived in Paris to take part in a planned coup to overthrow the king.

1 August 1792
RHINE FRONT
Prussian forces began to cross the Rhine around Coblenz. They were to cross the French frontier near Longwy.

FRANCE: HOME FRONT
News of the Brunswick Manifesto swept through Paris, galvanising popular opinion that the monarchy was acting with the Allies. The Assembly ordered the people to ready themselves for war. Louis had in fact remained loyal to his country and had refused to bend to demands from his closest supporters that he call upon foreign aid to put down the Assembly.

3 August 1792
FRANCE: POLITICS
Forty-seven of the forty-eight Paris sections signed a petition calling for the removal of the king. The Assembly, under pressure, agreed to discuss the matter. The Brunswick Manifesto, rather than cowing the French people, had spurred them into urgent action.

8 August 1792
FRANCE: POLITICS
The Paris sections chose a new Commune and began to make secret plans to storm the Tuileries, the seat of the Assembly. The anger of the mob was inflamed further by the writings of Marat's radical newspaper, *Journal de la République Française*. Robespierre was elected to the Paris Commune.

9 August 1792
FRANCE: POLITICS
The Assembly debated the issue of the king's removal from office but could agree nothing.

10 August 1792
FRANCE: POLITICS
The Commune began its effort to storm the Tuileries, elements of the mob invading the Legislative Assembly and taking control. Royalist were driven out of office and in some cases murdered. The Commune carried out its plan to invade the Tuileries, where the Royal Family were being held for their own protection. Faced by a fervent mob bent on murder, the Swiss Guard pulled back but then opened fire with their muskets. This merely fired the mob's fury and they stormed the Tuileries, massacring

600 of the 900 Guards. Lafayette considered marching on Paris with his Army of the North in an effort to restore order.

The Legislative Assembly, now virtually held prisoner by the Commune and the mob, was forced to suspend the king and order him imprisoned.

11 August 1792
FRANCE: POLITICS
After the events of the previous day, an Executive Council of six ministers was established to oversee elections to the Convention. Over the next six weeks, actual power was divided between the Paris Commune and the Council, called the Provincial Executive Committee, headed by the popular Jacques Danton.

12 August 1792
FRANCE: REVOLUTION
The Royal Family was placed in the Temple Prison.

15 August 1792
FRANCE: COUNTER-REVOLUTION
As troops arrived to conscript peasants in western France, Jean Cotterreau, also known as Jean Chouan, led a revolt in the name of the king and against the nationalists. Thus began the Chouan revolt which was to rage for a number of years to come.

17 August 1792
FRANCE: REVOLUTION
Lafayette abandoned his army at Sedan and fled to the Austrians. General Charles Dumouriez took command of the Army of the North.

19 August 1792
PRUSSIAN OFFENSIVE
The Duke of Brunswick crossed the frontier into France from the Austrian Netherlands. He headed an army of 80,000 Prussian, Austrian, German and émigré soldiers.

20 August 1792
PRUSSIAN OFFENSIVE
Austrian and Prussian forces reached Longwy after a leisurely advance from the Rhine. The French garrison was bombarded lightly by the Prussians. The Allies prepared to continue their advance towards Verdun.

Lafayette surrendered to the Austrians and was imprisoned. He was considered to hold Revolutionary beliefs and therefore was thought of as an enemy of the monarchist regimes of the coalition.

23 August 1792
PRUSSIAN OFFENSIVE
Longwy fell to Brunswick's forces after the briefest of sieges. The demoralised Army of the Centre withdrew before the Prussian advance. The withdrawal of this force, and advance of the Allies, compelled the 23,000 French troops deployed at Sedan, now commanded by Dumouriez, to begin manoeuvring so as to link up with the Army of the Centre. Brunswick would need to act fast if he was to attack the French armies in isolation and before they could unite.

28 August 1792
FRANCE: HOME FRONT
The Provincial Executive Committee, acting for the Legislative Assembly, allowed house-to-house searches for arms and people suspected of anti-Revolutionary sympathies.

2 September 1792
PRUSSIAN OFFENSIVE
Verdun fell to Brunswick's army. The French commander, Colonel Beaurepaire, in despair at the state of his defences, shot himself upon the arrival of the Prussians. The Allied forces now moved to cross the Argonne Forest before marching upon Chalos and then Paris.

General François Kellermann arrived to take command of the French Army of the Centre.

2–6 September 1792
FRANCE: CIVIL UNREST
Alarm at the fall of Verdun led to panic in Paris. The mob believed that the prisons were packed full of royalist sympathisers and to prevent their liberation by the advancing Allies if they reached Paris more than 1,400 people were systematically executed in the Luxembourg Gardens. This atrocity became known as the September Massacres.

8 September 1792
PRUSSIAN OFFENSIVE
Brunswick entered the Argonne Forest as he continued his slow advance into the French interior. Dumouriez marched his troops behind the Argonne and deployed to protect the passes while also ordering Kellermann to march from Metz to St Menehould, where the two French armies would later unite.

10 September 1792
PRUSSIAN OFFENSIVE
An Austrian corps under Clerfayt penetrated Dumouriez's defences in the Argonne and turned the French front. Dumouriez now began the difficult task of forming a long front from the Argonne to Chalons while also linking up with Kellermann.

12 September 1792
PRUSSIAN OFFENSIVE
Dumouriez continued his march towards Kellermann as he strove to unite the Army of the Centre with his Army of the North in an effort to halt Brunswick. Both French units had roughly 30,000 men.

19 September 1792
PRUSSIAN OFFENSIVE
Dumouriez and Kellermann united at St Menehould and immediately received news of the arrival of the Allied force close to their positions. In fact, the Allied force had managed to interpose itself between the French armies and Paris, compelling both armies to deploy with fronts reversed.

20 September 1792
PRUSSIAN OFFENSIVE
With General Dumouriez temporarily absent from his army, General Kellermann, with a combined force of 59,000 men and fifty-four cannon, met Brunswick's 34,000 on a reversed front on the heights of Valmy. With fog obscuring the battlefield, the French were deployed along the ridge but with a dangerous gap between their two forces. Brunswick immediately moved to attack Kellermann in order to cut his line of retreat and separate the two French armies once more. A minor cavalry engagement warned Kellermann of the approach of the Allies and also allowed Dumouriez to move part of his army to close the gap in his line, which had become apparent as the mist burned off in the morning sun. There then followed an artillery exchange, during which the hitherto panic-stricken French levies held their ground and even managed an unsuccessful attack in an effort to capture some of the forward Prussian guns. Seeing the French falling back to their original positions, the Prussians formed up and moved to attack but they also failed to push on and withdrew to their original positions.

Present with the army, King Frederick William of Prussia called for another attack, which failed under the increasingly accurate fire of the French cannon. By dusk the battle had ended, with the French still in possession of the field. The Prussians lost fewer than 200 men killed and 600 wounded, and the French no more than 500 casualties. However, Brunswick left the field to the French and began to slowly withdraw his army back to the frontier.

The Cannonade of Valmy, and the victory it brought, proved to be a tour de force for the Revolution. Not only had the invading Prussians and their Allies been turned back in their march on Paris, but the new citizen armies, acting in conjunction with the regular army, at last proved they had the mettle to beat the armies of the old regime. Little did they know, but the face of warfare in Europe was about to change as manpower took over from manoeuvre. As Goethe, who had been present at the battle, later said to his comrades: 'From this place and from this day forth commences a new era in the world's history, and you can all say that you were present at its birth.'

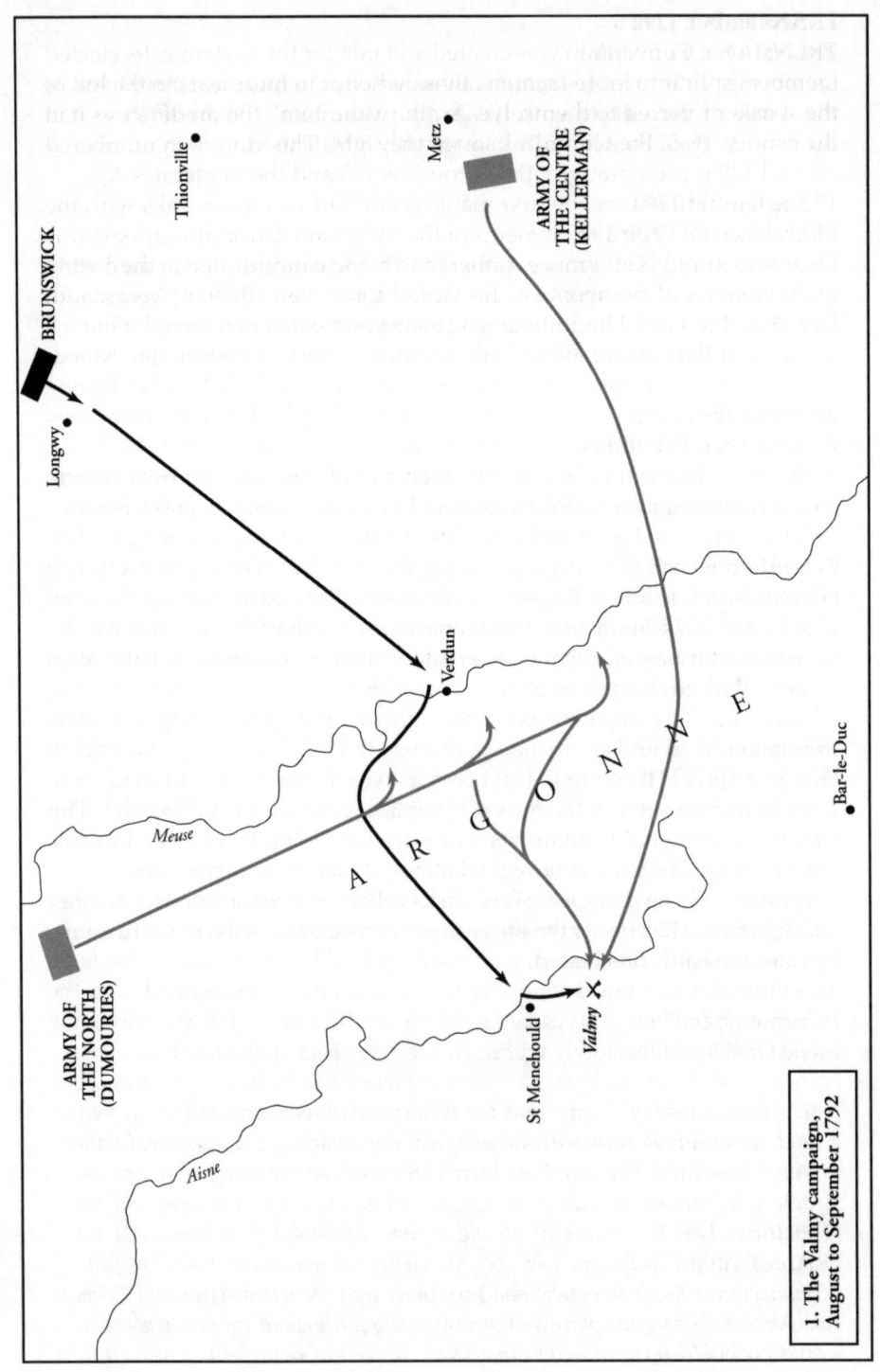

1. The Valmy campaign, August to September 1792

FRANCE: POLITICS
The National Convention was created and met for the first time. Its elected members split into loose factions, those who sat in high seats to the left of the speaker referred to themselves as 'the Mountain', the moderates sat in the centre, while the Girondins sat on the right. The Mountain numbered around 145 representatives, the Girondins 165 and the moderates 435.

The Girondins were the dominant faction but had loose links with the radical Jacobin Club and elements of the Mountain. Girondin support was dispersed throughout France, rather than being concentrated at the centre. Their dominant members in the Convention were Brissot, Vergniaud, Isnard and Roland. Dumouriez was their foremost general in the field

The leading members of the Mountain were Robespierre, Marat, Desmoulins and Danton and also included men such as Fouché, Egalité (formerly the Duc d'Orléans) and Saint-Juste. They had strong connections with the Paris Commune and had centralised their support in Paris.

The moderate centre, which was used by both the left and right during their efforts to gain superiority, included men such as Sieyes and Gregoire.

21 September 1792
FRANCE: POLITICS
The Convention abolished the monarchy. A committee headed by the Girondin Jean Baptiste Mailhe was established to determine what was to be done with the king.

25 September 1792
FRANCE: POLITICS
The Convention declared France a Republic, 'one and indivisible'. The factions of the republican movement were for the moment united in fear of a break up of France into federal states. A largely Girondin-dominated committee, whose members were Brissot, Vergniaud, Gensomme, Barère, Paine, Petion, Danton and the Marquis de Condorcet, was set up to establish a republican constitution.

29 September 1792
SOUTHERN FRONT
French forces under General Anselme attacked the Piedmontese and occupied Nice. Another force under General Montesquieu overran Savoy. French troops had moved following demonstrations by Jacobin factions in these areas and in response to the Piedmontese attacks.

11 October 1792
FRANCE: POLITICS
A new committee was established to draw up a new constitution. Danton and Abbé Sieyes were on the committee, but most of its other members were Girondins.

October–November 1792
RHINE FRONT
Following the retreat of Brunswick's army, and the recapture of Verdun and Longwy, General Adam Justine invaded Germany from Alsace and reached Mayence and Frankfurt-am-Main.

BELGIAN FRONT
Dumouriez moved north into Belgium with the 45,000 men and 100 guns of his Army of the North. He forced the Austrians to raise their siege of Lille. The Austrians then retired their army to Jemappes.

21 October 1792
RHINE FRONT
Mayence (Mainz) fell to Custine's forces.

6 November 1792
BELGIAN FRONT
Dumouriez, with 45,000 men, launched a surprise attack and struck the Austrians in their winter quarters at Jemappes, near the town of Mons. The Austrian army, commanded by Albert of Saxe-Teschen, had just 13,000 men and suffered a heavy defeat, losing 1,500 of its men to a French loss of 2,000 casualties. The French continued their advance deeper into the Austrian Netherlands and over the course of the next month occupied all of the territory between the frontier and Antwerp and Namur.

11 November 1792
CENTRAL FRONT
Kellermann was appointed to command the Army of the Alps.

13 November 1792
FRANCE: POLITICS
The debate on Louis XVI's fate began. The Mountain pushed for his execution while the Girondins took a more moderate line, proposing exile or similar measures.

14 November 1792
BELGIAN FRONT
Vigorously pressing his attacks, Dumouriez captured Brussels.

19 November 1792
FRANCE: POLITICS
The Convention issued a decree that aimed to 'aid all peoples who desire to recover their liberty'[1] by overthrowing their monarchs, in effect declaring that France would export its Revolution where it could. This generated widespread hostility from the rest of Europe.

20 November 1792
FRANCE: POLITICS
After supposed new documentary evidence against Louis was unearthed, Robespierre urged the Convention to condemn him to death immediately as an enemy of the state. This was rejected and instead it was decided to take a vote on the king's fate on a charge of conspiracy against the nation.

23 November 1792
BELGIAN FRONT
French gunboats moved to capture Antwerp.

27 November 1792
FRANCE: HOME FRONT
Savoy was incorporated into France, following an invasion by General Anselme.

29 November 1792
HOLLAND: POLITICS
The Dutch government made a formal appeal to Britain for help against the French.

1 December 1792
RHINE FRONT
Brunswick launched a counter-attack with an army of 60,000 men and began to drive Custine back from his positions near Frankfurt towards the Rhine.

FRANCE: POLITICS
Jacques Roux raged against the 'aristocracy of the rich' which now dominated French government. His 'Enragés' were vigorously attacked by both the Girondins and the Jacobins.

2 December 1792
RHINE FRONT
Frankfurt fell to Brunswick's forces as Custine retired to winter quarters in Mainz.

11 December 1792
FRANCE: POLITICS
Louis' trial began. He denied the conspiracy charges against him. The trial would last into mid-January 1793.

13 December 1792
BELGIAN FRONT
Dumouriez went into winter quarters.

17 December 1792
FRANCE: REVOLUTION
As the French began to export their Revolutionary zeal, a Jacobin Club was established in Naples in Italy.

21 December 1792
BRITAIN: POLITICS
MPs in the House of Commons urged war against France, ostensibly to protect the rights of Louis, but also to check the growing strength of the Revolutionary regime.

27 December 1792
FRANCE: POLITICS
The Girondins proposed a referendum on Louis' fate.

* 1793 *

FRANCE: ARMED FORCES
After years of neglect the French fleet was in a terrible condition. It was dispersed around the country's main ports but was poorly equipped and short of officers. Of seventy-six ships of the line, barely a third were actually available for action. At Brest the fleet had twelve ships of the line ready for action, and seven fitting out, at Toulon it had six ready for action and seven fitting out, while at Rochefort there were three ready for action and one fitting out.[2]

15 January 1793
FRANCE: POLITICS
The Convention voted on Louis' case. He was found guilty of conspiracy against the people of France by 683 votes to thirty-nine. The members of the Convention now had to debate his sentence.

16 January 1793
FRANCE: POLITICS
The Girondins again proposed a referendum to determine Louis' sentence but were defeated by the Jacobin-dominated Mountain, which was successful in its demand for the death sentence.

17 January 1793
FRANCE: POLITICS
Following an all-night session, the Convention voted by 387 to 334 to have Louis put to death. The Girondin efforts to prevent the death sentence undermined their already low popularity with the Parisian populace.

21 January 1793
FRANCE: REVOLUTION
King Louis XVI, whose fall had begun in 1789, finally met his fate in the Place de la République as he went under the guillotine.

30 January 1793
INTERNATIONAL POLITICS
Following the execution of Louis, the British joined the First Coalition. The British, Dutch and Spanish withdrew their ambassadors from France.

1 February 1793
ALLIED PLANNING
Brunswick's Austro-Prussian army of more than 50,000 deployed along the Rhine. It aimed to defeat Custine at Mainz. A second Austrian army of 43,000 men, under Prince Frederick of Saxe-Coburg, planned to recover the Austrian Netherlands.

INTERNATIONAL POLITICS
France declared war on Britain and the United Provinces (Holland). She was already at war with Prussia, Austria and Piedmont

14 February 1793
SOUTHERN FRONT
France annexed Monaco.

15 February 1793
HOLLAND: POLITICS
Dutch republicans called for the liberation of Holland by the French. Dumouriez welcomed the call as he planned to invade the Netherlands with his hitherto victorious army.

24 February 1793
FRANCE: POLITICS
The Convention issued a decree calling for conscription to support the manpower requirements of the army. Some 300,000 soldiers were to be called upon during March.

March 1793
FRANCE: CIVIL UNREST
There were widespread food riots in Paris and shortages throughout the rest of France. The Enragés became increasingly active in Paris.

BELGIAN FRONT
France annexed Belgium. A weak British expeditionary force landed in the Low Countries under the command of Frederick Augustus, Duke of

York and second son of King George III. Altogether the force had only six infantry battalions. Their aim was to provide moral and military support to the Dutch.

1 March 1793
BELGIAN FRONT
Prince Frederick Josias of Saxe-Coburg led an Austrian army of 43,000 men across the Meuse river and invaded Belgium. The Duke of York's Anglo-Hanoverian army co-operated with the Austrian army in its advance.

Dumouriez, who had been planning to invade the Netherlands, had to turn and face this new threat.

RHINE FRONT
Brunswick, now with 60,000 men, hemmed Custine in at Mainz. The Allies also deployed additional troops along the length of the Rhine.

2 March 1793
BELGIAN FRONT
French forces abandoned La Chapelle. Dumouriez no longer had a numerical superiority against the Austrians and, knowing the weakness of his volunteer soldiers, was compelled to avoid a set-piece battle.

5 March 1793
BELGIAN FRONT
The French pulled out of Liège.

7 March 1793
FRANCE: POLITICS
France declared war on Spain. The Spanish joined the First Coalition.

9 March 1793
FRANCE: HOME FRONT
The Girondin factions in the Convention called for a levy of massed armed forces. A levy of 300,000 men was granted although a decree to support this action would not come into force until August.

FRANCE: POLITICS
An attempted revolt by the Enragés in Paris failed.

10 March 1793
FRANCE: REVOLUTION
The Convention established the Extraordinary Criminal Tribunal to act against enemies of the Republic.

11 March 1793
FRANCE: COUNTER-REVOLUTION
The Vendée revolt broke out in reaction to the Convention's demands for a levy of troops. Counter-Revolutionary peasants, led by members of the clergy and nobility, linked up with the Chouans in western France and had initial success, gaining control of the royalist countryside and laying siege to republican towns and cities, such as Nantes and Angers.

18 March 1793
BELGIAN FRONT
Dumouriez, despite reservations due to his lack of overwhelming numbers, attacked the Austrians at Neerwinden with 41,000 men. After a bitter struggle the French suffered a severe defeat at the hands of Saxe-Coburg. The Austrians lost 3,000 men and the French 4,000. Many of the volunteers in the Army of the North began to desert. Brussels, and the greater part of Belgium, fell to the Austrians soon after as the French army in Belgium melted away.

FRANCE: POLITICS
The Convention decreed capital punishment against many of the issues upon which the Enragés protested.

21 March 1793
BELGIAN FRONT
General Dumouriez, while trying to pull the remnants of his forces back to the French frontier fortresses, was defeated by the Austrians at Louvain.

25 March 1793
RHINE FRONT
Prussian forces under Brunswick laid siege to Custine's forces in Mayence.

26 March 1793
FRANCE: CIVIL UNREST
The Convention established the Committee of Public Safety as its national executive. It was headed by Danton, now a leading Mountain figure. Jacobin influence throughout the Convention continued to grow.

April 1793
BELGIAN FRONT
The British sent another eleven cavalry regiments to the Low Countries to join the Duke of York in his efforts to aid the Dutch. Altogether the cavalry force numbered just 2,500 men, bringing British strength to some 17,000 men, the bulk of whom were enrolled Hanoverians.[3]

FRANCE: COUNTER-REVOLUTION
The Vendée revolt spread to Brittany as rebel guerrillas attacked republican towns.

4 April 1793
BELGIAN FRONT
Dumouriez, disgusted at the performance and desertion of his citizen army, and fearing for the safety of France in the hands of the Revolution, planned to join forces with the Austrians and march on Paris to depose the Convention. His army though refused to follow him, his senior officer and political representatives accusing him of treason.

5 April 1793
BELGIAN FRONT
Dumouriez denounced the left-wing government in Paris and deserted his army in order to go over to the Allies. General Picot Dampierre took over command of the Army of the North, which was in retreat to Valenciennes.

FRANCE: POLITICS
Dumouriez's treachery played straight into the hands of the Jacobins and helped them to discredit the declining Girondin faction in the Convention.

6 April 1793
FRANCE: POLITICS
The Committee of Public Safety was tasked with establishing security through the use of terror against the internal and external enemies of France.

Mid-April 1793
BELGIAN FRONT
Dampierre withdrew the Army of the North away from the frontier and to cantonments around Dunkirk, Cassel, near Lille and Bouchain, from where it could be restructured and strengthened.

23 April 1793
FRANCE: POLITICS
Marat was arrested on the orders of the Revolutionary Tribunal as the gulf between the Girondins and the Jacobins deepened.

24 April 1793
FRANCE: POLITICS
Marat was released as the Girondins came under pressure.

End-April 1793
BELGIAN FRONT
Rather than force a vigorous campaign against the demoralised French

army in the north, Saxe-Coburg led his Austrian forces into operations against the French covering forces at Valenciennes. The British were to concentrate their efforts upon Dunkirk.

May 1793
FRANCE: CIVIL UNREST
Federalist revolts began to spread through France in reaction against the radical central government.

1 May 1793
BELGIAN FRONT
Under pressure from the Representatives on Mission that were present with his army, Dampierre opted for an offensive to drive the Allies away from Valenciennes and Condé. An attack upon Saxe-Coburg's forces near Quievrain succeeded in driving the Austrians back initially before General Mack recovered the situation and drove the French back to the starting point.

8 May 1793
BELGIAN FRONT
General Dampierre attacked the Austrians under General Clerfayt at Raismes. Becoming embroiled in the close fighting, Dampierre was killed by an Austrian shot.

10 May 1793
BELGIAN FRONT
The French army retired in good order to Valenciennes after the loss of their commander. General Custine was appointed to command the Army of the North. His first task was to rally the army and instil discipline into the troops.

Mid-May 1793
BELGIAN FRONT
Custine gained the agreement of the Convention to the massing of French armies around Valenciennes in preparation for a blow into the Low Countries.

18 May 1793
SPANISH FRONT
Spanish forces defeated the French at Mas d'Eu.

FRANCE: POLITICS
The Commission of the Twelve was created by the Girondins to root out extremists in the Paris Commune. Its primary aim was to eliminate the Hebertists and Enragés.

20 May 1793
CENTRAL FRONT
Kellermann was appointed to command the new Army of the Alps and Italy.

21–23 May 1793
BELGIAN FRONT
Saxe-Coburg, deployed at Famars close to Valenciennes, defeated Custine's Army of the North. The Anglo-Hanoverians attacked south of the town while the Austrians moved up from the west and north. Custine was shortly recalled to Paris and General Jean Houchard replaced him as commander.

28 May 1793
FRANCE: POLITICS
The Insurrectionary Committee was established.

30 May 1793
FRANCE: CIVIL UNREST
There were anti-Girondin riots in Paris.

31 May 1793
FRANCE: POLITICS
The Girondins were undermined by the Jacobins and began to flee Paris. Those who remained behind were in immediate danger.

2 June 1793
FRANCE: POLITICS
The Convention, dominated by the Jacobins, declared the Girondin faction enemies of the people and expelled them. The Commune summoned the National Guards to restore order to Paris and prevent any Girondin escape. Brissot, Paine and Vergniaud were arrested. Roland managed to escape and fled to Belgium.

Mid-June 1793
FRANCE: CIVIL UNREST
Following the fall of the Girondin faction in Paris, the opponents of the Mountain and Jacobins in the provinces took matters into their own hands. Bordeaux renounced the authority of the Revolutionary government. Revolts spread as nearly three quarters of the eighty-eight departments of France declared themselves independent of Paris

In the Vendée the revolt by the rebel army of nearly 100,000 had gained control of large areas of Poitou, Anjou and Brittany. However, instead of progressing their rebellion by moving towards Paris, they laid siege to the Jacobin stronghold of Nantes.[4]

On Corsica, nationalists rebelled against the centre. The Bonaparte family fled their Ajaccio home for Marseille. The Bonaparte brothers were active Jacobins.

10 June 1793
BELGIAN FRONT
Condé surrendered to Saxe-Coburg's forces after a protracted siege.

13 June 1793
FRANCE: ARMED FORCES
Napoleon, having spent the previous few years in command of militia forces on Corsica, resumed his commission with the French regular army as a captain.

17 June 1793
BELGIAN FRONT
The plan to mass the French armies at Valenciennes was dropped due to protests by the generals of the armies along the Rhine and elsewhere, and the growing threat of the Vendée revolt.

19 June 1793
FRANCE: CIVIL UNREST
Vendean rebels occupied Angers.

28 June 1793
BELGIAN FRONT
Allied forces captured Valenciennes as General Ferrand ordered his isolated force to surrender. The British government now directed its forces, commanded by Frederick Augustus, Duke of York, to lay siege to Dunkirk.

July 1793
MEDITERRANEAN FRONT
British forces landed in Corsica.

FRANCE: CIVIL UNREST
The revolt in Bordeaux collapsed and Jacobins secured the city once more.
   In the Vendée the Republicans began to deploy regular army units against the rebels. Jean Baptiste Carrier, acting on the orders of the Committee of Public Safety, arrived in the region to galvanise Jacobin resistance.

10 July 1793
BELGIAN FRONT
Condé fell to the advancing Austrians.

FRANCE: POLITICS
Danton was removed as leader of the Committee of Public Safety. The committee was dominated by radical left-wingers.

13 July 1793
FRANCE: CIVIL UNREST
Charlotte Corday, a woman from Caen with Girondin connections, stabbed and killed the Jacobin leader of Lyon, Jean Paul Marat, as he lay in his bath. Corday was later guillotined.

17 July 1793
FRANCE: CIVIL UNREST
Anti-Jacobin activity broke out in Lyon.

24 July 1793
FRANCE: CIVIL UNREST
General Carteaux attacked the counter-Revolutionary forces in Avignon. Napoleon Bonaparte was among the army attacking the rebels.

RHINE FRONT
Mayence fell to Brunswick's 63,000 Prussians as the Allied force drove the French back.

27 July 1793
FRANCE: CIVIL UNREST
Maximilien Robespierre, who had called for the death of the enemies of the republic, joined the Committee of Public Safety.

August 1793
FRANCE: CIVIL UNREST
The Convention declared total war on its enemies and mobilised the people under the slogan 'Liberty or Death'. Marseille and Lyon, which declared for the monarchy, were attacked.

WAR AT SEA
The French fleet, commanded by Admiral Morard de Galles, sailed into the Atlantic. The British Channel fleet under Admiral Lord Richard Howe attempted to intercept but could not close with the French.

1 August 1793
FRANCE: COUNTER-REVOLUTION
The Convention ordered the destruction of the Vendean rebels and appointed General Kléber and an army of 100,000 men to destroy them and the federal rebels.

8 August 1793
BELGIAN FRONT
A minor action with the Allies prompted the French Army of the North to retire upon Arras. The Allies now turned their attentions to Dunkirk,

marching upon Ypres and Tournai as they turned north. Fighting in this theatre was now to be concentrated on Lille and Dunkirk.

9 August 1793
FRANCE: COUNTER-REVOLUTION
Kellermann laid siege to Lyon with elements of his Army of the Alps and Italy.

10 August 1793
BELGIAN FRONT
Carnot arrived to support the command of the Army of the North. He was to order a vigorous push into Flanders to disrupt Allied plans to reduce the French fortresses in this region.

18 August 1793
BELGIAN FRONT
As the British marched north, the Prince of Orange came under heavy attack near Lincelles, following the capture of Menin by French forces based at Lille. General Lake attacked the French forces near the town and drove them back but both sides had suffered heavy losses.

20 August 1793
FRANCE: ARMED FORCES
Kellermann was appointed to command the Army of the Centre. This force was currently engaged with the Prussians on the Rhine front.

21 August 1793
FRANCE: COUNTER-REVOLUTION
Toulon rose in revolt and declared for the monarchy. The monarchists had co-operated with the Girondins during the revolt but they emerged the stronger of the two factions and gained control of the town.

22 August 1793
BELGIAN FRONT
The Allies deployed around Dunkirk and Bergues and began the investment of the French forces. General Freytag, leading a contingent of Hanoverian troops, pushed the French out of their defences between Fumes and Bergues.

23 August 1793
BELGIAN FRONT
A subordinate of Houchard's, Jourdan, attacked Freytag's forces and disrupted the Anglo-Hanoverian efforts against Dunkirk and Bergues.

FRANCE: HOME FRONT
Lazare Carnot proposed the decree of the *leveé en masse* to the Convention, which allowed the conscription of the entire male population of France.

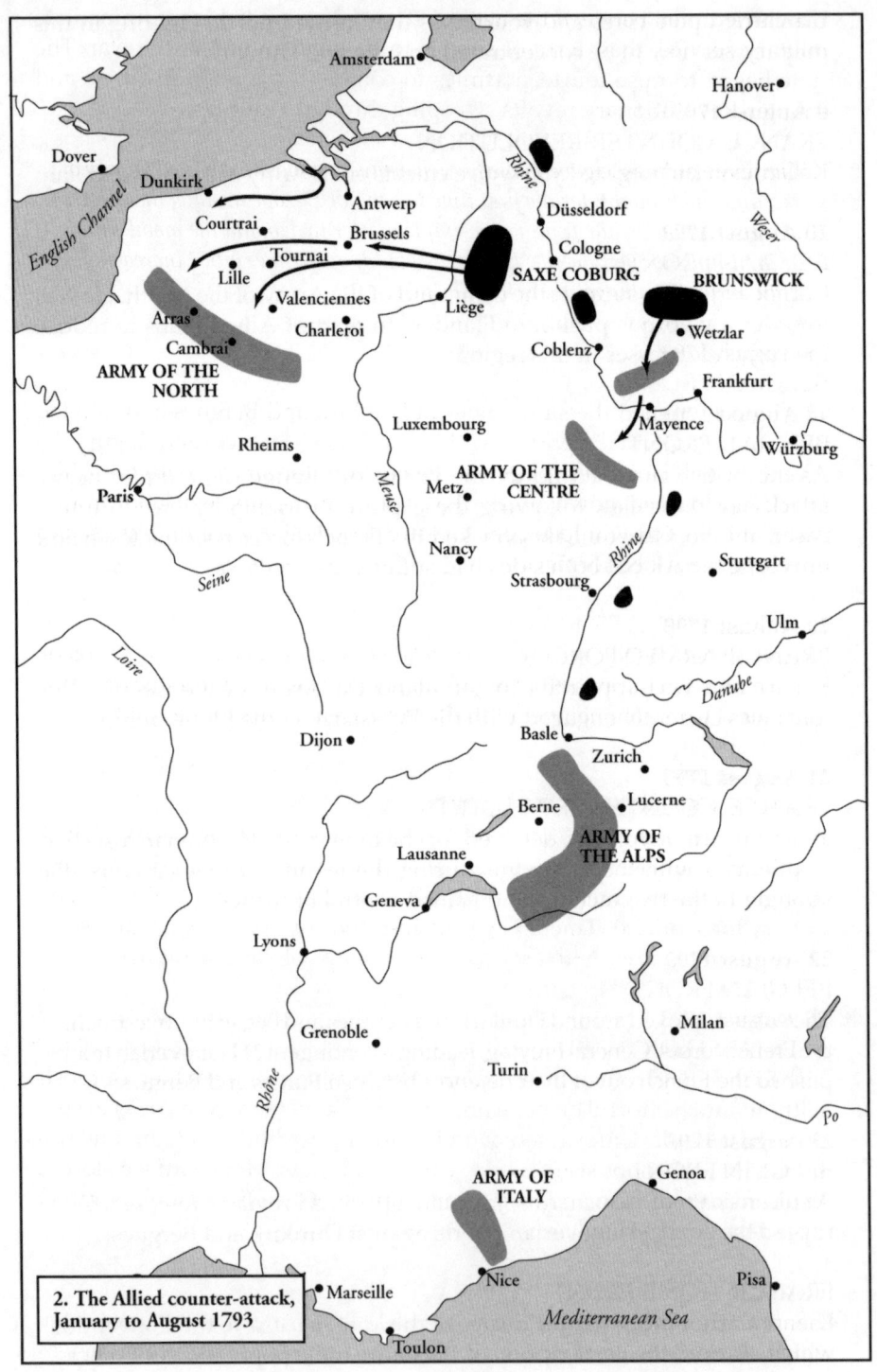

Dover

English Channel

Amsterdam

Hanover

Rhine

Weser

Dunkirk

Antwerp

Düsseldorf

Courtrai

Brussels

Cologne

Tournai

SAXE COBURG

BRUNSWICK

Lille

Valenciennes

Liège

Arras

Charleroi

Coblenz

Wetzlar

Cambrai

ARMY OF THE
NORTH

Frankfurt

Luxembourg

Mayence

Würzburg

Rheims

Meuse

Metz

ARMY OF THE
CENTRE

Paris

Nancy

Rhine

Stuttgart

Seine

Strasbourg

Ulm

Loire

Danube

Dijon

Basle

Zurich

Berne

Lucerne

Lausanne

ARMY OF
THE ALPS

Geneva

Lyons

Rhône

Grenoble

Milan

Turin

Po

Genoa

ARMY OF
ITALY

Marseille

Nice

Pisa

Toulon

Mediterranean Sea

2. The Allied counter-attack,
January to August 1793

48

Unmarried men between the ages of 18 and 25 were liable for immediate military service, their term of service to be the duration of the war. The state began to raise fourteen armies to combat the foreign invaders and counter-Revolutionary revolts sweeping through France.

The leveé en masse *gave to the French army an almost unlimited supply of recruits and brought, for the first time to a major European state, the spectre of conscription. While it proved a simple matter to demand the mobilisation of thousands of men for the armies, it would, over time, prove increasingly difficult to actually get them into the field.*

25 August 1793
BELGIAN FRONT
The French opened the sluice gates at Dunkirk and Bergues and flooded the country around the ports in order to aid their defences and disrupt the Allied efforts. Houchard planned a major counter-attack. With the Allies effectively pinned down on the coast due to the flooded land around them, the French would wheel forward from Lille towards Fumes and envelope the Allied force.

FRANCE: COUNTER-REVOLUTION
The revolt of Marseille was crushed by General Carteaux's forces. Napoleon was a captain in the army that overcame the rebels. He came to the attention of a fellow Corsican member of the Terror regime, Christophe Saliceti.

27 August 1793
FRANCE: COUNTER-REVOLUTION
Admiral Sir Samuel Hood, with the twenty-one ships of the British Mediterranean Fleet, accompanied by a Spanish squadron under Admiral Juan de Langara, entered the port and landed an Anglo-Spanish expeditionary force of 12,000 men. The British seized control of the naval arsenal in the town together with around seventy ships of various ratings.

28 August 1793
BELGIAN FRONT
The French began their attack from Lille, pushing in the Allied outposts without much effort. The main French army moved up from Arras to support the assault. Unfortunately, rather than push forwards, the undisciplined French troops scattered in search of plunder. Houchard was forced to reconsider his plan and instead aimed to simply relieve Dunkirk rather than destroy the Allied army.

FRANCE: THE TERROR
General Custine was guillotined. His only crime was to have been defeated in battle by the Austrians near Valenciennes. However, he was

an aristocrat by birth and his skilful handling of his army before the defeat did not sit well with the Convention.

30 August 1793
BELGIAN FRONT
Leaving 37,000 men to secure their base at Arras and Douai, Houchard planned to move upon Cassel with a force of 50,000.

September 1793
WAR AT SEA
With his sailors proving mutinous and difficult to control, Admiral de Galles abandoned his efforts to patrol in the Atlantic and returned to port. He had managed to avoid being engaged by the stronger British fleet. De Galles resigned his command shortly afterwards.

FRANCE: COUNTER-REVOLUTION
Carrier arrived in Nantes and led the Jacobin punishment of the rebels, putting the royalists and Girondins held in the city jails in chains and placing them on barges on the Loire river. He then ordered the barges to be sunk. Hundreds died this way.

5 September 1793
FRANCE: POLITICS
Demonstrations organised by the Paris Commune demanded decisive action of the Convention and the Committee of Public Safety. The hard line advocated by Robespierre, including the arrest of suspected enemies of the state and the creation of a Revolutionary army, was to be followed.

6 September 1793
BELGIAN FRONT
Houchard's Army of the North began its attack towards Cassel. A struggle developed with the Allied advance guards before Hondchoote. General Freytag, commanding the forward Allied contingent, was wounded during the fighting. He was succeeded by Wallmoden.

7 September 1793
BELGIAN FRONT
The French consolidated their positions around Hondchoote, Houchard leaving around 24,000 men to face the Allied force while he moved the remainder upon Dunkirk to relieve the besieged garrison.

FRANCE: COUNTER-REVOLUTION
General Kléber and his army deployed against the Vendean rebels, moving upon Nantes.

Republican forces under General Carteaux invested Toulon. Despite having 30,000 men, he failed to prosecute the siege vigorously.

8 September 1793
BELGIAN FRONT
The French defeated the Anglo-Hanoverian forces in another clash at Hondschoote. Houchard's assault force of 24,000 overwhelmed the 13,000 Hanoverians led by Wallmoden and compelled them to withdraw. Both armies lost around 3,000 men.

While the Allies held up the French advance at Hondchoote, the Duke of York raised the siege of Dunkirk, though he was compelled to abandon his siege train.

11 September 1793
BELGIAN FRONT
Saxe-Coburg continued his efforts against Houchard, taking Le Quesnoy near Menin.

13 September 1793
BELGIAN FRONT
General Houchard launched a counter-attack around Menin and defeated the Dutch contingent of the Anglo-Hanoverian army, commanded by the Prince of Orange, before the Austrians of Saxe-Coburg could march to his aid.

15 September 1793
BELGIAN FRONT
Houchard pressed his forces forward in order to attack the Austrians. Unfortunately he missed his target but one of his detachments was attacked by Beaulieu at Courtrai and suffered a defeat which caused it to withdraw from Menin.

16 September 1793
FRANCE: COUNTER-REVOLUTION
General Doppet, now commanding the Republican forces at Toulon, appointed Napoleon to command his artillery forces. Napoleon had excellent connections within the Jacobin regime, connections that were to aid his rise to power during these turbulent times.

17 September 1793
FRANCE: THE TERROR
The Convention passed a law (the Law of Suspects) that enabled it to arrest anyone who held suspected anti-republican opinions or undertook actions against the state. To reinforce the activities of the Committee of Public Safety a Committee of General Security was also established. It was

even more extreme than the Public Safety Committee and incorporated a new Revolutionary Tribunal to try perceived enemies of the people.

19 September 1793
FRANCE: COUNTER-REVOLUTION
Kléber attacked the Vendean rebels at Torfu but was defeated.

20 September 1793
BELGIAN FRONT
Houchard abandoned his attacks in Belgium and concentrated his 45,000 men upon Gaverelle. The Allies meanwhile made preparations to attack Mauberge.

22 September 1793
BELGIAN FRONT
Houchard was dismissed from his command and arrested for not pressing his attacks into the Netherlands hard enough. He was later executed under the guillotine. General Jean-Baptiste Jourdan was appointed to command the Army of the North.

End September 1793
BELGIAN FRONT
The Allies laid siege to Mauberge.

October 1793
BELGIAN FRONT
Lazare Carnot, Minister of War, joined the Army of the North to co-ordinate its efforts to defeat the Allies in Belgium. He ordered Jourdan to relieve Mauberge, which was under siege by 26,000 Austrians. The remainder of the Allied force, some 40,000 men, was arrayed in a cordon to protect against a French relief attack.

RHINE FRONT
Austrian and Prussian forces stormed the Weissenburg Lines and secured the Rhine frontier.

FRANCE: CIVIL UNREST
The Terror gripped France as the Committee for Public Safety purged its supposed enemies. Robespierre was a major figure in the Committee but did not hold absolute power. His main supporters were Saint Just and Couthon. Other members included Billaud-Varenne, Collot d'Herbois, Carnot and Barère. Although the Committee was supposed to be subject to the Convention, it wielded real power in Paris.

To add to France's woes, the harvest of 1793 had been particularly poor. In order to avert widespread famine the French began to look abroad to purchase grain.

2 October 1793
FRANCE: COUNTER-REVOLUTION
Couthon, a leading member of the Committee of Public Safety, arrived to force the siege of Lyon to be conducted more vigorously.

9 October 1793
FRANCE: COUNTER-REVOLUTION
The Republicans recaptured Lyon. Couthon left Collot d'Herbois and Joseph Fouché to organise the execution of the rebel leaders and any supposed traitors. This was done by tying them to stakes and firing cannon at them. More than 2,500 were executed.

15 October 1793
BELGIAN FRONT
Jourdan, with 45,000 men, attacked the Allied forces around Mauberge, striking them near Wattignes. The Allies had the better of the day, driving off Jourdan's assaults.

16 October 1793
BELGIAN FRONT
Jourdan renewed his attacks at Wattignes and after hard fighting drove in Saxe-Coburg's left flank. The Austrian forces began to retire and were compelled to abandon the siege of Mauberge. During two days of bitter fighting the French lost 5,000 men and the Allies some 3,000.

FRANCE: THE TERROR
Marie Antoinette was executed. The former Mountain representative Egalité (Duc d'Orléans) was also executed.

17 October 1793
BELGIAN FRONT
Jourdan dug in around Mauberge, mistakenly expecting the Allies to counter-attack after the previous day's battle.

18 October 1793
FRANCE: ARMED FORCES
Napoleon was promoted to chef de bataillon.

31 October 1793
FRANCE: THE TERROR
More than twenty Girondins' including their leaders Vergniaud and Brissot, were executed by guillotine.

4 November 1793
FRANCE: COUNTER REVOLUTION
The Vendéan rebels defeated French regular troops at Fougères.

16 November 1793
FRANCE: THE TERROR
The unfortunate General Houchard was guillotined in Paris.

17 November 1793
SOUTHERN FRONT
General Jacques Dugommier took command of the Republican forces surrounding Toulon.

28–30 November 1793
RHINE FRONT
Prussian forces under Brunswick defeated the French under General Lazare Hoche at Kaiserslautern. Hoche had concentrated his army and had taken the offensive in the Alsace in an effort to push Wurmser's Austrians back to the line of the Rhine.

12 December 1793
FRANCE: COUNTER-REVOLUTION
The Vendéan rebels again defeated the French regular forces operating against them, this time at Le Mans.

14 December 1793
SOUTHERN FRONT
Following a plan proposed by Bonaparte, the French forces besieging Toulon captured Fort Eguillette, which commanded the anchorages.

15 December 1793
SOUTHERN FRONT
The French began to bombard the Allied ships in Toulon harbour.

18–22 December 1793
RHINE FRONT
French forces (under Pichegru and Hoche) counter-attacked along the Rhine frontier and broke through the Austrian and Prussian Weissenburg defences. Hoche continued his advance towards Landau while Pichegru pushed towards Mayence.

18 December 1793
SOUTHERN FRONT
The British began to evacuate their forces from Toulon as the French army surrounding the port continued to pour fire down on them.

19 December 1793
SOUTHERN FRONT
Dugommier recaptured Toulon. As they withdrew, the British had destroyed or removed as much material as possible, but the Spanish contingent left fifteen ships of the line in the port as they departed.

Captured rebel leaders and any suspects identified by the Jacobin representative, Augustin Robespierre, brother of the leader of the Committee of Public Safety, and his followers (including Paul Barras) were executed by firing squad. Once again hundreds of people were killed.

22 December 1793
RHINE FRONT
Hoche defeated the Prussians under Brunswick at Froschwiller.

FRANCE: ARMED FORCES
Following his success at Toulon, Napoleon was promoted to Brigadier-General.

Napoleon's natural military ability had shown itself for the first time at Toulon. Using his military instincts, and a healthy dose of good luck at being in the right place at the right time, he had achieved a significant result against the enemies of the Revolution.

23 December 1793
FRANCE: COUNTER-REVOLUTION
The Vendée revolt was crushed at the battle of Savernay, near Nantes. Over the coming weeks some 3,000 rebel soldiers, ragged starving peasants, were executed. A vicious guerilla war continued throughout the Vendée for many months.

26 December 1793
RHINE FRONT
Wurmser's Austrians were defeated by Hoche at Geisberg, thereby clearing the Alsace region of Allied forces. By the end of the year Mayence had been recaptured and the Rhine frontier secured for France once more.

* 1794 *

January 1794
ALLIED PLANNING
The Allied forces aimed to adopt a plan put together by the Austrian Chief of Staff, Baron Karl Mack von Leiberich. His simple intention was to force the annihilation of the French armies and the defeat of the Republican regime. In Belgium Saxe-Coburg was to concentrate around Ypres.

FRENCH PLANNING

Carnot continued to reorganise the French army and planned to launch a series of offensives throughout the year to clear the Allies from French territory. The Army of the North was to push forward upon Brussels while the Army of the Moselle was to secure Liège. The Army of the Ardennes was to deploy in the area between the two attacking armies.

2 February 1794
FRANCE: ARMED FORCES

Carnot issued orders, his *Amalgame*, on army conduct. 'The general instructions are always to manoeuvre in mass and offensively; to maintain strict, but not overtly meticulous discipline ... and to use the bayonet on every occasion.' This dictum was largely prompted by the lower level of discipline in the new citizen formations. The infantry regiments were converted into three battalion units, each regiment having one regular and two volunteer battalions. These new units were titled Demi-Brigades. The 1st and 3rd Battalions of the new regiments were volunteer units and the 2nd a regular unit. From this formation the classic *ordre mixte* deployment evolved, the 2nd battalions usually deployed in the centre of the line while the 1st and 3rd battalions deployed in column on either flank. A typical Demi-Brigade should deploy six artillery pieces, ninety-six officers and 3,300 men.[5]

Large-scale mobilisation had given France a manpower availability of 750,000 men. Her armies were now better organised and indoctrinated to attack wherever and whenever possible. The French armies had also adopted a flexible system of changing from line to column in attack and of using extensive screens of skirmishers to disrupt the enemy armies.

6 February 1794
ITALIAN FRONT

Napoleon was appointed to command the artillery forces of the Army of Italy. The Army of Italy, some 67,000 men commanded by General Dumerbion, was planning to drive the Piedmontese from Oneglia, some miles along the coast from Nice. This town was hampering French efforts to supply their troops from the sea. Dumerbion had 21,000 of his men available for the attack, the remainder being tied down on security duties.

March 1794
FRANCE: THE TERROR

Alexandre de Beauharnais was arrested, as was General Hoche.

BELGIAN FRONT

General Charles Pichegru was appointed to command the 70,000-strong Army of the North.

10 March 1794
RHINE FRONT
Jourdan was appointed to command the Army of the Moselle.

15 March 1794
FRANCE: THE TERROR
The Hebertists, a major faction in the Paris Commune, were overthrown by Robespierre. Hebert and his followers were arrested after trying to raise the Commune against the Committee of Public Safety.

24 March 1794
FRANCE: THE TERROR
Robespierre, through the Revolutionary Tribunal, had the Hebertists executed. Popular feeling turned against the Committee of Public Safety but they were powerless to prevent Robespierre from eliminating his opponents.

30 March 1794
FRANCE: THE TERROR
Turning against the Danton faction, Robespierre, with the support of Collot d'Herbois and Billaud-Varenne, had Danton, Desmoulins and other supposed enemies arrested.

April 1794
FRANCE: THE TERROR
Robespierre ordered all foreigners and nobles to leave Paris.

WAR AT SEA
Following the poor harvest of 1793 the French had purchased grain in the Americas and prepared to sail it to France in a fleet of more than 120 vessels. Admiral Villaret de Joyeuse, with the vessels of the Brest Fleet, was ordered to sail out to meet the fleet and escort it to France.

The British were aware of the grain fleet and ordered Admiral Howe to intercept it with his fleet. Howe had some twenty-six ships of the line.

BELGIAN FRONT
Pichegru and Jourdan began their invasions of Belgium. The Army of the North began its push towards Lille on a broad front. Jourdan's Army of the Moselle moved upon Liège and Namur from its base around Luxembourg.

ITALIAN FRONT
The Army of Italy successfully drove the Piedmontese from Oneglia and secured the Col di Tenda. Masséna, commanding the central column of the French attack, handled his troops particularly well.

ALPINE FRONT
Kellermann's Army of the Alps secured the Little St Bernard Pass and Mont Cenis.

5 April 1794
FRANCE: THE TERROR
Danton and Desmoulin were executed. The Committee of Public Safety, dominated by Robespierre, was in control of Paris and France, although popular support had been lost through their excesses.

Mid-April 1794
BELGIAN FRONT
Jourdan's advance towards Liège had been held up by Beaulieu's Austrians at Arlon and suffered a minor reverse. Jourdan pauses to regroup so that he could renew the offensive with greater force at the beginning of May.

24 April 1794
BELGIAN FRONT
The Anglo-Austrian cavalry force of just 300 men under General Ott attacked and defeated a French cavalry force at Villers-en-Cauchies near Cambrai. Pursuing the broken French force, Ott then attacked the main force of 12,000 infantry and captured its cannon. Panicked, the French retreated hastily, losing some 1,200 men to an Allied loss of just seventy men.

The French offensive towards Belgium had bogged down in a series of separate engagements. The left wing of the army had succeeded in thrusting forwards upon Lille while the centre was held by the Allies around Landrecies and the right secured the junction with the Army of the Ardennes near Charleroi.

26 April 1794
BELGIAN FRONT
British and Austrian forces defeated elements of the Army of the Ardennes, some 24,000 strong, at Beaumont. The French lost twenty-two artillery pieces during their hasty retreat.[6]

30 April 1794
SPANISH FRONT
The French launched a new offensive against the Spanish. Dugommier's Army of the Pyrennes crossed the Tech river as it took the initiative.

4 May 1794
BELGIAN FRONT
Jourdan, with 41,000 men, resumed his advance from Longwy against the Allies, whose forces were dispersed on a wide front. Saxe-Coburg was

deployed with 65,000 men at Landrecies, Kaunitz with 27,000 at Mauberge, Beaulieu at Arlon with 8,000 while a further 9,000 men were at Trier. The right wing of the French Army of the North was situation around Mauberge with 38,000 men while its centre, with 24,000, was at Guise.

6 May 1794
SPANISH FRONT
Saint-Laurent fell to the Army of the Pyrenees. The French moved towards the coast.

10 May 1794
BELGIAN FRONT
British cavalry defeated a sizeable French infantry force at Willems. The left wing of the Army of the North was around Lille and Courtrai, between two Allied forces, one at Tournai and the other at Thielt.

11 May 1794
BELGIAN FRONT
Pichegru attacked the Allies at Courtrai and defeated the Austrian force led by Clerfayt.

15 May 1794
BELGIAN FRONT
The Allies, with the left wing of the French Army of the North embedded in their own right, decided to use their forces to converge upon the French and annihilate them. Having brought up reinforcements from their own left wing around Mauberge, the Allies had massed a sizeable force.

17 May 1794
BELGIAN FRONT
The Allies began their offensive against the French troops at Lille and Courtrai but were embroiled in bitter fighting.

18 May 1794
BELGIAN FRONT
The Allies under Saxe-Coburg, 74,000 strong, were defeated at Tourcoing by Souham's 70,000. Souham was temporarily commanding Pichegru's Army of the North. The French lost 3,000 men during the fighting to an Allied loss of 5,500 men and sixty cannon.

19 May 1794
BELGIAN FRONT
After their reverse at Tourcoing the Allies fell back upon Tournai to concentrate their forces.

21 May 1794
BELGIAN FRONT
Souham pushed his army forwards towards Tournai to strike at the Allies once more. Jourdan continued his advance from Longwy upon Arlon and Neufchâteau. Beaulieu put up stiff resistance to the French advance.

22 May 1794
BELGIAN FRONT
The French drove into the outlying Allied positions near Tournai and made slow but steady progress. Pichegru returned to the army and resumed command. Souham commanded the main column of the army.

23 May 1794
BELGIAN FRONT
There was further fierce but inconclusive fighting between the French and the Allies at Tournai. The French, with 45,000 troops, lost 6,000 men, while the Allies, 50,000 strong, lost 3,000. Both armies retired from the field but the French Army of the North had managed to remain in the field despite being outnumbered, a significant sign of its growing confidence.

RHINE FRONT
Mollendorf's Prussians defeated the French at Kaiserslautern but failed to follow up the victory.

28 May 1794
BELGIAN FRONT
Jourdan reached Ciney near Dinan as Beaulieu fell back to ensure the security of the Allied flank.

29 May 1794
BELGIAN FRONT
Jourdan received orders to capture Dinan and Charleroi before moving to secure Namur.

SPANISH FRONT
Collioure fell to Dugommier's Army of the Pyrennes. Spain had lost all of its gains in France.

WAR AT SEA
Admiral Howe, with his twenty-six ships, intercepted Villaret de Joyeuse's fleet of twenty-six warships some 400 miles out in the Atlantic. In a running fight the British tried and failed to break the French line.

30 May 1794

WAR AT SEA

There was limited action as Howe again tried to cross the French line but the onset of fog prevented the British carrying through their attack.

31 May 1794

WAR AT SEA

Fog again prevented any further British attacks upon the grain fleet.

June 1794

BELGIAN FRONT

The British landed a force of 7,000 men under Lord Moira at Ostend to reinforce their units already fighting the French.

1 June 1794

WAR AT SEA

Howe managed to bring about a mêlée with Villaret's vessels. In a bitter struggle the French lost one ship sunk (the *Vengeur*) and six captured. Thirteen more were heavily damaged. The British fleet suffered eleven ships badly damaged. Manpower losses were 7,500 French sailors killed, wounded or captured to a British loss of 300 killed and 900 wounded. Despite his losses, Villaret had accomplished his mission, the grain fleet reaching France unmolested. Villaret held off the British long enough before breaking off the action to return the Brest.

Although a tactical victory of British seamanship over the French navy, strategically the French had achieved their objective, the safe passage of their grain fleet. Despite this, the British hailed the action as a glorious victory.

3 June 1794

BELGIAN FRONT

Elements of the French Armies of the Moselle, Ardennes and North linked up to form a massed force of 96,000 men against the Allied left. They became known informally as the Army of the Sambre & Meuse.

4 June 1794

FRANCE: POLITICS

Robespierre was elected President of the Convention.

10 June 1794

FRANCE: POLITICS

Robespierre coerced the Convention into passing a new Law of Suspects (the Law of 22 Prairial). This law enabled the state to arrest people for very little and gave them no defence. Opposition to Robespierre secretly began to galvanise, some members of the Convention, such as Fouché, Barras, Carrier and Tallien, fearing for their lives.

12 June 1794
BELGIAN FRONT
Jourdan crossed the Sambre and invested Charleroi with 55,000 men of his Army of the Sambre & Meuse. The Allies had split their force into two parts, Saxe-Coburg with the bulk to the north facing Pichegru's Army of the North, while the Prince of Orange held 45,000 on the line Mauberge–Charleroi–Namur.

16 June 1794
BELGIAN FRONT
An Allied counter-attack around Charleroi forced Jourdan to raise his siege and pull back across the Sambre.

17 June 1794
BELGIAN FRONT
French forces attacked the Allies at Hooglede but fared badly. However, the French troops rallied and managed to defeat the Allies, compelling them to withdraw to the north.

18 June 1794
BELGIAN FRONT
Jourdan crossed the Sambre once more and again invested Charleroi and its garrison of 3,000 men.

24 June 1794
BELGIAN FRONT
Saxe-Coburg drew forces off his right wing to reinforce the left. He now assembled some 52,000 men close to Charleroi in order to prevent Jourdan from advancing farther and to relieve Charleroi.

25 June 1794
BELGIAN FRONT
Charleroi fell to Jourdan. Saxe-Coburg continued his relief attack, unaware that the town had fallen.

26 June 1794
BELGIAN FRONT
Still unaware that Charleroi had fallen the previous day, Saxe-Coburg continued his effort to relieve the garrison. Jourdan's 73,000 men, released from their siege activities, were surprised by the Allied attack near Fleurus and after initially being pushed back, managed to defeat the Allied right wing. General Jean Baptiste Kléber, commanding the French left, drove the Prince of Orange from the field while Jourdan counter-attacked in the centre. Fighting

continued fiercely with the French gaining ground in the centre and on the left while the Allies pushed back the French right. With the battle going against him, and with news reaching him that Charleroi had already fallen, Saxe-Coburg called off his attack. Both sides had lost around 5,000 men.

The victory at Fleurus seemed to indicate that the French Republic was no longer in mortal danger, and therefore that the Terror was no longer necessary to assure the stability of France against both external and internal enemies. The conspiracy to depose Robespierre, and the excesses of his regime, began to gain momentum.

27 June 1794
BELGIAN FRONT
Saxe-Coburg began to withdraw his forces from Belgium as the Austrians abandoned their fight for their Netherlands province.

2 July 1794
BELGIAN FRONT
Jourdan was appointed commander of the Army of the Sambre & Meuse. The army was around 80,000 men strong.

10 July 1794
BELGIAN FRONT
Brussels fell to the French.

23 July 1794
FRANCE: THE TERROR
Alexandre de Beauharnais was executed.

26 July 1794
FRANCE: THE TERROR
Robespierre made what would be his last speech in the Convention, calling for his enemies to be purged.

27 July 1794
FRANCE: THE TERROR
There was a revolt against Robespierre in the Convention (the coup of 9 Thermidor). Its members voted for and ordered the arrest of Robespierre, his brother Augustin, and his allies, Saint Just, Couthon, Hanriot and Dumas, plus others in Robespierre's faction on charges of crimes against the Republic.

Robespierre and his brother, Saint Just and Couthon were arrested and held in the Hôtel de Ville while in Paris the Commune tried to rally support against the Convention, but to no avail.

BELGIAN FRONT
Liège and Antwerp fell to the armies of Jourdan and Pichegru. Austria

abandoned the Netherlands for good. The French success in Belgium opened up the northern wing of the Prussian forces fighting along the Rhine.

28 July 1794
FRANCE: THE TERROR

During the early hours of the morning Robespierre was declared an outlaw and the leadership of the Commune was ordered arrested. Troops of the National Guard broke into the Hôtel de Ville and attacked Robespierre and his group. Robespierre was shot in the jaw.

By the afternoon the execution of Robespierre had taken place, the dictator dying along with Couthon, Saint Just and his brother under the blade of the guillotine. A further eighteen supporters of Robespierre were also executed.

29 July 1794
FRANCE: THE TERROR

More than seventy people, mainly Robespierre supporters in the Commune leadership, were executed. The Terror was brought to a bloody end.

31 July 1794
FRANCE: POLITICS

The Convention reorganised the Committee of Public Safety. It continued to include Barère, Collot d'Herbois, Carnot and Billaud-Varenne but was joined by Jean Tallien and a number of new members following the execution of Robespierre and his followers. They commonly became known as the Thermidoreans. The Convention was now dominated by moderate men such as Sieyes and Jean Cambacères, but also some realigned radicals, Paul Barras and Joseph Fouché to name but two.

1 August 1794
RHINE FRONT

The French began to form the Army of the Rhine and Moselle under General Jean Moreau.

9 August 1794
FRANCE: POLITICS

Due to his connections with the Jacobins and the brother of the deposed and murdered Robespierre, Napoleon was arrested and jailed at Antibes.

10 August 1794
MEDITERRANEAN FRONT

Corsica fell to the British after a slow campaign across the island.

FRANCE: POLITICS

The Revolutionary Tribunal was reorganised along normal legal lines rather than as an instrument of terror.

13 August 1794
SPANISH FRONT
General Augereau defeated the Spanish at San Lorenzo de la Muga.

17 August 1794
SPANISH FRONT
General Moncey was appointed to command the Army of the Eastern Pyrennes.

20 August 1794
FRANCE: POLITICS
Napoleon was released from jail without charge. He returned to serve with the Army of Italy.

24 August 1794
FRANCE: POLITICS
The Convention reduced the power of the Committee of Public Safety, leaving it with responsibility only for matters of war and foreign policy.

28 August 1794
RHINE FRONT
The Prussians were defeated at Friedelsheim by Moreau. Moreau had launched an invasion of the Rhineland aimed at driving the Prussians back to the river.

29 August 1794
BELGIAN FRONT
The French recaptured Valenciennes.

Early September 1794
ITALIAN FRONT
Austrian forces in Italy and Piedmont, now acting in union with the Piedmontese, took the offensive against the Army of Italy and drove it back along the Riviera. Dego was threatened.

5 September 1794
RHINE FRONT
Mollendorf's Prussians were defeated by Moreau at Battenburg.

13 September 1794
RHINE FRONT
The Prussians were again defeated by Moreau at Herzheim.

15 September 1794
BELGIAN FRONT
The French defeated the Austrians at Boxtel in the Netherlands.

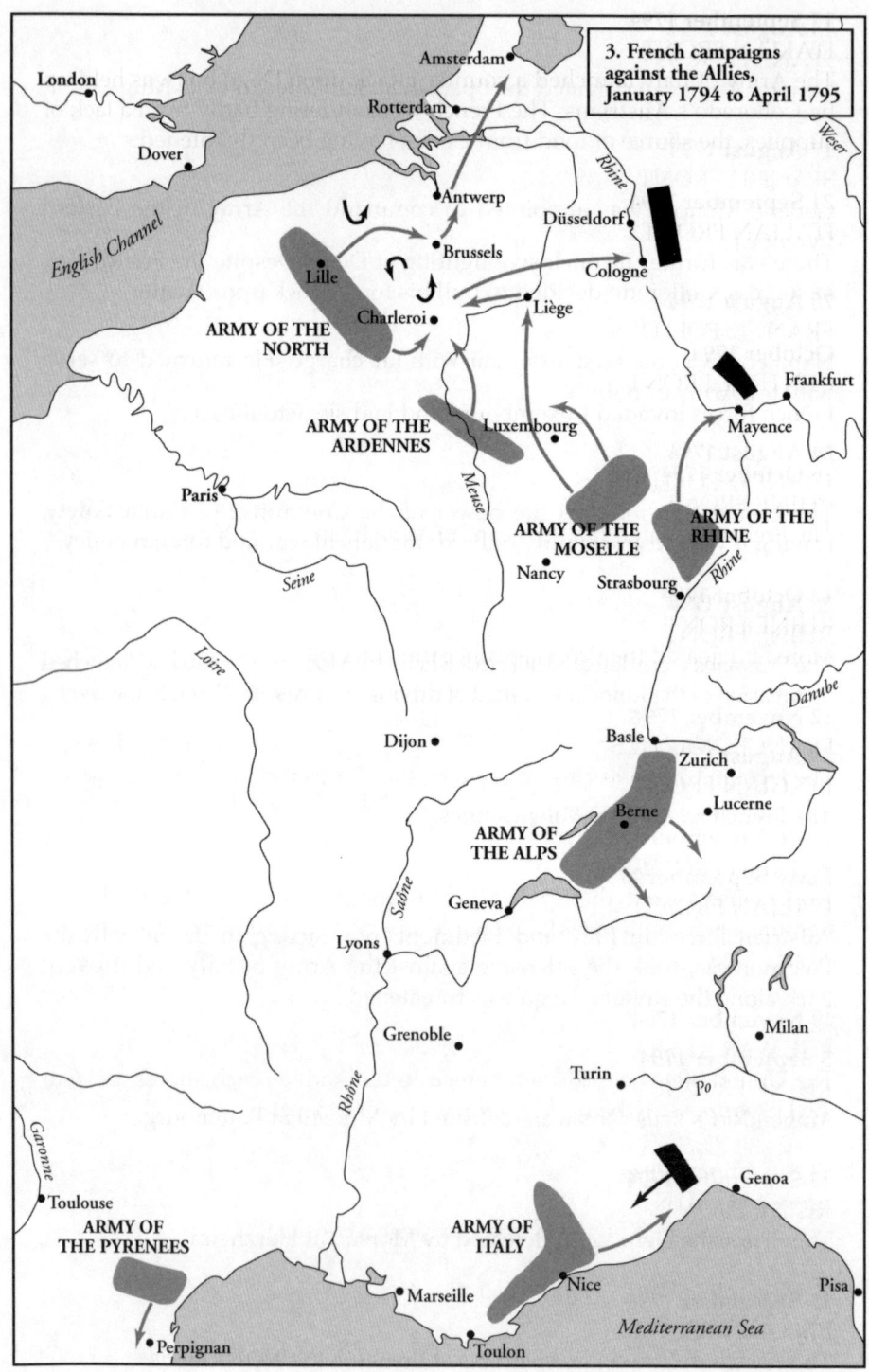

3. French campaigns against the Allies, January 1794 to April 1795

London

Dover

English Channel

Amsterdam

Rotterdam

Antwerp

Düsseldorf

Brussels

Cologne

Lille

Liège

Charleroi

ARMY OF THE
NORTH

Rhine

Weser

Frankfurt

ARMY OF THE
ARDENNES

Luxembourg

Mayence

Paris

ARMY OF THE
MOSELLE

ARMY OF THE
RHINE

Meuse

Nancy

Strasbourg

Seine

Rhine

Danube

Loire

Dijon

Basle

Zurich

Berne

Lucerne

ARMY OF
THE ALPS

Saône

Geneva

Lyons

Grenoble

Milan

Rhine

Turin

Po

Garonne

Genoa

Toulouse

ARMY OF
THE PYRENEES

ARMY OF
ITALY

Nice

Pisa

Marseille

Perpignan

Toulon

Mediterranean Sea

17 September 1794
ITALIAN FRONT
The Army of Italy launched a counter-attack upon Dego but was held up by Colloredo's Austrians. The French were suffering badly from a lack of supplies, the source of food from Genoa having been threatened.

21 September 1794
ITALIAN FRONT
There was further inconclusive fighting at Dego. Despite the French lack of success, Colloredo decided to pull his forces back upon Acqui.

October 1794
CENTRAL FRONT
French forces invaded Luxembourg and laid siege to the city.

16 October 1794
RHINE FRONT
The French defeated the Prussians at Monsheim.

17 October 1794
RHINE FRONT
Moreau defeated the Prussians once more at Zell.

12 November 1794
FRANCE: POLITICS
The Jacobin Club was closed down by the Convention.

17–20 November 1794
SPANISH FRONT
Augereau attacked the Spanish fortifications at Figueras. Amid heavy fighting, Dugommier was killed while observing the attack from Montague Noire.

19 November 1794
THE WAR AT SEA
The United States and Britain agreed to blockade French shores, despite the US supposedly being in an alliance with France.

27 November 1794
SPANISH FRONT
Perignon captured Figueras and laid siege to Rosas.

29 November 1794
RHINE FRONT
Moreau defeated the Prussians at Mainz and invested the city.

ITALIAN FRONT
General Dumerbion was removed from command of the Army of Italy and General Schere appointed in his place. The army now numbered 54,000 men, with just 17,000 available for field operations.

December 1794
SOUTHERN FRONT
The French drove the Piedmonese out of Savoy once more and advanced upon Savona.

FRANCE: POLITICS
As the Convention continued to dismantle the apparatus of the Terror, Carrier, author of the murders in Nantes during the Vendée revolt, was tried and executed. The activities of other Terrorist Committee members, Barère, Billaud-Varenne, Collot d'Herbois and Vadier, were investigated.

* 1795 *

The wars fought for the very survival of France were now past and, with the ending of the Terror and the defeat of the royalist rebels and federal cities, France was able to switch its attention from the interior to using its energy to export its Revolutionary zeal across Europe. Despite having formed a coalition against the French, the Allied powers were not united in their war aims, preventing them from conducting a coordinated campaign on all fronts.

January 1795
BELGIAN FRONT
Pichegru pushed deeper into the United Provinces.

THE OPPOSING FORCES
The *levée en masse* had brought hundreds of thousands of French citizen soldiers into the field. Against an Austrian army of 300,000 men, deployed between the Austrian Netherlands, Italy and home provinces, a British army of 120,000, mainly deployed to protect the British Isles and Empire, with very limited numbers committed to the continent, and a Prussian force of 225,000 men, the French now fielded some 700,000 men in the various armies on their frontiers.

15 January 1795
FRANCE: ARMED FORCES
Kellermann was reinstated in the Army following the fall of the Robespierre regime.

23 January 1795
BELGIAN FRONT
Amsterdam fell to Pichegru's army. In a unique event of military history, advancing French cavalry captured the ice-bound Dutch fleet anchored at Texel. Dutch naval power was a crucial gain for the French as their own fleet was so badly depleted following the purges of the Revolution and the Terror.

February 1795
GERMAN FRONT
The demoralised British expeditionary force, having retreated through Belgium and the Netherlands, marched towards Bremen in order to link up with the Royal Navy and be evacuated to Britain. British performance had been limited and had brought to light a number of glaring deficiencies in the army's equipment and leadership.

FRANCE: CIVIL UNREST
As news of the fall of the Jacobins spread throughout France, the people of Lyon, who had suffered badly following their revolt against Jacobin rule, massacred all the Jacobins they could find.

3 February 1795
SPANISH FRONT
Perignon captured Rosas as his campaign in the Pyrenees continued.

17 February 1795
FRANCE: COUNTER-REVOLUTION
General Hoche brought a temporary peace to the Vendée after he negotiated terms with the rebel leader, François de Charette. Although the Vendée revolt had been crushed at the end of 1793, guerrilla war had continued against the republican forces throughout the region, compelling the army to keep a strong presence there.

21 February 1795
FRANCE: POLITICS
A decree was passed by the Convention separating the Church from the state. The work of the Convention now undid some of the rulings of the Revolutionary assemblies in an effort to create stability throughout France.

March 1795
INTERNATIONAL POLITICS
Following the defeat of the Dutch and the occupation of Holland, the Convention ordered the creation of the Batavian Republic. This new republic, which would be created in May, was to be an important and long-term ally and satellite of France, being created around 'old' Holland.

MEDITERRANEAN FRONT
An expeditionary force from the Army of Italy, including Napoleon among their number, attempted to regain control of Corsica, but was forced to abandon its efforts due to the presence of the Royal Navy.

3 March 1795
CENTRAL FRONT
Kellermann was once again appointed to command the Army of the Alps and Italy. General Scherer took command of French forces operating against the Spanish in the Pyrenees

April 1795
FRANCE: ARMED FORCES
Napoleon, having returned to Paris after the abortive attempt to regain Corsica, was appointed to command the artillery of the Army of the West, which was fighting royalist forces in Brittany. He requested a post with the Army of the Alps instead and, when this was refused, applied for sick leave.

1 April 1795
FRANCE: POLITICS
The coup of 12 Germinal took place. The *sans-culottes* of Paris, the poorest elements of the city's populace, invaded the Convention and demanded the constitution of 1793 be adopted. General Pichegru restored order by placing the city under martial law.

5 April 1795
RHINE FRONT
France and Prussia signed the Peace of Basel. Prussia, led in her negotiations by the prime minister, Count von Haugwitz, recognised French claims to the left bank of the Rhine while France agreed to the neutralisation of North Germany. This was the first treaty agreed by one of the old states of Europe with the new regime in France. Prussia now adopted a position of neutrality with the French, and took no part in the subsequent wars fought by Austria.

14 April 1795
BELGIAN FRONT
The British Netherlands expedition, having finally reached Bremen, completed its evacuation from mainland Europe.

16 April 1795
INTERNATIONAL POLITICS
The Peace of Holland was signed in The Hague, ending the conflict between France and the United Provinces.

6 May 1795
SPANISH FRONT
Perignon was defeated at Bascara.

16 May 1795
INTERNATIONAL POLITICS
The Treaty of Basel was signed, formally ending hostilities between France and Prussia. Spain and Saxony signed shortly afterwards as the First Coalition fell apart.

The Treaty of the Hague confirmed the Peace of Holland. Holland became the Batavian Republic, independent from France but with a French garrison of 25,000 troops in her territory, and tied to France through military alliance.

20 May 1795
FRANCE: CIVIL UNREST
The rising of 1 Prairial began. Once again the disaffected and hungry *sans-culottes* of Paris rose against the Convention, invading the Tuileries and murdering a deputy. As the crowd began to disperse the National Guard secured the Tuileries. General Menou was then called in with his army units to restore order.

21 May 1795
FRANCE: CIVIL UNREST
A mob of 20,000 *sans-culottes* attempted to invade the Tuileries once again but was held at bay by Menou's troops.

23 May 1795
FRANCE: CIVIL UNREST
Menou unleashed his 20,000 troops against the mob and dispersed them.

30 May 1795
SPANISH FRONT
Scherer replaced Perignon as commander of the Army of the Pyrennes.

8 June 1795
FRANCE: ÉMIGRÉ FORCES
The Dauphin, who had assumed the title Louis XVII, died in the Temple Prison in Paris, a prisoner of the Republic. King Louis XVI's brother would assume the title Louis XVIII. He was in exile at Verona.

8–12 June 1795
WAR AT SEA
A British fleet under Admiral William Cornwallis, escorting a transport fleet carrying an émigré invasion force to Quiberon Bay, managed to prevent a French sortie to attack the invasion force. Admiral Villaret, with twelve ships, was held at bay by five British blockade ships.

23 June 1795
WAR AT SEA
Admiral Villaret again attempted to intercept the invasion fleet but was intercepted by Admiral Lord Hood with twelve ships off Ile de Groix, near Lorient. The French lost three ships captured and had to break off the battle.

24 June 1795
FRANCE: ÉMIGRÉ FORCES
Louis XVI's brother, the Comte de Provence, declared himself Louis XVIII in a proclamation issued at Verona.

26 June 1795
CENTRAL FRONT
Luxembourg fell to the French after an eight-month siege.

27 June 1795
WESTERN FRANCE
The British landed an émigré force of 5,000 men under the command of Puisaye and d'Hervilly, at Quiberon near Vannes. They linked up with around 15,000 Chouans who were still under arms despite the agreement brokered by Hoche. Their aim was the spark a Royalist revolt in Brittany. British ships also blockaded Brest. Unfortunately the émigré force had landed at an appalling site, situated on an easily isolated peninsula.

July 1795
RHINE FRONT
Pichegru was appointed to command the Army of the Rhine and Moselle. He had 90,000 men deployed in Alsace and around Mainz and faced Wurmser's 85,000 Austrians. Jourdan had a further 100,000 French troops in his Army of the Sambre & Meuse, deployed west of Coblenz. He faced an equal number of Austrian soldiers under the command of Marshal Clerfayt. With Prussia out of the war, the Austrians were fighting to prevent French expansion into southern Germany, traditionally an area of Austrian influence.

The French plan was for Jourdan to attack from Neuweid towards Dusseldorf and the Main while Pichegru was to secure Mannheim and the line of the Neckar.

ITALIAN FRONT
The Austrians and Piedmontese unleashed a major offensive aimed at driving the French back along the Riviera and out of their gains in Piedmont. Vado was taken and Genoa isolated.

16–20 July 1795
WESTERN FRANCE
Hoche's Army of the West, with 13,000 men, comprehensively defeated

the émigré force on the Quiberon peninsula. The royalists lost 8,200 men in hard fighting to a French Republican loss of just 500 men.

Following the battle the Convention sent Tallien as its representative to try the prisoners. He ordered the execution of nearly 800 émigrés.

22 July 1795
INTERNATIONAL POLITICS
The French and Spanish made peace at Basle. Another member of the Coalition fell aside. Slowly but surely the French were gaining the upper hand, securing their borders against foreign invasion.

August 1795
FRANCE: POLITICS
Pichegru initiated secret negotiations with émigré forces. France made peace with Saxony, Hesse-Cassel and Hanover.

5 August 1795
FRANCE: POLITICS
Lazare Carnot resigned from the Committee of Public Safety in protest at the Thermidorean foreign policy.

21 August 1795
FRANCE: ARMED FORCES
Napoleon joined the Bureaux Topographique, enabling him to stay close to political events in Paris.

22 August 1795
FRANCE: POLITICS
A five-man group (Louis de la Revellière-Lepeaux, Jean François Reubell, Louis Letourneur and Lazare Carnot but dominated by the scheming Paul Barras), calling themselves the Directory, began to built up its strength in the failing government. Letourneaux concentrated on naval affairs, Carnot on the army, Reubell called for French expansion to her natural frontiers and Revellière-Lepeaux on education. Barras effectively controlled the Directory but Reubell also strove for dominant power.

September 1795
FRANCE: ARMED FORCES
Napoleon was appointed to head a military mission to reorganise the Turkish artillery. He prepared to leave for the East.

ITALIAN FRONT
General Augereau was transferred from the now peaceful Spanish frontier to the Army of Italy. Scherer, released from his command in the Pyrenees, resumed command of the Army of Italy.

FRANCE: CIVIL UNREST
There was renewed unrest in Paris against the Convention.

3–6 September 1795
RHINE FRONT
Archduke Charles, brother of Emperor Francis of Austria, defeated Jourdan's Army of the Sambre & Meuse at Wurzburg as the French attempted their invasion of Germany. Pichegru, in league with the Allies, had betrayed the French plans.

27 September 1795
FRANCE: POLITICS
The Convention approved the constitution of 1793 but the populace of Paris was determined to bring down the legislative body no matter what.

1 October 1795
FRANCE: POLITICS
France annexed the Austrian Netherlands (Belgium).

3 October 1795
FRANCE: CIVIL UNREST
As the Directory continued to build its power base in place of the increasingly unpopular Convention, Paul Barras was charged with the defence of the Tuileries against the increasingly violent mobs in Paris. He decided to appoint Napoleon Bonaparte to command the army forces in Paris. Barras knew Napoleon from his time at the siege of Toulon.

4 October 1795
FRANCE: CIVIL UNREST
Napoleon took command of the 5,000 troops available in Paris. Realising that his soldiers would be unable to stand without heavy weapons in support, he sent his cavalry commander, Major Joachim Murat, to collect some cannon and bring them back to his positions around the Tuileries.

5 October 1795
FRANCE: CIVIL UNREST
A crowd of 35,000 built up throughout the day, their aim being to break into the Tuileries. Royalists had hijacked the protests and attempted to overthrow the Convention. Using his cannon against the mob, Napoleon dispersed them with a 'whiff of grapeshot'. Hundreds were killed as they attempted the surge towards his guns. The power of the Parisian mob was broken for good. Napoleon gained a reputation for himself as a soldier who would use any means to carry out his orders ruthlessly. Moreover, he had saved the fledgling Directory from destruction along with the defunct Convention.

RHINE FRONT
Jourdan again attempted to press his invasion towards Frankfurt. Clerfayt outmanoeuvred him and defeated him in battle near Hochst. Jourdan now began to pull his troops back towards the Moselle.

16 October 1795
FRANCE: ARMED FORCES
Napoleon was promoted to the rank of major-general by a grateful Directory.

26 October 1795
FRANCE: POLITICS
The Convention dissolved itself in favour of a new Legislative Corps of 750 members. The Corps was split into two Councils, one of 250 members, the Council of Elders and another of 500, named the Council of 500. The Directory took control of the governance of the state. Their main aim was the military expansion of France. Carnot remained Minister for War. Barras strove to gain hegemony but met competition from Reubell.

27 October 1795
FRANCE: ARMED FORCES
Napoleon was appointed Commander-in-Chief of the Army of the Interior. With little field experience, and none against foreign enemies, his rise to power had been both surprising and meteoric.

29 October 1795
RHINE FRONT
Austrian forces under Marshal Charles von Clerfayt defeated Pichegru's blockading force at Mayence. The Austrians now moved to invade the Palatinate.

November 1795
RHINE FRONT
Pichegru, long having been in league with royalists and the Austrians, defected to the Allies.

ITALIAN FRONT
The Army of Italy launched a counter-attack from its base around Nice in an effort to retake Vado and reopen communications and lines of supply with Genoa.

15 November 1795
WESTERN FRONT
A British attempt at a landing with 2,500 troops on the Poitou coast was foiled and they were forced to withdraw.

22–24 November 1795
ITALIAN FRONT
Elements of the Army of Italy, led by Masséna, defeated an Austro-Piedmontese force under Wallis in defensive positions near Loana. Scherer failed to follow up on the success and merely returned to positions along the Riviera.

21 December 1795
RHINE FRONT
Marshal Charles von Clerfayt agreed to a general armistice along the Rhine front.

The Revolutionary Wars had raged unabated since the spring of 1792. France had been brought to the very brink of collapse but, through the Terror of the Robespierre regime and the Revolutionary zeal of her citizen armies, disaster had been held off. Recovering both internally and abroad, the French had managed to quash the revolts which had swept three quarters of the nation while also defeating the Allies along the Rhine and in the Netherlands. As her enemies left the field one by one, the stability and security of the new French Republic seemed more assured. Through the midst of civil disorder and external threat, Napoleon Bonaparte had risen rapidly through the ranks of the army. It was this man who would upset the Directory's plans for the continuation of the war in the most unexpected way.

Notes

1. Connelly Owen, *The French Revolution and Napoleonic Era*, p. 114
2. Haythornthwaite, *Napoleon's Military Machine*, p. 160 on the deployment of the effective units of the French Navy.
3. Ibid, p. 106
4. Connelly Owen, *The French Revolution and Napoleonic Era*, p. 130
5. Haythornthwaite, *op cit*, p. 27
6. Ibid, p. 107

CHAPTER III

The Rising Star of France

France had emerged as a united force from the Revolutionary Wars. With the Directory in command, the French aim remained to take the war to her enemies. An invasion of Italy was to divert Austrian attention from the main French effort, an invasion of southern Germany, the overall plan being no less than the envelopment of the Austrian forces and capture of Vienna. Napoleon was to launch the diversionary attack in the south with his small Army of Italy while Moreau led the southern French pincer into Bavaria and the Tyrol, and Jourdan advanced to the north to effect the northern arm of the pincer through Germany.

* 1796 *

February 1796
FRANCE: POLITICS
The Directory began to suppress the resurgent Jacobins and other opponents of their regime. Royalist groups began to emerge to challenge the republicans through political means.

February–March 1796
FRANCE: COUNTER REVOLUTION
General Hoche made good progress against the Vendée rebels, capturing a number of their leading figures, including Georges Cadoudal.

FRANCE: MILITARY PLANNING
The French began to build up their forces along the Rhine in line with Carnot's planned two-pronged offensive into Germany. Jourdan, with 72,000 men, was to draw the Austrian forces under Archduke Charles away from Moreau, whose army of 78,000 men was to invade Bavaria. Once Charles had been drawn away, Jourdan was to destroy the Austrian army and then push forward to link up with Moreau. They would then both advance east to link up with the Army of Italy as it pushed up from northern Italy. One of the main considerations pushing the French to

advance beyond their own borders, and the Rhine in particular, was their capacity to feed their armies through their reliance on forage.

2 March 1796
FRANCE: ARMED FORCES
Napoleon Bonaparte, 27 years old, was appointed to command the Army of Italy, replacing General Barthelemy Scherer. His appointment had been gained largely through his association with Barras.

9 March 1796
FRANCE: POLITICS
Napoleon married Josephine de Beauharnais, former mistress of Paul Barras and widow of the terror victim Alexandre. Josephine's son, Eugene, would eventually become a loyal follower and member of Napoleon's inner circle.

27 March 1796
ITALIAN FRONT
Napoleon arrived to command his army. It comprised Masséna's division (which included the smaller divisions of La Harpe and Meynier) with 12,000 men, Seurier's division with 9,450 men, Augereau's division with 6,200 men, Stengal's cavalry force of 3,500 and some 3,800 artillerymen and engineers. Macquard's division, with around 3,400 men, and Garnier's division with another 3,400, were deployed behind the main forces, guarding the coastal and northern approaches to Nice while to the rear, guarding his lines of communication, Napoleon had around 12,000 men. This gave the Army of Italy a total deployment of some 62,000 men with sixty field cannon and twenty-four light cannon. For operational use there were around 42,000 men available, spread out from Nice.

Napoleon's three main divisional commanders, Generals Jean Serurier, Pierre Augereau and André Masséna, were all more experienced in higher commands than their new commander in chief. Serurier was of aristocratic birth and had been an officer in the Royal Army while Augereau, of peasant birth, had risen through the ranks. Masséna was a former smuggler who had also risen through the ranks. Berthier, another aristocrat with a long record of service in the Royal Army, was Napoleon's chief of staff and had travelled with him to join the Army of Italy. Also with the Army of Italy was Joachim Murat, in the cavalry arm, and Marmont, with the artillery. This grouping brought together a number of men who would follow Napoleon in the following two decades.

The Austrian forces facing the French numbered 35,000 men under General Beaulieu. They were deployed south-west of Milan. The Piedmontese, under Baron Colli, had a further 25,000 men south of Turin. Thus, both Allied armies were widely separated on the Lombard Plain, enabling Napoleon to identify the opportunity to deliberately interpose his own force between these two and defeat them one at a time. The Piedmontese were further distracted by the presence of Kellermann's Army of the Alps, 18,000 strong, to their west near Lake Geneva.

10 April 1796
ITALIAN FRONT

With Napoleon's army moving up from Nice to Savona, the Austrians launched an attack with 10,000 men to the west of Genoa, around Voltri, in order to strengthen their seaward flank. The French unit on this flank, numbering 3,000 men under General Cervoni, part of Napoleon's Army of Italy, managed to hold off the Austrian attacks and conducted a skilful withdrawal to avoid encirclement.

In preparation for his offensive against the Austrians and Piedmontese, Napoleon reorganised his support units into two cavalry divisions and an artillery reserve.

12 April 1796
ITALIAN FRONT

Napoleon, with 10,000 men in the van, launched a rapid advance and crashed into the Austrian right flank force of 9,000 men at Montenotte. Beaulieu was defeated, losing 2,500 men to a French loss of just 800. There was also sporadic fighting close to Millesimo as Augereau, with 9,000 men, began his move against the Piedmontese.

13 April 1796
ITALIAN FRONT

Detaching Masséna to cover Beaulieu, Napoleon moved to attack Colli's army. Augereau attacked Provera at Cosseria. Joubert, one of the junior French commanders, was wounded during the fighting.

Masséna was aggressive in his movements and captured the town of Dego from the Austrians. He then allowed his men to forage widely.

14 April 1796
ITALIAN FRONT

With his 12,000 men widely scattered around Dego, Masséna was caught by surprise by an Austrian attack with a concentrated force of 5,700 men. The Austrians pushed forward and recaptured the town, and with it all of Masséna's cannon.

Provera, commanding a sizeable detachment of Piedmontese troops, surrendered to Augereau after being defeated at Millesimo.

15 April 1796
ITALIAN FRONT

Napoleon concentrated his forces against the Austrians at Dego and drove them out of the town after a day of hard fighting. The bitter struggle cost the Austrians 3,000 casualties to a French loss, over two days, of 1,500 men.

16 April 1796
ITALIAN FRONT
Baron Colli counter-attacked with his Piedmontese forces, striking Augereau around Ceva. Bitter fighting erupted as the French attempted to stem the Piedmontese advance. Napoleon turned his army away from Dego and began to march to Augereau's aid, rather than pursue the retreating Austrians.

17 April 1796
ITALIAN FRONT
Colli continued to attack Augereau at Ceva, forcing the French to give ground.

19 April 1796
ITALIAN FRONT
In further heavy fighting the French resumed their attack but were held up around San Michele.

21 April 1796
ITALIAN FRONT
Colli, under increasing French pressure, tried to pull his 13,000-strong army back to high ground before Mondovi. Having arrived to reinforce Augereau, Napoleon attacked with a combined force of 17,500 men. The initial French attack was halted but a renewed assault drove the Piedmontese back off the ridge.

22 April 1796
ITALIAN FRONT
Colli retreated from Mondovi, opening up the Piedmont plain to advancing French forces.

23 April 1796
ITALIAN FRONT
With his small army battered and demoralised, Colli sought terms for an armistice with Napoleon.

27 April 1796
ITALIAN FRONT
Informed of the collapse of the Piedmontese, and realising that his advanced position was exposed to French attack, Beaulieu withdrew his forces towards the crossing over the Po river at Valenza.

28 April 1796
ITALIAN FRONT
Napoleon agreed an armistice with Piedmont. It became known as the Armistice of Cherasco.

2 May 1796
ITALIAN FRONT
Beaulieu crossed the Po, retreating to the north bank. He then spread his forces out on a sixty-mile front to protect against a French assault.

5 May 1796
ITALIAN FRONT
Napoleon, pursuing the retreating Austrians now that the Piedmontese were out of the war, demonstrated along the Po east of Valenza in an effort to distract Austrian attention.

6 May 1796
ITALIAN FRONT
Having attracted Austrian attention to the Po around Valenza, Napoleon marched his army rapidly east. Beaulieu was unaware of this change in the French area of operations.

7 May 1796
ITALIAN FRONT
Having crossed the frontier into the neutral Duchy of Parma and marched seventy miles in two days, Napoleon launched a thrust across the Po at Piacenza, well behind the Austrian flank. With their left wing threatened, the entire Austrian defence all along the Po river line was undermined.

8 May 1796
ITALIAN FRONT
Napoleon defeated Beaulieu at Fombio. The Austrians began to retreat, abandoning Pavia and Milan.

10 May 1796
ITALIAN FRONT
Napoleon, driving north into the crumbling Austrian positions with some 18,000 men, defeated Beaulieu's rearguard of 9,000 men in a hard fought action at Lodi. The Austrians fought desperately to prevent the French using the bridge at Lodi to cross the Adda river, ranging artillery along the causeway to inflict heavy losses on the French attackers. The first attack was repulsed but, with Napoleon himself involved in the fighting, siting artillery pieces, a renewed assault by General Masséna carried the French across the bridge. Both armies had suffered around 1,000 casualties in the fighting.

With their position in northern Italy perilous, the Austrians conducted an ordered withdrawal towards the Tyrol and Venice.

15 May 1796
ITALIAN FRONT
Napoleon entered Milan in triumph. The Austrian garrison retired to the citadel and held out for a further six weeks.

21 May 1796
ITALIAN FRONT
Piedmont made peace with France. King Victor Amadeus II surrendered Savoy and Nice.

26 May 1796
ITALIAN FRONT
The Army of Italy formed new Demi Brigades.

29 May 1796
ITALIAN FRONT
Napoleon advanced to the Mincio river with 28,000 men. Beaulieu had 19,000 stretched out along the Mincio between Lake Garda and Mantua and a further 11,000 anchored inside Mantua itself.

30 May 1796
ITALIAN FRONT
Napoleon broke through the Austrian defences on the Mincio, defeating Beaulieu's detachment of 6,000 men at Borghetto. The Austrian force was scattered and quickly retired towards the Adige river and into the safety of the Tyrol.

Northern Italy with the exception of Mantua was lost. Inside Mantua, 13,000 Austrian soldiers, with 500 cannon, were trapped.

In a campaign lasting less than two months Napoleon had achieved a stunning victory. Piedmont had been knocked out of the war in a matter of days and the Austrians swept from northern Italy. Using his starving army aggressively to bring the enemy to battle, Napoleon had demonstrated his brilliance, and convinced not only his officers, but also himself, of his greatness. The Allies had not experienced war like this, with the primary French aim being the destruction of the enemy field army rather than the acquisition of territory.

June 1796
MEDITERRANEAN FRONT
French successes in northern Italy compelled the British Mediterranean Fleet to abandon its base at Leghorn.

4 June 1796
GERMAN FRONT
The French prepared to begin their offensive into Germany. They deployed Jourdan's 78,000 strong Army of the Sambre & Meuse and Moreau's 76,000 strong Army of the Rhine and Moselle against the Austrians in Germany.

Jourdan faced around 80,000 men under Archduke Charles along the Middle Rhine while Moreau faced General Latour, who had a further 55,000 on the Upper Rhine.

ITALIAN FRONT
Napoleon left Serurier to lay siege to Mantua while he deployed the bulk of his army along the line of the Adige.

10 June 1796
GERMAN FRONT
Jourdan crossed the Rhine at Dusseldorf. This was the start of the French offensive into Germany. Napoleon's victories in Italy had succeeded in drawing Austrian attention to the south but there were still sizeable contingents deployed in southern German and along the Rhine.

16 June 1796
GERMAN FRONT
Archduke Charles defeated forward elements of Jourdan's army in a hard fought action at Wetzlar. Having attracted Charles to him, Jourdan slowly began to fall back towards the Rhine.

21 June 1796
ITALIAN FRONT
Beaulieu handed over command of his remaining forces in Italy to General Dagobert Wurmser.

23–27 June 1796
GERMAN FRONT
Moreau's Army of the Rhine and Moselle began to cross the Rhine at Strasbourg. Informed of this new assault, Charles left 36,000 men under General Alexander Wartensleben to watch Jourdan before moving south with another 20,000 to confront Moreau. Charles had split his weaker force in an effort to cover two stronger opponents.

INTERNATIONAL POLITICS
The Armistice of Bologna ended the brief conflict between France and the Vatican. Napoleon had managed to extract a large tribute from the Papacy to fund the Directory's war effort.

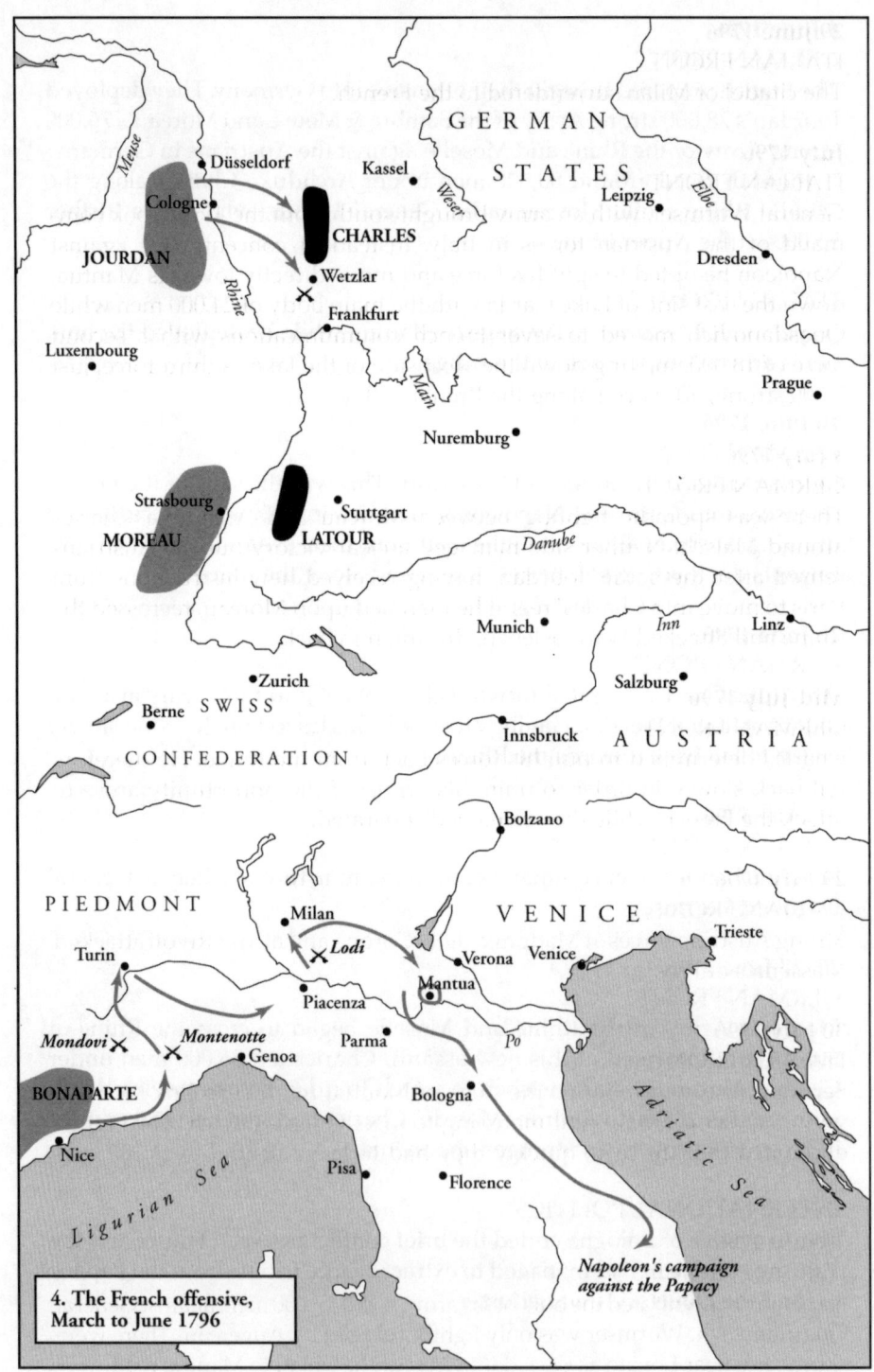

4. The French offensive,
March to June 1796

Napoleon's campaign
against the Papacy

29 June 1796
ITALIAN FRONT
The citadel of Milan surrendered to the French.

July 1796
ITALIAN FRONT
General Wurmser, with an army brought south from the Tyrol, took command of the Austrian forces in Italy. Instead of concentrating against Napoleon he opted to split his force and move directly towards Mantua, down the east side of Lake Garda with the main body of 24,000 men while Quasdanovich moved to sever French communications with a second force of 18,000, moving down the west side of the lake. A third force, just 5,000 strong, advanced along the Brenta valley.

9 July 1796
GERMAN FRONT
There was sporadic fighting between Moreau and Archduke Charles around Malsch. Neither side managed a clear victory but the Austrians retired after the battle. Jourdan, having received new instructions from Paris to move into Charles' rear if he marched upon Moreau, recrossed the Rhine and attacked Wartensleben, driving him back.

Mid-July 1796
GERMAN FRONT
Charles determined to pull his forces back from the Rhine. He therefore fell back slowly in order to unite his armies if the opportunity arose to attack the French while they remained separated.

29 July 1796
ITALIAN FRONT
Strong Austrian forces at Madonna della Corona and also at Rivoli attacked Masséna's outposts.

30 July 1796
ITALIAN FRONT
Serurier hastily abandoned the siege of Mantua in order to link his force with Napoleon's main unit marching to meet Quasdanovich. The French evacuated their force so quickly they had to leave behind over 100 cannon.

31 July 1796
ITALIAN FRONT
Napoleon concentrated the bulk of his army, some 47,000 men, against General Quasdanovich. Wurmser was only lightly covered by Augereau. There were skirmishes near Lonato as Quasdanovich cut the Milan to Mantua road.

1 August 1796

GERMAN FRONT

The advance into Germany had eaten away at French strength, Moreau now having fewer than 50,000 men while Jourdan had just 45,000. Charles had been able to bring up reinforcements and now had 34,000 men. Wartensleben, still falling back before Jourdan, also had around 30,000 men.

2 August 1796

ITALIAN FRONT

Fighting broke out again near Lonato as Napoleon's forces began to concentrate against the Austrians.

3 August 1796

ITALIAN FRONT

Napoleon, with 10,000 men, attacked Quasdanovich's 18,000 men at Lonato. The Austrians, moving forward in three columns, were defeated in detail and suffered 3,000 casualties. A further 3,000 men were isolated and forced to surrender. The remainder beat a hasty retreat to the north along Lake Garda. French losses were around 2,000 men.

General Augereau's division fought a successful delaying action against Wurmser at Castiglione in order to prevent him linking up with Quasdanovich.

GERMAN FRONT

Charles left Latour with 30,000 men to continue the fighting withdrawal against Moreau while he moved with 28,000 to join up with Wartensleben.

4 August 1796

ITALIAN FRONT

Leaving minor forces to cover the retreating Quasdanovich, Napoleon turned his army about to concentrate against Wurmser.

5 August 1796

ITALIAN FRONT

Napoleon, with 35,000 men, attacked Wurmser's 15,500 near Castiglione. The French, with Masséna on the left, Augereau on the right and Kilmaine's cavalry on the extreme right wing, struck the Austrian frontally. Serurier's division marched up from the rear but attacked earlier than planned, alerting Wurmser to the envelopment Napoleon hoped to spring around him. Amid heavy fighting the Austrians held their own until Masséna charged forward with the French artillery and smashed the Austrian left. The French then wheeled around, rolling the Austrian front upon itself. Despinois then arrived with French reinforcements to add to the fury, striking the Austrian right wing hard. Wurmser ordered the retreat of his broken force. The Austrians then retired across the Mincio, and from there, back into the Tyrol although some of the scattered elements of Wurmser's force, around 6,000 men, made it to Mantua. This battle had cost Wurmser 3,000 casualties and Napoleon just over 1,000.

11 August 1796
GERMAN FRONT
Wartensleben fought a bitter drawn battle at Neresheim but was again compelled to withdraw.

12 August 1796
GERMAN FRONT
Archduke Charles was pushed back across the Danube between Ulm and Donauworth by Moreau's advancing forces. Wartensleben also pulled back upon Amberg. Charles determined on a new plan to concentrate against Jourdan's rear. Jourdan was close to Nuremberg and moving towards Ingolstadt.

14 August 1796
GERMAN FRONT
Charles deployed Latour, with 30,000 men, to cover Moreau while he moved with 27,000 against Jourdan. He recrossed the Danube and advanced to the north.

19 August 1796
INTERNATIONAL POLITICS
The First Treaty of San Ildefonso brought France and Spain into alliance. The threat posed by the combined Spanish and French naval forces compelled the British to abandon the Mediterranean before the end of the year.

24 August 1796
GERMAN FRONT
Charles attacked Jourdan's flank and rear with his 27,000 while Wartensleben held the French frontally. Jourdan, with 34,000, had been pushing Wartensleben's 19,000 back near Amberg. The battle was fierce and Jourdan was compelled to withdraw or risk being trapped by the two Austrian forces, losing 2,000 men to an Austrian loss of just 500.

Moreau, realising he was facing a minor part of the Austrian force, launched an immediate attack and defeated Latour at Friedberg.

ITALIAN FRONT
Napoleon left 8,000 men to renew the siege of Mantua while he pushed
north towards Trent with his remaining 34,000. The Austrian garrison
of Mantua had grown to 17,000 after fugitives had joined it from
Wurmser's defeated army.

25 August 1796
GERMAN FRONT
Learning of Moreau's victory, Jourdan regrouped his force near Wurzburg.
Charles attempted to envelop Jourdan once again but moved too slowly.
Moreau pushed forward towards Munich.

29 August 1796
GERMAN FRONT
Learning of Latour's defeat, Archduke Charles despatched 10,000 men
from his own command as reinforcements. Charles was left with just
50,000 men to face Jourdan.

September 1796
ITALIAN FRONT
Wurmser had regrouped his army in the Tyrol and prepared to launch
another effort to recover northern Italy and relieve Mantua. Despite having been defeated already due to the division of his forces, Wurmser made
the same mistake again. This time he sent General Davidovich with 20,000
men to defend the Tyrol from French attack while he led the main force
of 26,000 men down the Brenta Valley towards Mantua. Napoleon was
unaware that the Austrians had regrouped and planned to renew their
offensive.

2 September 1796
ITALIAN FRONT
Napoleon defeated Davidovich at Caliano on the Adige river and pushed
towards Trent.

3 September 1796
GERMAN FRONT
Archduke Charles, with 44,000 men, attacked Jourdan's 30,000 at
Wurzburg. Outmanoeuvred, Jourdan's flanks were enveloped and he
went down badly. Struggling to disengage, the French lost 3,000 men
killed or wounded and a further 4,000 captured, plus seven cannon lost,
before breaking off the battle and retiring towards the Rhine. Austrian
losses were just 1,500 men. Jourdan now retired his army to the line of the
Lahn river.

When Moreau learned of Jourdan's defeat and withdrawal, he broke off his pursuit of Latour and, over the course of the next six weeks, began to fall back. Charles attempted, unsuccessfully, to intercept him.

ITALIAN FRONT
Napoleon continued to attack Davidovich and push him back towards Trent.

4 September 1796
ITALIAN FRONT
Masséna, leading Napoleon's advance with a force of 20,000 men, defeated Davidovich's 10,000 at Roveredo. The Austrians suffered 3,000 casualties to a French loss of just 800.

5 September 1796
ITALIAN FRONT
Napoleon continued his advance, driving the Austrians back through Trent. He then learned of Wurmser's advance and began a forced march back down the Brenta valley to overtake the Austrian advance.

7 September 1796
ITALIAN FRONT
The French defeated a minor Austrian force at Primolano.

8 September 1796
ITALIAN FRONT
Napoleon, with 22,000 men, intercepted Wurmser at Bassano. Augereau and Masséna each attacked the Austrian flanks, isolating a division of the enemy force, compelling it to surrender. Wurmser fought his way free with a sizeable force and pushed towards Mantua. The defeat had cost him 4,000 captured and thirty-five guns but the remainder of his army was split apart, 12,000 running for Mantua with Wurmser while another 3,000 fled to the east.

13 September 1796
ITALIAN FRONT
Wurmser broke through to Mantua. The garrison swelled to 28,000 with his arrival.

14 September 1796
WAR AT SEA
A French squadron under Admiral Richery evaded the British blockade of Toulon and escaped from the Mediterranean. Richery then sailed to Newfoundland where he prayed on Canadian commercial shipping.

15 September 1796
ITALIAN FRONT
The Austrians attempted to prevent the French renewing the siege of Mantua but were repulsed by Masséna and General Charles Kilmaine. The Austrians lost 4,000 men in the fighting and the siege was closed once more.

16 September 1796
ITALIAN FRONT
Battle of San Giorgio.

24 September 1796
ITALIAN FRONT
Baron Josef Alvintzy was appointed to command the Austrian forces in Italy. He also decided to split his army and advance on a number of fronts.

1 October 1796
ITALIAN FRONT
French forces completed the blockade of Mantua, some 9,000 French troops containing 28,000 Austrians.

8 October 1796
INTERNATIONAL POLITICS
Spain declared war on Britain.

26 October 1796
GERMAN FRONT
Moreau re-crossed the Rhine at Hunningen.

1 November 1796
ITALIAN FRONT
Alvintzy renewed the offensive into northern Italy. He sent Davidovich with 16,000 men down the valley of the Adige while he moved himself with 27,000 upon Vicenza. He intended the two forces to link up at Verona before advancing to relieve Mantua. Napoleon was aware of the Austrian intent and moved his 30,000 men between the two enemy forces. General Vaubois, with 8,000, was deployed to cover Davidovich while Napoleon took 18,000 to tackle Alvintzy. He held another 4,000 men in reserve.

6 November 1796
ITALIAN FRONT
The French, with 20,000 men, met the Austrians in battle at Bassano for a second time. The Austrian force of 28,000 suffered 2,800 casualties to a French loss of 3,000.

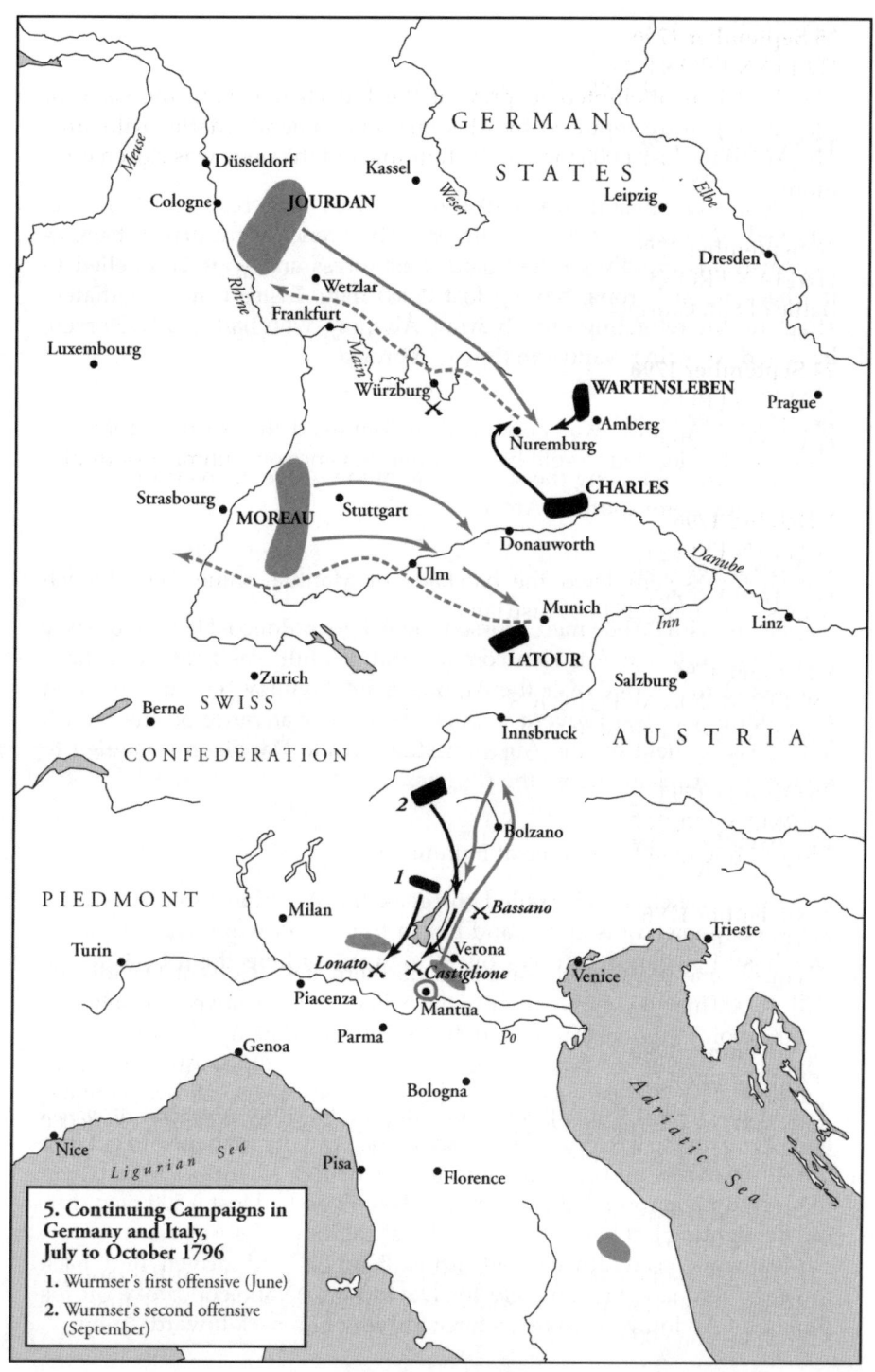

**5. Continuing Campaigns in
Germany and Italy,
July to October 1796**

1. Wurmser's first offensive (June)

2. Wurmser's second offensive
(September)

7 November 1796
RUSSIA: SUCCESSION
Paul was declared Tsar of the Russian Empire.

12 November 1796
ITALIAN FRONT
Napoleon's advance guard, 12,000 men led by Augereau and Masséna, attacked Alvintzy's 12,000 at Caldiero. The French were driven back as the Austrians rapidly concentrated their forces and were compelled to fall back upon Verona, having lost 2,000 men. Instead of immediately attacking the retreating French army, Alvintzy, who had lost 1,500 men, hesitated, allowing Napoleon time to regroup.

14 November 1796
ITALIAN FRONT
Napoleon pushed along the south bank of the Adige in an effort to reach the crossing point south of Arcola.

15 November 1796
ITALIAN FRONT
Napoleon, with 20,000 men, crossed the Adige at Ronco. He then quickly turned north to cut Austrian communications but was held up in hard fighting at the bridge over the Alpone river. Alvintzy sent an advanced force under General Provera to delay Masséna's advance on the French left. Masséna held off the Austrian attack while Napoleon struggled to establish a firm base across the Alpone.

16 November 1796
ITALIAN FRONT
Repeated French attacks failed to break the Austrian force at Arcola. Masséna renewed his attack and began to force Provera back. Alvintzy was busy bringing his forces out of danger, pulling them back to the east.

17 November 1796
ITALIAN FRONT
Augereau crossed the Alpone south of Arcola while Masséna attacked once more on the left. Simultaneously French cavalry managed to get into the Austrian rear and caused panic and confusion. Alvintzy's force began to break up and retreated to the north. Napoleon had lost 3,500 men during the fighting but had inflicted 6,200 casualties on the Austrians.

Meanwhile, Davidovich had struck Vaubois and driven him back towards Verona. Unfortunately for Davidovich, Napoleon broke off his pursuit of Alvintzy to strike his force, driving him back towards Trent.

19 November 1796
ITALIAN FRONT
Davidovich was shut up in Trent by Napoleon's forces.

22 November 1796
ITALIAN FRONT
The French, with 15,000 men, attacked an Austrian force of 7,000 near Rivoli. French casualties were just 200 men lost to an Austrian loss of nearly 900.

1 December 1796
WAR AT SEA
The British Mediterranean Fleet, fourteen ships of the line commanded by Admiral Jervis, pulled back to its base at Gibraltar. Captain Horatio Nelson evacuated the British forces from Elba later in December. From Gibraltar the British concentrated on harassing Spanish shipping on the Atlantic coast. The British had been severely outnumbered by the Franco-Spanish naval concentration at Toulon. Spanish naval strength brought their combined fleet to thirty-eight vessels.

15 December 1796
WAR AT SEA
Admiral de Galles broke through the British blockade of Brest with an invasion fleet of thirty warships and twenty transports, carrying Hoche's 13,000 badly trained and hastily assembled third rate troops. They were intended for an invasion of Ireland. Unfortunately bad weather and poor seamanship scattered a large part of the force.

21 December 1796
WAR AT SEA
Galles' invasion force arrived at Bantry Bay but more bad weather prevented the French landing their forces in Ireland. The proposed invasion was now abandoned. During the ill-fated expedition the French lost five ships to bad weather and six more to British attacks.

* 1797 *

7 January 1797
ITALIAN FRONT
Austrian troops began to move from Bassano and Padua. Incredibly, Alvintzy had again divided his forces for this latest offensive. Alvintzy marched down the Adige valley with 28,000 men while 15,000 more moved upon Verona and Mantua from the east. To counter this threat Napoleon concentrated the bulk of his forces, some 10,000 men under

General Barthelemy Joubert, near Rivoli while Masséna was moving up from Verona with 6,000 men and Generals Antoine Rey and Claude Victor were also marching towards Rivoli with another 6,000. Augereau screened Verona and the Adige with another 9,000 men while General Serurier invested Mantua with 8,000. Wurmser remained trapped in Mantua with his disease-ravaged army.

13 January 1797
ITALIAN FRONT
The Austrian forces moving upon Verona were repulsed by Masséna and compelled to retreat.

14 January 1797
ITALIAN FRONT
Alvintzy, with 28,000 men, launched an attack against Napoleon's 10,000 men on the Rivoli plain. The Austrian forces moved in six columns, three attacking the French frontally and one each attacking the flanks. The final column aimed to march around to the French rear. The main Austrian assault struck Joubert hard and after heavy fighting forced the French back. As the Austrians then began to drive in the French right wing, Masséna marched up with his 6,000 men, having moved from before Verona overnight to support Napoleon. He launched an immediate attack and halted the Austrians in their tracks. The French right and centre then counter-attacked and began to drive the Austrians back, surrounding one of the flank columns. After hard fighting, the Austrians began to retreat, followed closely by Napoleon. Alvintzy attempted to rally his forces but was then struck by Murat's cavalry and forced to give up the field. Austrian losses exceeded 12,000 men including 8,000 captured. The French lost just over 3,000 men.

15 January 1797
ITALIAN FRONT
Napoleon launched a pursuit of the broken Austrian army, completing the disintegration of the main enemy field force.

16 January 1797
ITALIAN FRONT
The Austrians had sent two columns behind the main French forces, one in the direction of Verona and one towards Mantua. The Verona column had already been defeated on 13 January but General Provera leading the Mantua column of 9,000 men managed to evade Augereau to reach the outskirts of the city. Provera attacked from outside while Wurmser led a sortie from the town with 5,000 men. After hard fighting Serurier drove Wurmser back. Napoleon and Masséna hurried back to Mantua from Rivoli and joined forces with Augereau. This combined force then

fell upon Provera and in a bitter struggle forced the Austrians to surrender. Total French losses were 2,000 casualties to an Austrian loss of 6,000 men.

2 February 1797
ITALIAN FRONT
Mantua fell as Wurmser surrendered his exhausted force. Some 18,000 of the 28,000 men in the town had died from disease and enemy action. The French had lost 7,000 men, again mainly due to sickness and disease.

14 February 1797
WAR AT SEA
The Spanish sent a fleet of twenty-seven vessels from the Mediterranean to join the French fleet at Brest. From here the Franco-Spanish force aimed to carry an invasion force into England.

Under the command of Admiral Jose de Cordova, the Spanish fleet was intercepted off Cape St Vincent by the fifteen ships of Admiral Sir John Jervis's former Mediterranean fleet. The Spanish, sailing in a group of nine vessels and another of eighteen vessels, was cut in two by Jervis, and the larger of the two groups was attacked. The Spanish van attempted to come about but was held off by Captain Nelson, with his vessel HMS *Captain*. Nelson captured two Spanish vessels by boarding. Overall the Spanish lost four ships captured and another ten damaged, plus 5,000 sailors killed, wounded or captured. The British fleet suffered only minor damage and the loss of around three hundred sailors, of whom fewer than one hundred were killed.

15 February 1797
WAR AT SEA
Cordova managed to escape from Jervis and took refuge in Cádiz, where the British blockaded them. The threat of invasion was dispelled.

19 February 1797
INTERNATIONAL POLITICS
Treaty of Tolentino. The Vatican agreed to pay France an indemnity to prevent occupation.

22–24 February 1797
WAR AT SEA
There was an attempted French invasion of Britain at Fishguard. A force of 1,400 troops of *La Légion Noire*, so called due to their dyed black uniforms and the fact that half of the force comprised men just released from prison, aimed to raise disaffected British farmers in revolt.

Once ashore, the French troops, who lacked the most basic supplies, looted the surrounding farms, where they found beer and wine. The inevitable result was that the bulk of the invasion force became thoroughly drunk. At this unfortunate moment the British mustered their forces and surrounded the French. The forlorn invaders then surrendered, their campaign having lasted just two disastrous days.

10 March 1797
ITALIAN FRONT
Napoleon began his invasion of Austria following his conquest of northern Italy. Joubert, with 12,000 men, contained the 14,000 Austrian troops and 10,000 Tyrolean riflemen in the Tyrol, while Napoleon's main force, some 41,000 strong, confronted Archduke Charles, who had 27,000 men deployed along the line of the Tagliamento.

16 March 1797
ITALIAN FRONT
Napoleon began to cross the Tagliamento, pushing his forces forward towards the Tarvis Pass. An Austrian blocking force of 5,000 men was brushed aside, suffering 700 casualties to the French loss of 500 men.

18 March 1797
ITALIAN FRONT
Harried by Napoleon, Archduke Charles pulled his forces back behind the Isonzo.

23 March 1797
ITALIAN FRONT
Masséna defeated part of Archduke Charles' army at Malborghetto, compelling the Austrians to abandon the line of the Isonzo. Napoleon led his forces across the Julian and Carnic Alps in pursuit. Joubert drove back the Austrian forces in the Tyrol and made for Linz.

6 April 1797
ITALIAN FRONT
Napoleon reunited his army at Klagenfurt, having successfully crossed the Alps. The French then began to move towards Vienna.

7 April 1797
ITALIAN FRONT
The Austrians requested a truce as Napoleon continued to concentrate his forces close to Vienna.

12 April 1797
ITALIAN FRONT
The Austrians renewed the truce to continue negotiations to end the hostilities with the French.

16 April–15 May 1797
WAR AT SEA
The Royal Navy base at Spithead was rocked by a mutiny of the enlisted sailors against the brutality of their officers and poor conditions and food.

17 April 1797
ITALIAN FRONT
A revolt broke out in Verona against French rule.

GERMAN FRONT
French forces crossed the Rhine. Hoche, replacing Jourdan as commander of the Army of the Sambre & Meuse, crossed at Dusseldorf and Coblenz. Archduke Charles had left the German front for Italy, leaving Latour's Army of the Upper Rhine and Werneck's Army of the Lower Rhine to face the French.

18 April 1797
GERMAN FRONT
Hoche's Army of the Sambre & Meuse defeated part of Werneck's Army of the Lower Rhine at Neuweid (Lahn).

INTERNATIONAL POLITICS
Peace of Loeben. This began preliminary peace terms between Napoleon and the Austrian Emperor. French forces were less than a hundred miles from the Austrian capital. Napoleon conducted the negotiations without any reference to the Directory. While the negotiations continued the French pulled back behind the line of the Isonzo.

20 April 1797
GERMAN FRONT
Moreau crossed the Rhine at Kehl. Werneck was driven in by the French advance and threatened with envelopment by Hoche's advance. Only the Peace of Loeben, which largely brought hostilities in Germany to a close, saved Werneck from isolation and defeat.

May 1797
FRANCE: POLITICS
Elections throughout France returned a sizeable number of royalists to the Legislative councils. The Council of Elders elected a royalist, Jean-Jacques Barthelemy, to replace Letourneur on the Directory.

12 May 1797
ITALIAN FRONT
A democratic republic was established by the French in Venice.

12 May–13 June 1797
WAR AT SEA
Another mutiny broke out among the British ships moored at Nore. Eventually brought under control, the mutineers succeeded in gaining better conditions.

16 May 1797
ITALIAN FRONT
French troops led by Napoleon occupied Venice.

15 June 1797
ITALIAN FRONT
The French established the Ligurian Republic around Genoa.

9 July 1797
ITALIAN FRONT
The Cisalpine Republic was established around Milan.

August 1797
FRANCE: POLITICS
After elections in May had brought the royalists into the Councils, the corrupt Directory moved to ensure its command of the state through armed force. The directors called upon Napoleon to secure the safety of the Republic. He dispatched General Augereau to Paris to assist.

2 September 1797
FRANCE: POLITICS
The Clichy Club, a group of disgruntled moderates, planned a coup against the Directory.

3 September 1797
FRANCE: POLITICS
Augereau was appointed to command the Directory's forces in Paris by Barras, Reubell and La Revellière.

4 September 1797
FRANCE: CIVIL UNREST
Augereau arrested the Directory's opponents, the leaders of the Clichy Club, in the Councils. Barras and his two colleagues imposed their will upon the Councils and upon the other members of the Directory.

9 September 1797
FRANCE: POLITICS
The Directory continued to tighten its grip on power in France by eliminating its opponents. Barthelemy and Carnpot were exiled and Pichegru

arrested before being exiled. The Directory's suppression of their opponents became known as the coup of 18 Fructidor. To replace their exiled
members, Neufchâteau and Douai joined the Directory.

18 September 1797
GERMAN FRONT
Hoche, commanding the Army of the Sambre & Meuse, died at Wetzlar.

11 October 1797
WAR AT SEA
A Batavian Fleet of twenty-six vessels under Admiral Jan de Winters was
attacked by a British Fleet of sixteen ships under the command of Admiral
Adam Duncan at Camperdown as it emerged from the Texel in order to
join the French fleet at Brest. The Dutch had intended to join the French
before sailing for Ireland with a force of 15,000 men and large quantities of
supplies to aid Irish rebels. Duncan attacked the Dutch aggressively and
broke their fleet into small pockets. During the ensuing fight eleven Dutch
ships were captured and 5,000 men killed wounded or captured. While
the British did not lose any ships, they did suffer heavy damage.

16 October 1797
FRANCE: ARMED FORCES
Napoleon was offered the command of the Army of England, the army
being assembled for a proposed invasion of the British Isles.

17 October 1797
ITALIAN FRONT
The Treaty of Campo Formio confirmed the Peace of Loeben. Austria
recognised the existence of the Cisalpine Republic and surrendered
the Austrian Netherlands to France. In compensation she received the
Republic of Venice. The Austrians also recognised French rule on the left
bank of the Rhine.

10 December 1797
FRANCE: POLITICS
Napoleon returned to Paris to an overwhelming reception from the people.
His ruthlessness during the 'whiff of grapeshot' episode was forgotten but
in him, following his independent dictation of terms to the Austrians, the
members of the Directory saw a political threat.

29 December 1797
INTERNATIONAL POLITICS
The Second Coalition united Russia and Britain against France. Austria
would join later.

* 1798 *

January 1798
FRANCE: MILITARY PLANNING
The Directory pressed ahead with its plans for an attack on England and appointed Napoleon as commander of the forces assembling at Dunkirk. Napoleon was doubtful as to the practicality of the plan due to British control of the seas. He instead was hatching a plan with Talleyrand to seize Egypt in order to threaten British interests in India and lay the foundations for the establishment of a French Empire.

January–March 1798
SWISS FRONT
French troops moved into and pacified the Swiss cantons after republican forces began agitating against the ruling regimes.

22 January 1798
HOLLAND: POLITICS
The French established the Batavian Republic in Holland.

February 1798
FRANCE: MILITARY PLANNING
Napoleon proposed a plan for the invasion of Egypt in order to threaten British interests in the Orient. Opinion in the Directory was split; Reubell, who did not trust Napoleon, wanted to keep him in France where he could be watched, but the others felt it would be safer all round to remove him to the far off Orient.

11 February 1798
ITALIAN FRONT
French forces occupied Rome after republican insurgents in the city called for aid.

15 February 1798
ITALIAN FRONT
The French proclaimed the creation of the Roman Republic.

20 February 1798
INTERNATIONAL POLITICS
Pope Pius VI was deported to France.

2 March 1798
GERMAN FRONT
The French fought at Fribourg.

5 March 1798
FRANCE: MILITARY PLANNING
The Directory approved Napoleon's plan to invade Egypt and abandoned their plans for an invasion of England. Napoleon began to assemble a new army at Toulon. The concentration of forces at Dunkirk continued in an effort to divert British attention from the Mediterranean.

26 March 1798
SWISS FRONT
The French occupied Zurich unopposed.

29 March 1798
SWISS FRONT
French forces completed the occupation of Switzerland, beginning the reorganising of the country as a republic.

April 1798
FRANCE: POLITICS
Elections throughout France returned many Jacobin deputies to the provinces, although the Directory retained control of Paris. Opposition to the Directory was mounting among the public and army. Neufchâteau left the Directory and was replaced by Treilhard.

12 April 1798
EGYPTIAN FRONT
Bonaparte was appointed to command the newly assembled Army of the Orient.

26 April 1798
SWISS FRONT
The French annexed Geneva while also declaring the creation of the Helvetian Republic following the completion of their reorganisation of the Swiss cantons.

8 May 1798
WAR AT SEA
The British Mediterranean Fleet, commanded by Admiral Nelson, re-entered the Mediterranean.

11 May 1798
FRANCE: POLITICS
The coup of 22 Floreal took place. The Directory annulled the April elections and endorsed its own candidates, finally breaking any last vestiges of support the Directors might have had.

19 May 1798
EGYPTIAN FRONT
Bonaparte and his 35,000-strong Army of the Orient (24,000 infantry, 4,000 cavalry, 3,000 artillerymen plus services) sailed for Egypt from Toulon. The French invasion fleet of nearly 400 vessels was escorted by thirteen ships of the line and six frigates commanded by Admiral François Brueys.

BELGIAN FRONT
There was an abortive British landing at Ostend.

23 May 1798
IRISH REBELLION
The '98 rebellion in Ireland began with insurrection in County Wexford led by Wolf Tone and Napper Tandy.

9 June 1798
IRISH REBELLION
British forces under General Needham defeated the Irish rebels at Arklow. The British began to savagely repress the uprising.

MEDITERRANEAN FRONT
The French Egyptian task force arrived off Malta and made ready to attack.

10 June 1798
MEDITERRANEAN FRONT
The Knights of St John refused a French request to dock at Malta for supplies, giving Napoleon an excuse to attack. Some 28,000 French troops landed on the islands and secured Valetta, the small Maltese army of 4,000 surrendering without a fight.

12 June 1798
IRISH REBELLION
The Irish rebels were defeated at Vinegar Hill, near Enniscorthy, County Wexford, by British forces under General Lake. The rebels surrendered following their defeat.

15 June 1798
MEDITERRANEAN FRONT
Having secured Malta and installed a 4,000-strong garrison, Napoleon and his fleet continued their journey to Egypt.

1 July 1798
EGYPTIAN FRONT
The French landed at Marabout, close to Alexandria, in Egypt.

2 July 1798
EGYPTIAN FRONT
Napoleon defeated the Turks under Coraim at Alexandria, assaulting and capturing the city.

5 July 1798
EGYPTIAN FRONT
Napoleon began his advance upon Cairo, sending 10,000 men down the Nile on barges while another 15,000 marched across the desert.

15 July 1798
EGYPTIAN FRONT
Napoleon reunited his army at the tip of the Nile delta before preparing to push on to Cairo.

17 July 1798
EGYPTIAN FRONT
Napoleon defeated a minor Mameluke force at Shubra Khir.

21 July 1798
EGYPTIAN FRONT
Napoleon, with 23,000 men of whom only 2,700 were cavalry, deployed in five mobile divisional squares as he advanced upon the Mameluke army north of Giza. The Mamelukes, some 60,000 strong, were split by the Nile. Ibrahim Bey was deployed on the east bank and could only watch as Murat Bey, with 6,000 cavalry and fifty cannon, plus thousands of ill-disciplined infantry, launched a totally undisciplined attack, striking Reynier's and Desaix's squares. Napoleon threw in Vial's and Bon's squares while Dugua's was held in reserve. The Turks were routed and fled the field. French losses were less than 300 while the Turks lost more than 3,000.

23 July 1798
EGYPTIAN FRONT
French troops entered Cairo.

25 July 1798
EGYPTIAN FRONT
Cairo fell to the French.

1 August 1798
EGYPTIAN FRONT
Nelson, with thirteen ships, attacked the unprepared French fleet of seventeen vessels under Brueys in a vulnerable anchorage in Aboukir Bay. Having anchored their fleet between the land and some rocks, the French were unable to respond to the British attack. Nelson led his ships between the French fleet and the land and proceeded to attack unopposed, the French having failed to man their landward guns. After sustained British fire the French had suffered severe losses. Only three of the French ships escaped. Brueys was killed when his flagship, the *Lorient,* caught fire and exploded. The French army in Egypt was now isolated.

19 August 1798
FRANCE: POLITICS
The French and the Helvetian Republic signed an alliance.

22 August 1798
IRISH REBELLION
French forces, numbering 1,200 men and four cannon, under the command of General Humbert, landed at Killala Bay in County Mayo. They aimed to support the Irish rebellion but the British had already largely defeated the Irish.

25 August 1798
IRISH REBELLION
Humbert defeated the British under General Lake at Castlebar.

September 1798
MEDITERRANEAN FRONT
Malta rose in revolt against the French. The French garrison, commanded by General Vaubois, attempted to quell the revolt but was gradually driven back into Valetta.

5 September 1798
FRANCE: HOME FRONT
France introduced conscription. Under the Jourdan Law all men between 18 and 40 must register and those between 18 and 25 were liable to be called up for military service.

IRISH REBELLION
Humbert defeated Lake at Collooney.

8 September 1798
IRISH REBELLION
Humbert was surrounded and forced to surrender to General Cornwallis at Ballinamuck.

9 September 1798
INTERNATIONAL POLITICS
Turkey declared war on France.

23 September 1798
IRISH REBELLION
The British under Trench defeated the Irish rebels at Killala.

7 October 1798
EGYPTIAN FRONT
General Desaix, chasing the broken Mameluke army south, caught and defeated it at Sediman, fifty miles south of Cairo.

12 October 1798
WAR AT SEA
A British fleet under Sir John Borlase Warren intercepted a French squadron, commanded by Admiral Bompard, aiming to reinforce General Humbert, who had already surrendered. The French squadron was destroyed, seven of the nine ships being sunk or captured.

OCCUPIED NETHERLANDS
A revolt broke out in the Brabant region against the French occupation and the conscription of men into the army. The rebels expected British help to arrive within the next couple of weeks.

21 October 1798
EGYPTIAN FRONT
An unexpected revolt in Cairo was suppressed.

OCCUPIED NETHERLANDS
The British attempted to land an army at the mouth of the Schelde river to aid the Brabant rebels. Four days of fighting followed as the British attempted to gain a foothold.

23 October 1798
OCCUPIED NETHERLANDS
The Brabant rebels were defeated by the French and lost control of Mechelen.

24 October 1798
OCCUPIED NETHERLANDS
The British effort to land a force in the Schelde to support the Brabant rebels failed, leaving the rebels to face the French forces alone.

November 1798
ITALIAN FRONT
General Joubert renewed French attacks in Piedmont, overrunning most of the country.

15 November 1798
MEDITERRANEAN
Minorca fell to the British.

19 November 1798
IRISH REBELLION
The Irish leader, Wolf Tone, died.

22 November 1798
OCCUPIED NETHERLANDS
A rebel army of 17,000 suffered a heavy defeat at Diest, losing more than 1,000 killed.

29 November 1798
INTERNATIONAL POLITICS
Ferdinand IV, Bourbon King of Naples, dismayed at the French treatment of the Pope and their establishment of republics throughout Italy, declared war upon France by invading the Roman Republic. A Neapolitan army, some 60,000 strong under the command of the Austrian, General Karl Mack von Leiberich, captured Rome.

1 December 1798
INTERNATIONAL POLITICS
Naples made a treaty with England.

3 December 1798
BRITAIN: POLITICS
The British government introduced Income Tax to finance the war effort.

ITALIAN FRONT
Neapolitan forces, commanded reluctantly by the Austrian General Mack, invaded the Papal States and quickly pushed on to Rome.

4 December 1798
INTERNATIONAL POLITICS
France declared war on Naples in retaliation for the invasion of Roman territory.

5 December 1798
OCCUPIED NETHERLANDS
Brabant rebels were compelled to evacuate their forces from Hasselt. However, the French attacked during the withdrawal and killed half of the 4,000-strong force. This defeat largely brought the rebellion to an end, the Brabant rebels having lost more than 15,000 killed during the fighting.

8 December 1798
ITALIAN FRONT
In northern Italy, French troops entered Turin.

15 December 1798
ITALIAN FRONT
A mixed force of 30,000 French and Italian troops, led by General Championet, drove back the Neapolitans and recaptured Rome.

23 December 1798
INTERNATIONAL POLITICS
The Russians and Turks made a treaty against France.

24 December 1798
INTERNATIONAL POLITICS
The British and Russians concluded a treaty against France. The Knights of St John, ousted from Malta, appealed to Russia for aid against the French. Emperor Paul I eagerly agreed, the Russian monarch being the driving force behind the developing anti-French coalition. Napoleon's invasion of Egypt was deemed a threat to Russian interests against the Ottomans.

29 December 1798
INTERNATIONAL POLITICS
The Second Coalition was formed. Britain, Austria, Russia, Naples, the Ottoman Empire and the Vatican were united against France. The Allies planned to take the war to the French in a number of theatres. An Allied army under the Duke of York would invade the Netherlands and eject the French while Archduke Charles led an Austrian force into Germany and Switzerland. The Russian Marshal, Alexander Suvarov, would lead a Russo-Austrian army into Italy and drive the French back. Altogether the Allies had some 300,000 men available, plus the less reliable Neapolitan forces in Italy.

Two years of conflict had seen the emphasis of the wars turn from a fight for the survival of the republican regime to the expansion of French territory throughout Western and Central Europe. The emergence of Napoleon Bonaparte following his lightning campaign across northern Italy, and the ongoing invasion of North Africa and the Near East, had convinced the Allies of the need for another coalition to halt the seemingly limitless ambitions of the French. The following year would see fighting spread from the Rhine frontier, through Switzerland and Italy and in the Orient.

CHAPTER IV

The War of the Second Coalition and the Rise of Bonaparte

With French power firmly established from the Low Countries to northern Italy and the Orient, the Allies determined to take the war back into France itself. However, the organisational talent of Carnot would counter this by seizing the initiative and taking the war directly to the Allies.

* 1799 *

FRANCE: MILITARY PLANNING
The French war effort, led once again by Carnot, opted to go onto the offensive against the massing armies of the Second Coalition. Carnot, with a total force of around 200,000 men at his disposal, would launch an attack in Italy with General Scherer's 60,000-strong army, a second assault through Germany with Jourdan's 46,000-strong Army of Mayence, which was deployed around Constance, and a third offensive in Switzerland, where Masséna had a further 30,000. To defend the Batavian Republic were 24,000 French and Batavian troops under General Brune.

ALLIES: MILITARY PLANNING
To oppose the expected French offensives the Allies deployed 80,000 Austrian troops under Archduke Charles to oppose Jourdan, Hotze with 13,000 at Bregenz, Auffenberg with 7,000 at Chur and 5,000 more at Feldkirch, all to oppose Masséna's forces in Switzerland. Behind these units were a further 47,000 men under Bellegarde in the Tyrol, deployed near Innsbruck and Landeck.

11 January 1799
ITALIAN FRONT
Pushing steadily south, Championnet captured Capua as Mack's Neapolitan army fell apart. So tenuous had his position become due to the rioting of the populace, Mack fled to the French in fear of his life.

20 January 1799
ITALIAN FRONT
French troops reached Naples. The Bourbon monarch fled to Sicily.

24 January 1799
ITALIAN FRONT
Championnet stormed Naples and comprehensively defeated the Neapolitan forces.

29 January 1799
ITALIAN FRONT
Following the collapse of the Neapolitans, the French established the Parthenopean Republic. They were supported by local republican elements.

31 January 1799
EGYPTIAN FRONT
Napoleon assembled his forces for an attack against the Turkish forces, under Achmed Pasha, building up in Syria. The French were to invade with a force of 13,000 men. Napoleon left 5,000 men in Cairo and 4,000 with General Desaix to pacify the south.

6 February 1799
EGYPTIAN FRONT
Napoleon launched his invasion of Palestine.

8 February 1799
EGYPTIAN FRONT
French forces reached El Arish. The garrison of 3,200 men refused a demand to surrender so the French were compelled to invest the fort. They only had light artillery cannon available which could do little damage to the defences.

18 February 1799
EGYPTIAN FRONT
Napoleon, with 13,000 men, brought up heavier artillery pieces and began to bombard El Arish.

19 February 1799
EGYPTIAN FRONT
Ibrahim Aga surrendered his army in El Arish, having suffered 700 casualties. Napoleon, who had lost fewer than 400 men, allowed the Ottomans to march out of the fort under parole not to fight again. The Ottoman delaying action had enabled their other forces throughout Syria and Palestine to mobilise.

March 1799
ITALIAN FRONT
The Austrians, with 67,000 men commanded by General Paul Kray, began an offensive aimed at taking back northern Italy. General Scherer, with 41,000 men available on the Mincio river, moved north to drive the Austrians back before they could be reinforced by the Russians.

SWISS FRONT
The Russians invaded Switzerland but Masséna had already moved, crossing the Rhine at Mayenfeld and marching quickly into the Vorarlberg and Grison. His aim was to cover the flank of Jourdan's army as it invaded Germany. Most of the Austrian forces at Chur, some 7,000 men, were captured.

GERMAN FRONT
An Austrian army advanced towards France through the Black Forest.

1 March 1799
INTERNATIONAL POLITICS
The united powers of the Second Coalition formally declared war on France.

3–7 March 1799
EGYPTIAN FRONT
Bonaparte invested and stormed Jaffa with 18,000 men. The garrison of 4,500 men, led by Abou-Saad, was defeated and the town captured. Some 2,500 Turkish troops surrendered but upon discovering that a large number of them were from the supposedly paroled garrison of El Arish, were executed on Napoleon's orders. Another 2,000 Turks had died in the fighting.

5 March 1799
ITALIAN FRONT
Scherer drove north to the Adige but was badly defeated by Kray at Magnano, near Verona. The French lost 4,000 killed and 4,500 captured during the bloody fighting. Kray lost some 3,800 men killed and wounded, and a further 1,500 captured. Under orders from supreme command, Kray allowed the French to retire.

6 March 1799
SWISS FRONT
Masséna attacked an Austrian forward post of 1,000 men at Luziensteig.

7 March 1799
SWISS FRONT
Masséna continued his vigorous attacks against Auffenberg's forces. The French commander had detached a smaller force under Oudinot to hold off Hotze, and it fought a bloody action at Feldkirch.

10 March 1799
GERMAN FRONT
Jourdan's Army of the Mayence crossed the Rhine at Kehl and moved to attack Archduke Charles.

MEDITERRANEAN FRONT
British forces were sent to garrison Sicily.

12 March 1799
INTERNATIONAL POLITICS
Austria declared war on France.

17 March 1799
EGYPTIAN FRONT
French forces reached Acre as they pushed deeper into Syria.

18 March 1799
EGYPTIAN FRONT
The French besieged Acre with an army of 12,000. The Ottoman garrison of 5,000 men, commanded by Djezzar, was aided by the capable British naval captain, Sydney Smith.

21 March 1799
GERMAN FRONT
Archduke Charles, with around 70,000 men, checked Jourdan's advance at Stockach. Despite his setback, Jourdan determined to attack once more and moved forward.

23 March 1799
SWISS FRONT
Masséna again attacked the Austrian forces at Feldkirch with 15,000 men, but was repulsed. Keeping part of his army to invest Feldkirch, he then sent General Lecourbe, with 10,000 men, forward down the Inn valley to threaten the Tyrol.

GERMAN FRONT
Archduke Charles had separated his army when Jourdan, with 38,000 men, launched his vigorous attack at Stockach. Fighting desperately to prevent the French driving in his right wing, Charles fought a delaying action until the remainder of his army could join him. As they arrived the battle began to go against the French, Charles bringing 60,000 men together, smashing the French centre and driving Jourdan's army back. French losses were 3,600 to 6,000 Austrian.

SWISS FRONT
Lecourbe, reinforced by a detachment under Desoulles, attacked the Austrian and Tyrolean forces at Naunders and Tauffers. In hard fighting the French took 6,000 prisoners and sixteen cannon, effectively wiping out the Austrian regular units facing them.

26 March 1799
GERMAN FRONT
Following his reverse at Stockach, Jourdan began to withdraw to the Rhine. Charles failed to follow up his victory with a vigorous pursuit.

April 1799
SWISS FRONT
The French setbacks in Germany and Italy enabled the Austrians to bring more forces to bear against Lecourbe's small army in the Tyrol and Masséna's units in Switzerland. In the Inn valley, the Austrians struck Lecourbe with armies under Generals Bellegarde and von Hotze and drove him back to the Rhine. Bellgarde gained control of Chur and Hotze of Luziensteig.

4 April 1799
ITALIAN FRONT
Suvarov deployed into Italy with 17,000 men and took command of the Russian and Austrian forces.

16 April 1799
EGYPTIAN FRONT
Napoleon, aware that the Turks were sending a force to relieve Acre, despatched General Kléber with a reconnaissance force to establish their position and strength. Kléber encountered the 35,000 Turks under Achmed Pasha near Mount Tabor and launched an attack with 1,500 men. However, the Turks managed to recover and forced Kléber to deploy into defensive squares. A day of bitter fighting followed.

17 April 1799
EGYPTIAN FRONT
Pasha launched further undisciplined attacks at Mount Tabor. The Turks had by now fully surrounded Kléber's small division of 1,500 men but were then struck in their rear by Napoleon with some 2,500 men. In heavy fighting the Turks were defeated, losing 500 men, and had to abandon their relief attack. The French had suffered just sixty casualties.

17 April 1799
ITALIAN FRONT
Suvarov began his offensive in Italy. He planned to push west with 90,000

men while leaving Kray with 20,000 to pin down the French in Mantua and Peschiera. Moreau took command of the French forces in northern Italy as Scherer was replaced.

20 April 1799
ITALIAN FRONT
The small French garrison of Brescia surrender to the advancing Russo-Austrian army.

21 April 1799
ITALIAN FRONT
Allied troops reached Cremona but the advance now began to slow.

26 April 1799
ITALIAN FRONT
Moreau ranged his army along the Adda to protect Cassano, Lecco and Lodi. Suvarov moved to attack the French, who numbered just 20,000 men, all along their line.

27 April 1799
ITALIAN FRONT
Suvarov, with 65,000 men, attacked and routed Moreau at Cassano. An Austrian detachment under Melas forced a crossing of the river. Moreau, realising his position was lost, left behind a rearguard under Serurier to hold up the Allied advance while the main part of the army withdrew. Vigorous Allied attacks succeeded in surrounding Serurier, whose force was entirely destroyed. The battle had cost the Austrians some 6,000 casualties, but the French had lost 7,000 captured plus a further 3,000 killed or wounded. Moreau's army was shattered and retreated to the Ticino in considerable disorder.

28 April 1799
ITALIAN FRONT
Suvarov captured Milan, his Cossacks leading the Allied troops into the city. Turin was captured shortly afterwards.

May 1799
GERMAN FRONT
Jourdan resigned his command, which was given over to Masséna. He then merged his army with the Army of Mayence to create the new Army of the Danube, and then entrenched his force near Zurich. Masséna was tasked with defending the French line from Mayence to Switzerland.

Archduke Charles and General Hotze deployed some 90,000 men around Lake Constance but due to detachments only 35,000 were available to Charles, and 20,000 to Hotze. They moved slowly upon Masséna's positions.

ITALIAN FRONT
With the French forces in northern Italy scattered to hold on to their possessions, the Allies spread out their armies in order to besiege the many French garrisons. Moreau was largely locked up in Genoa. French forces in the south reassembled, and some 33,000 men under the command of General Jacques Macdonald began to march north.

17 May 1799
EGYPTIAN FRONT
The French raised their siege of Acre and made preparations to withdraw from Syria. Napoleon's army was in dire straits as it was ravaged by plague. The unsuccessful siege had cost the French 4,000 men and the Ottomans 2,000.

21 May 1799
EGYPTIAN FRONT
The French army began its retreat to Egypt.

25 May 1799
SWISS FRONT
Masséna fended off Austrian attacks, led by Charles, at Thur. Hotze was advancing against Masséna's flank and compelled the French to break off the action.

26 May 1799
SWISS FRONT
Charles and Hotze united their forces and moved to attack Masséna along the Toss river.

27 May 1799
SWISS FRONT
Masséna was pushed away from the Toss river by the Austrians and over the course of the next few days withdrew by stages to positions around Zurich.

June 1799
ITALIAN FRONT
Moreau began to launch diversionary attacks from Genoa in order to draw Suvarov to him. Macdonald had reached northern Italy and began to manoeuvre to catch Suvarov between himself and Moreau.

4 June 1799
SWISS FRONT
The Austrians under Archduke Charles and General Hotze, with 42,000 men, attacked Masséna's 25,000 men along their five-mile front before Zurich.

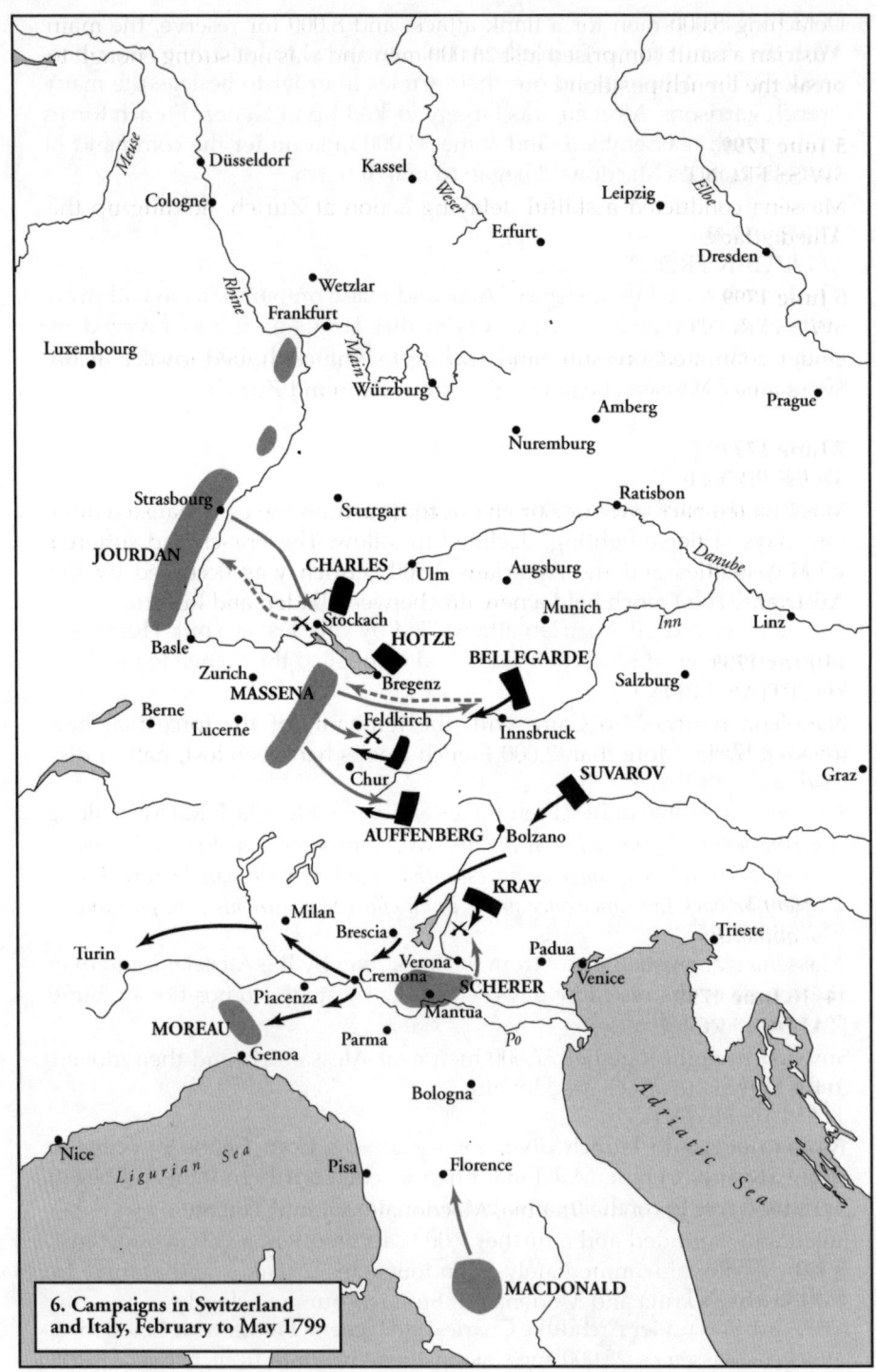

6. Campaigns in Switzerland
and Italy, February to May 1799

Detaching 8,000 men for a flank attack, and 8,000 for reserve, the main Austrian assault comprised just 26,000 men and was not strong enough to break the French positions.

5 June 1799
SWISS FRONT
Masséna conducted a skilful delaying action at Zurich, holding up the Allied attacks.

6 June 1799
SWISS FRONT
Under continued pressure, and fearing for the continued loyalty of his Swiss allies, Masséna began to give ground around Zurich.

7 June 1799
SWISS FRONT
Masséna fell back west of Zurich but the Austrian forces, exhausted after four days of fierce fighting, declined to follow. The French had suffered 1,700 casualties and the Austrians 3,500. Zurich was occupied by the Austrians. The French held a new line between Baden and Lucerne.

14 June 1799
EGYPTIAN FRONT
Napoleon returned to Cairo with the remnants of the force that had invaded Syria. More than 2,000 French troops had been lost, half to disease.

His failure in Syria had been the first real setback for Napoleon. With his army overstretched and lacking essential supplies, he began to turn his attention back to France once more, in an effort to ensure his own position of authority.

14–16 June 1799
ITALIAN FRONT
Suvarov brought together 37,000 men near Alessandria and then moved to the Trebbia to attack Macdonald.

17–19 June 1799
ITALIAN FRONT
In bitter fighting on the Trebbia, Macdonald, with 35,000 men, lost 6,000 killed and wounded and a further 9,000 captured while Suvarov lost just 5,500. Macdonald immediately abandoned his advance and started to withdraw to Parma and Modena but Suvarov pursued closely.

18 June 1799
FRANCE: POLITICS
The coup of 30 Prairial, undertaken by the members of the legislative councils, forced the Directory to dismiss La Revellière-Lepeaux and Douai. Treilhard was also voted off the panel of directors. To replace them were appointed Sieyes and Roger Ducos, both of whom held moderate views, and General Moulin and Louis Gohier who were Jacobins. Barras still held the balance of power. The Jacobin presence on the Directory enabled them to appoint Jacobin ministers in the Councils and regain popular support throughout Paris. General Bernadotte was appointed Minister of War. Robert Lindet became Minister of the Interior.

22 June 1799
INTERNATIONAL POLITICS
The Austrians and British signed an alliance. Britain began to bankroll the Austrian war effort.

July 1799
FRANCE: ARMED FORCES
Between January 1791 and July 1799 the French conscripted 1,570,000 men to the colours.

ITALIAN FRONT
Macdonald managed to link up with Moreau's force near Genoa, but both generals were then pushed back towards the French Riviera by Suvarov's army. French losses during scattered fighting were more than 5,000 men.

15 July 1799
EGYPTIAN FRONT
An Ottoman force of 18,000 men, commanded by Mustapha Pasha, assembled at Rhodes and, escorted by British and Russian warships, sailed for Egypt and landed at Aboukir. The Ottomans then entrenched their army to await the arrival of additional cavalry and artillery forces.

25 July 1799
EGYPTIAN FRONT
Bonaparte had concentrated 8,000 men near Aboukir and attacked the entrenched Ottomans. The first Ottoman position was easily carried but French attacks were held up at the second defence line. General Jean Lannes then led a second attack that penetrated the Ottoman positions. Murat's cavalry also broke the Ottoman line, capturing the Turkish commander. In a furious battle the Ottoman force was almost wiped out, only 2,500 making it to the safety of the citadel. French losses were just over 1,000 men.

August 1799
FRANCE: POLITICS
Sieyes continued his efforts to curb the growing power of the Jacobins. After bringing Barras and Ducos into his fold he managed to get the Jacobin Club closed down once again. He then appointed his close friend Joseph Fouche as Minister of Police and appointed General Lefebvre to command the Army of the Interior.

2 August 1799
EGYPTIAN FRONT
The last defenders of Aboukir citadel surrendered to Napoleon's force.

5 August 1799
SWISS FRONT
Masséna attacked into Switzerland once again, pushing back Archduke Charles's left wing as he advanced.

ITALIAN FRONT
Moreau was relieved of command of the Army of Italy and Joubert was appointed in his place.

14 August 1799
SWISS FRONT
Masséna had advanced east again but, once more, Archduke Charles defeated him at Zurich. Lecourbe, operating in the French right with 25,000 men, drove the Austrians from St Gotthard and Furka passes. The Austrians lost 8,000 men in the fighting

15 August 1799
ITALIAN FRONT
Joubert, with 35,000 men, launched a counter-attack at Novi against Suvarov's 50,000. In hard fighting Joubert was killed and his army broke apart, suffering 11,000 casualties. Suvarov then launched a full scale offensive and drove the French back to the Apennines.

16–17 August 1799
SWISS FRONT
The Austrians attempted to overrun Masséna's left wing at Dottingen but were repulsed.

23 August 1799
EGYPTIAN FRONT
Bonaparte relinquished his army and, together with Generals Berthier, Lannes and Murat and a personal bodyguard of 200 men, including Marmont and Bessières, left Egypt for France aboard a fast frigate. He

managed to slip past the British fleet. The Army of the Orient was handed over to the command of General Jean-Baptiste Kléber. Napoleon was determined to impose his will upon the increasingly ineffectual Directory and the resurgent Jacobins, and gain a dominant position in the French government.

27 August 1799
NETHERLANDS FRONT
An Anglo-Russian expedition under the Duke of York landed south of the Texel river in Holland. The force consisted of 12,000 men with six hundred cannon. The Allies advanced and pushed back the Franco-Batavians under General Brune.

30 August 1799
NETHERLANDS FRONT
A British squadron intercepted a Dutch fleet on the Texel. The Dutch surrendered without a fight.

September 1799
ITALIAN FRONT
The Allied forces in Italy were left under the command of the Austrian general Michael Melas. Suvarov turned north with 20,000 men to stop Championnet's Army of the Alps, which was pushing south towards Italy through the Mount Cenis Pass. Melas had around 60,000 men still in northern Italy.

ALLIED COMMAND
The Allies revised their plans. Charles was to move north through Germany to aid the Anglo-Russian forces in the Netherlands while Suvarov would move from Italy to Switzerland to defeat Masséna. The Allied forces in Switzerland, commanded by the Russian, General Korsakov, were reduced to 40,000 following Charles's departure.

FRANCE: POLITICS
General Jourdan, supporter of the Jacobins, attempted to declare 'the nation in danger' in order to gain extraordinary powers. He was defeated in the councils. Alarmed at Jacobin efforts, Bernadotte was removed from his post as Minister of War. Sieyes now began to cast about for a new military man who could head an administration controlled by himself and his colleagues (Fouché, Ducos, Talleyrand and Barras).

16 September 1799
NETHERLANDS FRONT
General Brune, with 22,000 French and Batavian troops, defeated York's badly organised 35,000 Anglo-Russians at Bergen-op-Zoom. The Allies lost 4,000 men, mainly Russians, to a French loss of 3,000.

Mid-September 1799
SWISS FRONT
Masséna, with a total force of 75,000 men, attacked in the region of Zurich and central Switzerland with 40,000 while a division under Lecourbe, with 12,000, held the St Gotthard Pass to prevent Suvarov's 58,000 men from joining up with General Korsakov's 20,000. The French army was deployed on a wide arc from Basel to the St Gotthard Pass. Smaller divisions of French forces under Thureau and Chabran secured the Valais and Basel.

25 September 1799
SWISS FRONT
Korsakov was heavily attacked at Zurich. Masséna's vanguard, commanded by Oudinot, struck the Austrians hard and crossed the Limmath river.

26 September 1799
SWISS FRONT
There was hard fighting along the Limmath as the French pressed their attack against the Allies around Zurich. In hard fighting Korsakov lost 8,000 men and 100 guns and was compelled to withdraw. Masséna lost 4,000 men but recaptured the town. Soult led a secondary French attack which successfully crossed the Linth river and defeated Hotze's 25,000 Austrians, the Austrian commander being killed during the fighting.

26 September 1799
SWISS FRONT
Suvarov reached the St Gotthard Pass but was blocked by Lecourbe. In heavy fighting he managed to smash his way through the French positions but found Korsakov had been defeated. His efforts to break through had cost him 14,000 casualties.

30 September 1799
SWISS FRONT
Suvarov continued to retire to the upper Rhine. Tsar Paul then relieved him of his command and abandoned his offensive, compelling Charles to abandon his march to the Netherlands.

RUSSIA: POLITICS
The increasingly irrational Tsar Paul believed the Austrians were fighting the French purely for the benefit of themselves, in order to recover the territories they had lost in the wars of the First Coalition. In anger he ordered his armies to withdraw from the war.

2 October 1799
NETHERLANDS FRONT
The Duke of York attacked the French again and this time defeated Brune

at the Second Battle of Bergen-op-Zoom. Each force lost around 2,000 men. The Allies moved on to capture the Batavian fleet, the main aim of this campaign. Much of the fleet would be destroyed or taken as prizes in order to prevent the French from using it in the future.

6 October 1799
NETHERLANDS FRONT
General Brune, deploying his army on the coast, defeated the Duke of York in a hard fought action at Castricum. Brune lost 2,500 men to an Allied loss of 3,500. York began to withdraw, having achieved his aim of destroying the Dutch fleet.

9 October 1799
FRANCE: POLITICS
Napoleon and his companions landed at Fréjus as they returned to France. The French people were demoralised by the war and difficult conditions at home, brought about by the Directory's corruption and neglect of the economy.

16 October 1799
FRANCE: POLITICS
Napoleon reached Paris and immediately became immersed in Sieyes' plan to overthrow the Directory. His brothers Joseph and Lucien were already at work in the Councils but were not advocating that their brother become the titular head of the regime. Sieyes continued to look for a suitable candidate to be his military man and after much searching had originally settled on Joubert but he was killed in battle in August. His eyes now turned to Napoleon.

The populace again greeted Napoleon's return with cheers following his victories in Egypt and at Aboukir. The Directory was forced to overlook the abandonment of his army, which they had been aiming to censure him on.

18 October 1799
NETHERLANDS FRONT
The Allies signed the Convention of Alkmaar with the French, bringing about the evacuation of the Anglo-Russian forces from the Lowlands. The British returned some 8,000 prisoners they were holding.

November 1799
INTERNATIONAL POLITICS
After disagreements with Britain and France, Tsar Paul I withdrew Russia from the coalition.

4 November 1799
ITALIAN FRONT
The Austrians under Melas defeated the French Army of the Alps under

Championnet at Genoa. Virtually all of the territory gains achieved by Napoleon in 1796 and 1797 had been lost to the Allies.

9 November 1799
FRANCE: POLITICS
Barras, Ducos and Sieyes resigned from the Directory while Gohier and Moulin were arrested. Talleyrand summoned the Councils and asserted that the Jacobins were ready to seize power. The Council of Elders decided they would meet on 10 November to determine their course of action and in the meantime appointed General Bonaparte to command the forces around Paris. Bernadotte opposed his appointment but he was persuaded to desist by his brother in law, Joseph Bonaparte.

The actions of Sieyes and his conspirators became known as the coup of 18 Brumaire.

10 November 1799
FRANCE: POLITICS
Napoleon went before the Council of Elders and demanded a revision of the constitution. Sieyes had in fact planned to implement an entirely new constitution but did not feel that the Councils would accept this. The Elders grudgingly agreed to Napoleon's demands. He then went before the Council of 500, president of which was his brother Lucien. Despite their best efforts, the 500 erupted and Napoleon was knocked unconscious. Troops then stormed the chamber to restore order. After peace was restored, the few members of the Council still present voted to give executive powers to a group of temporary consuls. By the skin of its teeth the coup had succeeded and the Consulate was established.

Napoleon, Sieyes and Roger Ducos were appointed as provisional consuls but Napoleon quickly and unexpectedly emerged as the leading member of a triumvirate. Within a short time Napoleon managed to replace Sieyes and Ducos with Jean Cambacères and Charles Lebrun as his infant regime found its feet.

19 November 1799
NETHERLANDS FRONT
The British completed the evacuation of their forces from the Netherlands.

December 1799
FRANCE: ARMED FORCES
Napoleon began to assemble a new Army of the Reserve at Dijon.

14 December 1799
FRANCE: POLITICS
Bonaparte was appointed First Consul, backed up by the power of the army. France had effectively become a military dictatorship.

INTERNATIONAL POLITICS
Napoleon began to make overtures to the Allies that he wished to make peace. Recognising the split between the Allies and Russia, he began to persuade Tsar Paul of the usefulness of an alliance with France.

24 December 1799
FRANCE: POLITICS
A new constitution was issued in France. The Consulate officially began. General Louis Berthier became Napoleon's Minister of War and Chief of Staff.

> *Napoleon's rise to supreme power had been nothing short of startling. From his humble origins his sheer ambition and self-belief had brought him to the head of the foremost state in continental Europe. So great were to be his actions upon this period of history that it, and the wars that accompanied it, were to be named after him. The Napoleonic period had begun.*

* 1800 *

January 1800
FRANCE: ARMED FORCES
The *Garde des Consuls* was formed, with Murat as its commander. It would go on to comprise the Imperial Guard. At this stage it numbered just 2,000 men.

As First Consul, Napoleon began the expansion of the army, and of the artillery arm in particular. In 1800 it numbered 28,000 men. The system of civilian drivers of artillery trains was abandoned in favour of men who were under the colours. Of greatest importance though was Napoleon's development of the corps system, grouping divisions into autonomous units, within his armies.

ALLIED PLANNING
The Austrians aimed to renew their offensive in Italy while holding down the French in Germany. General Kray was to prevent Moreau from attacking in Germany by pinning him with a force of more than 120,000. Moreau had a similar sized force deployed along the Rhine from Switzerland to Alsace. Baron Melas, with another 100,000 Austrian troops, was to attack Masséna's 40,000 on the Riviera coast, pushing the French out of Italy once and for all.

FRENCH PLANNING
Napoleon, now in sole command of the French military, was free to make his own strategic plans. Assembling new armies, he planned to take the war aggressively to the Allies, turning first on the Austrians in an effort

to knock them out of the war. Moreau was to command the Army of the Rhine, with 146,000 men deployed along the Upper Rhine, while Masséna commanded the Army of Italy, with 56,000 men, between Mont Blanc and Genoa. In Holland, Brune commanded 25,000 men while there were a further 100,000 troops held in garrisons throughout France.

21 January 1800
EGYPTIAN FRONT
The Convention of El Arish between the French and the Ottomans proposed to end the fighting in Egypt. Kléber agreed to evacuate his forces from Egypt provided they were allowed free passage to France. The British rejected the convention.

25 January 1800
FRANCE: ARMED FORCES
Around Dijon Napoleon formed the new Army of the Reserve of 60,000 men, with which he would push through Switzerland then south into northern Italy. Then he and Masséna would crush Melas between them. The entire strategy undertaken by Napoleon was a massive gamble; success would establish a concrete foundation for his regime but failure would potentially leave him in a precarious political position.

1 March 1800
FRANCE: ARMED FORCES
Napoleon formally introduced the corps system into the French armies, issuing orders for General Moreau to divide the veteran Army of the Rhine into four all-arms corps.

20 March 1800
EGYPTIAN FRONT
General Kléber attacked and defeated the Turks under Vizier at Heliopolis. Cairo was recovered shortly after. The French forces in Egypt were now fighting for their own survival and nothing more, having been abandoned to their fate first by the Directory and now by Napoleon's regime.

5 April 1800
ITALIAN FRONT
The Austrians began their offensive into Italy. During the next two weeks they swept through northern Italy and battered Masséna's army before pushing him and 12,000 men back into Genoa. Melas, leaving General Ott with 21,000 men to besiege Masséna, led his force towards Nice, pushing the remnants of the French army, some 18,000 men under General Louis Suchet, back upon the coastal town.

8 April 1800
ITALIAN FRONT
Melas forced the French from Mont Cenis.

20 April 1800
ITALIAN FRONT
Masséna was isolated in Genoa by General Ott. Any possibility of supply by sea was prevented by a British naval blockade and, with his forces low on supplies, the prospects did not look encouraging for the French.

3 May 1800
GERMAN FRONT
Moreau invaded Bavaria and quickly met, and defeated, Kray at the Second Battle of Stockach.

4 May 1800
GERMAN FRONT
Kray pulled his forces back but was closely pursued by General Moreau.

5 May 1800
GERMAN FRONT
Moreau caught Kray's Austrians once again and this time defeated them at Moskirch.

6 May 1800
FRENCH COMMAND
Napoleon left Paris to join the Army of the Reserve.

15 May 1800
SWISS FRONT
Napoleon joined the main body of the Army of the Reserve as it began its crossing of the Alps. He led his 37,000 men through the Great St Bernard Pass but also sent 5,000 through the St Cenis Pass to divert Melas' attention. Moreau was ordered to send another 15,000, an entire corps, south from the German front via the Simplon and St Gotthard Passes, to join up with Napoleon in Lombardy.

16 May 1800
GERMAN FRONT
Moreau fought Kray for a third time, this time defeating him in battle at Ulm. Moreau was supposed to detach one of his corps and send it south but, not believing in the viability of Napoleon's plan, only sent a single division down.

ITALIAN FRONT
Lannes, leading the French advance through the Great St Bernard Pass, reached Aosta.

24 May 1800
ITALIAN FRONT
Having successfully crossed the Alps, Napoleon's army began deploying into Lombardy.

Late May 1800
ITALIAN FRONT
Melas learned of Napoleon's unexpected arrival in northern Italy and began to pull the 30,000 men facing Suchet back from Nice to confront him.

2 June 1800
ITALIAN FRONT
Napoleon's forces captured Milan.

4 June 1800
ITALIAN FRONT
In Genoa, Masséna surrendered his 7,000 starving soldiers to General Ott. The French army had run out of supplies. Having negotiated an excellent settlement, British ships took Masséna and his men by sea to the mouth of the Var river.

7 June 1800
ITALIAN FRONT
General Melas, deployed in force around Turin, had his lines of communication with the east cut as Napoleon continued to push forward.

9 June 1800
ITALIAN FRONT
General Jean Lannes, moving south with 8,000 men, defeated Ott's 18,000 at Montebello as they advanced north from Genoa. Lannes threw his forces into a vigorous attack and, when joined by General Victor's 6,000 troops, forced the Austrians to withdraw. Ott's force, having lost 3,000 men, fell back in disorder towards Alessandria.

11 June 1800
ITALIAN FRONT
Napoleon's army in Italy was reinforced by the arrival of General Desaix's division of 10,000 men. He despatched him towards Novi to prevent an Austrian withdrawal from Alessandria in the direction of Genoa. Napoleon sent a second division of his army north to cover the line of the Po river.

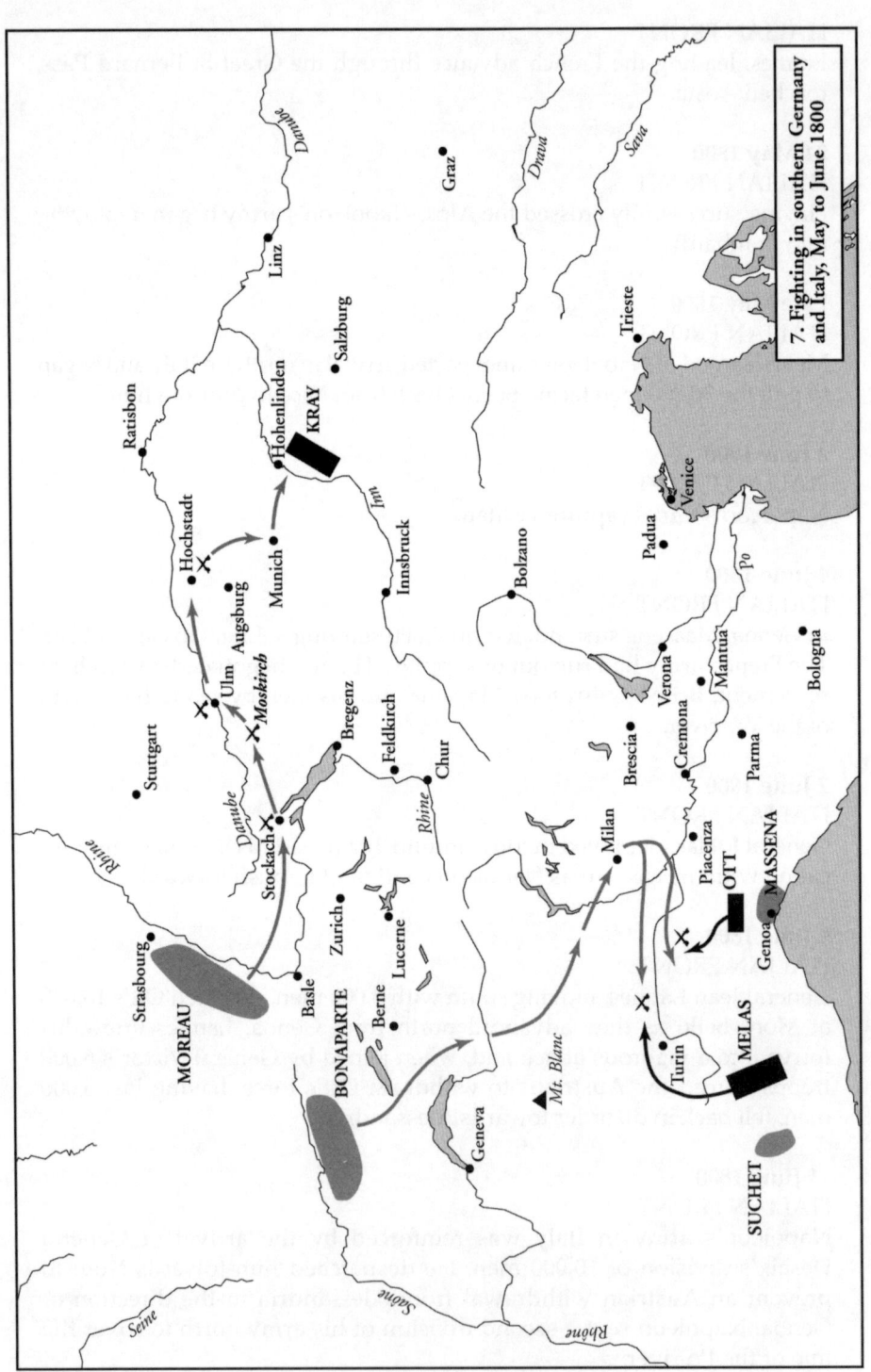

7. Fighting in southern Germany and Italy, May to June 1800

13 June 1800
ITALIAN FRONT
Melas had concentrated 31,000 men at Alessandria. Ott's badly demoralised troops joined him.

14 June 1800
ITALIAN FRONT
Napoleon mistakenly believed Melas and his army were still in Turin and were preparing to retreat. He therefore advanced with his units separated and unexpectedly, with just 18,000 men (the corps of Victor and Lannes and Murat's cavalry), ran into the main Austrian force a mile east of Alessandria, near Marengo. General Desaix was marching south on the road to Genoa as ordered.

Melas, who had just under 30,000 men available, opened the battle during the morning with an aggressive assault towards the east, pushing in the French right wing. Napoleon issued a series of urgent orders to his dispersed corps, calling them back to the sound of the guns. By 1pm, after some furious fighting, Victor's corps had been compelled to withdraw two miles while Lannes and Murat fought a fierce defensive action to prevent total collapse. By 3pm General Melas believed he had won the battle and incredibly handed over command to General Zach to mop up the French force.

Napoleon, with the aid of the Consular Guard, which had marched north to prevent Ott from encircling the French army, rallied his forces and with the arrival of Desaix's 10,000 at 5pm, launched a fierce counter-attack. Desaix, supported closely by Marmont's artillery, attacked the Austrians frontally while the French cavalry, led by General Kellermann, rolled up the northern Austrian flank. The Austrian army collapsed and was routed. Some 14,000 Austrian troops were killed, wounded or captured while the French lost 8,000, including the talented Desaix.

The victory at Marengo could so easily have ended in French defeat. Napoleon's new regime had survived its first significant military test, but it had been helped in no small part by the ability of the fallen General Desaix.

EGYPTIAN FRONT
General Kléber, the commander of French forces in Egypt, was murdered by an assassin in Cairo. Command of the ill-fated Army of the Orient passed to General Jacques Menou.

15 June 1800
ITALIAN FRONT
The French and Austrians concluded the Convention of Alessandria following the Austrian defeat at Marengo. Melas' army had been virtually

destroyed, leaving him with no option but to surrender. He agreed to evacuate his forces from Lombardy.

Napoleon left the Italian theatre for Paris, leaving General Brune in command of the army, with orders to consolidate the gains.

19 June 1800
GERMAN FRONT
Moreau continued to press the Austrians in Bavaria, defeating Kray at Hochstadt before advancing upon Munich. Kray managed to pull his forces back to positions behind the Inn river.

WAR AT SEA
There was an abortive British raid on Belle Isle.

15 July 1800
GERMAN FRONT
The French and Austrians concluded a ceasefire. General Kray was relieved of his command and Archduke John was appointed in his place.

26 August 1800
WAR AT SEA
There was an abortive British raid on Ferrol.

September 1800
INTERNATIONAL POLITICS
Tsar Paul began to mass forces against the Austrian border in support of Napoleon's efforts. He was also trying to sponsor an alliance of Russia, Sweden, Prussia and Denmark against Britain. The nobles of the Russian court became increasingly alarmed at Paul's policies.

5 September 1800
MEDITERRANEAN FRONT
After a two-year siege, the French garrison of Valetta in Malta surrendered to the British and Maltese rebels.

22 November 1800
GERMAN FRONT
The conflict in Germany was resumed following the end of the mutually agreed ceasefire. Archduke John aimed to destroy the French left wing and sever communications with France.

3 December 1800
GERMAN FRONT
General Moreau, with 90,000 men, unexpectedly ran into the Austrians near Hohenlinden, twenty miles east of Munich. The French reacted most

quickly and launched a vigorous attack upon John's advancing army of 83,000 Austrians and Bavarians. Neither army was concentrated, barely two thirds of each actually fighting. Moreau managed to isolate parts of the Allied force, launching skilful attacks on each flank, attacks that were led by Generals Ney and Grouchy. The French killed or captured some 14,000 men for a loss of just 2,300 men.

Mid-December 1800
GERMAN FRONT
Moreau advanced through southern Germany towards Vienna. General Guillaume Brune marched his Army of Italy across the Julian Alps to threaten the Austrians while General Macdonald invaded the Tyrol from Switzerland.

MEDITERRANEAN FRONT
The British embarked a force of 15,000 men, commanded by General Abercromby, at Malta for Rhodes, where they aimed to link up with the Turks and invade Egypt.

24 December 1800
FRANCE: POLITICS
There was an attempt on Napoleon's life. A Royalist supporter attempted to kill him with a bomb but failed in his efforts. The attackers aimed to restore the Bourbon dynasty but in actual fact gave Napoleon the excuse and opportunity he needed to eliminate opposition to his regime, particularly the Jacobins.

25 December 1800
GERMAN FRONT
The Austrians sued for peace as the French armies mauled their forces on the roads to Vienna.

30 December 1800
MEDITERRANEAN FRONT
The British expeditionary force to Egypt docked at Rhodes to link up with the Turks. Unfortunately the Turks were not ready so the British determined to invade alone although they waited in order to train their army for an assault landing before launching their invasion.

* 1801 *

1 January 1801
BRITAIN: POLITICS
Act of Union between Britain and a temporarily pacified Ireland created the United Kingdom.

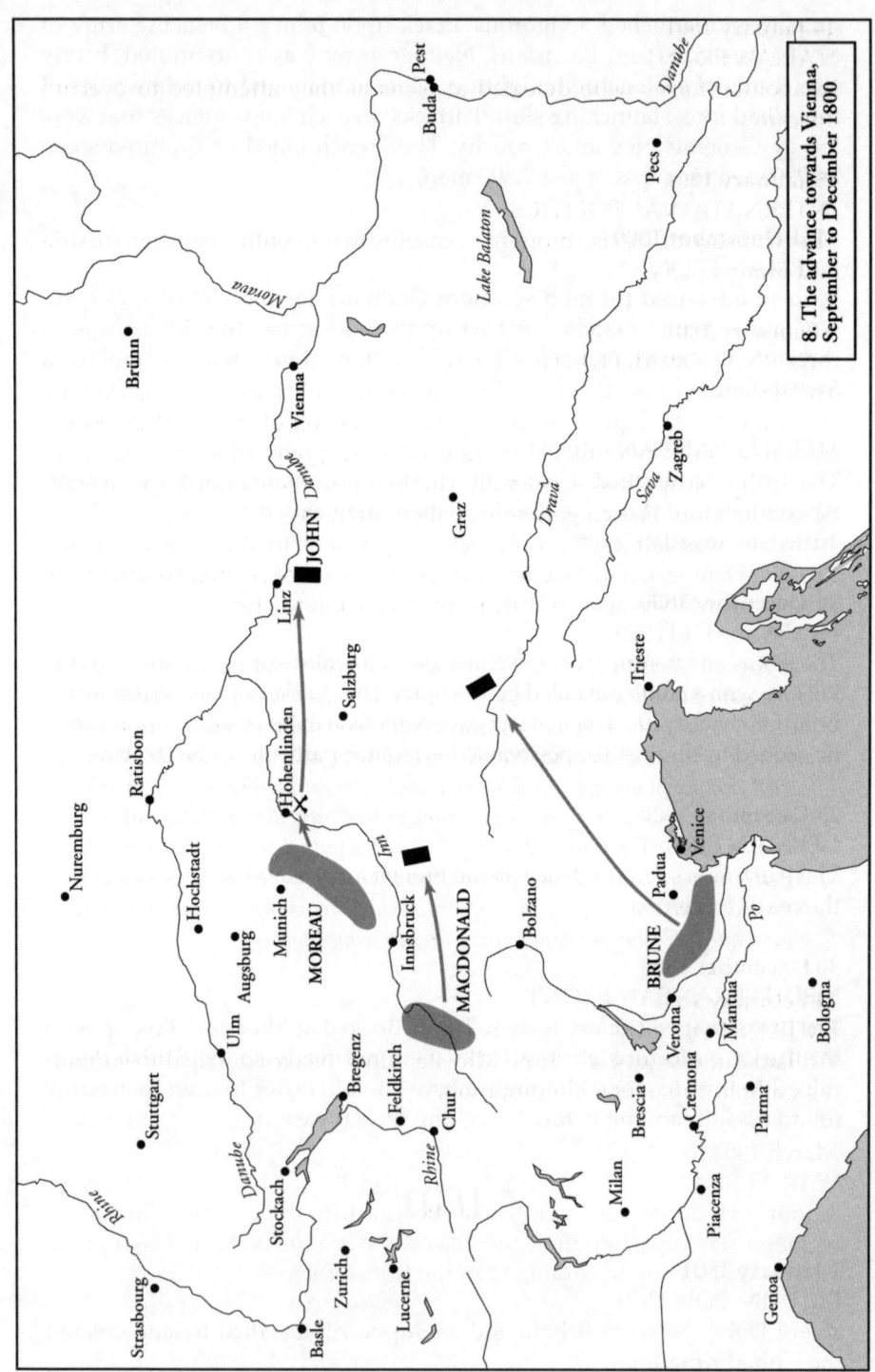

8. The advance towards Vienna, September to December 1800

14 January 1801
ITALIAN FRONT
Neapolitan forces were defeated at Siena as they attempted to overrun Tuscany.

15 January 1801
INTERNATIONAL POLITICS
The Armistice of Treviso brought a ceasefire in the conflict between Austria and France.

9 February 1801
INTERNATIONAL POLITICS
The Peace of Luneville ended the war between France and Austria. The Austrians finally agreed to the French possession of Italy and the Rhine frontier. More importantly, they agreed to a reorganisation of the German states. The Neapolitans, generally successful in their campaigns in Italy, agreed to admit French garrisons to their territory.

Britain was left as the only active opponent to the French. Russia, Prussia, Denmark and Sweden formed a League of Armed Neutrality to protect themselves against British commerce interdiction.

Throughout the period of the Second Coalition the French government had undergone significant upheaval. The Directory had fallen and Napoleon's fledgling regime had been established. Now essentially in sole political and military control of France, Napoleon had been able to undertake a concerted campaign against the Coalition and brought victory to French arms both north and south of the Alps. Austria had been decisively defeated by Napoleon himself in Italy at Marengo. Coupled with defeats in Germany the Austrians were left with no option other than to seek terms. This provided Napoleon with the opportunity to firmly establish his regime and undertake a fundamental reorganisation of the French armed forces.

14 February 1801
BRITAIN: POLITICS
William Pitt resigned as Prime Minister after the crown failed to support his Catholic Emancipation proposals.

March 1801
WAR AT SEA
Admiral Hyde Parker led a British fleet of fifty-three vessels, including eighteen warships, into the Baltic to end the League of Armed Neutrality. Nelson was second in command of the British force.

2 March 1801
EGYPTIAN FRONT
The British arrived off Aboukir and began to reconnoitre the proposed landing site. The French began to assemble a force to oppose the landing.

8 March 1801
EGYPTIAN FRONT
A British army of 18,000 under General Sir Ralph Abercromby landed at Aboukir but met fierce French resistance. The landings took place under heavy fire from French infantry, inflicting some 700 British casualties. General Moore, Abercromby's second in command, led the advanced party and routed the defending French force, capturing its cannon.

13 March 1801
EGYPTIAN FRONT
The advancing British, pushing forward towards Alexandria, ran into a French blocking unit. In hard fighting the French were compelled to retreat, having lost 500 men. French strength in artillery had cost the attacking British some 1,300 killed or wounded. Abercromby decided to abandon his advance upon Alexandria and instead fortified his positions at Aboukir.

22 March 1801
EGYPTIAN FRONT
The French attacked the British forces, which had taken up an entrenched position east of Alexandria. Menou's attack was very well planned. A feint on the left flank diverted British attention from the main attack on their right wing. Fierce fighting developed as the French pressed their attacks home. The British troops were struck hard by French cavalry and, unable to form squares in time, fought in dispersed order, suffering heavy losses. The men of the 28th Regiment were attacked to front and rear, compelling their second rank to face about to meet the attack while the front rank fought off the frontal assault. Disciplined British musketry inflicted heavy losses upon the attacking troops. Despite their best efforts, French soldiers managed to break the British line and captured General Abercromby. However, he was quickly rescued by the men of the 42nd Regiment. Later in the battle Abercromby was injured and had to be carried from the field. After further heavy fighting the French attack was repulsed and Menou pulled his force back upon Alexandria. Abercromby died of his wounds a week after the battle. French losses during the battle were 3,000 men while the British lost 1,300.

24 March 1801
RUSSIA: POLITICS
Tsar Paul I was assassinated during a palace coup. The Russian ruling class was becoming increasingly uncomfortable with Paul's continued

alignment with France. His son, Alexander I, assumed the throne but he was mentally unstable. However, he was a fierce opponent of the French Revolution, but would later become an admirer of Napoleon before the ill-fated invasion of 1812.

28 March 1801
EGYPTIAN FRONT
General Abercromby died of the wounds he had received in the battle of Alexandria. General Hutchinson took command of the British forces. He left 5,000 British and local Turkish troops to blockade the French in Alexandria before turning to march for Cairo.

2 April 1801
DANISH FRONT
Admiral Hyde Parker, with a fleet of thirty-three vessels, ordered Nelson to move his fleet into Copenhagen to attack the Danish fleet and port. The entry to the harbour was protected by strong defences and the British lost a number of ships, which ran aground while avoiding Danish fire. Nervous of his losses, Hyde Parker ordered the attack abandoned but Nelson disobeyed his orders and pushed his twelve ships through the fire into Copenhagen harbour and attacked the Danish fleet of eighteen vessels, commanded by Admiral Fischer.

In a furious fire-fight, the British destroyed the Danish force, capturing twelve ships and destroying the remainder. The Danes suffered 2,000 casualties and 2,000 captured but the British suffered 1,000 killed or wounded and many of their vessels were badly damaged. The League signed an armistice with the British shortly afterwards, preventing Nelson from continuing the journey to Revel to destroy the Russian fleet, as originally intended.

Nelson's audacious attack had smashed the League of Armed Neutrality in a single blow. However, skilful though Nelson was in the art of naval warfare, this act did nothing for the Continental perception of the British that they were fighting merely to protect their own interests and strengthen their own growing worldwide empire.

17 June 1801
INTERNATIONAL POLITICS
Tsar Alexander I signed a convention that ended the League of Armed Neutrality. Russia once more began to turn away from France and towards the Allies.

27 June 1801
EGYPTIAN FRONT
Cairo fell to Hutchinson's British army in Egypt.

6 July 1801
WAR AT SEA
A British fleet of eight vessels under Admiral Saumarez fought a drawn battle against a Franco-Spanish force of twelve ships under Admiral Linois at Algeciras.

12 July 1801
WAR AT SEA
During the night of 12–13 July Admiral Saumarez defeated the larger Franco-Spanish fleet in a second action off Algeciras. The British captured one ship while two of the Spanish ships engaged each other in error during the hours of darkness and were both destroyed.

15 July 1801
INTERNATIONAL POLITICS
Napoleon and the Papacy came to a concordat to settle the French breach with the Catholic Church following the earlier revolutionary years. The agreement recognised Catholicism as the religion of the majority of France, which aided Napoleon's popularity and his consolidation of power.

August 1801
EGYPTIAN FRONT
The British continued their advance through Egypt, capturing Alexandria.

31 August 1801
EGYPTIAN FRONT
Menou's 26,000-strong Army of the Orient, locked up in Alexandria, agreed to surrender to the British.

2 September 1801
EGYPTIAN FRONT
The French Army of the Orient concluded its surrender.

14 September 1801
EGYPTIAN FRONT
The British evacuated the French army from Egypt, escorting them to France.

1 October 1801
INTERNATIONAL POLITICS
Signing of the preliminaries of the Peace of Amiens between France and Britain.

* 1802 *

March 1802
FRANCE: ARMED FORCES
The Consular Guard numbered 5,300 men.

27 March 1802
INTERNATIONAL POLITICS
After much negotiation the Treaty of Amiens brought peace to Britain and France. The British agreed to restore many of the territories they had captured from France and evacuate Malta and Elba. France agreed not to send her troops into Naples and Switzerland, and to honour the independence of Portugal and Holland. The treaty had been negotiated by Joseph Bonaparte on behalf of France, and Lord Cornwallis for Britain.

For the first time in ten years the conflict in Europe was over. In accordance with the treaty, French forces soon began to withdraw from Naples and Switzerland. The required evacuation of Holland did not come about.

The Peace of Amiens enabled Napoleon to bring an end to a decade of conflict in Europe. He was now able to give his full attention to internal reorganisation, proving he was not only an excellent general but an able head of state and organiser of the nation's civil codes. However, the main thrust of French reform was for the improvement of the military, a fact not lost on the British, who also intended to use the peace to reorganise for war.

8 April 1802
INTERNATIONAL POLITICS
The Concordat agreed between the Papacy and France was finalised.

8–14 May 1802
FRANCE: POLITICS
Voting took place throughout France on the life consulship for Napoleon.

2 August 1802
FRANCE: POLITICS
Napoleon was appointed First Consul for Life after a plebiscite overwhelmingly came out in his favour. Of more than three and a half million votes, fewer then 10,000 were against the proposal. He would go on to draft a new constitution that concentrated power in his own hands and gave him the right to choose his successor. This came to dominate Napoleon's internal and external policies as he tried to place members of his family in hereditary positions throughout his empire.

Having spent the last ten years fighting a series of wars that had their origin in the deposition of the ruling monarch, France had effectively elected herself a king in all but name. Napoleon would spend the remainder of his reign fighting to secure his dynasty, a struggle that would lead France to hitherto unknown military greatness.

THE EMPIRE OF FRANCE
France annexed Elba.

11 September 1802
THE EMPIRE OF FRANCE
Piedmont was annexed by France.

15 October 1802
THE EMPIRE OF FRANCE
Napoleon announced the annexation by France of Switzerland. This was the latest in a series of moves that had unsettled an already sceptical British government.

* 1803 *

January 1803
INTERNATIONAL POLITICS
French forces completed the occupation of Switzerland. Napoleon implemented a new constitution by the Act of Mediation. The French also renamed the Cisalpine Republic the Italian Republic. Napoleon was appointed president.

In order to raise revenue at home, Napoleon negotiated the sale of Louisiana to the United States of America.

March–April 1803
INTERNATIONAL POLITICS
Napoleon attempted to exert pressure on the British to evacuate Malta, as covered by the terms of the Treaty of Amiens. The British responded by demanding that Napoleon evacuate his forces from Holland and Switzerland. Napoleon attempted to negotiate but his pride prevented him from backing down.

The First Consul's highhanded attitude had also begun to alienate Tsar Alexander. His attempts to interfere in a settlement in the Balkans between Russia and the Ottoman Empire drove Russia towards the British camp.

16 May 1803
INTERNATIONAL POLITICS
Britain, convinced Napoleon was acting to challenge her interests around the world, declared war on France and re-imposed her naval blockade.

Continental support for Britain was weak, the British being perceived to be acting to protect their own interests.

With Europe about to be plunged into more than a decade of conflict, it is useful to assess the military forces, both naval and land based, available to the main participants.

The Forces of the French Empire

FRANCE: ARMED FORCES

Napoleon had undertaken a massive reorganisation of the French army. He reinforced the introduction of the corps structure although corps could vary in strength considerably, being anywhere from 10,000 to 30,000 strong.

Each corps usually contained two infantry divisions (around 10,000 men each), a cavalry brigade of around 3,000 men and supporting artillery and supply trains. The infantry divisions had brigades as their sub-units and these in turn comprised regiments, the basic fighting formation of the army. A corps would normally comprise up to sixty artillery pieces, some deployed as corps artillery and the remainder split out between the lower units.

The army of 1803 contained seven corps with another, allied, corps held in reserve. In addition to the cavalry allocated to the various corps, army command held the bulk in a separate formation, the Cavalry Reserve of six divisions under Napoleon's command. An army Artillery Reserve was also created, usually numbering around 150 cannon. The ultimate reserve though, to be used to deliver a killing blow to the enemy, were the 8,000 infantry, cavalry and artillery troops of the Guard.

The *Maison*, Napoleon's mobile headquarters, was another excellent development but the direction of the strategy of the empire remained confined to Napoleon's person. Only he knew what operational strategy was intended, and while his subordinates were skilful, they lacked the genius of Napoleon or the knowledge of the wider plan. While Napoleon committed France to combat in one limited theatre at a time this did not prove an issue.

As part of the plan to strengthen the army in the future, an officer school for the army was established at Fontainebleau. In total the French army had a force of around 500,000 men.

THE ALLIES AND SATELLITES OF FRANCE: ARMED FORCES

The Dutch were allied with the French, as were the Italian and Ligurian Republics and Switzerland. The Dutch provided a fleet of fifteen battle-ships and a considerable number of troops integrated into French regiments. Switzerland, a satellite state, provided a number of infantry units amounting to 16,000 men. The Spanish deployed 130,000 men in forty-five infantry regiments and a fleet of thirty-two warships. Bavaria, soon to become a satellite of the French, had an army of 22,000 men.

The Forces of the Allied Powers

BRITAIN: ARMED FORCES
The Royal Navy, protector of British interests at home and abroad, fielded thirty-four battleships fit for operational duty and seventy-seven in reserve. She also had a considerable fleet of smaller warships. The army, always small by continental standards, numbered just 130,000 men at home and around the empire, therefore being severely overstretched and, generally, very badly led. Like the remainder of the continental armies, the British had failed to develop in line with the new French model and would learn the divisional and corps systems the hard way, through years of combat with the French. Perhaps the greatest deficiency the British suffered from was a lack of commitment to maintain the armed forces. At every opportunity parliament cut back military spending, leaving the army short of some of the most basic supplies.

AUSTRIA: ARMED FORCES
Austria had an army of 430,000 men and 1,000 cannon in fifty-seven line regiments, seventeen border regiments, thirty-two cavalry regiments and three artillery regiments. The artillery regiments contained a fraction of the total number of cannon, the bulk being distributed throughout the army rather than concentrated. Austrian military thinking remained fixed on the methods of the Seven Years War but she remained the most constant opponent of the French. The ruling Hapsburg dynasty, realising that their rule was dependent upon the strength of the army, always stopped short of committing to a knock out battle and would seek terms rather than risk losing their military formations in battle.

RUSSIA: ARMED FORCES
Russia had an army of around 400,000 men in 110 infantry regiments and Cossack cavalry units plus a seemingly limitless supply of manpower from the interior. The Russian units deployed into regiments while on campaign but there were no higher command functions below that of army commander. This made the Russian armies unwieldy in action. However, the Russian infantry were tenacious fighters, particularly in defensive positions.

PRUSSIA: ARMED FORCES
Prussia fielded an army of around 250,000 men, although there were only 140,000 available for field operations, the remainder being tied down in garrison and depot duties. Prussian military thinking rested upon the achievements of Frederick the Great so that her army was in effect massively outclassed by the new method of war adopted by Napoleonic France.

18 May 1803
FRANCE: ARMED FORCES
Napoleon created a new Army of the Ocean Coasts to protect against British attacks. The army would be highly trained and drilled.

23 May 1803
INTERNATIONAL POLITICS
Napoleon ordered the arrest of all British citizens in French territories.

26 May 1803
GERMAN FRONT
In retaliation for the British declaration of war, French troops marched into Hanover.

1 June 1803
GERMAN FRONT
France completed the occupation of Hanover. Napoleon had conducted a major reform of the map of Germany, reducing through negotiation some 360 smaller states to just forty. Bavaria and Wurttemberg were brought into the empire as client states. Some of the southern states, such as Bavaria and Wurttemberg, received large tracts of land in return for aligning themselves with France. Its also gave them a feeling of security, as they continued to fear the threat of Austrian aggression. These moves largely brought about the collapse of the Holy Roman Empire.

14 June 1803
ITALIAN FRONT
French forces occupied Naples.

24 September 1803
FRANCE: ARMED FORCES
Napoleon reintroduced regiments to the French army, taking the place of the Revolutionary demi-brigades.

9 October 1803
INTERNATIONAL POLITICS
The Franco-Spanish alliance was concluded. Napoleon planned to use the combined Franco-Spanish fleets to escort an invasion of England. Over the next two years the French would assemble a massive invasion fleet at Boulogne, Etaples, Wimereux, Ambleteuse, Calais, Dunkirk and Ostend.

* 1804 *

13 February 1804
FRANCE: POLITICS
The Cadoudal plot was uncovered. Georges Cadoudal and General Pichegru had returned from exile in an effort to depose Napoleon and install Louis XVIII as king. General Moreau unwillingly became involved.

19 February 1804
FRANCE: POLITICS
General Moreau was arrested.

28 February 1804
FRANCE: POLITICS
General Pichegru was arrested.

20 March 1804
INTERNATIONAL POLITICS
French secret agents crossed the border into Germany and kidnapped the Duc d'Enghien. They then took him back to France. The duke, a member of the Bourbon dynasty, was believed falsely to be the Royalist co-ordinator in Germany.

21 March 1804
FRANCE: POLITICS
The Duc d'Enghien was executed on Napoleon's orders. The execution sent shock waves through Europe, alarming the Bourbon regimes as well as Napoleon's increasingly nervous neighbours.

7 May 1804
BRITAIN: POLITICS
William Pitt became Prime Minister. He was vehemently opposed to Napoleon and aimed to conduct the war as vigorously as possible. Pitt's stance, combined with Napoleon's aggressive policy towards his neighbours, made war all but inevitable.

18 May 1804
FRANCE: POLITICS
Napoleon was elected Emperor of France, re-establishing a system of dynastic succession. France became an Empire.

19 May 1804
FRANCE: ARMED FORCES
The Marshalate was created. Napoleon promoted Generals Serurier,

Perignon, Lefebvre, Kellermann, Brune, Ney, Mortier, Augereau, Berthier, Bessières, Davout, Lannes, Marmont, Masséna, Jourdan, Moncey, Murat and Bernadotte to Marshals of France. The Consular Guard was renamed the Imperial Guard. An ambitious programme to expand the Guards began. Its current strength of 5,000 infantry, 2,000 cavalry and 1,000 artillery troops would soon rise.

June 1804
INTERNATIONAL POLITICS
Napoleon's declaration of himself as Emperor of the French accelerated the move by Tsar Alexander away from a French alliance and towards the British. Britain was making strenuous efforts to bring the European powers into an alliance against France but the prevailing suspicion persisted that the British wanted Europe to fight the war on her behalf.

11 August 1804
AUSTRIA: POLITICS
Francis II of the Habsburg Empire assumed the title Emperor Francis I of Austria following the break up of the Holy Roman Empire.

2 October 1804
WAR AT SEA
Sidney Smith raided the invasion barges assembling at the mouth of the Rhine. Using fire ships he managed to destroy a large number of the vessels the French had concentrated. The threat of a French invasion persisted however.

6 November 1804
INTERNATIONAL POLITICS
Russian and Austria signed a mutual defence agreement.

2 December 1804
FRANCE: POLITICS
Napoleon crowned himself Emperor of the French at Notre Dame in the presence of Pope Pius VII. He placed the crown upon his own head, demonstrating that he was under no one else's authority. After the upheaval of the Revolution and the abolition of the monarchy, he had effectively established a dynastic succession in France once again. Napoleon though looked farther than France and would plant his family members around Europe as monarchs over the coming decade.

14 December 1804
INTERNATIONAL POLITICS
Spain, under French pressure, declared war on Britain.

* 1805 *

March 1805
INTERNATIONAL POLITICS
Napoleon announced his intention to transform the Italian Republic into a kingdom and to assume the crown himself. The major European powers saw this latest move as yet more evidence that Napoleon would not halt his expansion of France and of his own personal power.

29 March 1805
WAR AT SEA
Villeneuve sailed from Toulon with twenty ships, having slipped past the British blockade during a period of bad weather.

30 March 1805
WAR AT SEA
Learning that the French had managed to break out from Toulon, Nelson believed they were making a break into the Mediterranean rather than the Atlantic. He therefore took his fleet to lie in wait off Sardinia.

11 April 1805
INTERNATIONAL POLITICS
The beginnings of the Third Coalition came to fruition as Britain managed to entice Russia into an alliance. By its terms Russia was committed to war if Napoleon did not agree to abide by the terms of the Treaty of Amiens. Sweden and some of the minor German states would also be drawn in over the course of the coming months.

FRANCE: ARMED FORCES
The large part of the Grande Armée was concentrated near Boulogne on the Channel coast in preparation for the invasion of England.

18 April 1805
WAR AT SEA
Nelson, having heard that the French fleet had passed through the Straits of Gibraltar some time ago, realised they were not in fact operating in the Mediterranean and set off into the Atlantic in pursuit. Villeneuve was already most of the way across the ocean.

14 May 1805
WAR AT SEA
Villeneuve reached Martinique, having drawn Nelson, whose ten ships were far behind due to his initial error in thinking the French would remain in the Mediterranean, across the Atlantic. The French fleet was

shortly joined by a Spanish contingent and made its way back to European waters.

26 May 1805
THE EMPIRE OF FRANCE
Napoleon crowned himself King of Italy in Milan Cathedral. The Italian Republic was converted into the new Kingdom of Italy. This dynastic move further confirmed the Allies' belief that Napoleon aimed to impose his own personal authority over Europe, galvanizing Austria's will to wage war in particular, the ruling Hapsburgs having been wavering between peace and war.

4 June 1805
INTERNATIONAL POLITICS
Napoleon annexed the Ligurian Republic, based around Genoa, for France. His forces also occupied the Duchy of Lucca. He placed his sister as monarch of Lucca, giving the British more ammunition to raise a new coalition among the European powers. Emperor Francis of Austria became increasingly alarmed at French progress in Italy.

7 June 1805
INTERNATIONAL POLITICS
Eugene de Beauharnais, Napoleon's stepson, was appointed Viceroy of Italy. Napoleon's continued domination of affairs in northern Italy was seen as a direct threat by Austria. Emperor Francis, until now adopting a position of neutrality, had realised finally that he must either act together with the growing alliance against France or wait and possibly be attacked by Napoleon in the future. The latter's declaration of his kingship alarmed the pope and the southern Italian states, leading them to believe that he would extend direct French rule over all of Italy.

22 July 1805
WAR AT SEA
Part of the British blockade fleet off Brest, some eighteen ships under Sir Robert Calder, checked Villeneuve and his Franco-Spanish fleet off Cape Finisterre. Villeneuve, who lost two ships to the British attacks, sailed for the ports of Ferrol and Corunna. This had a direct impact on Napoleon's plan to dominate the Channel in order to launch an invasion of England.

In the invasion ports along the English Channel the French had assembled a fleet of more than 2,300 transport vessels, enough to transport some 168,000 men and 9,000 cavalry.

28 July 1805
INTERNATIONAL POLITICS
Britain and Russian strengthened their alliance agreed earlier in the year.

Napoleon's assumption of the crown of Italy had pushed Russia over the edge, Tsar Alexander deeming this to be a real threat to Russian interests in the Balkans.

3 August 1805
FRANCE: ARMED FORCES
Napoleon arrived at Boulogne and took command of his army. He continued the pretence that he planned to invade England but his attention had already turned to tackling his European opponents.

9 August 1805
INTERNATIONAL POLITICS
The Third Coalition was formed as Britain managed to bring together Austria and Russia. Sweden also promised to act with the Coalition. Prussia was urged to join but would not commit. The Allies planned to amass Russian and Swedish forces in Pomerania, Austrian armies in Bavaria and Italy, British and Russian forces for an invasion of Naples and more Russian forces at the borders to march west to aid the Austrians.

After three years of peace, the patience of the European powers in the face of Napoleon's continued efforts to humiliate them through his foreign policy finally ran out. Having stood by while he placed his family on the thrones of various newly created states, the Allies now determined to bring the French Emperor back into line. However, Napoleon had not only conducted political consolidation but had raised the French army to a level of efficiency unknown in any other European army. His introduction of the corps and higher command systems were to prove crucial during the wars that followed the creation of the Third Coalition.

CHAPTER V

The Wars of the Third and Fourth Coalitions

In supreme command of France and her military might, Napoleon prepared to go to war with the Allies once more. With his army deployed against the Channel coast, he would stun his enemies with an audacious advance into central Europe.

18 August 1805
WAR AT SEA
Admiral Villeneuve, having been bullied mercilessly by Napoleon, sailed from Ferrol to Cádiz. He received Spanish reinforcements to replace his earlier losses. The British shadowed the French en route as they did not have strong forces immediately available.

24 August 1805
FRANCE: STRATEGY
Napoleon, aware of the Austrian intent to invade Bavaria, issued orders to his army to march east to the Rhine. There the army would pause to regroup before plunging into southern Germany to defeat the Austrians before the Russians could march west to reinforce them. He would then turn about to face the Russian threat.

In a separate effort to keep the Prussians from joining the coalition, Napoleon agreed to cede Hanover in return for Prussian neutrality.

27 August 1805
FRANCE: ARMED FORCES
The Grande Armée, some 210,000 strong, began to leave the Channel coast for Germany, abandoning finally any planned invasion of England to meet the more serious threat posed by the Continental Allies.

2 September 1805
ALLIED DEPLOYMENT
A Russian force some 55,000 men strong, commanded by General Mikhail Kutuzov, began to march west to aid the Austrian efforts against the French in southern Germany. He was expected to deploy into Bavaria

in late October. General Buxhowden moved west behind Kutuzov with another 60,000 men. General Bennigsen, with 40,000 men, began his march to aid the Prussians should they move upon Hanover and Holland. As yet, Prussia remained uncommitted to the coalition. Sweden had also promised to provide an army in their Baltic province of Swedish Pomerania.

10 September 1805
GERMAN FRONT
Austrian forces under General Mack and Archduke Ferdinand invaded Bavaria, advancing towards Ulm. Mack had seniority of command of the 89,000 Austrian troops and marched in the belief that he would be reinforced by the Russians a week before the French could march east from the Channel coast to oppose him.

The Bavarian army of 22,000 men, vastly outnumbered, fell back to the north to evade the advancing Austrians.

ITALIAN FRONT
Archduke Charles prepared to lead another Austrian force, this one 100,000 men strong, against Masséna in Italy. Archduke John had a further 33,000 men in the Tyrol, to act as the link between the Austrian forces in Italy and Germany.

23 September 1805
GERMAN FRONT
Under attack by the Austrians, Bavaria signed an alliance with France.

25 September 1805
GERMAN FRONT
The Grande Armée, some 170,000 infantry and 40,000 cavalry, had concentrated its forces and began crossing the Rhine. Bernadotte's I Corps formed the northern wing while Marmont's II Corps crossed at Mayence. Davout's III and Soult's IV Corps crossed farther south at Mannheim while Ney's VI Corps crossed at Karlsruhe. Lannes V Corps and Murat's Cavalry Corps crossed at Strasbourg.

Bernadotte was to push south to link up with Marmont at Wurzburg while Soult and Davout were to push south-east, via Halle, towards Munich and the Danube. Ney and Baden would also advance towards Munich from the west while Lannes formed the southern wing, pushing first to Stuttgart before also striking east for Munich. Murat would demonstrate with his cavalry to keep Mack's attention. Bavarian forces under General Wrede and General Deroi would push down from the Main river to Nurnberg before linking up with Bernadotte and Marmont.

Mack, still unaware that Napoleon had left the Channel coast, had his forces stretched out between Ulm and Munich. Of his 89,000 men, barely 50,000 were now available to him immediately.

ITALIAN FRONT
Archduke Charles deployed his army into the valley of the Adige, ranging his forces between Trent and Venice.

27 September 1805
WAR AT SEA
Villeneuve, goaded by Napoleon to act or face dismissal, sailed from Cádiz towards the Mediterranean. He knew that Nelson was waiting with his fleet of twenty-nine ships and aimed to try and evade him so that he could reach Cartagena and gather more reinforcements before sailing on for Italy.

1 October 1805
GERMAN FRONT
Baden signed an alliance with France while Prussia began to mobilise its forces.

2 October 805
GERMAN FRONT
The Grande Armée completed its crossings of the Rhine and pushed forward to envelop the Austrians.

3 October 1805
INTERNATIONAL POLITICS
Sweden joined the Third Coalition.

6 October 1805
GERMAN FRONT
Napoleon's forces reached the Danube, the left wing taking Ingolstadt and Neiberg while the centre converged on Munich. The whole now began a turning manoeuvre towards Augsburg and Landsberg, cutting the Austrians off from their lines of communication. Murat continued his cavalry demonstration through the Black Forest to keep Mack's attention while the rest of the Grande Armée swept around the Austrian flanks and into their rear. General Kutuzov's Russians were still two weeks march to the east and could not provide any aid to General Mack.

8 October 1805
GERMAN FRONT
Wurttemberg signed an alliance with France.

11 October 1805
GERMAN FRONT
General Dupont, with a detachment of just 4,000 men, deployed in a vulnerable and unsupported position around Haslach, was heavily attacked by General Mack with a force of 13,000 infantry and 12,000 cavalry. Mack completely

botched his attack and was repulsed with heavy losses. Dupont then took the offensive and managed to pin down the Austrian troops until dusk, when he then skilfully disengaged his army and regrouped with Ney's forces.

13 October 1805
GERMAN FRONT
Murat pulled his cavalry out of Elchingen to hand over coverage of this sector to Marshal Ney. The Austrians quickly moved to establish a break-out route and occupied the village.

14 October 1805
GERMAN FRONT
Ney's VI Corps launched a fierce attack upon Elchingen to prevent Austrian forces under Generals Werneck and Riesch breaking out. After heavy fighting the French retook the village and forced to Austrians to pull back to avoid complete destruction. After a bloody fight the Austrians had lost 4,000 men and the French some 3,000.

15 October 1805
GERMAN FRONT
With Mack contemplating surrender, Archduke Ferdinand led 6,000 cavalry on a break-out attempt from the Ulm pocket but met fierce French resistance. After heavy fighting barely 2,000 of the Austrian troopers escaped. Ferdinand was unable to escape and was held back in a separate encirclement from Mack.

17 October 1805
GERMAN FRONT
Mack agreed to surrender his army of 30,000 men at Ulm if the Russians had not reached him by 25 October. Napoleon had strategically defeated the main Allied land effort without having to fight a single large-scale action. The French now began their advance upon Vienna.

18 October 1805
ITALIAN FRONT
Masséna launched an attack across the Adige but Archduke Charles, advised of the deteriorating situation in Germany, had already begun to withdraw his army east to Caldiero.

19 October 1805
WAR AT SEA
Learning that Napoleon intended to replace him with another commander, and goaded by accusations of cowardice, Villeneuve put to sea once more, this time intending to sail into the Mediterranean. Nelson had intentionally drawn his ships back in order to lure the French into thinking it was safe to leave port.

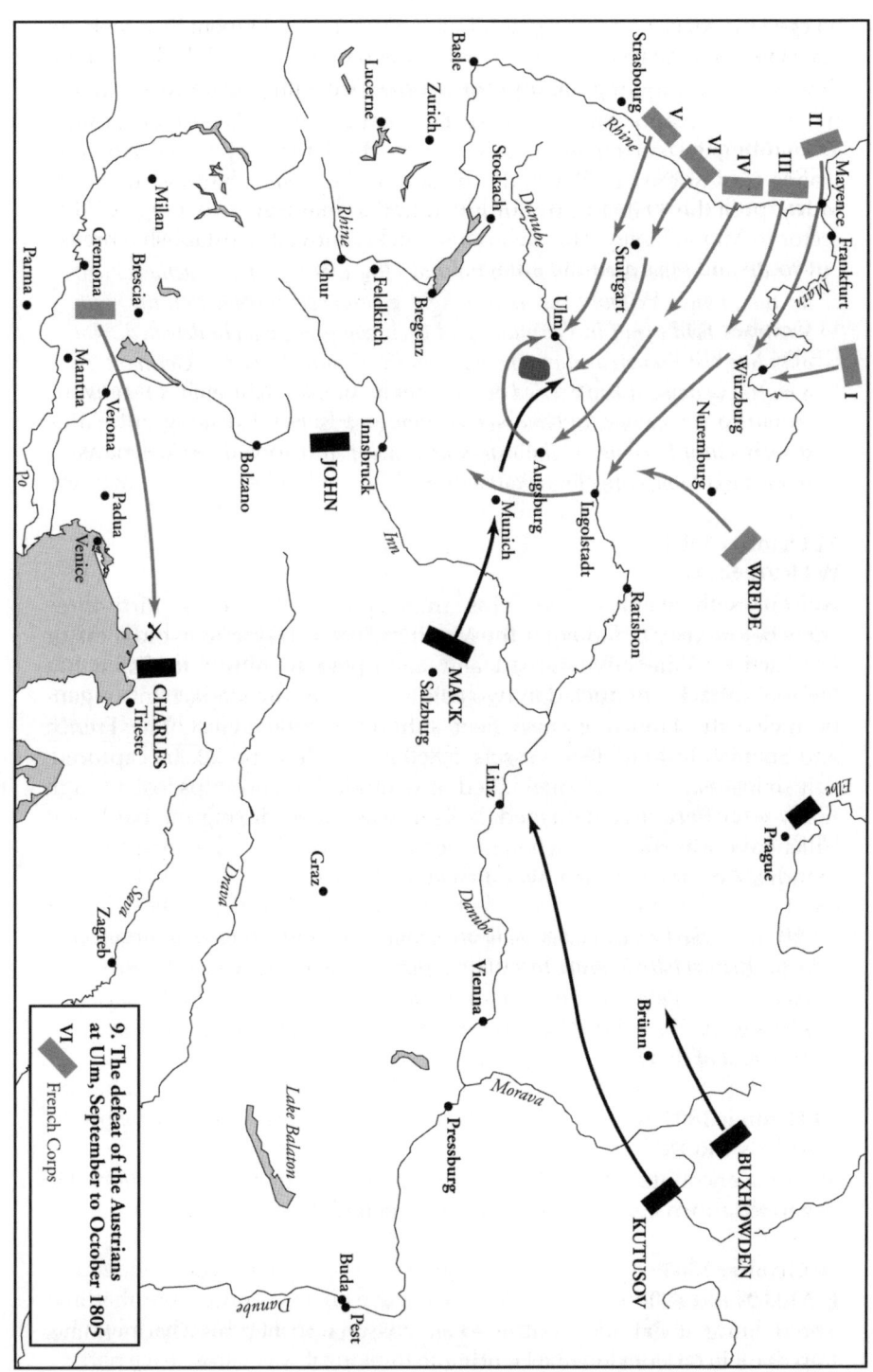

9. The defeat of the Austrians at Ulm, September to October 1805

VI — French Corps

20 October 1805

GERMAN FRONT

Not even waiting long enough for his time to expire, Mack surrendered his army to Napoleon. Archduke Ferdinand, with 13,000 men around Trochtelfingen, surrendered to Murat. A third force of 12,000 Austrian troops surrendered at Neustadt. In total the Austrians had lost in excess of 50,000 of the 89,000 men committed to the offensive.

The defeat of the Austrian army around Ulm was a fantastic achievement for the French. Without the need to fight a single set piece action the main Austrian field army in Germany had been comprehensively defeated. Not only had the French army marched from the Channel coast to Germany in a matter of days, it had carried out a series of complex manoeuvres that had outwitted its opponent. This victory though was but a stepping stone of greater glory to come, as the Russians continued their ponderous advance to the west to meet the French in battle.

21 October 1805

WAR AT SEA

Nelson, with twenty-seven ships, intercepted Villeneuve's thirty-three ships before they could enter the Mediterranean. Trying to avoid a major fleet action, Villeneuve turned and attempted to return to Cádiz but Nelson's attack, conducted in two columns, cut his fleet apart. In a gigantic mêlée the Franco-Spanish fleet suffered a total defeat. The French and Spanish lost eighteen vessels, 5,860 men killed and 20,000 captured. British losses were 1,500 men killed or wounded but no ships lost, though many were seriously damaged. Nelson was killed during the battle but Villeneuve was captured when his vessel was boarded. The Spanish commander, Admiral Gravina, was also killed.

Although the French had already abandoned their intention of an invasion of the British Isles in order to deal with their continental enemies, the British victory at Trafalgar meant they could no longer seriously consider such a plan again. The Royal Navy had demonstrated its supremacy against the strongest of the continental powers.

29 October 1805

ITALIAN FRONT

Masséna encountered Charles in his prepared positions near Caldiero. He began to launch attacks against the entrenched Austrian troops.

30 October 1805

ITALIAN FRONT

The fighting at Caldiero continued as Masséna pushed his attacks home. Losses on both sides were mounting.

31 October 1805
GERMAN FRONT
Kutuzov had arrived with 27,000 men and deployed alongside 16,000 Austrian troops along the Inn river.

ITALIAN FRONT
Masséna attacked for the third day running. By now the French had managed to gain the upper hand and, having suffered heavy losses, Charles began to pull his forces back towards the Julian Alps.

TYROLEAN FRONT
Archduke John was pressed back by the French and retreated, aiming to link up with Charles on the far side of the Julian Alps.

1 November 1805
AUSTRIAN FRONT
Napoleon launched his invasion of Austria. He left 50,000 men to cover his lines of communication.

3 November 1805
INTERNATIONAL POLITICS
Frederick William of Prussia met with Tsar Alexander of Russia and Emperor Francis of Austria. After a series of discussions, the Treaty of Potsdam confirmed the alliance of Prussia with Russia and Austria against France, reversing Prussia's ten-year period of neutrality. However, her lack of action throughout this period had left the other Allies suspicious of her motives.

4 November 1805
WAR AT SEA
The surviving French vessels from Trafalgar were defeated at Rochefort.

8 November 1805
AUSTRIAN FRONT
The French under Davout and Marmont defeated the Austrians under Merveldt at Zell.

9 November 1805
AUSTRIAN FRONT
Kutuzov pulled his forces back from the Inn and crossed the Danube at Mautern. Emperor Francis of Austria had requested that the Russian pull their forces back to protect Vienna rather than linking up in Moravia with Buxhowden.

11 November 1805
AUSTRIAN FRONT
Mortier, deploying a newly formed French VIII Corps of just 8,000 men, defeated a Russian delaying force of 40,000 led by General Miloradovich at Durrenstein.

14 November 1805
AUSTRIAN FRONT
Napoleon entered Vienna. The Austrians evacuated their forces from the city so hastily that Napoleon captured large quantities of weapons and supplies.

ITALIAN FRONT
Archduke Charles and John, with a combined army of 80,000 men, were blocked from retreating through the Julian Alps by Marshals Ney and Marmont, with 20,000 men. To the rear of the Austrian force, Masséna harassed them with his 35,000 men. The Austrians had no choice but to adopt a line of retreat into Austria and Hungary rather than towards the rest of the Austrian forces.

15 November 1805
AUSTRIAN FRONT
Leaving 20,000 men to guard Vienna, Napoleon pushed north with 73,000 and moved to attack the Russian rearguard of 8,000 men, commanded by General Bagration, near Oberhollabrunn. Kutuzov was hurriedly pulling back to the north, aiming to link up with Buxhowden near Brunn.

16 November 1805
AUSTRIAN FRONT
Napoleon defeated Bagration after a hard fought action at Oberhollabrunn.

17 November 1805
GERMAN FRONT
British forces began to land in Hanover.

19 November 1805
AUSTRIAN FRONT
Kutuzov united his force with Buxhowden's near Olmutz. The Russians now numbered 71,000 men, and were shortly joined by another 15,000 Austrians. Tsar Alexander took direct command of the Allied army, sidelining Kutuzov.

20 November 1805
AUSTRIAN FRONT
Napoleon concentrated his 65,000 men near Brunn in an effort to try and goad the Allies into attacking him. He needed to bring the Allies to bat-

tle before Archduke Charles, with 85,000 men, could march up from the south to threaten his rear.

ITALIAN FRONT
The British and Russians landed an expeditionary force near Naples. The Neapolitans were supposed to be allied with France but Queen Marie-Caroline was keen to act against Napoleon without actually breaking her ties. The king, Ferdinand, was weak and dominated by his wife. The British and Russians, together with a small number of Neapolitan troops, launched a tentative invasion of southern Italy.

27 November 1805
AUSTRIAN FRONT
As part of his plan to feign weakness Napoleon requested an armistice from the Allies.

28 November 1805
AUSTRIAN FRONT
The Allies, refusing the request for an armistice, took Napoleon's bait and began to concentrate their forces around him. Archduke Ferdinand had 18,000 men near Prague, while Emperor Alexander of Russia and Francis II of Austria were at Olmutz with the main army.

Napoleon deployed his army west of Austerlitz in a seemingly weak position so as to entice the Allies to attack.

30 November 1805
INTERNATIONAL POLITICS
The Prussian premier, Haugwitz, arrived at Napoleon's headquarters to present an ultimatum following the earlier French violation of the territory of Ansbach. Napoleon delayed seeing him formally until after the expected battle with the Russians.

1 December 1805
AUSTRIAN FRONT
The Austro-Russian forces, some 85,000 men and 278 cannon deployed at Austerlitz, ranged their forces at the foot of the Pratzen Heights against Napoleon's seemingly weak right flank. Napoleon had 73,000 men and 139 cannon deployed on a five-mile line. As a ploy to draw the Allies on, the French fell back from the Pratzen Heights, which were duly occupied by Kutuzov's men.

2 December 1805
AUSTRIAN FRONT
With Napoleon's army stretched out in a seemingly weak line from the Santon hill in the north to the northern tip of the Satschan lake, the Allies

prepared to launch their attack. Lannes held the French left wing with his V Corps (12,700 men and twenty cannon) while Soult commanded the centre with his IV Corps of 23,600 men and thirty-five cannon. Davout's III Corps secured the southern wing but was just 6,300 men strong. The Imperial Guard commanded by Bessières with 5,500 men, Bernadotte's I Corps with 13,000 men and twenty-four cannon, Oudinot's grenadier division of 5,700 men and Murat's cavalry (7,400 men) were held in reserve behind Lannes.[1]

Kutuzov planned to push General Buxhowden with 45,000 men across the Pratzen Heights to strike the French southern wing before rolling up the line. A diversionary attack by Bagration to the north would pin down Lannes. Kutuzov planned to move exactly as Napoleon had expected he would.

The Allies opened their attack in the early morning, striking Davout's corps hard and placing it under intense pressure. Shortly afterwards Bagration hit Lannes but was held up by a spirited French defence. With the Allies moving as predicted Napoleon unleashed his counter-attack. Marching forwards in the centre, Soult assaulted and captured the Pratzen Heights, slicing the Allied army in two. Kutuzov immediately recognised the danger and began a fierce counter-attack. In hard fighting Soult managed to hang on until reinforced by Bernadotte from the French reserve.

With the situation deteriorating rapidly, Kutuzov threw in his own reserve, the Russian Imperial Guards. Initially forcing the French back, they were repulsed by a ferocious counter-attack, the French cavalry falling upon them as they fell back. Napoleon now threw in his reserve, the Imperial Guard marching to reinforce Soult. He then sent this entire force wheeling south to catch Buxhowden between Davout and himself. In a bloody struggle the Russian force was smashed, men trying in their panic to cross the frozen Satschen lake in order to escape. Bombarded by French artillery, the frozen surface broke up, drowning hundreds of Russian soldiers.

Realising his army was not only defeated, but utterly smashed, Kutuzov ordered a retreat. Bagration managed to extricate his force in order but the rest of the army was scattered or captured by the French.

French losses during the battle were almost 10,000 men but the Allies lost 16,000 killed or wounded and a further 11,000 men and 185 cannon captured.

Austerlitz was the crowning glory in Napoleon's most successful year and a testament to the skill and professionalism of the revitalised French army. Not only had he defeated a major Austrian invasion of southern Germany without having to fight a single major engagement, he had enticed the Allies into attacking him at a site of his choosing and decisively defeated them exactly as planned.

4 December 1805
AUSTRIAN FRONT

Emperor Francis II of Austria surrendered unconditionally, leaving Tsar Alexander of Russia to withdraw his forces to the east.

15 December 1805
INTERNATIONAL POLITICS
After having kept him waiting for two weeks, Napoleon finally met Haugwitz of Prussia. On behalf of King Frederick William of Prussia, but without his knowledge, Haugwitz signed an alliance with France, the Treaty of Schonbrunn. By this treaty Prussia was to cede minor territories to France and Bavaria. When he learned of the treaty, Frederick William was dismayed as he had been negotiating to bring Prussia closer to Britain and Russia. In an effort to avoid antagonising both the Allies and the French, the Prussians determined not to ratify the treaty of Schonbrunn until a general peace had been agreed.[2]

The Prussian army, brought to readiness prior to Austerlitz, stood down in the face of French pre-eminence. Napoleon realised that the Prussians had been intent on attacking him earlier in the year and determined to force a war upon the Prussians as soon as he was ready. To lull them in the meantime he agreed that they could occupy Hanover. The Prussians assured the British that if they did occupy Hanover, it was only to ensure that the French did not remain in possession.

26 December 1805
INTERNATIONAL POLITICS
The Treaty of Pressburg ended the war between Austria and France. Austria was forced to accept humiliating terms, ceding the Tyrol to Bavaria and Venice and Dalmatia to the French controlled Kingdom of Italy. She also had to give up some of her German territories to the French satellites of Baden and Wurttemberg while recognising Napoleon's right to be King of Italy. Only Britain and Russia remained actively at war with France.

27 December 1805
ITALIAN FRONT
The French sent 40,000 men into Naples as the British and Russians began to withdraw their army. Napoleon aimed to overthrow King Ferdinand and his queen, Marie-Caroline, after their double-dealing with the Allies. He intended to place his brother Joseph on the Neapolitan throne.

* 1806 *

RUSSIA: ARMED FORCES
Following their disastrous defeat at Austerlitz, the Russians began an expansion and reorganisation of their army. The replacement of the Russian artillery was already ongoing under the direction of General Arakcheev.

14 January 1806
INTERNATIONAL POLITICS
Prussia began a diplomatic offensive aimed at ensuring some protection against the vulnerable position she found herself in. Haugwitz left for France to continue negotiations, while the Duke of Brunswick was sent to the Russians.

19 January 1806
ITALIAN FRONT
The British and Russians evacuated their forces from Naples.

23 January 1806
BRITAIN: POLITICS
William Pitt, prime minister of Britain and main proponent of the war against France, died. The succeeding parliament aimed to negotiate a peace with France if possible.

6 February 1806
WAR AT SEA
Admiral Duckworth defeated the French, with five vessels under Admiral Laissaque, off San Domingo. Three of the French ships were captured and the other two ran aground.

9 February 1806
ITALIAN FRONT
French forces closed in upon Naples. Ferdinand and Marie-Caroline fled the city.

11 February 1806
ITALIAN FRONT
Ferdinand and Marie-Caroline fled to Sicily. Joseph Bonaparte entered the city shortly afterwards to assume the crown of Naples.

13 February 1806
GERMAN FRONT
The British pulled their forces out of Hanover.

INTERNATIONAL POLITICS
Napoleon gave Prussia full rights to Hanover in return for her closing her ports to British ships. Haugwitz had been told in no uncertain terms he must either accept the previously issued assurances or face war. He agreed on behalf of King Frederick William.

15 February 1806
INTERNATIONAL POLITICS
Following his bullying interview with Napoleon, Haugwitz signed a new treaty with the French.

16 February 1806
ITALIAN FRONT
The British landed a force in Sicily to support Ferdinand IV.

24 February 1806
INTERNATIONAL POLITICS
The Franco-Prussian treaty of 15 February was ratified. Bernadotte moved French troops into Ansbach and the Prussians were urged to move their forces into Hanover.

4 March 1806
ITALIAN FRONT
Having overrun much of Naples, the French laid siege to the remnants of the Neapolitan army at Gaeta.

5 March 1806
BALKAN FRONT
Russian forces in the Mediterranean seized control of Cattaro.

INTERNATIONAL POLITICS
Napoleon began to conduct peace negotiations with the British in an effort to end the long-running war.

9 March 1806
ITALIAN FRONT
The ineffective and leaderless Neapolitan army was heavily defeated at Campo Tenese.

11 March 1806
ITALIAN FRONT
Joseph Bonaparte was proclaimed King of Naples by the Neapolitan gentry and city fathers.

15 March 1806
GERMAN FRONT
As part of his strategy to parcel up Germany into pockets of French influence, Napoleon created the Grand Duchy of Berg. He placed Marshal Murat in charge as duke.

18 March 1806
GERMAN FRONT
Prussian troops began to occupy Hanover, French troops handing over control of Hameln.

22 March 1806
ITALIAN FRONT
A recent series of civil disturbances led to open revolt in Calabria.

April 1806
INTERNATIONAL POLITICS
Napoleon began to put pressure upon the Dutch to either accept a constitutional monarch (a member of Napoleon's family of course) or be annexed by France. Talleyrand, acting behind Napoleon's back, secretly tipped off the Dutch leaders that Napoleon had every intention of imposing a monarchy on them.

1 April 1806
THE EMPIRE OF FRANCE
Joseph Bonaparte was crowned King of Naples.

15 April 1806
FRANCE: ARMED FORCES
The Imperial Guard was expanded with the creation of the 2nd Grenadier Regiment and 2nd Chasseurs à Pied.

12 May 1806
ITALIAN FRONT
The British captured Capri. They then moved on to launch an invasion of Calabria with 5,000 men, commanded by Sir John Stuart, to support the insurgents. The French forces in Naples were taken by surprise.

16 May 1806
WAR AT SEA
The Royal Navy, as directed by the Orders-in-Council, recommenced its blockade of French ports from Brest to the mouth of the Elbe.

26 May 1806
BALKAN FRONT
French forces occupied Ragusa (modern-day Dubrovnik).

5 June 1806
THE EMPIRE OF FRANCE
Napoleon gained the reluctant agreement of the Dutch that the Batavian Republic should be reconstituted as the Kingdom of Holland. He intended

1. Napoleon's whiff of grapeshot, Paris, 5 October 1795. (AKG)

2. *Bonaparte aiming the cannon at Lodi,* from the aquarelle by F de Myrbach.

3. General Abercromby in the midst of battle, Alexandria, 21 March 1801.

4. The dismasted *Redoubtable* fights on against HMS *Victory* and HMS *Temeraire* at Trafalgar, 21 October 1805.

5. Nelson is mortally wounded by sniper fire at Trafalgar.

6. Mack surrenders to Napoleon at Ulm, October 1805. (Print after E Boutigny)

7. The Last Stand of the 14th Line, Eylau, February 1806. (Print after L Doyer)

8. Madrid, 2 May 1808. The beginning of resistance to the French. (Fotomas Index)

9. The Siege of Saragossa. (Print after Jules Girardet)

10. Napoleon reviews the German's at Abensberg.

11. Marshal Lannes at Ratisbon, April 1809.

12. The Grande Armeé begins its march into Russia, June 1812.
(Print after F de Myrbach)

13. The Bravest of the Brave. Ney's command of the rearguard during the retreat from Russia, December 1812. (AKG)

14. The battle of Leipzig reaches it's climax, 18 October 1813.
(Print after F de Myrbach)

15. Napoleon leads his army, France, 1814 campaign. (Meissenier)

16. The Prussians storm Plancenoit during the battle of Waterloo.
(Print after C Röchling)

to place his brother Louis on the throne, believing him to be malleable to his wishes. The Napoleonic dynasty was spreading steadily across continental Europe.

17 June 1806
BALKAN FRONT
Russian forces from Cattaro had pushed against the French occupation of Ragusa and defeated the French army in a battle outside the town.

18 June 1806
BALKAN FRONT
Russian forces laid siege to Ragusa.

20 June 1806
THE EMPIRE OF FRANCE
Louis Bonaparte was declared King of Holland.

4 July 1806
ITALIAN FRONT
Stuart, with 5,000 British troops, defeated a French force of 6,000, under Reynier, at Maida in Calabria.

6 July 1806
BALKAN FRONT
A French relief force drove away the Russians and relieved the siege of Ragusa.

12 July 1806
INTERNATIONAL POLITICS
Napoleon undertook the formation of the Confederation of the Rhine. Sixteen German states swore allegiance to France and withdrew from the Holy Roman Empire. More states would join over the coming months. As part of the terms of the treaty, in the event of war France was to use an army of 200,000 men to protect the Germans while the Confederation would raise an army of their own, comprising 30,000 from Bavaria, 12,000 from Wurttemberg, 8,000 from Baden, 5,000 from Berg, 4,000 from Hesse-Darmstadt and a total of 4,000 from the other smaller states.[3]

In addition to settling affairs in Germany in favour of France, Napoleon also made new demands of the Prussians, that they cede more of their German territories. Furthermore, in an effort to reach an accord with the British, he let it be known that he was prepared to hand over Hanover, already promised to Prussia. This infuriated the Prussians when they found out. King Frederick William, believing that war was inevitable, made a secret pact with the Russians.

18 July 1806
ITALIAN FRONT
After a long siege the French forces in Naples captured Gaeta.

20 July 1806
INTERNATIONAL POLITICS
France and Prussia signed a peace treaty.

6 August 1806
INTERNATIONAL POLITICS
The Holy Roman Empire, having effectively ceased to exist through Napoleon's reordering of Germany, was dissolved. Emperor Francis II of the Holy Roman Empire renounced his titles and became Francis I of Austria.

9 August 1806
INTERNATIONAL POLITICS
Believing he would have the active support of the Russians, King Frederick William of Prussia made the decision to go to war with France. He began to make preparations to mobilise the army.

24 August 1806
INTERNATIONAL POLITICS
Tsar Alexander rejected a peace proposal from the French. Napoleon realised that Russia must be drawing towards an alliance with Prussia, posing an increased threat to France.

September 1806
INTERNATIONAL POLITICS
Negotiations between Napoleon and Frederick William III of Prussia broke down in the face of Napoleon's humiliation of the Prussian leadership during the formation of the Confederation of the Rhine and offer to hand Hanover to the British while it remained within the Prussian sphere. The Prussians expected Russian aid but the Russians had only just begun forming their armies around Brest-Litovsk.

12 September 1806
INTERNATIONAL POLITICS
King Frederick William of Prussia ordered his army into Saxony and occupied the state. He then forced the Saxons to join him against France. Napoleon had issued a warning to Frederick that any move against Saxony would result in war. He also urged the Prussians to disarm. Prussia assured the French of their peaceful intentions, lying as blatantly to them as Napoleon normally did in his diplomacy.

13 September 1806
GERMAN FRONT
Prussian forces, moving through Saxony, reached Dresden.

18 September 1806
GERMAN FRONT
Having realised that the Prussians were determined to go to war, Napoleon decided to deploy the Grande Armée into southern Germany to be in place to launch an offensive against Prussia.

19 September 1806
GERMAN FRONT
Napoleon issued orders for the movement of his forces towards the Saxon frontier.

25 September 1806
INTERNATIONAL POLITICS
The Prussian king dispatched an ultimatum to Napoleon, ordering him to evacuate all of his forces from Germany.

FRANCE: ARMED FORCES
Napoleon left Paris to join his army in Germany.

28 September 1806
GERMAN FRONT
Enroute to the army in Germany, Napoleon reached Mayence. He waited here for the Imperial Guard to catch up and would then proceed across Germany to his concentrations in Bavaria.

1 October 1806
INTERNATIONAL POLITICS
General von Knobelsdorf, the carrier of the Prussian ultimatum, reached Paris but found Napoleon gone. He then set off for the French encampments in Germany.

2 October 1806
GERMAN FRONT
Napoleon and his detachment of troops reached Wurzburg. He issued orders for the deployment of the army against the Prussians and Saxons and then continued his march.

6 October 1806
INTERNATIONAL POLITICS
The Prussians formed a Fourth Coalition with Britain, Russia and Saxony, and planned to campaign against the French. The Prussians and Saxons

fielded a joint army of 130,000 men under the command of the the aged Duke of Brunswick. Britain and Russian had not ceased hostilities since the formation of the Third Coalition, despite entering into tentative negotiations with Napoleon. Napoleon's inability to back down in any way prevented any peace being agreed.

While Napoleon had demonstrated his mastery of the military art, his headstrong foreign policy meant France was plunged into yet another conflict. While the Grande Armée remained the formidable fighting force it was, Napoleon could back his policy with force of arms. However, to guarantee security Napoleon needed to retain his edge over the European rivals, or moderate his hostile negotiating strategies.

7 October 1806
INTERNATIONAL POLITICS
General von Knobelsdorf reached Bamberg and delivered the Prussian ultimatum to Napoleon. An answer was demanded by 8 October.

GERMAN FRONT
Napoleon had the Grande Armée, 160,000 infantry, 10,000 artillerymen with 500 cannon and 30,000 cavalry, concentrated in southern Germany. Having already realised that Prussia was likely to attack he decided he would launch a pre-emptive strike and invade Prussia from Bavaria, the Bavarians providing a contingent of around 10,000 men. He would commit the bulk of his strength to the campaign, leaving 20,000 Dutch and French troops to hold on to the Netherlands while a 20,000-strong corps formed under Mortier's command along the Rhine front. Napoleon planned to strike north from Bavaria into Saxony in three columns, and defeat the Prussian army in the field before moving towards Berlin.

The Prussians were deployed in a cordon defence, some 95,000 Prussian infantry, 5,000 artillerymen and 30,000 cavalry and 20,000 Saxon troops, on a one hundred-mile front from Erfurt to Dresden, south of Leipzig. General Blücher commanded a detachment at Erfurt, Ruchel was at Gotha, Hohenlohe at Weimar and Saxon forces were grouped at Dresden. These forces were organised into two field armies, one under the 71-year-old Duke of Brunswick, the overall commander in chief, and the other under Prince Hohenlohe, who at 60 years of age was a youngster compared to most of the Prussian generals. Total artillery available stood at around 550 cannon but these were spread between the infantry regiments rather than concentrated in force. On the eve of the French offensive the Prussian high command had decided to re-order its force along a line through Weimar, Jena and Naumburg, causing needless confusion.

ITALIAN FRONT
Though peaceful at the moment, in order to keep watch on the Austrians,

Eugene de Beauharnais had an army of 40,000 throughout northern Italy. There was a Neapolitan army of dubious quality to the south, which could be called upon if required.

8 October 1806
GERMAN FRONT
In answer to the Prussian ultimatum, Napoleon invaded Saxony from north-east Bavaria, moving rapidly in three columns through the forests of the Teutoburg, his army stretching across a thirty-mile front. Soult's IV Corps, with 32,000 men, led on the right with Ney's VI Corps, 20,000 strong, following and the allied Bavarians, some 7,000 of them, behind him. Lannes' 21,000-strong V Corps led on the left with Augereau's II Corps, 17,000 strong, behind. Bernadotte's I Corps, with 21,500 men, led in the centre with Davout's 31,000-strong III Corps, the 6,500 men of the Imperial Guard behind. Murat's 17,500 reserve cavalry marched with the central column but were moving forward to screen ahead of the advance.[4]

WAR AT SEA
Admiral Sir Sidney Smith raided Boulogne.

9 October 1806
GERMAN FRONT
As the French emerged from the German forests into open country, Bernadotte's corps encountered and defeated the Saxons and Prussians under General Tauenzein at Schleiz. The Prussians withdrew to Auma but their men were exhausted. Despite being in their own territory the Prussian troops were suffering from a severe shortage of supplies, not being free to forage as their French counterparts were.

Murat's cavalry, so far held back among the infantry, pushed ahead of the main force to scout ahead and disrupt the Prussian forces.

The Prussians continued their redeployment, elements of the Saxon army continuing their move towards Jena while Hohenlohe had brought the army together to march from Weimar. Any attempt to launch an offensive to the south had been abandoned in favour of one to the west. General Ruchel was ordered west with 15,000 men to form the advance guard of the planned offensive. Knowledge of the French advance was virtually non-existent.

On the Lower Rhine, Prussian forces under the command of General Lecoq began a slow advance from Munster and Hameln towards Holland.

10 October 1806
GERMAN FRONT
Lannes' V Corps encountered the Prussian advance guard, some 8,000 men and forty cannon under Prince Louis Ferdinand at Saalfeld. Quickly

moving to the attack, Lannes brought 20,000 men to bear upon the small Prussian force. In a desperate battle the Prussians were quickly overrun. In an effort to extricate his force Prince Louis led a cavalry charge but he and nearly 1,000 of his men were killed during the fighting. Another 1,800 were captured. French losses were fewer than 200 men killed or wounded.

11 October 1806
GERMAN FRONT
Dismayed by the loss of his vanguard detachment, Brunswick ordered his army to fall back upon the Elbe. Ruchel's movement west was halted and his force ordered back to Weimar.

Due to his manoeuvres as he advanced, Napoleon transposed the forces on the right wing with those in the centre. The change of position was completed by 12 October.

12 October 1806
GERMAN FRONT
Napoleon completed the turning of the Prussian left flank. He had interposed his forces between the Prussian field army and Berlin and ordered Davout and Bernadotte to move west to cut the Prussian lines of communication. Napoleon, with the main part of the army, was to move upon Jena. Believing the main body of the Prussian army to still be in place he was actually moving against the smaller force, while Davout moved against the main part.

13 October 1806
GERMAN FRONT
Davout began to move west but Bernadotte, either misunderstanding his orders or deliberately refusing to operate in conjunction with Davout, whom he disliked, began to move to the south-west.

Late in the day Lannes reported strong Prussian forces near Jena, which Napoleon still mistakenly believed was the main Prussian field army. The Emperor believed the Prussians would pull back and offer battle in two or three days' time. Ruchel completed his deployment around Weimar.

14 October 1806
GERMAN FRONT
While Lannes, with 25,000 men, held Hohenlohe's attention at Jena, Napoleon marched as many forces as possible to join him. By mid-morning Augereau had arrived on Lannes' left, bringing French strength to 50,000 and by midday Soult and Ney, who deployed to the right, together with the reserve cavalry, had brought the total French strength up to 90,000 men.

Hohenlohe had just 33,000 men immediately available and frantically called for General Ruchel, with a further 15,000, to march to his support from Weimar.

The French launched vigorous attacks against the Prussian force and made steady progress as their forces concentrated. However, the arrival of Ney, who committed his units to a foolish attack, almost brought disaster. Charging forward, Ney's corps was isolated by Prussian cavalry and had to be rescued by a relief attack launched by Lannes and the French cavalry. Hohenlohe failed to take advantage of the French confusion and merely fought a delaying action while he waited for Ruchel. Under intense and sustained artillery fire, the Prussian infantry suffered crippling losses before Napoleon launched an all-out assault. By mid-afternoon the Prussian army was in full retreat, Ruchel's men being caught up in the general collapse. Prussian losses were 12,000 men and 112 cannon to a French loss of just 6,000 men.

To the north, at Auerstadt, Davout with the 27,000 men and forty cannon of his III Corps, was attacked by Brunswick's main force of 65,000 men and more than 200 cannon. In heavy fighting the French held off a series of unco-ordinated Prussian attacks, defeating each one in turn. Brunswick was mortally wounded, together with his deputy Mollendorf. King Frederick William took personal, but less than effective, control of the battle. At midday Davout launched a blistering counter-attack on each Prussian flank and drove the Prussians from the field. Prussian losses were 13,000 killed or wounded and another 25,000, almost the remainder of Brunswick's force, were captured. More than 100 cannon were also taken on the field. Davout had lost 7,000 men but had fought an outstanding battle against overwhelming odds.

Bernadotte, between the two battles, failed to march to the sound of the guns and aided neither force.

The dual battles of Jena and Auerstadt effectively destroyed the military machine created by Frederick the Great half a century earlier and proved the outstanding ability of the Grande Armée to advance rapidly and react quickly once the enemy was encountered. All that remained was for the French to pursue the remnants of the Prussian army until it was completely destroyed, then turn on their last major foe, the Russians.

15 October 1806
GERMAN FRONT

The Prussian army, defeated, demoralised and with discipline breaking down, retreated to the north. Napoleon ordered a close pursuit. Erfurt and 10,000 Prussian troops surrendered to Murat's cavalry. Throughout the weeks of the French pursuit, their soldiers were met with enthusiasm by the German people, who turned upon their own army in its hour of defeat. However, the developing rapacity of the French troops for plunder very quickly reversed this trend.

16 October 1806
GERMAN FRONT

A Prussian force under Duke Eugene of Wurttemberg, some 16,000 strong, marching en route for Magdeburg, had been ordered to change direction towards Leipzig. His force was now close to Halle.

17 October 1806
GERMAN FRONT

Duke Eugene's force was struck by Bernadotte near Halle and suffered a severe defeat. Prussian losses were more than 5,000 men to a French loss of just 800.

Napoleon ordered his brother Louis to move his forces off the defensive and invade Western Prussia from Wesel with a force of 10,000 men. The Franco-Dutch objective was Paderborn. Mortier, who was at Mayence with 5,500 men, was ordered to strike towards Fulda.

18 October 1806
GERMAN FRONT

The French continued their advance, the main direction of their movement being towards Magdeburg. Isolated skirmishes were fought between the rapidly moving French cavalry and the retreating Prussians, who were pulling back through the Harz Mountains towards Magdeburg.

King Frederick William left his headquarters at Magdeburg for Berlin. His plan was to draw his forces back behind the Elbe in order to establish a new defence line and bring up reinforcements from Silesia and Poland. He was also aiming to continue the fight long enough for the Russians to march west to join his forces.

19 October 1806
GERMAN FRONT

Lannes reached Dessau on the Elbe river but found the bridge there burned. Davout was at Duben as he pushed towards Wittenberg.

On the Lower Rhine front the Prussians learned of the disasters at Jena and Auerstadt and abandoned their limited advance upon Holland. Lecoq pulled his forces back upon Hameln.

20 October 1806
GERMAN FRONT

Soult and Murat reached the outskirts of Magdeburg. Hohenlohe had drawn his forces back into the city. Murat sent an emissary forward into the city to demand its surrender. He was taken through the Prussian lines and observed the disorder in their army and their lack of defences. The Prussians refused the surrender demand.

Marshal Ney reached Halberstadt as he closed up to support Soult. Davout crossed the Elbe at Wittenberg while Lannes had repaired the bridge at Dessau and established a bridgehead on the eastern bank. Murat and Bernadotte were pushing upon Dessau to support Lannes while Augereau and Grouchy were pushing their forces towards Wittenberg.

As discipline broke down in the Prussian army due to their catastrophic defeats, it also declined in the French army as fatigue and plundering took their toll. Senior commanders began to complain about the breakdown of discipline and took rigorous measures to bring the troops back into line.

21 October 1806
GERMAN FRONT
Having drawn up to the Elbe, Napoleon issued orders for the continuation of the advance upon Berlin. Soult and Ney were to invest Magdeburg and protect the extending French lines of communication while the bulk of the remainder pushed on ahead.

22 October 1806
GERMAN FRONT
The French completed the isolation of Hohenlohe's forces in Magdeburg. Hohenlohe had himself escaped with a small force and retreated towards the Oder river. Some 25,000 troops were trapped inside the city under the command of the 71-year-old General Kleist. The French believed there were just 8,000 Prussian troops inside the city.

23 October 1806
GERMAN FRONT
Soult demanded that Kleist surrender Magdeburg but the Prussians refused. However, the populace was against the troops defending the town and Kleist was keen to surrender without too much loss of face.

In Western Prussia, General Lecoq had brought his force back to Hameln and took up defensive positions prior to an evacuation to the east.

24 October 1806
GERMAN FRONT
Davout reached the suburbs of Berlin. Lannes also had troops at Potsdam and near Spandau, close to Berlin, but Napoleon had deemed that Davout should be the first to enter the city. Augereau had advanced to a position south of Potsdam while Bernadotte was approaching Brandenburg.

General Blücher, still falling back after the collapse of the Prussian army, crossed the Elbe at Sandau. Hohenlohe had brought his force back to Neustadt. Both groups were endeavouring to reach the Oder.

Lecoq abandoned his positions in Hameln and began to march for the Elbe.

25 October 1806
GERMAN FRONT
Davout entered Berlin and marched through the city to establish a camp on

the Spree river. His troops were enthusiastically greeted by the populace and the mayor. Spandau and its small garrison of 900 men surrendered to Lannes' troops. Bernadotte reached Brandenburg.

In an effort to catch the corps of General Yorck, Soult left the siege of Magdeburg to Ney and his 17,000 men, and marched to Tangermunde. Yorck managed to evade the French and cross the Elbe at Sandau, just behind Blücher.

26 October 1806
GERMAN FRONT
The Prussians again fought a rearguard action at Altenzaun,

27 October 1806
GERMAN FRONT
Napoleon entered Berlin. Hohenlohe ordered his forces to move upon Prenzlau. Blücher was to link up with the main force on the Oder. Murat and Lannes were pursuing the Prussians towards Stettin while Bernadotte had reached Oranienburg.

Learning of the French advance along the Elbe, Lecoq abandoned his march and turned his troops around for Hameln once more.

28 October 1806
GERMAN FRONT
Murat overtook the retreating Prussians north of Berlin. Hohenlohe, ill advised by General Massenbach, who was duped by Murat into believing that the Prussian force faced 100,000 French troops, surrendered his 12,000 men near Prenzlau.

Soult, still chasing the retreating Prussians up the Elbe, crossed at Tangermunde. Bernadotte was now at Furstenburg and believed he was close to catching Blücher.

POLISH FRONT
The Russians had completed the concentration of two armies around Brest Litovsk. General Bennigsen commanded one army of 55,000 while Buxhowden commanded the other, with 35,000. Buxhowden led his force into central Poland to oppose the French.

29 October 1806
GERMAN FRONT
Stettin fell to Lannes and Murat.

30 October 1806
GERMAN FRONT
Leading elements of Bernadotte's corps caught up with Blücher's rear-guards near Neustrelitz. A running fight took place as the Prussians held off repeated French attacks.

31 October 1806
GERMAN FRONT
Blücher linked up with a smaller Prussian force under General Winning. He deployed this larger force into two corps groups, each with around 10,000 men and issued orders for a movement back towards the Elbe to reach either Magdeburg or Hanover. Soult encountered the rearguards of General Winning's force and became embroiled in skirmishes.

To the west, Louis Bonaparte and Mortier converged upon Cassel.

1 November 1806
GERMAN FRONT
Bernadotte encountered Yorck's force, now part of Blücher's contingent, at Nossentin and became involved in a sharp action. After a stubborn fight Yorck fell back upon Alt Schwerin. Soult reached Waren as the French began to converge upon the Prussians. On the Oder, the fortress of Kustrin fell to the French while to the west Cassel was occupied by Mortier and Louis, who united their forces at Cassel and prepared to move upon Hanover. Louis had overall command.

2 November 1806
POLISH FRONT
Despite the fatigue of his troops following their advance throughout Prussia, Napoleon launched his invasion of Poland, pushing Davout forward towards Warsaw. He planned to advance with a total force of 80,000 men and consolidate his positions along the Vistula before moving upon the Russians. Lannes, Soult and Murat would follow Davout as their corps concentrated.

3 November 1806
GERMAN FRONT
Blücher made a stand with his rearguards south of Schwerin. Bernadotte was involved in more fighting while Soult marched as quickly as his fatigued men could go to try and link up with him.

4 November 1806
GERMAN FRONT
Blücher continued his hard march but the French allowed their troops some rest. After the running battles of the last few days the Prussian force had been reduced to 16,000 men. He now changed his line of march towards Lübeck.

5 November 1806
GERMAN FRONT
Prussian troops forced their way into Lübeck. Blücher demanded supplies for his starving and exhausted soldiers.

Marshal Ney gave notice to the Prussians that unless they surrendered Magdeburg he would begin a bombardment of the city.

6 November 1806
GERMAN FRONT
General Blücher surrendered his army to Bernadotte and Soult after they boxed him in at Lübeck. All that remained of the Prussian army was a force of 15,000 men under General Lestocq, which was moving east towards the Russian forces deployed close to the Vistula.

Learning of the surrender of Prenzlau, General Kleist opened negotiations to surrender his force to Ney's corps.

7 November 1806
GERMAN FRONT
Ney and Kleist agreed an armistice ahead of negotiations to surrender the garrison of Magdeburg. In the west the French approached the outskirts of Hameln, where General Lecoq was entrenched with 10,000 men.

9 November 1806
GERMAN FRONT
Louis returned to Holland, leaving command of his force of 12,000 men to Mortier.

GERMAN FRONT
As the French pushed east, Davout captured Posen. Jerome left a detachment of troops to lay siege to Glogau as he advanced.

10 November 1806
GERMAN FRONT
French troops moved into Magdeburg as the terms of surrender were agreed. To the west, Mortier brought up the bulk of his force to Hameln and invested the town with half his force. He then continued his march towards Hanover.

12 November 1806
GERMAN FRONT
The French troops commanded by Mortier occupied Hanover.

16 November 1806
GERMAN FRONT
The Prussians negotiated an armistice at Charlottenburg with the French. King Frederick William would disavow it and continue to fight on alongside the Russians.

18 November 1806
GERMAN FRONT
Davout reached Sempolno as he continued the advance towards Warsaw. Lannes reached Thorn, into which the retreating Prussian corps of Lestocq had retired.

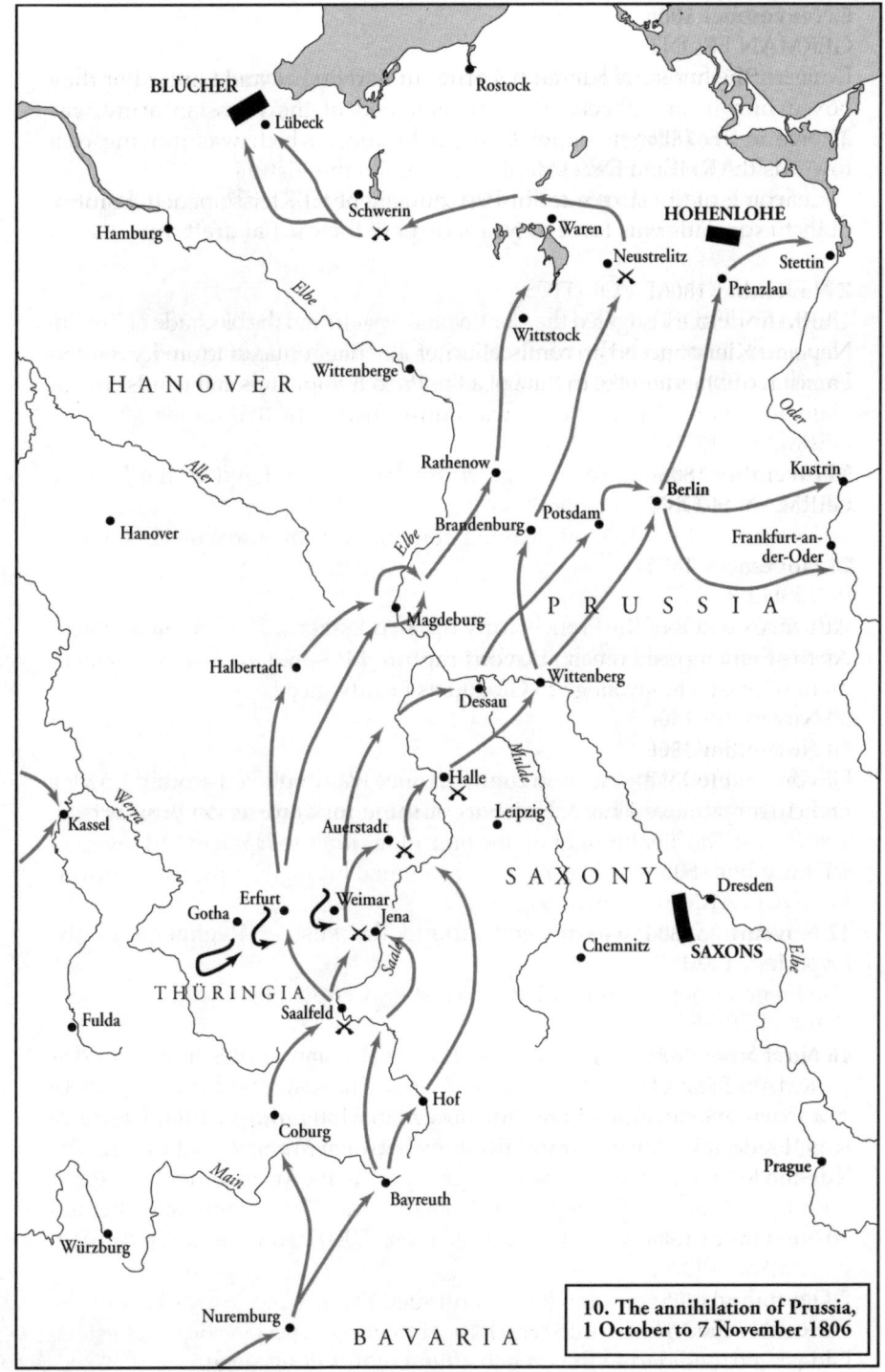

10. The annihilation of Prussia,
1 October to 7 November 1806

20 November 1806
GERMAN FRONT
Realising the futility of his stand, Lecoq surrendered Hameln to the French.

21 November 1806
FRANCE: ARMED FORCES
Napoleon issued a decree calling up the class of 1807 for service in January of that year. This was nearly a year ahead of their usual draft time.

INTERNATIONAL POLITICS
The Berlin decree instigated the Continental System and the blockade of Britain. Napoleon announced the confiscation of all British manufactured goods in French territories and the closure of all ports to British ships and goods.

GERMAN FRONT
Most of the Prussian fortress garrisons had surrendered to the French, netting some 32,000 prisoners.

28 November 1806
POLISH FRONT
Advance guards of the French army reached Warsaw. The Russians evacuated the city as the French marched in.

30 November 1806
GERMAN FRONT
Davout entered Warsaw in strength. Lannes was deployed around Lowicz and Augereau near Thorn. Ney was pushing forwards upon Bromberg.

1 December 1806
FRANCE: ARMED FORCES
The Young Guard was formed around the Fusilier Regiments of the Imperial Guard.

POLISH FRONT
General Kamenskoi began to redeploy his Russian armies in widely dispersed positions from Pultusk, Plock and Prassnitz, withdrawing them from their extended positions along the line of the lower Vistula. Their aim was to disrupt French communications between Warsaw and Berlin. The Russian force was divided into two groups, the 1st Army under Bennigsen with 68,000 men, including 15,000 cavalry and 270 cannon, and the 2nd Army under Buxhowden with 30,000 men, 7,000 cavalry and 210 cannon.

2 December 1806
GERMAN FRONT
Glogau surrendered to the French after a month-long siege.

POLISH FRONT
French troops crossed the Vistula at Warsaw and occupied Praga.

3 December 1806
POLISH FRONT
Over the next week Davout pushed his corps across the Vistula and on towards the Bug. Lannes moved up behind Davout to deploy into Warsaw and guard the Vistula.

6 December 1806
POLISH FRONT
Ney's Corps reached the Vistula at Thorn and drove Lestocq's Prussians back.

10 December 1806
INTERNATIONAL POLITICS
The Treaty of Posen formed an alliance between Saxony and France. The Elector of Saxony was proclaimed king.

18 December 1806
POLISH FRONT
Napoleon entered Warsaw. Bennigsen, deployed just to the north at Pultusk, moved to halt the French advance. The Emperor was determined to bring the Russians to battle and began to concentrate his army.

23 December 1806
POLISH FRONT
Napoleon launched his offensive against the Russians. He aimed to penetrate the Russian left wing and cut them off from their lines of communication with Russia. Lacking clear intelligence, the French unexpectedly ran into the Russians at Czarnowo. Bennigsen, with 15,000 men, was attacked by a French advance guard of 8,500 and, after heavy fighting, drew his force back. The Russians had lost 1,400 men to a French loss of 1,000.

26 December 1806
POLISH FRONT
Lannes, with 25,000 men, attacked Bennigsen's 35,000 men at Pultusk and, in a hard battle, pushed the Russians back. Bennigsen withdrew, having lost 5,000 men to a French loss of 8,000.

Murat and Augereau, with 38,000 men, were also heavily attacked at Golymin. General Gallitzin with 18,000 troops, had his men dug in in defensive positions around the village. Conducting an extremely rugged defence the Russians held up the French force and managed an ordered withdrawal, having lost around 1,000 men. The French also lost nearly 1,000 troops in the hard fought action.

27 December 1806
POLISH FRONT
With temperatures plummeting and informed directly by his troops of their state of exhaustion, Napoleon put his army into winter quarters. The French were spread out in defensive positions from Elbing, on the Baltic coast, to the Bug river. Strict orders were issued to the corps commanders to do nothing that would bring the Russians to battle.

30 December 1806
POLISH FRONT
Bennigsen had been placed in command of the joint Russian and Prussian armies, a force of around 85,000 Russians and 15,000 Prussian troops. He went into winter quarters, keeping his forces concentrated around Deusch-Eylau, Osterode and Allenstein in East Prussia.

The Russians were concentrating a new army in western Russia and aimed to commit this force to Poland and East Prussia in the spring.

In just three months the French had completely destroyed the military threat posed by the Prussians, occupied their territory and taken the war to the very borders of Russia. Exhausted after the mammoth marches, the French desperately needed a period of quiet to reinforce and recuperate.

* 1807 *

2 January 1807
POLISH FRONT
The Russian commanders agreed upon a plan to launch an offensive against the French in East Prussia. Leaving minor forces to cover the French between the Bug and the Narew, the bulk would pass through the East Prussian forests to attack the French left wing.

6 January 1807
POLISH FRONT
Bennigsen began to move his forces along the left bank of the Narew to redeploy in order to attack the French left wing.

7 January 1807
INTERNATIONAL POLITICS
The British issued further 'Orders in Council' in response to the Berlin Decrees, reinforcing the blockade of French territories by extending its scope to cover all French ports. The Royal Navy was also given the power to detain any vessels thought to be carrying goods for France.

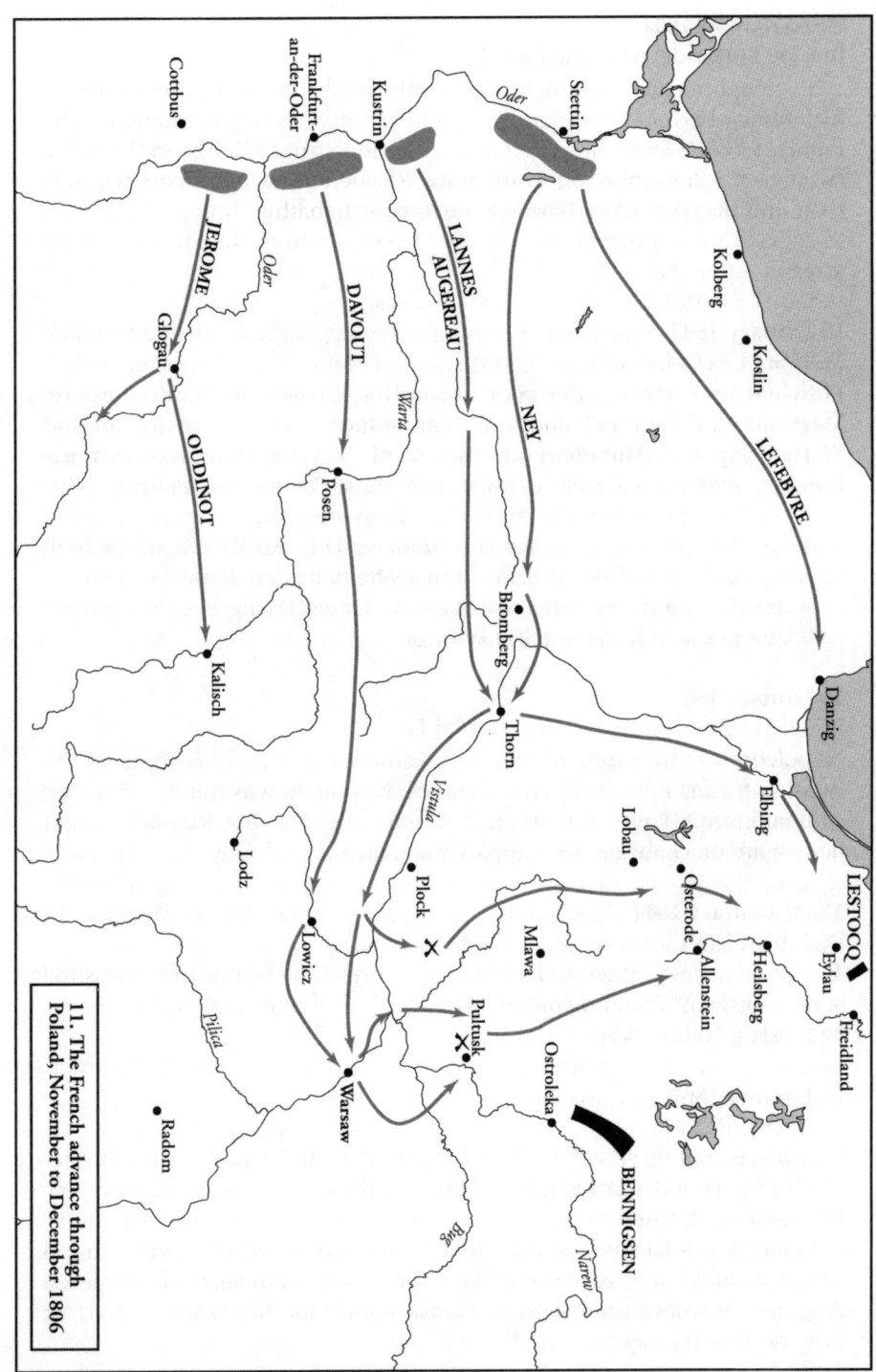

11. The French advance through Poland, November to December 1806

GERMAN FRONT
Breslau surrendered to the French.

12 January 1807
POLISH FRONT
Bennigsen's slow moving army, some 75,000 strong, reached the Bobra river and began to cross. The Russians were marching through the forests to conceal their movement as much as possible from the French cavalry screens.

15 January 1807
POLISH FRONT
With his men starving in the poor land of East Prussia south of Konigsberg, Marshal Ney had extended his cantonments to the north, around Wartenburg and Allenstein. He mistakenly came into contact with the Russians and caused them considerable alarm. Bennigsen, believing this to be a pre-emptive move to disrupt his own offensive, ordered an immediate assault, striking west towards Danzig. This movement struck both the corps of Ney and Bernadotte. Bernadotte had been deployed between Ney and the Baltic in order to cover the forces laying siege to Danzig against a possible Russian relief attempt.

16 January 1807
POLISH FRONT
Napoleon was informed of Ney's movement north and his contact with Russian forces. Furious at Ney's moves, Napoleon was not as yet aware of Bennigsen's larger intentions but, guessing that the Russians might launch an attack, began to redeploy his forces accordingly.

17–22 January 1807
POLISH FRONT
The Russians attempted to isolate Ney's corps but their advance was too slow and the Marshal managed to evade their moves and pull his forces back upon Neidenberg.

25 January 1807
POLISH FRONT
Bernadotte, falling slowly back to the west, defeated a Russian force under Markov, part of Bagration's detachment of the main force, at Mohrungen. Both sides lost around 1,100 men.

Lefebvre's X Corps was detached from Danzig and deployed around Thorn to block any Russian move to the west. Napoleon also ordered Augereau to concentrate around Plonsk while Oudinot was to march for Lowicz from his base around Kalisch.

26 January 1807
POLISH FRONT
Bennigsen's main army reached and occupied Mohrungen.

27 January 1807
POLISH FRONT
Bennigsen moved forward upon Allenstein, which was evacuated by Bernadotte's corps.

28 January 1807
POLISH FRONT
Napoleon became aware of the Russian advance and over-extension of their positions and immediately issued orders to attack towards Allenstein. Just west of the town, Benngisen ordered his army to halt so that his men could rest before continuing their advance.

30 January 1807
GERMAN FRONT
French forces laid siege to Stralsund on the Baltic coast.

31 January 1807
POLISH FRONT
The French were ready to launch their counter-offensive after a rapid concentration of their forces against Bennigsen's now exposed lines of communication. The Russian advance guard, led by General Bagration, continued to move west upon Deutsch Eylau. Prussian troops captured French orders that revealed Napoleon's plan to trap the Russian force.

1 February 1807
POLISH FRONT
Bagration passed the captured French orders on to Bennigsen, while his troops captured a second set of French orders, confirming French intentions. Bennigsen immediately decided to pull his forces back to the north to evade the French attack. Unaware that the Russians were informed of his intentions, Napoleon ordered his right wing to launch their attack.

2 February 1807
POLISH FRONT
Minor Russian forces were intercepted by Soult's and Murat's corps at Allenstein, the bulk having hastily evacuated their positions around the town. Bennigsen now drew his army up on positions on the heights near Ionkovo.

3 February 1807
POLISH FRONT
Soult attacked Bennigsen at Ionkovo, but aware that the French intended to outflank him, he began the evacuation of his main force. Ney and Augereau moved up from Allenstein towards Ionkovo. Bennigsen appointed Bagration to command the Russian rearguard and hold up the French pursuit. Bagration conducted a stubborn defence and repulsed French efforts to cut their line of retreat to the Alle.

4 February 1807
POLISH FRONT
Bennigsen issued orders to his army to continue to withdraw upon the Alle river and Preussisches-Eylau. Lestocq's Prussians had become detached from the main force and withdrew by a separate route. Bagration's rear-guard unit fought a continuous running battle with the French as he covered the main body's escape. Bitter fighting raged at Wolfsdorf as the Russians left behind a small detachment to hold up the French pursuit.

6 February 1807
POLISH FRONT
Bennigsen drew his army around Preussisches-Eylau. He had 67,000 men with 460 cannon. Bagration fought further rearguard actions against Davout at Heilsberg and the main part of the French army at Hof. Bagration detached Barclay de Tolly with a force of 7,000 men to hold Hof but they came under intense attack, losing 2,000 men.

7 February 1807
POLISH FRONT
Napoleon's advance corps, led by Marshals Soult and Murat, reached Bennigsen's positions at Preussisches-Eylau. The French force numbered 45,000 men and 200 cannon but Ney and Davout, with 26,000 men, were on the march. Lestocq's 9,000 Prussians were falling back before Ney, towards Bennigsen's concentration at Eylau. Napoleon launched a bloody attack late in the day and captured Eylau. Bennigsen decided this time to stand and fight, knowing that Lestocq was marching to him to reinforce his army.

Bagration abandoned his positions at Hof and fell back upon Preussisches-Eylau, delaying the arrival of additional French forces to aid Napoleon's attacks.

8 February 1807
POLISH FRONT
Napoleon deployed his force around Eylau to meet an expected Russian attack. Soult held the left flank with Augereau on the right and the cavalry, under Murat, in reserve behind. Bennigsen deployed his army with a large

infantry reserve in the centre and two massed cannon batteries to the fore. He began his attack under cover of a fierce blizzard, striking the French left wing hard. While bitter fighting raged the French and Russian artillery traded barrages.

In an effort to delay the Russians until Davout and Ney could join him, Napoleon sent Augereau to attack in the centre. Augereau's entire corps, with St Hillaire's division in support, marched boldly forward through the snow. Losing their way in the blizzards, the French crashed into the Russian centre and one of the massed batteries. Bloody fighting ensued as the French were repulsed with massive losses, Augereau being badly wounded during the fighting. The Russian centre, commanded by von Sacken, led a fierce counter-attack that pushed its way into Eylau before being halted. During the Russian advance the 14th Line Regiment, in Napoleon's centre, was isolated and destroyed. With the battle going against him Napoleon threw in his cavalry reserve. Murat, with nearly 11,000 men, led a massive charge in two columns and smashed his way through the Russian centre before reforming into a single column to ride back through the Russian line once again to rejoin the French line. The French cavalry charge, costing them 1,500 killed or wounded, had staved off total defeat and thrown the Russian centre into confusion.

At this point Davout, en route to join Napoleon's main army, arrived to reinforce the French right. Launching a fierce attack against Bennigsen's left flank the Russian line began to buckle. However, before the French could roll up the Russian line Lestocq arrived with 9,000 of his men and halted Davout's advance. The fighting seemed to go against the French once more but late in the day Ney arrived on the Russian right. Before the French could attack in force the light faded and Bennigsen disengaged his battered force.

After the most bloody battle of his career Napoleon placed his army back into winter quarters to rest and refit. Although he had halted the Russian offensive his army was so badly damaged as to be unable to pursue. French losses exceeded 17,000 killed or wounded and 1,000 captured while the Russians lost around 22,000 killed or wounded and 3,000 captured.

9 February 1807
POLISH FRONT
Bennigsen began to pull his forces back to the east. Bagration again covered the withdrawal. In his communications with Tsar Alexander, Bennigsen claimed a major victory at Eylau.

19 February 1807
TURKISH FRONT
The British pushed a naval squadron through the Dardanelles but came under heavy fire.

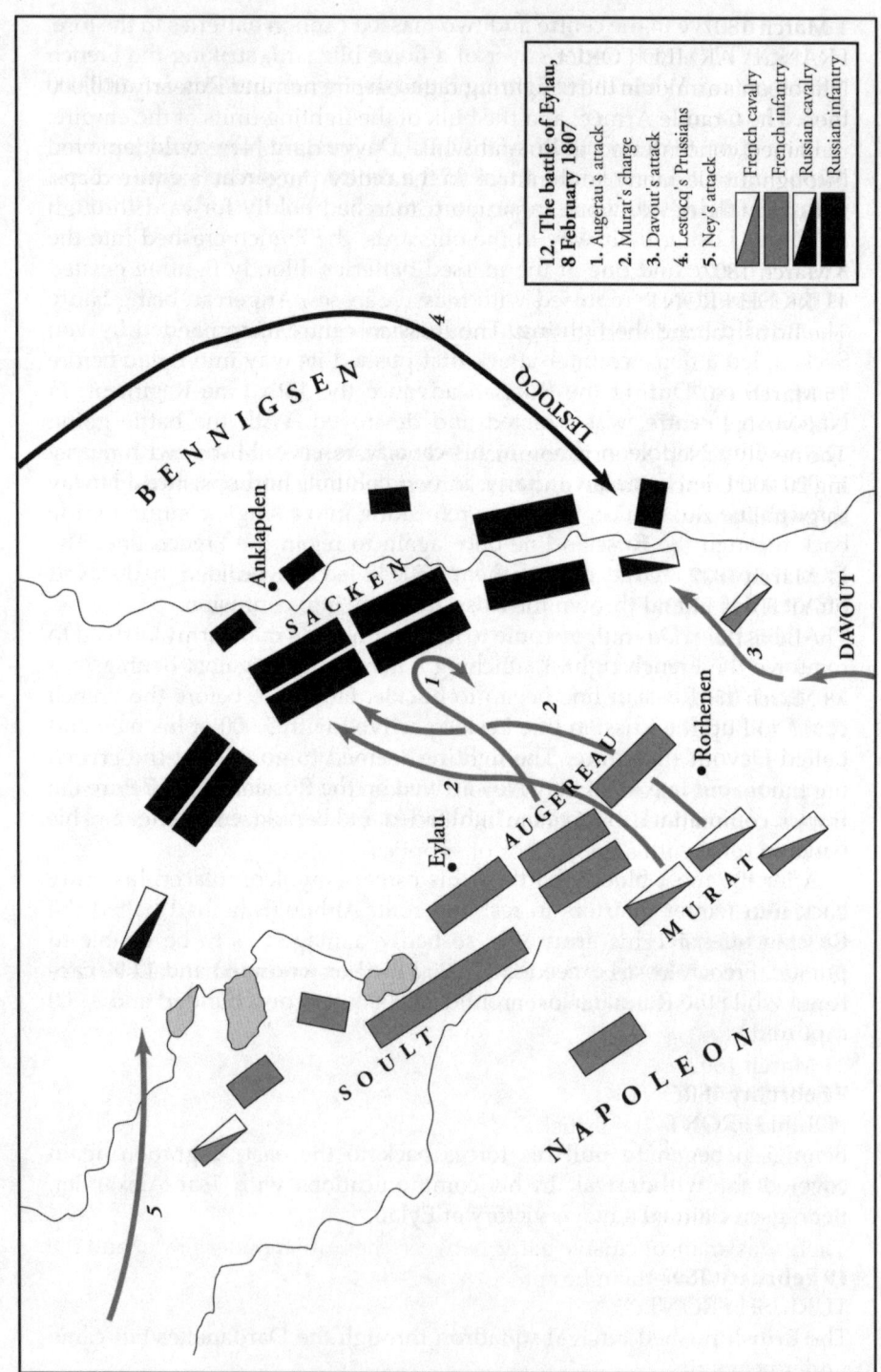

12. The battle of Eylau, 8 February 1807

1. Augerau's attack
2. Murat's charge
3. Davout's attack
4. Lestocq's Prussians
5. Ney's attack

French cavalry
French infantry
Russian cavalry
Russian infantry

BENNIGSEN

LESTOCQ

Anklapden

SACKEN

Eylau

AUGEREAU

Rothenen

DAVOUT

MURAT

SOULT

NAPOLEON

1 March 1807
FRANCE: ARMED FORCES
Napoleon's armies in the field around the empire numbered nearly 600,000 men. The Grande Armée, and the bulk of the fighting units of the empire, remained concentrated in Poland while a secondary force was deployed throughout Germany, to reinforce the Grande Armée when required and to occupy the newly won Prussian territories.

3 March 1807
TURKISH FRONT
The British abandoned their attempt to secure the Dardanelles.

15 March 1807
GERMAN FRONT
The newly raised X Corp, commanded by Marshal Lefebvre and comprising 20,000 French, Italian and newly recruited Polish troops, moved to lay siege to Danzig.

17 March 1807
EGYPTIAN FRONT
The British landed in Egypt.

18 March 1807
POLISH FRONT
Lefebvre, with 18,000 men, completed the investment of Danzig, occupying the heights overlooking the port. Inside the city were 16,000 Prussian troops commanded by General Kalkreuth in well-established defensive positions and with a good stock of supplies.

20 March 1807
GERMAN FRONT
French forces laid siege to Kolberg. The defence of the port was skilfully conducted by General Gneisenau.

21 March 1807
EGYPTIAN FRONT
Alexandria fell to the British.

20 April 1807
EGYPTIAN FRONT
There was an inconclusive battle between the British under Fraser and the Ottomans at Rosetta in Egypt.

26 April 1807
INTERNATIONAL POLITICS
King Frederick William of Prussia and Tsar Alexander of Russia agreed in a meeting at Bartenstein not to make a separate peace with the French. Their aim of expelling the French from Germany was far from realistic.

10 May 1807
POLISH FRONT
An Anglo-Russian force of 8,000 men landed close to Danzig under the command of Marshal Kamenskoi. The difficulty of the terrain prevented the Allied force from linking up with the garrison.

12 May 1807
POLISH FRONT
Marshal Lannes reinforced the French forces close to Danzig and contained Kamenskoi's force with 15,000 men. In a bloody assault the Allied force was defeated. It managed to stabilise its bridgehead but had no hope of relieving Danzig.

25 May 1807
POLISH FRONT
Unable to effect the siege of Danzig, Kamenskoi's force was withdrawn from its bridgehead close to the city.

26 May 1807
POLISH FRONT
Following the absolute failure of the relief attempt, General Kalkreuth opened negotiations with Lefebvre to surrender Danzig.

27 May 1807
POLISH FRONT
Danzig surrendered to the French.

June 1807
INTERNATIONAL POLITICS
Napoleon demanded that Portugal and Denmark close their ports to British goods by joining the Continental System.

2 June 1807
POLISH FRONT
Bennigsen left General Lestocq with a Corps of 20,000 men to contain Bernadotte around Braunsberg and then secretly began to redeploy his army in order to attack Marshal Ney.

3–4 June 1807
POLISH FRONT
Bennigsen concentrated his forces against Marshal Ney. Ney became aware of the build-up of Russian forces opposite his positions.

5 June 1807
POLISH FRONT
Bennigsen launched his offensive aimed at destroying Ney's concentration south of Konigsberg. The Russian army had been reinforced after the battles of the winter and now fielded 90,000 infantry and 8,000 cavalry. Napoleon was concentrating his main army around Allenstein but now became aware of Bennigsen's new attack and moved against him.

6 June 1807
POLISH FRONT
Napoleon's 147,000-strong army began its redeployment against Bennigsen.

7 June 1807
POLISH FRONT
Bennigsen sent advance units south from Heilsberg. Napoleon planned to wheel his forces around upon the Russians and cut their lines of retreat to Konigsberg or the sea. Bernadotte was to pin down Lestocq.

8 June 1807
POLISH FRONT
With Soult and Murat forming the advance guard, Napoleon unleashed his army upon Bennigsen. Russian advance guards were swept aside as the French pushed forward upon Heilsberg. Bernadotte's orders failed to arrive so he remained inactive against Lestocq.

9 June 1807
POLISH FRONT
Bennigsen had failed to catch Ney unawares. Instead the Russian force pushed forward to Heilsberg, where they took up a fortified position.

10 June 1807
POLISH FRONT
Murat reached Bennigsen's main positions at Heilsberg but failed to identify that the Russians had entrenched. Soult's infantry duly launched an attack in support and met unexpectedly heavy resistance. Napoleon, bringing up the remainder of his 65,000 men, attacked and defeated Bennigsen's dug-in 53,000. However, the cost had been high, the French suffering 12,000 casualties to a Russian loss of 9,000.

11 June 1807
POLISH FRONT
Bennigsen expected a renewal of the battle around Heilsberg but Napoleon moved the III Corps to threaten the Russian flanks. Bennigsen was compelled to withdraw upon Bartenstein to avoid encirclement, leaving significant quantities of supplies behind.

12 June 1807
POLISH FRONT
Bennigsen, turning sharply, pulled back towards Friedland on the Alle river. Napoleon thought the Russians were pulling back upon Konigsberg and ordered a rapid pursuit. Murat, Soult and Davout were sent to capture Konigsberg and defeat the Russians while Lannes moved to cover the Alle.

13 June 1807
POLISH FRONT
Napoleon, not realising he had managed it, interposed his army between Bennigsen, at Friedland, and Lestocq, at Konigsberg. Reconaissance then made it clear that Bennigsen had not in fact withdrawn upon Konigsberg but was on the Alle at Friedland.

FRANCE: THE MARSHALATE
General Victor was promoted to Marshal.

14 June 1807
POLISH FRONT
Lannes, with a force of 17,000, attempted to occupy Bennigsen's attention at Friedland while Napoleon brought his main body south as quickly as possible. The Russians, with 61,000 men available and another 20,000 close by, crossed the Alle river and attacked Lannes. Attacked by 46,000 men who had crossed the river, the French were hard pressed until Napoleon arrived. Building up some 80,000 men with 120 cannon, Napoleon prepared to launch a crushing blow. Bennigsen had also managed to bring up additional forces so he committed 60,000 men and 120 cannon, but they had the Alle to their rear.

Deploying Grouchy and Mortier on the left wing, Lannes in the centre and Ney on the right, Napoleon aimed to push Bagration, holding the southern half of the Russian line, back into the Alle. Ney attacked around 5pm, striking Bennigsen by surprise. The Russians fought back fiercely and slowed the French advance. Ney's force was damaged by Russian artillery on the far side of the Alle and was then struck by a Russian cavalry counter-attack. At this point Napoleon committed Victor with his reserve to reinforce Ney. In hard fighting the French again pushed Bagration back, but this time the French artillery of Victor's corps played havoc with the tightly packed Russian troops. The Russian left broke up and fled back through Friedland in an effort to escape.

Realising all was lost Bennigsen committed his Imperial Guard to protect his line while the main body withdrew. French pressure continued but the Russians managed to pull many of their men back to the east. Fighting continued into the night as the Russian withdrawal was completed.

Russian losses during the battle had been severe, some 25,000 men being lost together with eighty cannon. Napoleon's forces lost around 12,000 men.

15 June 1807
POLISH FRONT
Bennigsen continued his retreat to the east. Lestocq, realising that he would be left unsupported and already under attack around the city, evacuated Konigsberg and retreated towards Tilsit. Murat, with 25,000 men, pursued the Prussians closely.

19 June 1807
POLISH FRONT
Napoleon reached Tilsit. The Prussian army had been pulled back across the river to avoid capture. With their field army totally defeated, the Russians asked for terms.

25 June 1807
INTERNATIONAL POLITICS
Napoleon had an initial meeting with Tsar Alexander at Tilsit. The Russian monarch was taken with Napoleon and agreed to meet in July for further negotiations aimed at ending the war.

7–9 July 1807
INTERNATIONAL POLITICS
Napoleon met with Tsar Alexander and King Frederick William III on a raft moored in the middle of the Neimen river near Tilsit. Napoleon and Alexander got along very well, finding their mutual distrust and dislike of the British an excellent basis upon which to build their relationship.

The Treaty of Tilsit formed a Franco-Russian/Prussian alliance. Russia, who came away rather well from the agreement, agreed to join the Continental System, and recognised the French proposal to create a Grand Duchy of Warsaw and the French kingdoms in Italy and the Confederation of the Rhine. Russia received territory in East Prussia and a proposal to partition the Ottoman Empire between France and herself.

Prussia was absolutely humiliated, losing her historic territorial gains in Poland to the newly created Grand Duchy of Warsaw and all of her territory between the Rhine and Elbe to the Confederation of the Rhine. Prussia was to remain under French occupation until an indemnity of 140,000,000 francs had been paid, and her army was reduced to just 42,000 men.

The Treaty of Tilsit was used by Napoleon to bring about the creation of many of his satellite states, forming a sizeable buffer between France and her habitual enemies in the east. In Germany the Kingdom of Westphalia was created out of Prussian territories east of the Elbe together with parts of other states. Jerome Bonaparte was placed on the Westphalian throne while far to the east, although still a member of the Confederation of the Rhine, the Grand Duchy of Warsaw was organised.

Only the British remained actively committed to opposing Napoleon. Their domination of the seas enabled them to interdict French commerce and largely undermine the Continental System.

22 July 1807
INTERNATIONAL POLITICS
By the Treaty of Dresden the French brought about the creation of the Grand Duchy of Warsaw.

31 July 1807
INTERNATIONAL POLITICS
Having forced Denmark to accept the Continental System, Napoleon demanded that she enter into an alliance with France or be invaded.

DENMARK: ARMED FORCES
The greatest threat posed to Britain if Denmark joined the French alliance was the Danish fleet. With modern vessels and highly trained crews, the Danish fleet of fifty-eight vessels posed a very real danger to the Royal Navy.

August 1807
FRANCE: POLITICS
Talleyrand resigned his post as foreign minister. He had become increasingly concerned at Napoleon's expansionist aims and, despite secretly acting against this whenever possible, had failed to curb his ambition. Napoleon's treaty with Russia and his increasing demands upon Portugal convinced Talleyrand that Napoleon was not acting with France's best interests at heart. Napoleon was pleased at Talleyrand's resignation, as he was becoming more and more impatient at his continual obstruction. He appointed de Champagny as the new foreign minister.

2 August 1807
FRANCE: ARMED FORCES
Napoleon issued orders for General Junot to form a corps of observation along the Spanish frontier.

10 August 1807
GERMAN FRONT
French forces captured Stralsund as the Swedes withdrew from Pomerania.

16 August 1807
DANISH FRONT
Reacting to Napoleon's order to close their ports, Britain invaded Denmark, landing forces on Zealand. The British were worried that the Danish fleet was going to fall into Napoleon's hands as a result of his earlier orders, proving a threat to British interests and security in Europe.

29 August 1807
DANISH FRONT
General Wellesley, leading a small British force, defeated the Danes under Castenskiold at Kjoge (Roskilde).

2–7 September 1807
DANISH FRONT
A British army under Cathcart defeated the Danes under Peimann at Copenhagen. The British had conducted a protracted bombardment of the Danish capital.

7 September 1807
DANISH FRONT
The Danish surrendered to the British following the bombardment of Copenhagen. The British captured, and sailed away with, thirty-five Danish warships, effectively neutralising the effectiveness of the Danish fleet.

INTERNATIONAL POLITICS
The British action in Denmark influenced the Portuguese to leave their ports open to British trade. In Denmark it pushed the government towards an alliance with France.

14 September 1807
EGYPTIAN FRONT
The British evacuated their forces from Alexandria.

19 September 1807
EGYPTIAN FRONT
The British expedition to Egypt was withdrawn.

20 October 1807
INTERNATIONAL POLITICS
The French declared war on Portugal. French forces had already begun to march through Spain.

27 October 1807
INTERNATIONAL POLITICS
By the Treaty of Fontainebleau, Napoleon and Manuel Godoy, first minister of Spain, secretly agreed to ally against Portugal. Godoy was acting out of self-interest, realising that he owed his position solely to the presence of the aged, and slightly mad, King Charles IV.

The treaty worked entirely for Napoleon, enabling him to march forces through Spain in order to impose the Continental System on Portugal by force of arms. Spain was promised territory in Portugal once the French armies had completed their occupation.

30 October 1807
INTERNATIONAL POLITICS
Encouraged after the defeat at the hands of the British, Denmark signed an alliance with France.

By their pre-emptive strike, the British had pushed the Danes into a reluctant alliance with France. These aggressive British tactics confirmed to many continental states their Britain was acting to defend her own economic interests and not in the interests of her supposed Allies.

November 1807
IBERIAN FRONT
General Andouche Junot, with 30,000 men, marched through Spain to attack Portugal. The French army quickly crossed the border and pushed through Portugal towards Lisbon.

23 November 1807
THE EMPIRE OF FRANCE
The First Decree of Milan was issued. It stated that any ship that had been in a British port or had been boarded and searched by the British was liable for seizure by the French or their allies.

29 November 1807
IBERIAN FRONT
The Portuguese royal family embarked for Brazil. The governance of Portugal was left in the hands of the Council of Regency. They appealed to Britain for help in the war against the French.

1 December 1807
IBERIAN FRONT
Lisbon fell to the French as the occupation of Portugal was completed. The security of the French occupation depended on the continued alliance with Spain. Throughout December, French troops began to mass on the Franco-Spanish border and seized the border fortresses.

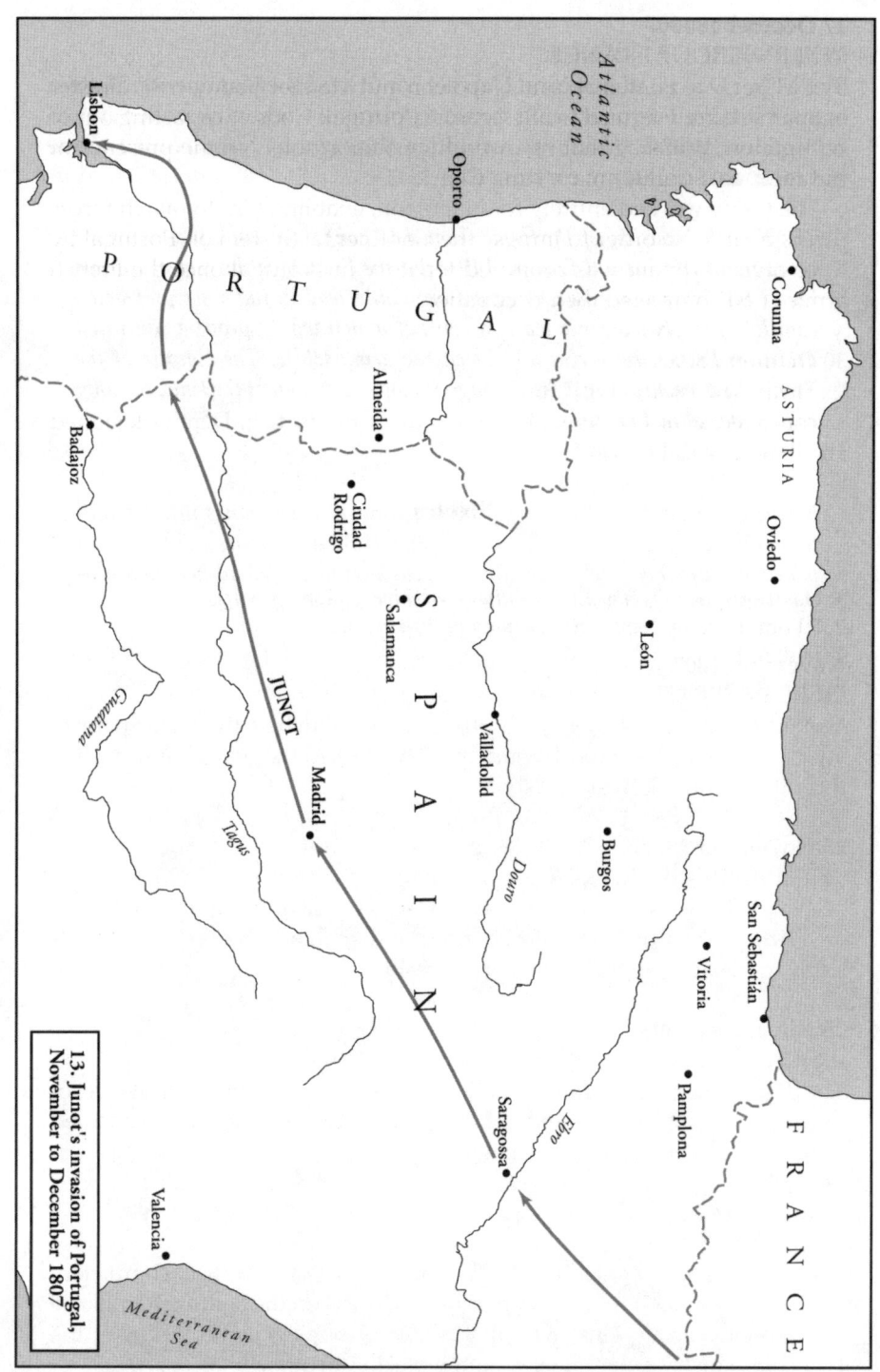

13. Junot's invasion of Portugal,
November to December 1807

17 December 1807
THE EMPIRE OF FRANCE
The Milan Decree (the Second Decree) confirmed the Continental System against Britain, Portugal being forced to join as she was now under French occupation. British trade was forbidden throughout Napoleonic Europe but rampant smuggling continued.

The French invasion of Portugal seemed to confirm French pre-eminence throughout continental Europe. Little did the French or the rest of Europe know, but Napoleon's latest aggression would lead to the most protracted conflict of the Napoleonic wars, a conflict which would prove a continual drain on French resources and bleed the army white. The Empire of the French had reached its height. Though it was not known at the time, the long road to defeat had begun.

Notes

1. Haythornthwaite, *Napoleon's Military Machine*, p. 188
2. F Loraine Petre, *Napoleon's Conquest of Prussia*, p. 6
3. Ibid, p. 10
4. Ibid, p. 74

CHAPTER VI

Warfare from Iberia to Austria

With their empire stretching from the Atlantic in the west to the far reaches of the Russian frontier in the east, the French seemed to have achieved total hegemony over continental Europe. Only Britain remained active against them now that Portugal had been crushed in a rapid campaign and Russia had been brought into the French sphere through political negotiation. However, Spain, a long-standing ally of the French, would prove to be the nation that would prove a thorn in the side of Napoleon's grand ambition.

* 1808 *

January–February 1808
IBERIAN FRONT
The French continued to infiltrate units into the border marches with Spain. Marshal Murat headed the French forces that were slowly making their way forward to the Ebro river.

18 January 1808
INTERNATIONAL POLITICS
Talleyrand had a secret meeting with the Austrian ambassador to Paris, Clemens Metternich, during which he assured the Austrian of his desire to see Austria acting as a balance between the power of France and Russia. Talleyrand, who had already attempted to act against Napoleon without being outwardly disloyal, had begun his treasonous path.

2 February 1808
ITALIAN FRONT
French troops occupied Rome.

16 February 1808
IBERIAN FRONT
French troops secured Pamplona.

18 February 1808
FRANCE: ARMED FORCES
Napoleon issued a decree detailing the reorganisation of the army. Infantry battalions were reduced from nine to six companies (four fusilier, one light and one elite grenadier) but regiments were strengthened from three battalions to four. One of the impacts of this change was an increased demand for officers and NCOs for the new fourth battalion. To try and keep up with this demand the officer school established by Napoleon at Fontainebleau was moved to St Cyr and its two-year course shortened to a few months.

20 February 1808
IBERIAN FRONT
Barcelona fell to the French as they continued their steady advance into Spain.

21 February 1808
RUSSIA
Russian forces attacked Sweden, invading the Finnish provinces. Denmark also prepared to attack the Swedes.

March 1808
IBERIAN FRONT
Publicising what was already happening, and using the excuse that their armies were to protect the coasts against British commerce and would reinforce Junot's army in Portugal, Murat led his army of 100,000 men towards Madrid and into the Spanish interior.

Manuel Godoy attempted to organise resistance to the French moves but his position of pre-eminence in the Spanish court was about to be ended.

5 March 1808
IBERIAN FRONT
San Sebastian was occupied by French troops.

13 March 1808
IBERIAN FRONT
French troops began their march on Madrid. The arrival of the French prompted the Spanish court into action, it being split into pro- and anti-French factions. The pro-French faction was headed by the king's son, Prince Ferdinand, while the anti-French faction was headed by the deeply unpopular Godoy on behalf of King Charles.

15 March 1808
ITALIAN FRONT
The French annexed Tuscany, Piacenza and Parma.

17 March 1808
SPAIN: POLITICS
Troops loyal to Ferdinand staged a coup at Aranjuez and deposed Charles IV. Ferdinand was placed on the throne in an effort to prevent the French deposition of the entire Bourbon regime. Ferdinand was proclaimed King Ferdinand VII. One of his first moves was to seek French support, calling for their aid against his opponents. Unknown to Ferdinand, Charles also appealed to the French to help restore him to his throne.

23 March 1808
IBERIAN FRONT
French troops entered Madrid. There was at this stage no real resistance by the populace or military.

24 March 1808
IBERIAN FRONT
Ferdinand marched into Madrid with his followers and imprisoned the hated Godoy. The new Spanish king aimed to ally himself with the French but Napoleon had his eyes on the throne for his own family. By now there were more than 100,000 French troops in Spain, securing large areas of the border marches.

25 March 1808
IBERIAN FRONT
Murat reached Madrid with his escort of Imperial Guards. He was given an enthusiastic welcome by the people, the crowds believing that he had arrived to secure the throne for Ferdinand. The French had around 40,000 men in and around the city. Murat was under instructions to send the entire Spanish royal family to Bayonne, where Napoleon was camped, for talks.

20 April 1808
IBERIAN FRONT
In an effort to gain the support of the French for his regime, Ferdinand met Napoleon at Bayonne.

end-April 1808
IBERIAN FRONT
Napoleon took into French custody the entire Spanish royal family and proposed to install his brother Joseph on the Spanish throne. Civil disobedience began to spread throughout the country, protests breaking out in Madrid, Burgos and Vittoria.

2 May 1808
IBERIAN FRONT
Violent anti-French protests broke out in Madrid as rumours spread that the French were about to transport the Spanish royal family out of the city. Murat ordered his troops to open fire on the protesters and sparked a massive revolt. Spanish civilians attacked the French forces across the city but the French countered by firing artillery and muskets into the crowds, killing hundreds. The Mamelukes in French service massacred anyone they could find, man, woman or child.

6 May 1808
IBERIAN FRONT
Under pressure from the French, Ferdinand agreed to surrender his throne.

10 May 1808
IBERIAN FRONT
As both Ferdinand and Charles renounced all rights to the Spanish throne, Joseph Bonaparte was announced the new King of Spain. Joseph was reluctant to leave his Kingdom of Naples, but acquiesced to his brother's demand.

16 May 1808
ITALIAN FRONT
France annexed Rome.

23 May 1808
IBERIAN FRONT
Uprisings broke out in Cartagena and Valencia against French rule or in support of the old Spanish regime. At this point the French controlled only the border regions, Catalonia, Aragón and a corridor of territory to Madrid. General Dupont began his march towards Andalusia with an army of 13,000 men, his aim being to secure Seville and Córdoba.

6 June 1808
IBERIAN FRONT
Joseph Bonaparte, arriving in Bayonne, was crowned king of Spain, giving up his Kingdom of Naples to Murat, Napoleon's brother in law. With insurrection beginning to sweep the French controlled areas of the peninsula, Murat decided that he would begin a gradual withdrawal to the line of the Ebro before pushing into the interior in force once more.

In Portugal civil disturbances broke out against French rule. With Spain already on fire, the French position in Portugal appeared precarious.

INTERNATIONAL POLITICS

The overthrow of the Bourbon court in Spain reverberated around Europe. Austria and Russia were shocked at the action and wondered if they might be next. In Austria the reaction was extreme; the war party in the Austrian court began to strenuously argue the case for a pre-emptive strike against Napoleon. Over the coming months Emperor Francis would be convinced that war with France was the only option. Metternich also sent information from Paris, which predicted that Napoleon was on the road to war again.

8 June 1808
IBERIAN FRONT
Córdoba fell to the French.

12 June 1808
IBERIAN FRONT
A small French force of 2,500 men defeated and routed a force of 5,000 Spanish irregulars at Cabezon. French losses were fewer than fifty killed or wounded.

15 June 1808
IBERIAN FRONT
Dupont reached Andujar but found his lines of communication to Madrid threatened by Spanish rebels.

15 June–17 August 1808
IBERIAN FRONT
General Verdier laid siege to Saragossa but Palafox's Spanish forces retained control of the city.

28 June 1808
IBERIAN FRONT
French attacks upon Valencia were repulsed by the efforts of Spanish irregulars.

5 July 1808
IBERIAN FRONT
Dupont had sent a detachment of troops to La Carolina in order to secure his lines of communication. The main part of the French force deployed along the Guadalquivir river in order to secure it against the Spanish forces of General Castaños which were assembling.

9 July 1808
IBERIAN FRONT
Having assembled his ministers for his new Spanish administration,

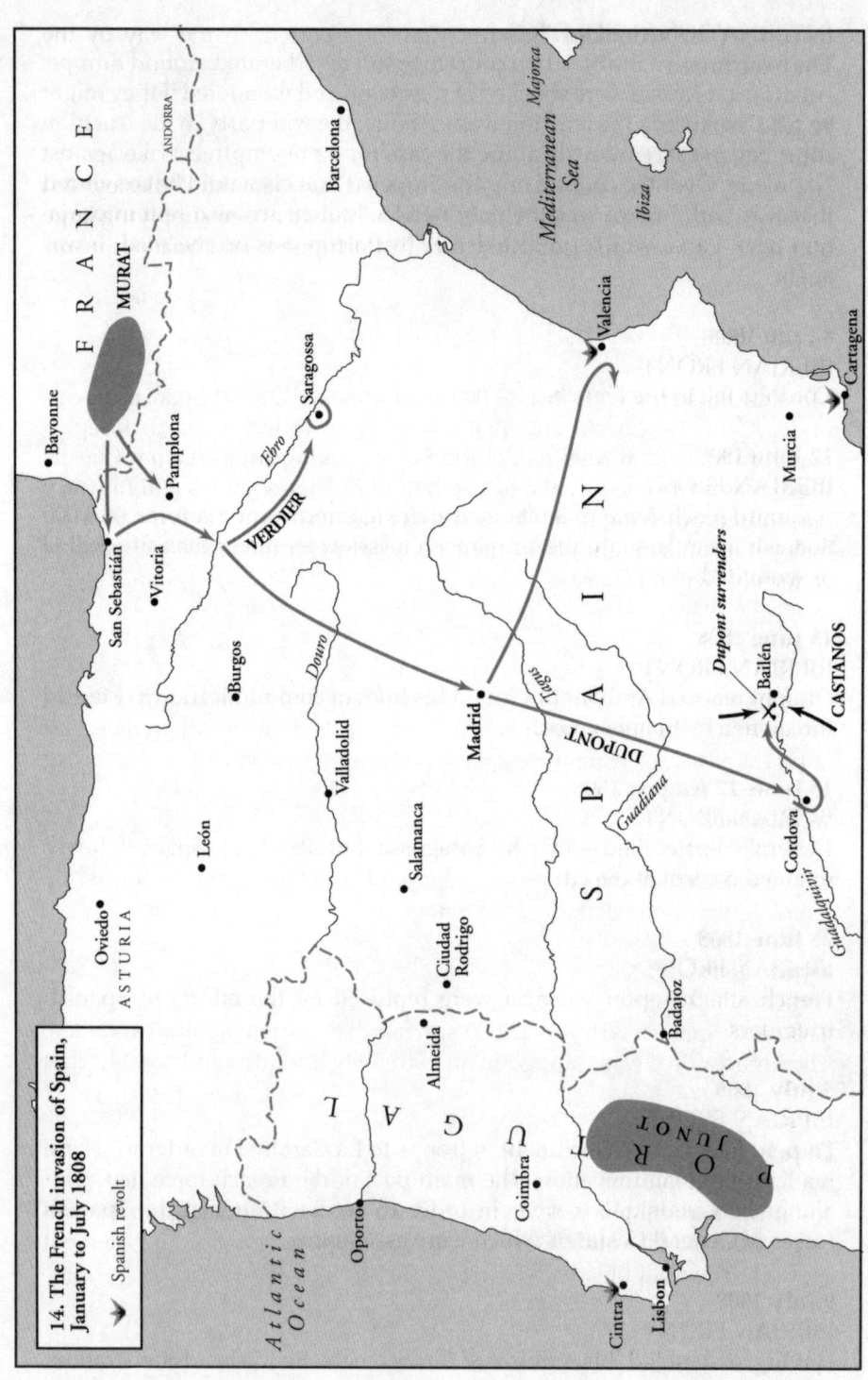

14. The French invasion of Spain, January to July 1808

→ Spanish revolt

Joseph set out from Bayonne for Madrid, escorted on the way by the Imperial Guard.

12 July 1808
IBERIAN FRONT

A British expeditionary force, commanded by General Wellesley, left Britain headed for Portugal. The British had already been supplying large quantities of arms and supplies to both Portuguese and Spanish insurgents.

14 July 1808
IBERIAN FRONT

Marshal Bessières with just 13,000 men attacked 21,000 Spanish troops under Generals Cuesta and Blake who were trying to block Joseph's march to Madrid at Medina del Rio Seco. Lacking support from Cuesta, Blake was confronted by the full weight of Bessières' attack and his force was routed. Suffering 3,500 casualties to a French loss of 1,000, the Spanish had yet again brought about their own defeat through the inexplicable actions of General Cuesta.

15 July 1808
IBERIAN FRONT

Castaños attacked Dupont at Andujar on the Guadalquivir river. Meanwhile, another Spanish detachment attacked the French in their rear at La Carolina, severing their lines of communication.

18 July 1808
IBERIAN FRONT

Under continued Spanish pressure Dupont withdrew from the line of the Guadalquivir and fell back upon Bailen.

19 July 1808
IBERIAN FRONT

Castaños' Spanish army of 32,000 surrounded Dupont's forces at Bailen. The French force was trapped in an extremely arid area and was short of water.

20 July 1808
IBERIAN FRONT

Joseph Bonaparte entered Madrid but was met by a quiet and resentful population. To the south, Dupont tried to break out from the encirclement around Bailen but failed after ferocious and costly fighting.

21 July 1808
IBERIAN FRONT
Dupont continued his unsuccessful breakout efforts at Bailen. Realising he and his army could not break out, he requested a ceasefire.

22 July 1808
IBERIAN FRONT
After negotiations which guaranteed the return of the French troops to France, Dupont surrendered his army to Castaños. Despite their promise of safe conduct out of Spain, the French troops were set upon by Spanish irregulars and were massacred. This was the first surrender of a French army and came as a shocking blow to French morale but heartened the enemies of France throughout Europe.

> *The surrender at Bailen shocked both France and her enemies. Not since the start of the Revolutionary wars had the French suffered such a humiliating reverse. The hitherto seemingly invincible armies of Napoleon had been thwarted in their effort to bring the Spanish under control. However, it was not just the surrender of the French that was significant, but the actions of the Spanish afterwards, the brutality shown to the prisoners setting the tone of the conflict in Iberia.*

25 July 1808
IBERIAN FRONT
The massacre of Evora.

1 August 1808
IBERIAN FRONT
A British force led by Sir Arthur Wellesley began landing at Mondego Bay, in Portugal, with around 9,000 men.

Joseph Bonaparte, following the policy that Murat had decided upon some time before, evacuated his forces from Madrid and began to withdraw to the Ebro.

AUSTRIA: ARMED FORCES
The Austrians had undertaken military preparations against a French attack. Their forces numbered 316,000 regular troops, 60,000 reserves, 185,000 German militia and 100,000 Hungarian militia. The war faction began to use the size of the army as an argument that it must either be used or risk bankrupting the state.

FRANCE: ARMED FORCES
Intelligence from secret agents throughout Europe flooded into France on the rearmament of the Austrians.

5 August 1808
IBERIAN FRONT
A further 5,000 British troops, released from service in Andalusia follow-ing the Spanish victory at Bailen, joined Wellesley's main army which continued to land in Portugal.

6 August 1808
IBERIAN FRONT
Spanish forces laid siege to Barcelona.

8 August 1808
IBERIAN FRONT
The British army in Portugal completed its landing. Of the total force, 5,000 moved towards Cádiz under General Spencer, the remaining 14,000 towards the Tagus river under Wellesley, and from there on to Lisbon.

15 August 1808
IBERIAN FRONT
The first skirmishes took place between British and French forces in Portugal close to the town of Obidos. Junot began to move his forces out of Lisbon to confront the British.

The French armies in Spain had been heavily reinforced throughout July and August and now numbered around 150,000 men.

INTERNATIONAL POLITICS
Napoleon confronted Metternich and demand to know why the Austrians were rearming. Metternich excused the assembly of forces as nothing more than Austria adhering to the terms of her agreements with France. Napoleon was not deceived but was of the mistaken opinion that the Austrians would not again risk a conflict after their defeat of 1805.

16 August 1808
IBERIAN FRONT
General Delaborde deployed his force near Rolica to oppose the British march upon Lisbon.

17 August 1808
IBERIAN FRONT
As the British advanced in Portugal, the French forward forces under General Delaborde attempted to delay them. Establishing his small force of around 4,500 men in rugged terrain near Roliça, he repulsed a premature attack by the British 29th Regiment. Wellesley then ordered a general attack on the French positions, and after hard fighting, compelled Delaborde to withdraw. The British had lost 500 men during the fighting to a French loss of 700 men.

20 August 1808
IBERIAN FRONT
General Burrard took command of the British forces from Wellesley. He ordered the advance on Lisbon to be abandoned until General Moore arrived. Junot meanwhile had concentrated his forces after moving out of Lisbon and now moved to attack the British near Vimiero.

21 August 1808
IBERIAN FRONT
General Burrard had declined to come ashore after taking control of the army in Portugal. When Junot launched his attack against the British, Wellesley was left to conduct the defence. Moving forward with 14,000 men and twenty-four cannon, the French struck the British along Vimiero ridge. Wellesley, with 17,000 men, managed to repulse two French attacks before the British cavalry launched a counter-attack. Pushing forward too far, the British troopers were cut off. The French then turned again and attacked the British left wing. Failing to crush the British flank the French were compelled to withdraw, having lost 2,000 men and fourteen guns during the fighting. British losses were just over 700 men but General Burrard refused to allow a pursuit of the French.

30 August 1808
IBERIAN FRONT
General Dalrymple arrived to take overall command of the British forces in Portugal. Despite the fact that Junot was cut off from his lines of communication, Burrard and Dalrymple negotiated the Convention of Cintra, allowing Junot to leave Portugal aboard British ships, complete with all of his baggage and the plunder he had taken from Portugal. In disgust the British parliament recalled the three generals present in the Iberian Peninsula to London to face an enquiry. Wellesley was exonerated and returned to Portugal later in the year.

September 1808
FRANCE: POLITICS
Napoleon entrusted Talleyrand with a diplomatic position once more. Talleyrand was to be Napoleon's representative in talks with Tsar Alexander at Erfurt later in the month.

6 September 1808
ITALIAN FRONT
Murat took the crown of Naples, assuming the title Joachim I.

26 September 1808
IBERIAN FRONT
Major-General Sir John Moore, having landed in Portugal with British

reinforcements, was placed in operational command of the British forces in the peninsula.

Moore planned to lead his 35,000-strong army into the Spanish interior to retake Madrid. The British plan was to operate in conjunction with the Spanish on the line of the Ebro. Moore almost immediately met with difficulties when dealing with the Spanish regulars. Napoleon determined to collect reinforcements and take control of the situation in Spain himself.

27 September 1808
INTERNATIONAL POLITICS
Talleyrand met with Tsar Alexander on behalf of Napoleon at Erfurt. Napoleon was due to meet with Alexander the following day. Alexander had travelled with the French ambassador to Russia, Cauliancourt, a man in Talleyrand's mould who was busy convincing the Russian monarch of the dangers of an unbridled Napoleon.

28 September 1808
INTERNATIONAL POLITICS
Napoleon and Alexander met at Erfurt but did not discuss formal issues. After the meeting Alexander secretly met with Talleyrand, who urged him to stand up to Napoleon's ambitions.

29 September 1808
INTERNATIONAL POLITICS
Napoleon had further meetings with Alexander but became increasingly annoyed as Alexander was no longer as pliable as he had been at Tilsit. Napoleon presented Alexander with a handwritten treaty between the two powers. Alexander again met secretly with Talleyrand later that day and together they devised a scheme to foil Napoleon's draft treaty. The talks continued for another two weeks.

4 October 1808
MEDITERRANEAN FRONT
Murat invaded Capri with a force of 2,000 men, aiming to eject the British.

12 October 1808
INTERNATIONAL POLITICS
After two weeks of difficult negotiations, the Convention of Erfurt reinforced the Treaty of Tilsit. Alexander half-heartedly promised Russian aid against any war with Austria but to Emperor Francis he wrote a note explaining his true intentions. Alexander was becoming more difficult for Napoleon to control, the Russian Tsar, with considerable help from Talleyrand and the anti-French faction at home, having realised that Napoleon's ambitions would never be sated.

18 October 1808
MEDITERRANEAN FRONT
Capri fell to Murat's forces.

25 October 1808
IBERIAN FRONT
A French counter-attack defeated Spanish forces at Logrono.

26 October 1808
IBERIAN FRONT
Moore left Lisbon as his army began its march towards the Ebro. Conditions were difficult as the roads were in terrible condition and cooperation from the Spanish was almost non-existent.

29 October 1808
IBERIAN FRONT
Marshal Lefebvre, with 21,000 men, attacked the Spanish under General Blake, with 19,000 men, at Zornoza. Neither army had deployed properly for battle but Blake's decision to remove his cannon enabled the French to quickly rout his force. For the loss of fewer than 600 men the French inflicted 1,500 casualties on the Spanish.

November 1808
FRANCE: POLITICS
Fouché entered into the conspiracy against Napoleon with Talleyrand, meeting secretly with him for talks. Fouché, head of Napoleon's police, was concerned at the Emperor's lack of an heir and had been pressing for him to divorce Josephine. He decided that should anything happen to Napoleon, Murat should be appointed emperor. Murat's wife, Napoleon's sister Caroline, was also the mistress of the Austrian attaché, Metternich, who therefore had a good idea of what was happening at the French court. Murat had been approached about the scheme and was in agreement.

4 November 1808
IBERIAN FRONT
Napoleon entered Spain and regrouped his forces. He had transferred the Imperial Guard, three corps from Germany, the cavalry reserve, two Italian, a Polish and a German division, to Spain to quell the peninsula's revolt once and for all. Massing at the border he advanced with his Marshals (Ney, Lannes, Soult, Mortier and Lefebvre, some of whom had already committed their forces) and a force of 194,000 men. Total French commitment in Spain and Portugal now reached 300,000 men.

5 November 1808
IBERIAN FRONT
Retreating after his defeat at Zornoza, Blake received reinforcements and with 24,000 men turned about to strike Victor's 12,000 near Valmaceda. Taken by surprise, the French were totally routed and, having lost 500 men, retired in considerable disorder. Blake regrouped his force and continued his retreat.

10 November 1808
IBERIAN FRONT
Napoleon defeated an Anglo-Spanish force at Gamonal. Victor attacked Blake's forces at Espinosa de los Monteros.

11 November 1808
IBERIAN FRONT
Victor defeated Blake and forced him back from Espinos de los Monteros.

13 November 1808
IBERIAN FRONT
The British advance guard reached Salamanca.

15 November 1808
IBERIAN FRONT
Moore halted his army at Salamanca in order to concentrate his forces. General Baird had landed at Corunna and was marching to the interior to reinforce the British units.

23 November 1808
IBERIAN FRONT
Lannes, with 31,000 men, caught a Spanish force of 19,000 men under Castaños at Tudela as Napoleon conducted the main advance upon Madrid. Lannes quickly shattered the Spanish line and routed the enemy force. For a loss of just 700 men the French had inflicted 4,000 casualties upon the Spanish.

28 November 1808
IBERIAN FRONT
Moore abandoned his effort to reach the Ebro and decided to withdraw his army to Portugal. Unfortunately he was beset by appeals for help from the Spanish and pressure by British government officials in Madrid not to withdraw.

30 November 1808
IBERIAN FRONT
The French army led by Napoleon stormed the Somosierra Pass, striking the Spanish blocking force of 9,000 men under General San Juan. Sending 400 Polish lancers forward, Napoleon swept the Spanish aside and opened up the route into Spain. The Poles lost half their number during the fighting but so impressed Napoleon they were immediately elevated to Guards status.

December 1808
FRANCE: POLITICS
Fouché's alignment with Talleyrand became known publicly, alerting loyalists to a possible threat to Napoleon's position.

4 December 1808
IBERIAN FRONT
Napoleon captured Madrid as the Spanish surrendered the city without a fight.

6 December 1808
IBERIAN FRONT
Unaware that the Spanish had surrendered Madrid to Napoleon, Moore determined to advance upon the city to take some of the pressure off the Spanish irregular forces fighting the French. Napoleon determined to expel the British from Spain and believed the campaign would then be over.

16 December 1808
IBERIAN FRONT
St Cyr marched a relief force to Barcelona and raised the siege.

20 December 1808
IBERIAN FRONT
The second siege of Saragossa began. Lannes encircled Palafox's army of 45,000 inside the city. Napoleon began his march north from Madrid to attack the British.

21 December 1808
IBERIAN FRONT
Four hundred British cavalry, led by General Paget, attacked and defeated a French cavalry force of 600 men under Debelle, part of Marshal Soult's corps, at Sahagún. The French lost nearly 300 men to a British loss of fewer than fifty men.

The French had by this time fully redeployed so that they could attack the British army with upwards of 150,000 men. While Soult attacked the British frontally, Ney was to push around their flank and into the rear.

23 December 1808
IBERIAN FRONT
Moore realised he was the focal point for the French attacks and abandoned his own attacks towards Madrid. Aware of his extremely precarious situation, he prepared to withdraw his forces.

INTERNATIONAL POLITICS
With Napoleon's attentions fixed on the Iberian front, the Austrians determined to regain their lost territories in Germany and to restore the Holy Roman Empire. They began to assemble their forces for an invasion of Bavaria in the spring of 1809. They had been encouraged by Talleyrand's assurances to Metternich that they should attack, while Napoleon's attention was fixed in Spain.

24 December 1808
IBERIAN FRONT
Moore ordered a retreat to Corunna. He turned his columns westward for their march to his sea base. It was a march of some 220 miles, through rugged and mountainous country, with the French hanging in the rear or pushing past his flank.

25 December 1809
IBERIAN FRONT
The British army retreated from Sahagún. Baird retreated with the main body directly towards Astorga while the Light Brigade fell back via Benevente and then Astorga.

26 December 1808
IBERIAN FRONT
The Light Brigade under General Paget comprised the rearguard of Moore's retreating army. With a force of 600 men, General Lefebvre-Desnouettes launched an attack aimed at cutting the British line of retreat. In a running fight the French pursued the retreating British cavalry but were then trapped in a well-executed ambush at Benevente. For a minor British loss the French lost more than 150 of their men, including General Lefebvre-Desnouettes, who was captured.

31 December 1808
IBERIAN FRONT
The British retreat reached Astorga. Moore determined that the Light Brigade would retreat directly east to Vigo while the main body of the army would push north-west towards Corunna.

* 1809 *

January 1809
FRANCE: ARMED FORCES
In Germany, Napoleon raised a new Army of the Rhine with 60,000 men. It began to concentrate around Nuremburg. Aware that Austria was on the warpath, he placed Berthier in command of these forces and recalled a number of Marshals from Spain (Lannes, Lefebvre and Bessières).

1 January 1809
IBERIAN FRONT
As the British army retreated, the Light Brigade reached Ponferrada while the main body had fallen back upon Villafranca, where it halted to restore order, discipline having begun to deteriorate. During its retreat it had passed through Bembibre, where a large body of British troops looted the town and got drunk. More than 1,000 men had to be left behind as the retreat continued to Villafranca.

FRANCE: POLITICS
Napoleon, alerted by a courier sent by loyalists in Paris, decided to leave Spain for Paris to put down the conspiracy against him by Talleyrand, Fouche and his sister Caroline. He would leave with the Guard once the British had been defeated, convinced the Iberian Peninsula was quelled, apart from a few minor mopping up operations. Soult would be left to finish off the retreating British.

2 January 1809
IBERIAN FRONT
Most of the British troops left behind at Bembibre were killed when the French attacked. The main body remained at Villafranca as order was restored. Unfortunately, the store houses in Villafranca were looted by the British and discipline broke down even further.

3 January 1809
IBERIAN FRONT
The British began to retire from Villafranca. A rearguard was left behind to prevent the French crossing the Coa river at Cacabelos. The French quickly moved up to attack, General Colbert pushing his men forward to exert intense pressure on the British line. In heavy fighting the French commander was killed and their attack faltered. The British then extracted their rearguard and continued their retreat but order had largely broken down in the army, many men again becoming drunk on the alcohol they had looted in Villafranca.

4 January 1809
IBERIAN FRONT
The main body of the British army had fallen back to Nogales. Discipline again began to break down but the rearguard defended vigorously, led by General Paget.

5 January 1809
IBERIAN FRONT
Moore's army had reached Constantino as it continued its painful march towards Corunna.

6 January 1809
IBERIAN FRONT
The British were back at Lugo, where they held for two days in another effort to restore order. By now the army was a band of stragglers.

7 January 1809
IBERIAN FRONT
The Light Brigade, withdrawing upon Vigo, reached Orense, just fifty miles from their destination. Other British and Portuguese forces took Cayenne.

8 January 1809
IBERIAN FRONT
The British column marching for Corunna reached Astariz, just forty miles away.

9 January 1809
IBERIAN FRONT
The British reached Betanzos, just ten miles from Corunna. Again they halted to regroup before completing their march. After marching through difficult terrain, in bad weather, the British had lost 4,000 men.

11 January 1809
IBERIAN FRONT
Moore's army reached Corunna and awaited the arrival of the British fleet.

12 January 1809
IBERIAN FRONT
The Light Brigade reached Vigo safely and began to re-embark to escape the French pursuit.

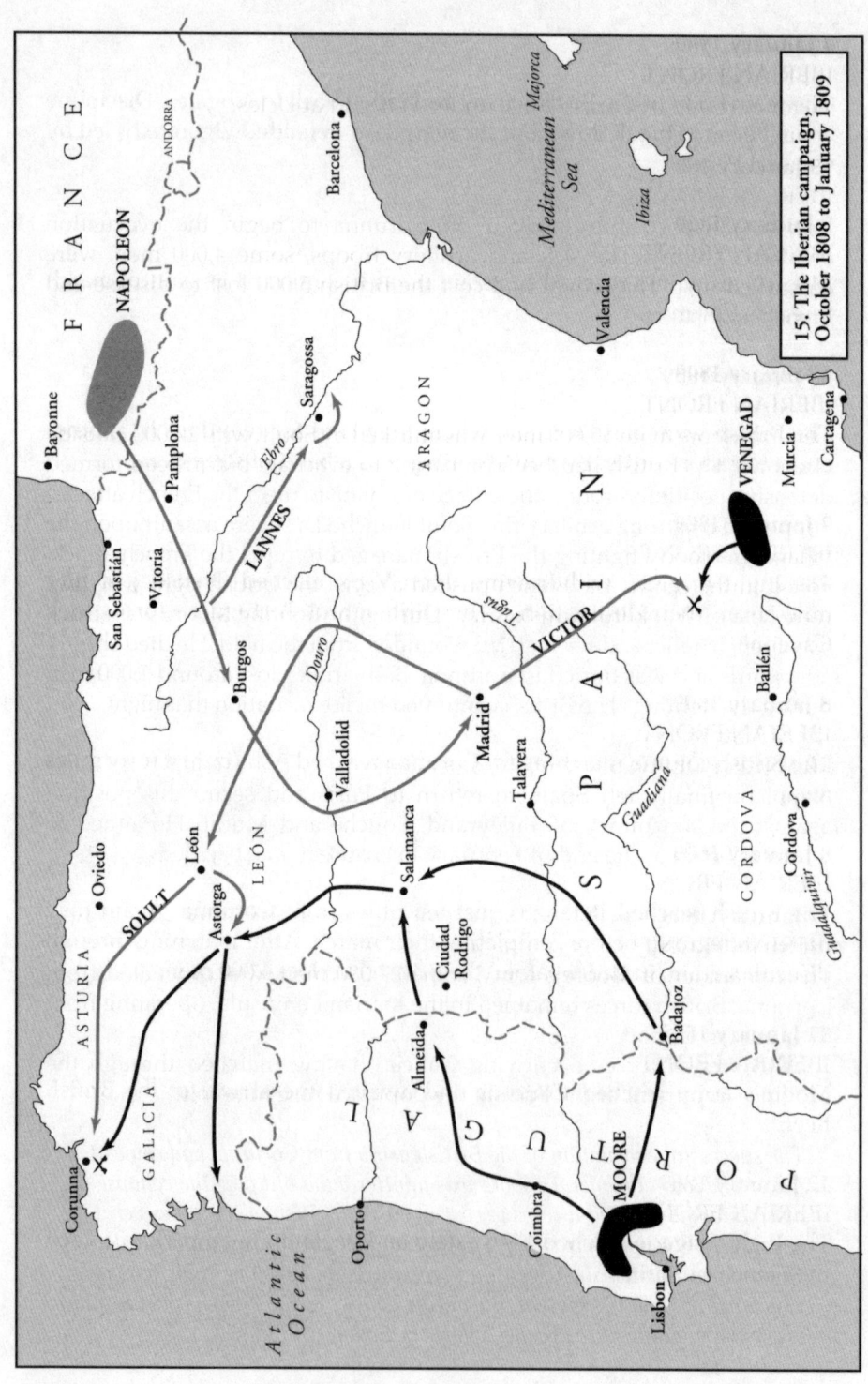

15. The Iberian campaign,
October 1808 to January 1809

13 January 1809
IBERIAN FRONT
Victor defeated a Spanish force under Venegad at Ucles.

15 January 1809
IBERIAN FRONT
British transport ships arrived off Corunna to begin the evacuation of Moore's army. The sick and artillery troops, some 4,000 men, were embarked first. The retreat had cost the British 5,000 lost to disease and French action.

16 January 1809
IBERIAN FRONT
General Moore, with 15,000 men, was attacked by Soult, with 20,000, outside Corunna. The British had been preparing to evacuate but instead formed defensive positions around the village of Elvina to meet the French attacks. Supported by strong artillery fire, Soult launched a severe assault upon the village. In bloody fighting the British managed to repel the French attack. Foiled in the centre, the French pushed against the British right wing but were held off by skilful British firing. During the fighting Moore was struck by a French bullet and was carried wounded from the field. He died shortly afterwards and was buried in Corunna. Both armies lost around 1,000 men during the fighting. The British continued their evacuation that night.

FRANCE: POLITICS
Napoleon finally left Spain to return to Paris and secure his position against the conspiracy of Talleyrand, Fouché and Murat. He aimed to return to Spain at the end of February to ensure it was pacified.

17 January 1809
IBERIAN FRONT
The remainder of Moore's army, some 27,000 men, was evacuated from Corunna. British forces remained in the Iberian Peninsula, operating from their base at Lisbon.

With French forces occupying Galicia, having marched through the province in pursuit of the British, the populace rose in revolt.

The successful evacuation of the British army from Corunna had come at a price. The loss of General Moore was a bitter blow but also the collapse of discipline had exacted a terrible cost upon the British army. However, the departure of Napoleon from the Spanish conflict left the war unfinished and allowed the Spanish insurgents to reorganise and resume their ferocious resistance against occupation. Byzantine politics at the French court would prove the undoing of the French efforts in Spain.

24 January 1809
FRANCE: POLITICS
Napoleon arrived in Paris and reasserted his authority. He laid plans to punish Talleyrand later and issued a severe warning to Fouché, accepting his excuses and leaving him in office. His sister Caroline and Murat were forgiven their indiscretion.

FRANCE: ARMED FORCES
Aware of Austrian intentions to go to war in the next few weeks, Napoleon began to mobilise forces in Germany. Berthier was sent to raise a new Army of the Rhine, 90,000 men strong.

INTERNATIONAL POLITICS
Napoleon was aware of Austrian plans to go to war with France and let it be known to Metternich.

27 January 1809
IBERIAN FRONT
Lannes launched a vigorous attack and penetrated the outer defences of Saragossa. The Spanish continued to resist fiercely.

28 January 1809
FRANCE: POLITICS
Napoleon assembled the Council and before its delegates delivered a tirade of abuse against Talleyrand. Angered all the more by Talleyrand's refusal to respond, he declared he was 'shit in a silk stocking' and once again dismissed him from office.[1]

February 1809
WAR AT SEA
The French managed to sail a fleet of eight ships under Admiral Willaumez out of Brest to reinforce the Lorient and Rochefort squadrons. Six ships were intended for Lorient and two for Rochefort.

1 February 1809
AUSTRIA: POLITICS
The Austrians, via their attaché Metternich, received information on French deployments from a secret contact. The contact turned out to be none other than the recently dismissed Talleyrand.

2 February 1809
AUSTRIA: ARMED FORCES
Archduke Charles, now commander of all Austrian land forces, began the reorganisation of the army into corps along French lines, but did not fully give up the rationale of 18th-century principles. Eleven corps were raised,

nine line corps for front line action and two for the reserve. Line corps had two or three divisions each and a total deployment of around 30,000 men. The Austrians still failed to fully implement a flexible skirmish screen, instead raising skirmishers that were tied tightly to their main units. Although the change to a corps structure was undoubtedly the correct thing to do, to carry it out on the eve of war was a dubious decision. It meant that the commanders of the corps and their armies went into battle with units that had not trained in manoeuvre, fighting or marching as a new formation. However, while Charles led the reorganisation of the army, he did not want to take it to war at the moment, but was being led into it by the crown.

8 February 1809
AUSTRIA: POLITICS
Emperor Francis took the final decision to go to war with France.

19 February 1809
IBERIAN FRONT
After a harrowing siege the Spanish army at Saragossa surrendered to Marshal Lannes. Some 35,000 civilians had died during the siege.

The French now had to contend with wide-scale guerrilla actions throughout the Iberian Peninsula, draining their strength and resources. Commitment to the peninsula had risen to some 350,000 troops.

March 1809
FRANCE: ARMED FORCES
The Tirailleurs-Chasseurs of the Young Guard were created. Napoleon continued the concentration of forces in southern Germany. Davout's III Corps was close to Ratisbon while Masséna's IV Corps was at Frankfurt. Lefebvre held his VII Corps between these two units. This latter formation was made up of Bavarian troops.

WAR AT SEA
The British intercepted the French shipping out of Brest and forced the entire force to put in to Rochefort, bringing French strength at the port up to fifteen vessels. The British blockaded the French in with thirty-seven of their own ships.

INTERNATIONAL POLITICS
Austria attempted to bring a coalition together against the French. A historic agreement with Prussia to provide support failed, King Frederick William of Prussia declining to mobilise his army alongside the Austrians. In an effort to bring the smaller German states on board and destabilise the Confederation of the Rhine, Austria proclaimed a war of German liberation.

9 March 1809
SWEDEN: POLITICS
A palace coup attempted to topple King Gustav IV from his throne.

IBERIAN FRONT
Marshal Soult launched an invasion of Portugal from southern Spain.

13 March 1809
AUSTRIA: ARMED FORCES
The Austrian corps began moving forward to their attack positions close to the borders.

SWEDEN: POLITICS
King Gustav IV was placed under arrest by his palace guards. Duke Charles proclaimed a regency.

17 March 1809
AUSTRIA: POLITICS
More information reached the Austrians on the deployment, strength and organisation of the French armies facing them. Talleyrand again proved invaluable.

20 March 1809
IBERIAN FRONT
The French defeated a Portuguese force at Braga.

26 March 1809
WAR AT SEA
Gambier was reinforced by the arrival of Captain Cochrane's squadron of twelve ships. Gambier had devised a plan to attack the French in their seemingly invincible position off Rochefort using fire ships.

27 March 1809
IBERIAN FRONT
A French force led by Sebastiani defeated the Spanish at Ciudad Real.

28 March 1809
IBERIAN FRONT
Marshal Victor, with 18,000 men, enticed the Spanish under General Cuesta to attack his heavily fortified positions at Medellin. A Spanish cavalry charge against the French left disintegrated and the mounted troops fled the field. Victor then launched a counter-attack and the Spanish army completely collapsed. More than 10,000 Spanish troops were lost to a French loss of fewer than 700 men.

Far to the west, Spanish forces recaptured Vigo.

29 March 1809
IBERIAN FRONT
Oporto fell to Soult after a short siege. The French troops sacked the town thoroughly.

April 1809
IBERIAN FRONT
Wellesley was promoted and became commander-in-chief of all British forces remaining in Portugal, with Prince William of Orange one of his aides. Marshal William Beresford was appointed to command the Portuguese forces operating alongside the British, at the request of the Portuguese Council of Regency. Wellesley had around 26,000 men close to Lisbon while Beresford had another 16,000. His orders from the government dictated that he could defend Portugal but could not enter Spanish territory without permission.

8 April 1809
TYROLEAN FRONT
The Austrians supported a revolt against Bavarian rule in the Tyrol. Insurrection, led by the Tyrolean patriot Andreas Hofer, swept throughout the region over the coming weeks, largely freeing it from Franco-Bavarian administration. The result of the revolt was that French communications from Germany to Italy were severed.

GERMAN FRONT
The Confederation of the Rhine rejected the Austrian proclamation of a German war of liberation and remained loyal to their ties with France.

9 April 1809
INTERNATIONAL POLITICS
The Fifth Coalition was formed by Britain and Austria. Austria delivered a message to the French informing them that they intended to advance their forces and would consider any resistance to be enemy actions. This uncharacteristic, rapid action was to take Napoleon entirely by surprise.

10 April 1809
GERMAN FRONT
Austria invaded Bavaria on two axes with an army of 200,000 men. The main Austrian advance, led by Archduke Charles, was across the Inn river, towards Ratisbon. This strike comprised six corps with approximately 150,000 men. The secondary assault was from Bohemia with two corps, a total force of 50,000 men led by General Bellegarde. Berthier commanded the French forces in Germany, some 176,000 strong, against the Austrians but allowed his army to be outmanoeuvred and split apart.

ITALIAN FRONT
Archduke John led an army of 50,000 regular troops and 50,000 militia, deployed in two corps, across the Julian Alps into Italy. Eugene de Beauharnais had 15,000 French and 37,000 Italian troops available against this force. John's objective was to reconquer northern Italy while also raising a revolt in the Tyrol.

POLISH FRONT
The Austrians deployed a further corps, around 40,000 men, in southern Poland, around Cracow, under the command of Archduke Ferdinand. They aimed to invade the Grand Duchy of Warsaw in order to try and draw Russia into the war on the Austrian side. The Poles had a force of 17,000 men to oppose the Austrian invasion.

11–12 April 1809
WAR AT SEA
During the night the British fleet under Gambier launched an attack upon the French at the Basque Roads near Rochefort. With Captain Cochrane co-ordinating the attack by the fire ships, the British inflicted a heavy, but not overwhelming, defeat upon the French.

12 April 1809
TYROLEAN FRONT
Innsbruck fell to Tyrolean insurgents. The French garrison was forced to surrender. A Bavarian garrison at Wilten was also compelled to surrender, clearing the Tyrol of the French and their allies.

13 April 1809
FRANCE: POLITICS
Napoleon left Paris for the German front.

15 April 1809
POLISH FRONT
Archduke Ferdinand led his corps into the Grand Duchy of Warsaw.

16 April 1809
GERMAN FRONT
Napoleon reached Stuttgart with a large part of his army. He took control of the situation from Berthier and planned an immediate counter-offensive. The Austrians, whose slow advance in the south had reached Landshut, had managed to split Berthier's forces so Napoleon began by regrouping his army. Austrian troops occupied Munich.

ITALIAN FRONT
Archduke John, with 40,000 of his men, was attacked by Beauharnais at Sacile but managed to repulse the French force and then threaten their flanks. The French were forced to retreat to the Piave river.

17 April 1809
GERMAN FRONT
Charles began to march his army north to link up with Bellegarde, who had conducted an equally slow advance from Bohemia. Napoleon continued to regroup his forces. Davout's III Corps and Lefebvre's Bavarian Corps were to assemble east of Ingolstadt and hold the Austrians while Lannes, with a newly formed corps in the centre of the line, and Masséna struck the Austrian centre and left.

18 April 1809
GERMAN FRONT
Napoleon, according to plan, had concentrated most of his army between Ingolstadt and Ratisbon, and began to advance against the over-extended Austrian centre and left at Abensberg.

19 April 1809
GERMAN FRONT
Davout's III Corps, with 28,000 men, was attacked by Hohenzollern, also with 28,000 men, at Tengen. Despite pleading for reinforcements, Hohenzollern was left unsupported and Davout was able to link his corps up with Napoleon's main force. In a bloody battle both armies had lost around 4,000 men.

POLISH FRONT
Archduke Ferdinand defeated a Polish force under Prince Poniatowski at Raszyn.

20 April 1809
GERMAN FRONT
Napoleon, with 131,000 men, attacked Archduke Charles' 161,000 at Abensberg. After a fierce attack the Austrian force was cut in two. Napoleon pursued the retreating left wing, some 35,000 men led by General Johann Hiller, with his main body towards Landshut, while Davout, with the 36,000 men of his III Corps, occupied the attention of Charles' 80,000 at Ratisbon. Austrian losses had been 2,700 killed or wounded and another 4,000 captured.

21 April 1809
GERMAN FRONT
Lannes' VII Corps, with 40,000 men, caught up with Hiller at Landshut. The Austrian force fought a fierce rearguard action but Napoleon sent in Masséna's corps of 57,000 to cut off the Austrian line of retreat and

pushed through the town and across the Isar river. Masséna's push into the Austrian rear almost isolated their entire force. Hiller disengaged as quickly as possible but had lost 10,000 men and most of his supplies. Napoleon now switched his attention to Archduke Charles while Bessières, with 20,000 men, continued the pursuit of Hiller.

POLISH FRONT
Austrian forces penetrated to Warsaw as Archduke Ferdinand overran much of the Grand Duchy.

22 April 1809
GERMAN FRONT
Archduke Charles turned some 75,000 of his men about and attacked Davout's 20,000 north of Eckmuhl. Throwing more than half of his army against the French left, Charles sent the remainder to cut off the approach of the Grande Armée. Davout put up a stout defence, the French holding steady for long enough for Napoleon to march to their aid. Reinforced by the arrival of Lannes with 30,000 men to his right, Davout launched a full-scale assault and smashed the Austrian left. Lefebvre then arrived and attacked the Austrian right wing, compelling Charles to begin the withdrawal of his army to the north, across the Ratisbon bridge over the Danube. Exhausted, the French troops were unable to pursue. The ferocious fighting had cost the French 6,000 men while the Austrians lost 12,000 men, including 5,000 captured.

IBERIAN FRONT
Wellesley assumed command of the Anglo-Portuguese army at Lisbon. It had 23,000 men but was short of artillery and transports. The French deployed Soult's army at Oporto with 24,000 men while Marshal Victor had another 30,000 at Badajoz. Wellesley split his army into three units, 12,000 to secure Lisbon under the command of General MacKenzie, 6,000 under the command of Beresford to prevent Marshal Soult from linking up with Marshal Victor, and 18,000 with Wellesley, who was near Coimbra.

23 April 1809
GERMAN FRONT
Lannes, with 37,000 men, stormed Ratisbon as Charles attempted to evacuate the ragged remnants of his army north across the Danube. Fighting the determined Austrian rearguard, Lannes was twice repulsed before the city walls but a third attack, led by General Morand after Lannes had been restrained by his staff from attacking himself, carried the French into the town. French losses were around 2,000 men to a Austrian loss of 6,000 killed, wounded or captured, virtually their entire force in the city.

24 April 1809
GERMAN FRONT
Napoleon, leaving Davout north of the Danube to protect his lines of communication, marched south towards Eckmuhl in order to then push towards Vienna.

Charles united his forces with General Bellegarde's. Despairing after his defeat at Ratisbon, Charles recommended to Emperor Francis that he seek peace terms with the French.

28 April 1809
GERMAN FRONT
Nationalist German forces under Schill invaded Westphalia to aid the revolt against the French that had started a few days earlier.

May 1809
GERMAN FRONT
There were further German uprisings in Brunswick and Hanover, following Westphalia in her efforts to overthrow French rule.

3 May 1809
AUSTRIAN FRONT
Masséna, with 22,000 men, caught up with Hiller's retreating 40,000 men at Ebersberg on the Traun river. Launching his attack across the river, the French suffered heavy losses but eventually managed to capture Ebersberg and its castle. The Austrians counter-attacked but were held off so Hiller abandoned his attack and resumed his retreat. During the bitter fighting the Austrians had lost 2,000 men killed or wounded and 4,000 captured to a French loss of 3,000.

5 May 1809
INTERNATIONAL POLITICS
In accordance with the terms of her treaty obligations, Russia declared war on Austria.

8 May 1809
ITALIAN FRONT
The French under Eugene defeated Archduke John's army at Campana.

10 May 1809
IBERIAN FRONT
Wellesley moved to attack Soult's forces in northern Portugal, forcing the French commander to pull his troops back over the Douro to Oporto.

11 May 1809
IBERIAN FRONT
British forces began secretly crossing the Douro river to threaten Soult's 24,000 men at Porto. The French had disabled the bridges over the river to deny them to the British.

AUSTRIAN FRONT
Hiller's retreating units crossed the Danube and joined the main body of the Austrian army once more.

12 May 1809
IBERIAN FRONT
Realising that the British had stolen across the river, Soult launched an attack with 13,000 men out of Oporto. Dug in in well entrenched positions, the British repelled the first assault and managed to push additional forces across the river. Threatened by the build up of British forces, Soult decided to abandon Oporto entirely. The battle had cost the French 600 casualties to a British loss of just 120 men.

AUSTRIAN FRONT
French troops entered Vienna. The Austrians evacuated their capital to avoid a battle, leaving behind vast amounts of supplies and weaponry in their magazines and store houses.

13 May 1809
AUSTRIAN FRONT
Napoleon entered Vienna unmolested. Charles had begun regrouping his forces on the northern bank of the Danube, deploying 96,000 men and 260 cannon.

14 May 1809
POLISH FRONT
Prince Poniatowski led a Polish counter-attack against the Austrians. While Ferdinand remained committed to the Grand Duchy of Warsaw, Polish forces invaded Austrian Galicia. Lublin fell.

15 May 1809
POLISH FRONT
Having pushed north from Warsaw, Ferdinand was repulsed before Thorn.

17 May 1809
INTERNATIONAL POLITICS
France annexed the Papal States, including Rome. Pope Pius VII was allowed to retain control of the Vatican.

18 May 1809
AUSTRIAN FRONT
Napoleon began the construction of a single bridge, in three spans, across the Danube at Lobau Island.

POLISH FRONT
Polish forces led by Poniatowski captured Sandomierz.

19 May 1809
AUSTRIAN FRONT
The French completed the construction of their crossing point at Lobau.

TYROLEAN FRONT
French forces led by Marshal Lefebvre recaptured Innsbruck.

20 May 1809
AUSTRIAN FRONT
The French began to cross the Danube. Masséna led the crossing with his IV Corps and established positions around the villages of Aspern and Essling. Faulty French reconnaissance failed to pick up the presence of the Austrian army just a few miles away.

Austrian efforts to cut the Lobau bridge succeeded, preventing Napoleon sending further troops across the north bank to reinforce Masséna. This was not seen as a serious threat though. Eventually the bridge was repaired sufficiently for Lannes to cross with his corps.

POLISH FRONT
Polish forces captured Zamosc.

21 May 1809
AUSTRIAN FRONT
Archduke Charles concentrated 95,000 men and 200 cannon upon Aspern and Essling and launched a surprise attack upon the French bridge-head. Neither Masséna around Aspern, nor Lannes around Essling, had established strong defensive positions with their 24,000 men and were surprised when their units were attacked. Bessières held the French centre with his strung out cavalry corps.

Hiller attacked on the right wing, while Bellegarde and Hohenzollern attacked in the centre and Rosenberg on the right. Charles held Lichtenstein in reserve.

The fighting raged fiercely all day, during which time the Austrians captured Aspern, but the French managed to organise an effective defence and brought reinforcements across, bringing their strength up to 32,000 men by the end of the day.

22 May 1809
AUSTRIAN FRONT
Pushing parts of Davout's III Corps across the Danube overnight, Napoleon strengthened his units on the north bank at Aspern and Essling. At dawn he launched a strong counter-attack and recovered control of Aspern. Regrouping, Napoleon them launched another attack with Lannes' corps against the Austrian centre. Furious fighting raged and the French attack was only repulsed when Charles personally led a counter-attack. The French were compelled to fall back and relinquish control of Essling.

Realising his position was untenable, and with his only supply line being cut regularly by Austrian sabotage attempts, Napoleon ordered the bridgehead to be evacuated. Launching a savage counter-attack in an effort to cover the withdrawal, the French managed to successfully pull back to Lobau Island and the south bank of the Danube. During the withdrawal an Austrian cannon ball struck Lannes, severing his leg. Much to Napoleon's distress his marshal and friend died later in the day.

During two days of bitter fighting the French had lost 23,000 men while the Austrians lost 20,000.

The reverse at Aspern-Essling had come as a rude awakening to the French. Archduke Charles had used his superior numbers to good effect, compelling the French to give up their bridgehead. The reliance upon a single line of supply had proved a significant factor in Napoleon's decision to abandon the north bank of the Danube. He would now spend time erecting bridges and undertaking thorough preparations before another crossing was attempted.

IBERIAN FRONT
The British abandoned their pursuit of Soult's army from Oporto. The French had lost 4,500 men in ten days of running skirmishes. British losses were fewer than 200 men. Wellesley now requested permission from London to take the war into Spain.

An independent Spanish force was defeated by the French at Santiago.

23 May 1809
IBERIAN FRONT
Blake's Anglo-Spanish army defeated the French at Alcaniz.

24 May 1809
IBERIAN FRONT
The French laid siege to Gerona.

GERMAN FRONT
General Schill stormed Stralsund and captured the town.

28 May 1809
GERMAN FRONT
At Stralsund, General Schill and his Prussian troops were defeated by Dutch and Danish forces allied to France. Schill was killed in the fighting and his army destroyed.

31 May 1809
POLISH FRONT
Polish troops captured Lvov.

June 1809
ITALIAN FRONT
Archduke John evacuated the Austrian army from northern Italy. Eugene immediately pursued. The French commander deployed Macdonald's I Corps with 15,600 men, Grenier's II Corps with 16,200 men, Baraguay d'Hillier's III Corps with 13,000 men and Grouchy's corps with 12,000 men.[2]

AUSTRIAN FRONT
Following his setback at Aspern-Essling, Napoleon concentrated his army in force between Vienna and Lobau Island. He began the construction of a number of timber bridges on the east side of Lobau Island, to carry his 200,000 men to the north bank of the Danube.

The Grande Armée currently deployed the Imperial Guard with 11,000 men, Oudinot's II Corps with 22,500 men, Davout's III Corps with 36,300 men, Masséna's IV Corps with 25,400 men, Lefebvre's VII Bavarian Corps with 21,300 men, Vandamme's VIII Wurttemberg Corps with 18,500 men, Bernadotte's IX Saxon Corps with 20,300 men, Jerome Bonaparte's X Westphalian Corps with 14,200 men and Bessières' Reserve Cavalry Corps of 10,900 men.[3]

Charles failed to follow up on his success and remained immobile around Aspern, expecting the French to try and cross there again.

POLISH FRONT
Archduke Ferdinand pushed into Poland once more and penetrated as far as Warsaw. The Poles mobilised in order to launch a counter-attack.

GERMAN FRONT
Rebel forces led by the Duke of Brunswick occupied Dresden. With Austria clearly losing the war, the Duke took his men north towards the North Sea coast, where they were evacuated by the Royal Navy.

SWEDEN: POLITICS
Duke Charles proclaimed himself King Charles XIII of Sweden. The former king, Gustav, was exiled.

9 June 1809
GERMAN FRONT
The Duke of Brunswick led forces into Saxony in order to aid the Austrians.

11 June 1809
GERMAN FRONT
Dresden fell to the Duke of Brunswick's small army.

14 June 1809
AUSTRIAN FRONT
Having retreated from Italy, Archduke John faced his force of 35,000 men about and made a stand on the Raab river. Eugene Beauharnais, pursuing closely with his 24,000 men, was supported by Marshal Macdonald with 9,000. Launching a diversionary attack to draw off the Austrian cavalry, Eugene quickly moved to strike the entrenched infantry. However, the diversionary attack was so successful that the Austrian horse was driven from the field, enabling the French cavalry to fall upon John's flank while the infantry assaulted the centre. Seeing his position was untenable, John abandoned his defensive line and pulled back upon Vienna. Austrian losses were 5,000 men to a French loss of 3,000.

15 June 1809
IBERIAN FRONT
Marshal Suchet defeated Blake's Anglo-Spanish army at Maria.

18 June 1809
IBERIAN FRONT
Wellesley reorganised the British army in Spain into divisional units for greater flexibility. Suchet defeated Blake again at Belchite.

POLISH FRONT
An Austrian counter-attack in Galicia recaptured Sandomierz.

19 June 1809
GERMAN FRONT
The Duke of Brunswick captured Leipzig as the Saxons were defeated.

22 June 1809
IBERIAN FRONT
The French began to evacuate their forces from Galicia.

3 July 1809
IBERIAN FRONT
Wellesley led his army across the Portuguese frontier and into Spain.

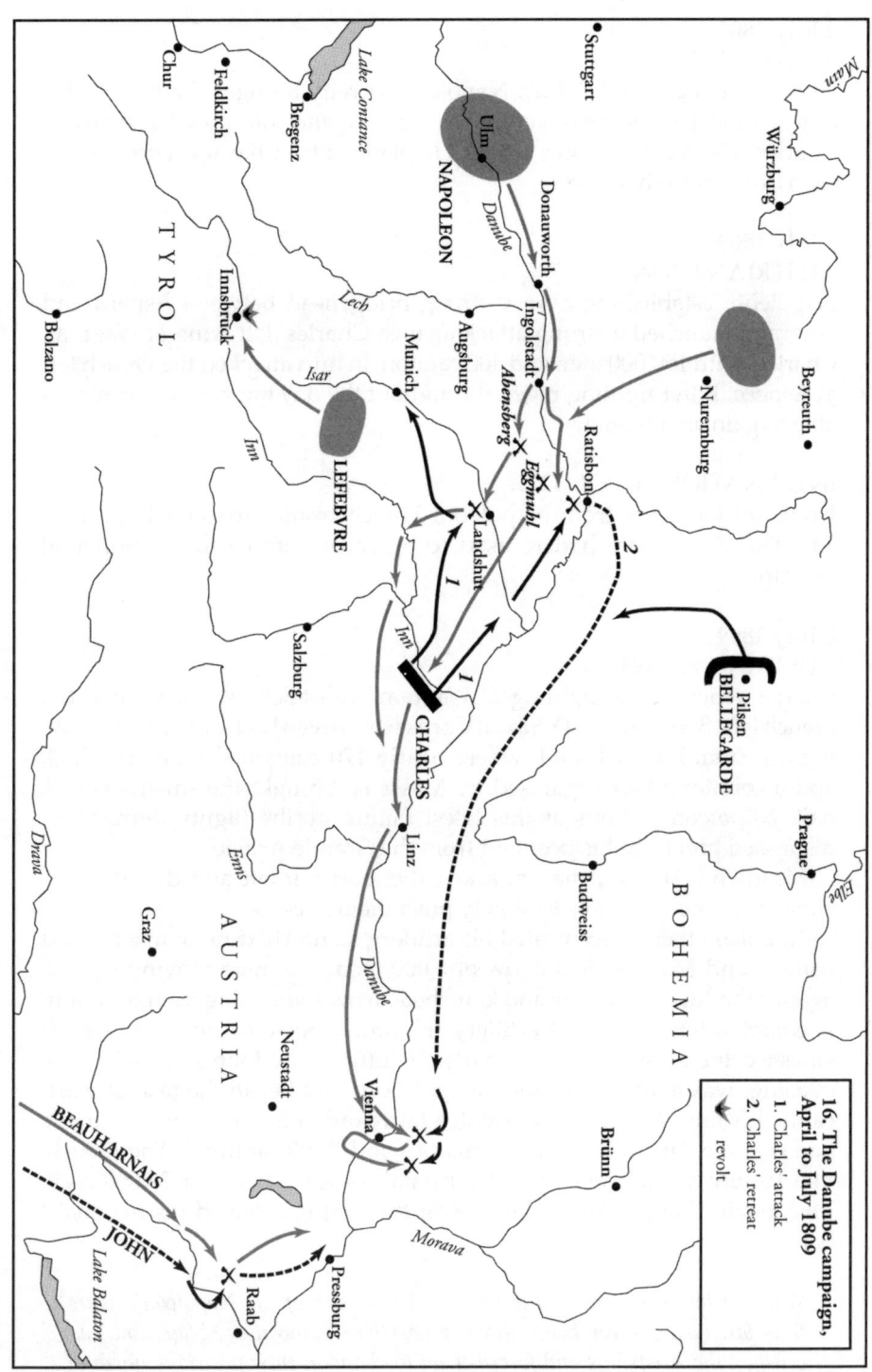

16. The Danube campaign, April to July 1809

1. Charles' attack
2. Charles' retreat
→ revolt

4 July 1809
AUSTRIAN FRONT
During the night of 4–5 July, Napoleon secretly brought the bulk of his army, some 160,000 men, across the Danube and interposed it between Charles' 150,000 and John's 15,000. He planned to strike at Charles before John brought up his forces.

5 July 1809
AUSTRIAN FRONT
Napoleon, establishing a very strong bridgehead between Aspern and Wagram, launched a strong attack against Charles' left wing at Wagram. Charles, with 150,000 men and 400 cannon, in turn attacked the French left at Aspern. Bitter fighting raged throughout the day but neither army was able to gain an advantage.

INTERNATIONAL POLITICS
Under instructions from Napoleon, French troops arrested Pope Pius VII. The Papal state had refused to agree or enforce the Continental System.

6 July 1809
AUSTRIAN FRONT
Charles renewed the fighting at Wagram with another attack upon the French left. Bernadotte's IX Saxon Corps was driven back but French flanking fire from Lobau Island, where nearly 170 cannon were entrenched, and a counter-attack organised by Masséna, brought the Austrians to a halt. Napoleon, furious at this latest failure by the flighty Bernadotte, dismissed him from his post and from the Grande Armée.

Meanwhile, Davout had attacked the Austrian left and despite ferocious resistance was able to slowly push them back.

Napoleon then concentrated his artillery, some 110 cannon in a massed battery, and Macdonald's corps of 8,000 men in a huge moving square, against the Austrian centre and launched an overwhelming frontal assault. A combination of massed artillery fire and a powerful infantry assault smashed the Austrian force. Charles, reinforced by John's arrival in the evening, was unable to restore his positions and began the task of extricating his men. He then undertook a fairly ordered retreat, but the battle had cost the Austrians 29,000 casualties and 7,000 captured. The French, due largely to their use of costly frontal assaults, had lost 37,000 men. Macdonald though, for his success in the centre, received his marshal's baton.

Wagram had been one of the most costly battles of the Napoleonic wars thus far. Using sheer brute force rather than manoeuvre, Napoleon had crushed the Austrians and forced them to abandon their positions north of the Danube. However, despite the severity of the defeat, the Austrians still had some fight left in them.

7–9 July 1809
AUSTRIAN FRONT
Napoleon pursued the defeated Austrians, capturing a further 19,000 prisoners.

10 July 1809
AUSTRIAN FRONT
Deploying his army in a strong defensive position at Zniam, Charles was attacked by Marmont. The French attack was held and as the Austrians brought up more troops, they moved to counter-attack. Heavy fighting continued through the afternoon but Marmont held the Austrians back until nightfall. During the night Masséna and Napoleon arrived to reinforce Marmont.

TYROLEAN FRONT
The revolt in the Tyrol continued but with French forces now freed up, they moved a large part of Eugene's army against the rebels.

11 July 1809
AUSTRIAN FRONT
The French, having been significantly reinforced, renewed their attacks at Zniam. Pinning down the Austrian force Napoleon ordered up Davout's and Oudinot's corps to crush the enemy flanks. Realising all was lost, Charles sought terms and negotiated an armistice. During two days of fighting both armies had suffered around 6,000 casualties.

12 July 1809
INTERNATIONAL POLITICS
The Franco-Austrian armistice was concluded at the Armistice of Zniam as Francis relented and made peace.

FRANCE: THE MARSHALATE
Generals Macdonald and Oudinot were promoted to Marshal.

15 July 1809
POLISH FRONT
Polish forces captured Cracow as the Austrians were driven farther back in Galicia.

17 July 1809
POLISH FRONT
The Poles inflicted another defeat upon the Austrians at Wieneawka.

The war of 1809 had ended in yet another defeat for the persistent Austrians. Charles' revitalised army had posed a greater threat to the French than ever before and coupled with a seeming lack of his usual brilliance, had inflicted upon Napoleon an unexpected and uncharacteristic reverse. Slowly but surely the Allied powers were learning from the French how to form their armies and fight their wars. The years of unending French victory were over, but the end was still a long way off.

Notes

1. James R Arnold, *Crisis on the Danube*, p. 24
2. Haythornthwaite, *Napoleon's Military Machine*, p. 189
3. Ibid.

CHAPTER VII

The Spanish Ulcer

Having disposed of a resurgent Austria, the French remained heavily committed to quelling the revolt that still ravaged the Iberian Peninsula. Faced not only with Spanish irregulars, but also a small but determined British and Portuguese army, the French had to fight on a number of fronts. The presence of Allied forces in the peninsula proved a persistent thorn in Napoleon's side, a thorn which over time would inflict a terminal wound.

20 July 1809
IBERIAN FRONT
Wellesley united his British army with the Spanish regular army led by General Cuesta, a man so inept and incompetent, he was at times thought to be working for the enemy. The Anglo-Spanish plan was to attack Victor's 22,000 men. Victor began a limited withdrawal in the face of the Allied advance.

23 July 1809
IBERIAN FRONT
After twice refusing to fight the French, Cuesta marched in pursuit of the withdrawing French forces. Wellesley refused to follow until the Spanish had provided the supplies they had promised for his men, who were now close to starvation.

26 July 1809
IBERIAN FRONT
Victor, realising he was faced by only the badly led Spanish army, turned upon them and pushed forwards. Cuesta retreated immediately. The French, under Joseph Bonaparte and Marshal Jourdan, had managed to link up with and reinforce Victor, whose force now numbered some 47,000 men.

27 July 1809
IBERIAN FRONT
Cuesta halted his retreat and drew up his army alongside Wellesley's at Talavera. The French vanguards reached the Allied positions and launched

a series of attacks. Initially driving the Spanish back, the British recovered their positions and stabilised the line.

28 July 1809
IBERIAN FRONT
The Allied army of 35,000 Spanish and 19,000 British troops, commanded by Wellesley and drawn up at Talavera, prepared to meet Victor's 47,000. The French began the battle early in the day with a vigorous attack but were repulsed by the British infantry, ranked in reverse slope positions. The fighting died down as the French regrouped their forces. Bringing the bulk of his army about to face the British, Victor left just a small detachment to watch the totally uncommitted Spanish troops.

During the afternoon the French launched another furious attack against the British. The fighting swung back and forth throughout the afternoon as neither side gained a decisive advantage. By nightfall the French retired from the field, having been fought to a draw. The Allies had lost 6,500 men, mainly British troops, during the fighting, while the French lost 7,400. Cuesta had once again proved his total unreliability as an ally.

29 July 1809
IBERIAN FRONT
Cuesta withdrew his Spanish army from Talavera. Wellesley was reinforced by the arrival of Crauford's Light Brigade but with Soult approaching his rear and the Spanish proving troublesome yet again, he decided to withdraw.

NETHERLANDS FRONT
There was a British landing at Walcheren. Forty-six warships escorted a fleet of 200 troops carriers. An army of 40,000 was landed near Antwerp under the command of the Earl of Chatham (the younger Pitt).

30 July 1809
GERMAN FRONT
The Duke of Brunswick captured Braunschweig. Jerome Bonaparte had largely reconquered Saxony and was pursuing the German troops.

1 August 1809
GERMAN FRONT
Brunswick defeated the French but, realising the long-term future for his troops was bleak, made a run for the coast and rescue by the Royal Navy.

2 August 1809
NETHERLANDS FRONT
British forces laid siege to Flushing.

8 August 1809
IBERIAN FRONT
Soult defeated a Spanish force under Cuesta at Arzobispo.

11 August 1809
IBERIAN FRONT
Joseph Bonaparte defeated a Spanish force at Almonacid de Toledo.

13 August 1809
TYROLEAN FRONT
Fierce rebel attacks compelled Marshal Lefebvre to abandon Innsbruck.

16 August 1809
NETHERLANDS FRONT
The British captured Flushing. The slow British attack had enabled Louis Bonaparte to heavily reinforce Antwerp. The British left 15,000 men to garrison Walcheren.

4 September 1809
IBERIAN FRONT
General Wellesley was announced as Viscount of Talavera and Wellington following his victory in Spain. He was continuing to withdraw his forces back to Portugal as co-operation with the Spanish was clearly impossible. From now on the British forces in Iberia would concentrate on the defence of Portugal rather than offensive action in Spain.

14 October 1809
INTERNATIONAL POLITICS
The Treaty of Schonbrunn brought peace between France and Austria. Austria was forced to surrender territory in Carinthia, Carniola and Croatia to France and gave up other lands to Bavaria and the Grand Duchy of Warsaw. Together with their existing territories in Dalmatia and Ragusa, the French created the Illyrian Provinces with some of these newly acquired lands, ruled directly from France. Austria was also compelled to join the Continental System and reduce her army to 150,000 men. Metternich, chancellor of Austria, realised that further resistance was futile for the time being and began a policy of close association with France.

Tsar Alexander, observing the harsh terms invoked upon Austria by Napoleon, became more convinced that Napoleon would eventually turn his attention to interfering in matters in Russia.

18 October 1809
IBERIAN FRONT
The Spanish, commanded by the Duke of Del Parque, defeated a French force at Tamames.

20 October 1809
IBERIAN FRONT

Wellington ordered the construction of the lines of Torres Vedras in order to protect his base at Lisbon against French attack. The defences would have three lines of fortifications, including more than 100 redoubts and 600 cannon.

25 October 1809
TYROLEAN FRONT

Bavarian troops recaptured Innsbruck as the Tyrolean revolt began to collapse.

19 November 1809
IBERIAN FRONT

In southern Spain the Spanish had concentrated their regular army in an effort to bring Soult to battle. Amassing 53,000 men, General Areizago was intercepted by Soult with 30,000 near Ocana. Suddenly shy of battle, the Spanish general attempted to pull his force back but was hit hard by the French. His centre collapsed during an overwhelming cavalry attack and his army also collapsed. The Spanish defeat was crushing, 5,000 being killed and 20,000 captured. French losses were fewer than 2,000 men. The remnants of the Spanish field army fled to concentrate around Cádiz, the capital of free Spain.

28 November 1809
IBERIAN FRONT

The French, led by Kellermann, defeated another Spanish force under the Duke of Del Parque at Alba de Tormes. Operations by the regular Spanish army were now largely at an end, the fight for their country being carried on by the guerillas and the Anglo-Portuguese army. Joseph Bonaparte believed that the war in Spain and Portugal was now virtually won and all that remained was to quash the resistance centred on Cádiz and Andalusia, and isolate the British. In Iberia the French deployed some 325,000 troops.

9 December 1809
NETHERLANDS FRONT

The British evacuated Walcheren. Their army had been ravaged by malaria, some 7,000 men being lost.

11 December 1809
IBERIAN FRONT

Gerona surrendered to the French.

15 December 1809
FRANCE: THE NAPOLEONIC DYNASTY

Anxious for a son and heir, Napoleon divorced Josephine.

* 1810 *

19 January 1810
IBERIAN FRONT
Joseph Bonaparte, Marshal Soult and Marshal Victor, coordinating their actions, began an offensive against the Spanish forces in Andalusia.

24 January 1810
IBERIAN FRONT
The people of Seville revolted against the rebel leadership.

29 January 1810
IBERIAN FRONT
The free Spanish authorities, centred on the Council of Regency, established their base in Cádiz.

31 January 1810
IBERIAN FRONT
Seville fell to Soult's army.

5 February 1810
IBERIAN FRONT
Having largely quelled the Spanish forces in Andalusia, Soult laid siege to Cádiz with 60,000 men. Wellington sent a contingent of 8,000 men by sea to reinforce the garrison of 2,000. The Spanish defence of the port was conducted by the Duke of Albuquerque.

8 February 1810
IBERIAN FRONT
Displeased with Joseph's performance and failure to quash the Spanish revolt, Napoleon established a number of military governorships in northern Spain. This effectively stripped Joseph of much of his authority.

20 February 1810
TYROLEAN FRONT
The Tyrolean revolt collapsed following the capture and execution of Andreas Hofer.

21 March 1810
IBERIAN FRONT
French forces laid siege to Astorga.

29 March 1810
IBERIAN FRONT
Oviedo fell to the French.

2 April 1810
THE EMPIRE OF FRANCE
Napoleon married the Archduchess Marie-Louise of Austria. Metternich had played a large part in promoting the marriage of the French and Austrian thrones. The marriage proved the final straw for Tsar Alexander of Russia as he had proposed an alliance through the marriage of Napoleon to Princess Anna.

13 April 1810
IBERIAN FRONT
French troops laid siege to Lerida.

17 April 1810
IBERIAN FRONT
Marshal Masséna took command of the French Army of Portugal. Masséna was well known for his extravagant looting.

22 April 1810
IBERIAN FRONT
Astorga fell to the French after a month-long siege.

24 April 1810
IBERIAN FRONT
The French defeated a Spanish force at Margalef.

14 May 1810
IBERIAN FRONT
Lerida fell to the French after another month-long siege.

15 May 1810
IBERIAN FRONT
French forces laid siege to Mequinenza.

6 June 1810
IBERIAN FRONT
Masséna laid siege to Ciudad Rodrigo, one of the frontier fortresses on the Spanish-Portuguese border.

8 June 1810
IBERIAN FRONT
Mequinenza fell to the French after a short siege.

1 July 1810
THE EMPIRE OF FRANCE
Louis Bonaparte, unhappy at the effect the Continental System was having on the Dutch economy and displeased that Napoleon had begun to move forces into his kingdom, abdicated. He went into voluntary exile in Austria.

9 July 1810
IBERIAN FRONT
Ciudad Rodrigo fell to Masséna. Wellington pulled back slowly before Masséna's advance, which, with Ney's VI Corps in the van, now proceeded towards Almeida. Soult consolidated his hold on Andalusia.

13 July 1810
THE EMPIRE OF FRANCE
Napoleon took the Kingdom of Holland directly into the Empire.

21 July 1810
IBERIAN FRONT
Masséna invaded Portugal with his 65,000-strong Army of Portugal. Soult began another offensive in southern Spain with his 60,000-strong Army of Andalusia. Co-operation between the two French armies was poor as the two marshals were rivals. Wellington opposed Masséna's attack at the border with a force of 18,000 English and 14,000 Portuguese troops.

24 July 1810
IBERIAN FRONT
Marshal Ney launched a full-scale assault upon General Crauford's troops which were protecting the British front along the Coa river. Crauford with just 4,700 men was struck by 24,000 French troops. Under intense pressure, the British were compelled to pull back but Ney had lost the opportunity to destroy the British force.

15 August 1810
IBERIAN FRONT
Masséna began to besiege Almeida after having reached the town some days before. Almeida guarded the northern approaches into Portugal and had to be captured to secure the French lines of communication should they advance any farther. Its garrison of 5,000 men prepared to withstand the French siege efforts.

21 August 1810
INTERNATIONAL POLITICS
Former French Marshal Bernadotte was elected Crown Prince of Sweden.

23–28 August 1810
WAR AT SEA
The British navy suffered a surprising defeat at the Ile de France.

26 August 1810
IBERIAN FRONT
Masséna opened the bombardment of Almeida. A lucky strike by a French projectile ignited the main magazine and destroyed a large part of the centre of the town, together with the munitions stored there. The British defence was thrown into chaos, having been stripped of their supplies for a long-term siege. The fortress commander could now only await relief by the main British army.

27 August 1810
IBERIAN FRONT
The French resumed their bombardment of Almeida and after a relatively short time forced the British to accept that they could not hold out and must surrender.

28 August 1810
IBERIAN FRONT
Masséna captured the border town of Almeida. Wellington began to withdraw his force back towards Lisbon but the French were slow to follow, Masséna not moving until mid-September. French strength in Iberia remained high, some 340,000 men being committed. Instead of centralising command, Napoleon had split these forces down into a number of regional armies, all reporting direct to him. These armies were designated the Army of Portugal, Army of Aragón, Army of Catalonia, Army of the North, Army of the Centre and Army of the South. Large parts of the French armies were tied down in protecting their lines of communication from guerilla attacks.

September 1810
INTERNATIONAL POLITICS
Tsar Alexander began to negotiate with the Swedes and with the Ottoman Empire in order to secure his borders in the event of war with the French.

18 September 1810
ITALIAN FRONT
Murat launched an invasion of British-controlled Sicily with a force of 35,000 men, carried aboard 300 transport ships. The invasion was repulsed once its initial detachment, a force of 3,000 Neapolitan soldiers, was ashore.

27 September 1810
IBERIAN FRONT
Wellington, with 26,000 British and 25,000 Portuguese troops and sixty cannon, in a reverse slope position, made a stand on Busaco ridge in an effort to delay Masséna's advance upon Lisbon. Masséna, with 66,000 men and 114 cannon, believed Wellington had left behind a rearguard only and therefore launched a badly conceived assault. Ney attacked on the left wing with the VI Corps while Reynier's II Corps attacked the right. Ney made good progress initially but was then caught by the British reverse slope tactic and his men went down in droves. A British attack then threw the French back down the hill. Reynier hit Picton's 3rd Division but was repulsed with heavy losses, being hit in the flank by the British 5th Division. Further French attacks were equally unsuccessful.

After a full day of bloody fighting, Masséna was compelled to abandon his attack. Wellington continued his withdrawal to Torres Vedras, having cost the French 4,500 men for a loss of just 1,300 of his own troops.

Wellington's use of the reverse slope had inflicted yet another costly defeat on the French. Thus far the British commander seemed to be an expert in defence, having beaten the French at Talavera and now Busaco. It remained to be seen if he would prove as adept in an offensive role.

28 September 1810
IBERIAN FRONT
Wellington withdrew his army from Busaco, having successfully held up Masséna's advance.

29 September 1810
IBERIAN FRONT
Unaware of Wellington's withdrawal, Masséna pulled his troops back to regroup.

1 October 1810
IBERIAN FRONT
Masséna resumed his advance towards Lisbon.

10 October 1810
IBERIAN FRONT
Masséna's advance was halted at the lines of Torres Vedras. Encountering the fortifications came as a complete surprise to the French. The British and Portuguese had also committed a scorched earth policy to the land north of the fortifications, denying the French food and supplies.

12 October 1810
IBERIAN FRONT
Masséna fully invested the lines of Torres Vedras, stretching his army out along its entire sixty-mile length.

15 October 1810
IBERIAN FRONT
The French under Sebastiani defeated a British force under Blayney at Fuengirola.

20 October 1810
SWEDEN: POLITICS
The Swedish parliament invited Marshal Bernadotte to become heir apparent to the Swedish throne. Bernadotte established a council of regency as Charles XIII's health declined.

3 November 1810
IBERIAN FRONT
The French defeated a Spanish force at Baza.

14 November 1810
IBERIAN FRONT
Masséna brought his army back from an immediate investment of Torres Vedras and concentrated around Santarem.

2 December 1810
WAR AT SEA
The British captured Ile de France.

13 December 1810
INTERNATIONAL POLITICS
France annexed Oldenburg and parts of Hanover and Berg.

16 December 1810
IBERIAN FRONT
Suchet laid siege to Tortosa.

31 December 1810
INTERNATIONAL POLITICS
France annexed the Valais.
  Tsar Alexander finally broke off his relationship with Napoleon, withdrawing Russia from the Continental System. Russian ports were immediately opened to all shipping.

* 1811 *

2 January 1811
IBERIAN FRONT
Tortosa fell to Suchet's army.

11 January 1811
IBERIAN FRONT
Soult laid siege to Olivenza.

23 January 1811
IBERIAN FRONT
Olivenza fell to the French.

27 January 1811
IBERIAN FRONT
Soult laid siege to Badajoz.

19 February 1811
IBERIAN FRONT
A Spanish force under General Mendizabal was defeated by Marshal Soult at the Gebora river.

20 February 1811
ITALIAN FRONT
Following the capture and execution of the rebel leader Parafante, the Calabrian revolt collapsed.

5 March 1811
IBERIAN FRONT
Masséna, having lost 13,000 men to disease and enemy action since October 1810, began his retreat from Santarem and Portugal. The French retreat was harried all the way by irregular forces and the vengeful population.

In an effort to break Marshal Victor's siege of Cádiz, the British and Spanish launched an amphibious attack into the French rear. An Anglo-Spanish force of 5,000 British troops under Thomas Graham and 10,000 Spanish under Count de la Pena landed near Barrosa. Aware of the Allied effort, Victor split his army and marched with 7,000 men to oppose the landing. Heavily outnumbered, the French were saved from almost certain destruction by the inexplicable actions of the Spanish contingent of the Allied army. While the Spanish stood idly by the British were left to fight a hard battle. Victor launched a fierce attack but his artillery became bogged down in marshy terrain and was unable to contribute to the fighting. Unsupported, the French infantry pressed their attack, which degenerated into a slogging match with

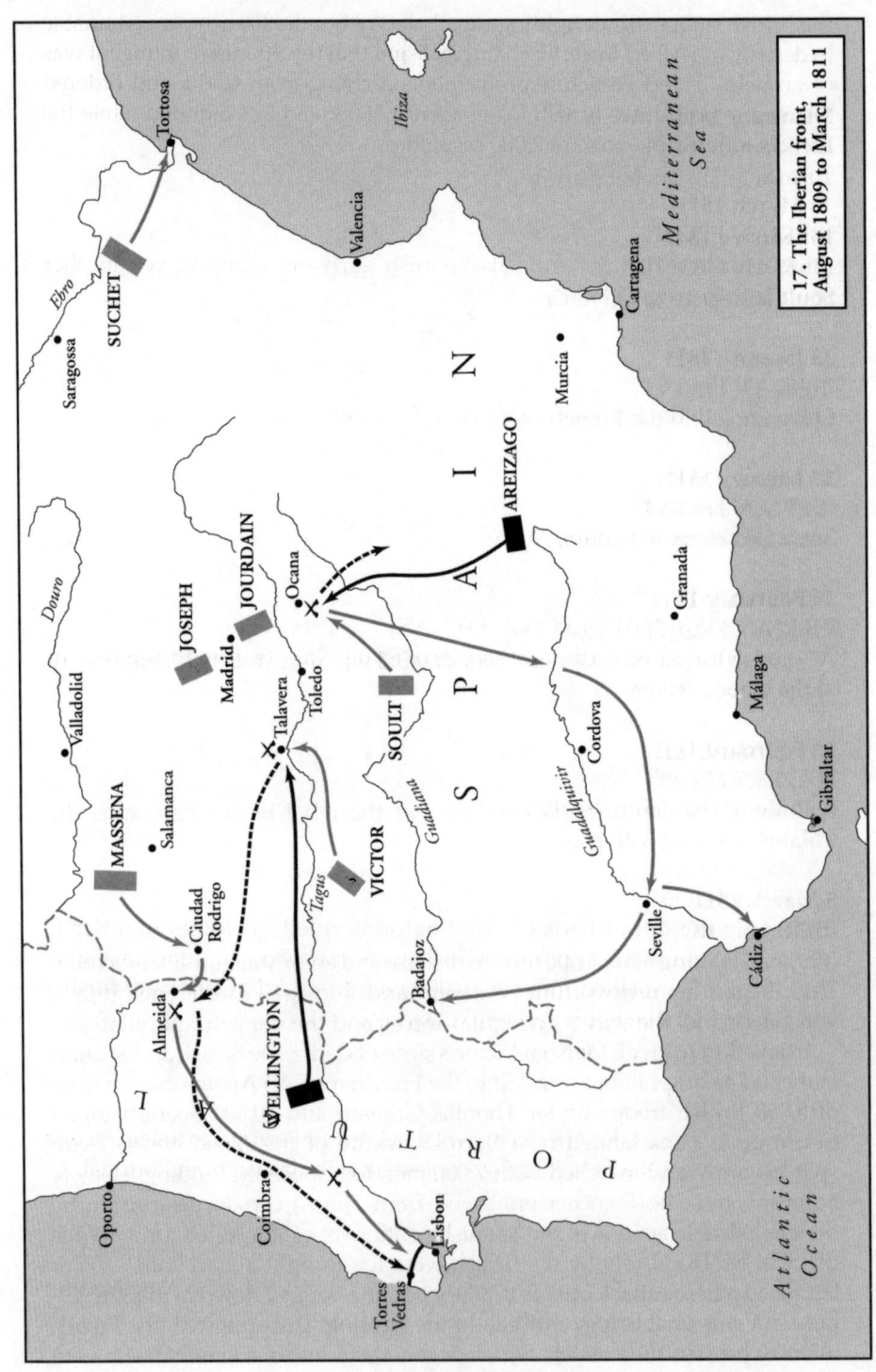

17. The Iberian front, August 1809 to March 1811

the British troops. Bitter fighting raged all day but the French proved unable to destroy the Allied force. Graham, realising that the Spanish contingent was of no help, feared French reinforcements arriving from Cádiz and ordered his men to withdraw. British losses were 1,200 killed or wounded while the French suffered in excess of 2,000 casualties.

11 March 1811
IBERIAN FRONT
Soult captured Badajoz from its Spanish garrison, securing yet another route into Portugal.

13 March 1811
WAR AT SEA
Hoste defeated a Franco-Italian naval force off Lissa.

14 March 1811
IBERIAN FRONT
Soult laid siege to Campo Mayor.

20 March 1811
FRANCE: THE NAPOLEONIC DYNASTY
Marie-Louise gave birth to a son, providing Napoleon with the heir he desperately desired.

25 March 1811
IBERIAN FRONT
Campo Mayor fell to Soult.

30 March 1811
IBERIAN FRONT
Following the fall of Badajoz, Wellington divided his forces in order to protect the southern approaches to Lisbon from French attack. General Beresford led an Allied force of 20,000 men to guard against any further attacks by Marshal Soult and retake Badajoz.

3 April 1811
IBERIAN FRONT
Wellington defeated Reynier's corps of the Army of Portugal in a sharp action at Sabugal. Masséna hastened to complete his withdrawal from Portugal.

7 April 1811
IBERIAN FRONT
Wellington advanced to the Spanish border and laid siege to Almeida and its 1,300-strong garrison. Masséna halted his withdrawal and made plans to march to the garrison's relief.

10 April 1811
IBERIAN FRONT
Spanish forces seized control of Figueras.

14 April 1811
IBERIAN FRONT
General Beresford recaptured Olivenza.

17 April 1811
IBERIAN FRONT
Following the Spanish capture of Figueras, the French sent in an army to lay siege to the town.

3 May 1811
IBERIAN FRONT
Wellington, with 35,000 men, met Masséna's relief attempt towards Almeida in a bloody battle at Fuentes de Oñoro. Masséna, with 49,000 men, committed some 5,000 in an attack upon Fuentes but was held up by a British force of 2,000. After bitter fighting the village was taken but the British reinforced their units and launched a vigorous counter-attack. After further hard fighting, the village was recaptured by British troops. British losses were nearly 300 men to a French loss of over 650.

4 May 1811
IBERIAN FRONT
Masséna spent the day grouping his army for a major attack on the 5th. French skirmishing kept the British and Spanish forces occupied.

5 May 1811
IBERIAN FRONT
Masséna launched a major assault upon the British lines around Fuentes. A combined infantry and cavalry attack routed an Anglo-Spanish cavalry force on the British right. Wellington threw additional troops in to stiffen his right wing and conducted a fighting withdrawal. However, he had already prepared stronger defences to his rear and halted on these. Meanwhile, Masséna unleashed another assault upon the village of Fuentes de Oñoro but was held up by a ferocious British defence. The British steadily strengthened their line throughout the day as Masséna threw in one attack after another. By evening the French were compelled to abandon their attacks and began to withdraw, having lost 2,200 men to a British loss of 1,500.

6 May 1811
IBERIAN FRONT
Beresford laid siege to Badajoz.

8 May 1811
IBERIAN FRONT
Suchet laid siege to Tarragona.

9 May 1811
IBERIAN FRONT
With the garrison of Almeida evacuated, Masséna pulled his force back from Fuentes de Oñoro, having lost 2,200 men to an Allied loss of 1,600 in the fighting at the beginning of the month. Masséna was shortly afterwards relieved of his command and replaced by Marmont.

10 May 1811
IBERIAN FRONT
Beresford raised the siege of Badajoz to face Soult, who was marching towards the town with a relief force. The French garrison took this as an opportunity to escape and broke out to link up with Soult.

15 May 1811
IBERIAN FRONT
Soult reached Albuera with 24,000 men, to find Beresford in defensive positions. He therefore planned to swing his army around the British right wing to cut the British off from the Spanish, who he thought were in the British rear.

16 May 1811
IBERIAN FRONT
Beresford, with 34,000 men (10,000 British, 10,000 Portuguese and 14,000 Spanish), faced Soult, with 24,000 men, near Albuera. Deploying the British troops in the centre, with the Portuguese to the left and the Spanish on the right, Beresford aimed to stop Soult reaching Badajoz.

Soult launched his flanking attack, but encountered the Spanish deployed on the British right. Being no match for the French troops, the Spanish were defeated. Soult almost rolled up the Allied front but Beresford hastily committed elements from his reserve to stabilise his front. These suffered severe losses as the French cavalry caught some of the units as they deployed. The Spanish contingent held in reserve, commanded by General d'España, refused to provide support, making a difficult situation far worse. Only the commitment of the last of the British reserves prevented the collapse of the British line, but bloody fighting then followed as the British and French troops slugged it out. In the end it was the French who gave way and began to withdraw. Soult managed to pull out the remainder of his force but had lost 8,000 men to a British loss of 7,000. The French then retired towards Seville, covering their withdrawal with cavalry screens.

25 May 1811
IBERIAN FRONT
The French cavalry screen, protecting their army as it withdrew upon Seville, launched a vigorous foray against the British and Spanish. The French force of 3,000 cavalry, commanded by General Latour-Maubourg, struck the Spanish contingent of the Allied force first. Suffering heavy losses the Spanish scattered leaving General Lumley's 2,000 British cavalry to fight the French. Latour moved forward via Usagre to attack the British while sending part of his force around on a flank attack. Realising the French had effectively negated their numerical superiority, Lumley launched a fierce attack and defeated Latour. The French were compelled to withdraw, having lost nearly 400 men to a British loss of less than fifty.

General Beresford reinvested Badajoz once again.

10 June 1811
IBERIAN FRONT
The siege of Badajoz was abandoned once again as Soult and Marmont threatened the British forces around the town.

17 June 1811
IBERIAN FRONT
With French strength continuing to build up Wellington began to pull his forces back into Portugal.

1 July 1811
FRANCE: THE MARSHALATE
General Suchet was promoted to Marshal.

28 July 1811
IBERIAN FRONT
Marshal Suchet captured Tarragona. French commitment in Spain had risen to 350,000 men. Soult deployed his Army of the South in Andalusia, Joseph Bonaparte commanded the Army of the Centre while Marmont had the Army of Portugal. Suchet had the Army of Aragón acting against the Spanish along the costas while Dorsenne commanded the Army of the North. Macdonald held down Catalonia with his Army of Catalonia. None of these forces acted in co-operation and most of their strength was drained combating the Spanish guerillas.

10 August 1811
IBERIAN FRONT
The French defeated a Spanish force at Las Vertientes.

11 August 1811
IBERIAN FRONT
Wellington pushed forward to the Spanish border and laid siege to the French troops in Ciudad Rodrigo.

19 August 1811
IBERIAN FRONT
After a long siege Figueras fell to the French.

23 September 1811
IBERIAN FRONT
Marmont relieved Ciudad Rodrigo as Wellington was forced to withdraw. Suchet laid siege to Sagunto.

25 September 1811
IBERIAN FRONT
As Wellington withdrew, Picton's 3rd Division, with around 1,000 men and 500 cavalry, covered the British rear. Marmont pursued energetically and his advance guard of 2,500 cavalry under General Montbrun managed to catch up with the British at El Bodon. Conducting a fighting withdrawal, the British held off the French attacks for the next seven miles, evading defeat and allowing Wellington to continue the uninterrupted withdrawal of the bulk of his force. Picton lost 150 men to a French loss of around 200 men.

25 October 1811
IBERIAN FRONT
Suchet defeated Blake's mixed Anglo-Spanish force outside Sagunto.

26 October 1811
IBERIAN FRONT
Sagunto fell to Suchet's army.

28 October 1811
IBERIAN FRONT
An Anglo-Portuguese force of 10,000 men, led by General Hill, attacked a French force of 4,000 under General Girard at Arroyo dos Molinos. Cutting off any lines of retreat, the British launched a furious assault into the town, crippling the French force. Managing to cut their way out, the French troops were vigorously pursued by the Allied force, losing 1,600 men. The British lost fewer than 100 men.

20 December 1811
IBERIAN FRONT
French troops laid siege to Tarifa.

23 December 1811
THE EMPIRE OF FRANCE
Napoleon began military preparations against Russia.

26 December 1811
IBERIAN FRONT
Suchet drove Blake's force back into Valencia.

31 December 1812
RUSSIA: POLITICS
Tsar Alexander placed limits on French trade in Russia. This move opened the breach between France and Russia even further.

* 1812 *

4 January 1812
IBERIAN FRONT
The French abandoned their siege of Tarifa.

Throughout Iberia the French had a number of armies under commanders who reported directly to Napoleon. Joseph, despite his position as king, commanded only those forces directly around Madrid. Marshal Marmont commanded the Army of Portugal, deployed near Salamanca, Marshal Soult the Army of Andalusia, General Caffarelli the Army of Navarre, General Decaen the Army of Catalonia and Marshal Suchet the forces grouped around Valencia. Joseph held only a small force around Madrid, around 20,000 men of the Army of the Centre.

8 January 1812
IBERIAN FRONT
Wellington laid siege to Ciudad Rodrigo once again as he launched his offensive into Spain.

9 January 1812
IBERIAN FRONT
Suchet defeated Blake at Valencia and captured the town.

10 January 1812
GERMAN FRONT
French troops marched into Swedish Pomerania. This move forced Bernadotte, Crown Prince of Sweden, towards the Allied camp.

14 January 1812
IBERIAN FRONT
The British rapidly captured the outer defences of Ciudad Rodrigo and moved to attack the town itself.

19 January 1812
IBERIAN FRONT
Opening two breaches in the citadel walls, the British stormed Ciudad Rodrigo. The French garrison, overwhelmed by the British attack, surrendered. The French commander, General Barrie, led the surrender of the French troops. British losses during the attack were 600 men killed or wounded, including General Crauford, killed during the assault.

The Spanish defeated a French force at Villaseca.

24 January 1812
IBERIAN FRONT
The French defeated a Spanish force at Altafulla.

26 January 1812
INTERNATIONAL POLITICS
France annexed Catalonia.

26 February 1812
INTERNATIONAL POLITICS
The French compelled the Prussians into an alliance ahead of the intended attack upon Russia.

10 March 1812
INTERNATIONAL POLITICS
Continuing to build up their alliance against Russia, the French concluded an alliance with the Austrians.

13 March 1812
FRANCE: ARMED FORCES
Napoleon passed a decree that organised the National Guard into three distinct groups. The first group comprised men between the ages of 20 and 26 from the classes of 1807 to 1812 who had not yet been called for active service. The second group comprised men between the ages of 26 and 40. The third and final group was men between 40 and 60 years of age. Napoleon demanded the formation of 100 cohorts of troops from the first group. Each cohort would consist of around 1,100 men.[1]

14 March 1812
FRANCE: ARMED FORCES
The number of National Guard cohorts demanded to be mobilised was reduced from 100 to eighty-four.

16 March 1812
IBERIAN FRONT
Wellington's army had moved south from Ciudad Rodrigo and laid siege to Badajoz. The French garrison numbered 5,000 men.

24 March 1812
INTERNATIONAL POLITICS
The Swedes concluded a secret agreement with the Russians.

25 March 1812
IBERIAN FRONT
The British attack the outer defences of Badajoz, capturing Fort Picurina after a bloody struggle.

4 April 1812
IBERIAN FRONT
Wellington learned that Soult was marching to relieve Badajoz so he determined to take the city as quickly as possible.

Napoleon, deeply involved in the preparations for his invasion of Russia, restored command of the armies in Spain to Joseph. Unfortunately the French commanders did not respect Joseph and refused to obey his commands, continuing to act entirely independent of their monarch and each other.

5 April 1812
IBERIAN FRONT
The British breached the walls of Badajoz in two places with their artillery fire and prepared to storm the city. Hasty repairs by the garrison caused the attack to be postponed but continued artillery fire opened a third breach. The French garrison of 5,000 men had already suffered 1,500 casualties during these early stages of the battle while the British attacking force lost 3,400 men.

5–9 April 1812
INTERNATIONAL POLITICS
The Convention of St Petersburg brought public agreement between Russia and Sweden for mutual aid in the event of Russo–French or Swedish–Danish conflict. Tsar Alexander had begun to increase the size of his armies as war with France became more likely.

6 April 1812
IBERIAN FRONT
At 10pm the British began their attack upon Badajoz, through the heavily fortified breaches in the city walls. British losses were extremely heavy as the French poured concentrated fire upon them. The main British attack though was conducted over the walls, the French having been largely

occupied with the defence of the breaches. Despite breaking into the city the French continued to resist fiercely. Only after the French commander had been driven into the citadel did the remnants of the garrison surrender. However, the British troops then sacked the town for two full days before order could be restored.

May 1812
FRANCE: ARMED FORCES
Napoleon began to concentrate his Grande Armée in Germany for the planned invasion of Russia. During the next six weeks some 650,000 men would assemble. Towards the end of the month the army began its march into Poland and East Prussia.

11 May 1812
BRITAIN: POLITICS
Prime Minister Spencer Perceval was assassinated.

17–28 May 1812
INTERNATIONAL POLITICS
The Conference of Dresden. Napoleon attempted to solidify his allies prior to the attack on Russia.

18 May 1812
IBERIAN FRONT
General Hill attacked the French forces in Almaraz.

19 May 1812
IBERIAN FRONT
Almaraz fell to Hill's attacks.

24 May 1812
FRANCE: ARMED FORCES
Napoleon made his decision to invade Russia.

28 May 1812
INTERNATIONAL POLITICS
Russia and the Ottoman Empire signed the Treaty of Bucharest. This enabled the Russians to release additional forces for the expected war with France.

June 1812
FRANCE: ARMED FORCES
The French had around 650,000 men assembled for the forthcoming campaign in Russia while another 250,000 were already committed to the fighting in Spain.

RUSSIA: ARMED FORCES
The Russian army introduced the corps system and continued with a series of reforms to their infantry units. General Barclay de Tolly led the reforms.

1 June 1812
IBERIAN FRONT
The French defeated a Spanish force at Bornos.

13 June 1812
IBERIAN FRONT
Having secured the Portuguese frontier, Wellington began his advance into the Spanish interior.

15 June 1812
IBERIAN FRONT
French troops abandoned Oviedo.

17 June 1812
IBERIAN FRONT
Wellington led his army to the Salamanca area and laid siege to the French-held forts around the town. Marmont, isolated and outnumbered, manoeuvred to avoid contact and called for help from Joseph and Caffarelli. Neither moved to his aid.

20 June 1812
INTERNATIONAL POLITICS
The Sixth Coalition was formed against the French.

Napoleon's continued aggressive foreign policy, combined with his marriage to Marie-Louise of Austria, had finally driven a wedge between France and Russia. Tsar Alexander, so agreeable at Tilsit in 1807, had now become a fierce opponent of France's hegemony over Europe. With the rebellion in Spain and the British presence in Portugal tying down increasing numbers of French troops, Napoleon determined to prosecute a new conflict at the other extremity of the continent, causing him to mass the greatest army he had ever brought together, utilising the resources not only of France, but of many of his European allies as well. The French invasion of Russia would be made with a force the size of which had not been seen in Europe before.

Note

1. F Loraine Petre, *Napoleon's Last Campaign in Germany, 1813*, p. 11

CHAPTER VIII

The Invasion of Russia

The French invasion of Russia took warfare to a new scale. Deploying nearly two thirds of a million men, the French aimed to smash the Russians in a mammoth campaign. Napoleon aimed to defeat the Tsar's armies close to the frontier and impel him to enter into a negotiated settlement. However, the French had not reckoned on Russian stubbornness and the sheer size of their kingdom.

23 June 1812
FRANCE: RUSSIAN FRONT DEPLOYMENT

For the invasion of Russia the French had called upon all the states of their empire to create a multi-national army. The invasion force consisted of flanking corps, largely comprising allied troops, while the armies in the centre, commanded by Napoleon and Jerome, would engage the main Russian forces.

On the French left wing, deployed at Tilsit on the Niemen river, was Macdonald's X Corps with 32,500 Polish, Bavarian, Westphalian and Prussian troops. Macdonald was to push towards Riga in order to protect the extending left wing of the central forces.

The first central army, commanded by Napoleon in person, comprised the I Corps under Marshal Davout, with 72,000 French, German and Polish troops, II Corps under Oudinot with 37,000 French, Portuguese, Swiss and Croat soldiers, III Corps under Marshal Ney with 40,000 French, Wurttemburg and Portuguese troops, IV Corps under Eugene de Beauharnais with 46,000 French, Croatian, Italian and Dalmatian troops, VI Corps under St Cyr with 25,000 men and the Imperial Guard, commanded by Mortier, with a strength of 47,000 men. To support the infantry there were three cavalry corps, all under the overall command of Marshal Murat. The I Cavalry Corps was commanded by General Nansouty and had 11,000 French and Prussian troopers while the II Cavalry Corps, also 11,000 strong, was commanded by General Montbrun and was made up of French, Polish and Prussian troops. The III Cavalry Corps had a strength of 10,000 troops from France, Bavaria and Saxony. The first part of this force, comprising the I, II, III Corps and I and II Cavalry Corps was to cross the Niemen around Kovno from 24 June with the aim of attacking the main Russian army commanded by Barclay de Tolly. Eugene was to lead the IV and VI Corps together with the III Cavalry Corps across from 30 June and would have the dual role of protecting the immediate right wing of Napoleon's army and also forming a junction between the former and Jerome.

The second army in the centre, commanded by Jerome Bonaparte, comprised the V (Polish) Corps under Poniatowski with 36,000 men, VII Corps under Reynier with 17,000 Saxon and mixed German troops, and the VIII Corps under the command of General Vandamme with 17,000 Westphalian and French troops. To support this force, which was advancing on the right of Napoleon's main force, was Latour-Maubourg's IV Cavalry Corps with 10,000 French, Bavarian and Saxon troops. Jerome's force was to cross the Niemen near Grodno and tackle Bagration's secondary Russian army. In order to entice Bagration forward against the rear of Napoleon's advancing force before attacking, Jerome was not to cross the Niemen until 1 July.

The right wing of the French army was made up of the reluctant Austrian Allies, a force of 40,000 men, designated the Austrian Auxilliary Corps. Schwartzenberg, commanding the Austrian force, was to cross the Bug river to protect the southern flank of the main armies against attack by Tormasov's forces to the south.

Behind the main forces, acting as reserves, was Victor's IX Corps with a mixture of 35,000 French, Westphalian, mixed Confederation of the Rhine and Saxon soldiers and Augereau's XI Corps with 50,000 French, Belgian and German troops.

To support the invasion through largely uncultivated countryside, Napoleon had massed a supply column of 25,000 vehicles with 90,000 horses and 10,000 oxen and brought with him significant quantities of supplies.

Napoleon's Grande Armée brought together more than 610,000 soldiers from all around the empire. Of the total number 200,000 were from 'old' France, Berg committed around 5,000 men, Baden 7,000, Naples 8,000 and Denmark over 10,000. Wurttemberg provided a force of 15,000 men as did the various smaller Confederation of the Rhine states, Bavaria some 25,000 men, Saxony about the same, Westphalia around 28,000, Switzerland 9,000 and Italy 30,000. The Polish commitment was significant, at 56,000 men. The reluctant allies, Prussian and Austria, provided 40,000 men each. There were also contingents of Dutch, Croatian, Dalmatian and Swiss troops.

RUSSIA: ARMED FORCES

The Russians had begun to reorganise their army along French lines and deployed a number of corps units, though unfortunately they had not learned how to use their corps effectively. They deployed three main field armies. Barclay de Tolly had 90,000 men in his First Army of the West, deployed north of the Niemen river around Vilna. His force comprised the I Corps, under General Wittgenstein, on the right wing, II Corps under Bagavout, III Corps under Tutchkov, IV Corps under Tolstoi, V Corps under Constantine and VI Corps, on the left wing, under Dokhturov near Grodno.

General Bagration, with the Second Army of the West, had 48,000 infantry deployed between Grodno and Volkovysk, split between the

VII Corps under General Raevski and VIII Corps under Borozdin together with Platov's 10,000 Cossacks in the IV Cavalry Corps.

South of the marshes, near Lutsk, was the Third Army of the West under General Tormasov of 30,000 men, which had not yet been reorganised into a corps structure. General Tshitshagov was deployed opposite the Turkish frontier in the Balkans with an army of 50,000 men. Some 30,000 men were deployed as a second line reserve along the Dvina and Dniepr rivers. Russian artillery strength, distributed between the three main field armies, numbered around 1,000 pieces. The Cossacks contributed a further force of 10,000 cavalry to the frontier armies.

In Finland the Russians had an army of 20,000 men while along their eastern frontiers there were another 30,000 troops, in the interior some 50,000 and in the many garrison towns another 50,000.[1]

Tsar Alexander was in command of the Russian armies but, shortly after the opening of hostilities, placed General Barclay de Tolly in overall command. Until such time, the Tsar was advised by the Prussian General von Phull. Phull's proposed plan in the face of a French invasion was for the First Army of the West to fall back from the frontier while the Second Army of the West struck at the enemy rear. The First Army was to establish a strong position at Drissa on the Dvina and gather to it substantial reserves for a set-piece battle against the invaders.

IBERIAN FRONT
Wellington captured the last of the Salamanca forts.

24 June 1812
RUSSIAN FRONT
Napoleon invaded Russia, starting the crossing of the Niemen with his own central army. Three bridges had been constructed across the river near Kovno, over which more than a quarter of a million men marched.

25 June 1812
RUSSIAN FRONT
Napoleon's army continued to cross the Niemen.

26 June 1812
RUSSIAN FRONT
Napoleon pushed Oudinot's II Corps off to the north to separate Wittgenstein's I Corps, on the right wing of Barclay de Tolly's First Army, from the main part and bring it to battle near Kedainiai. To provide support if it was required, Ney's III Corps would follow behind Oudinot.

Barclay de Tolly was well aware of the French movements and began the withdrawal of his forces to the Dvina. However, he was unenthusiastic about Phull's plan for an armed camp at Drissa and moved deliberately slowly.

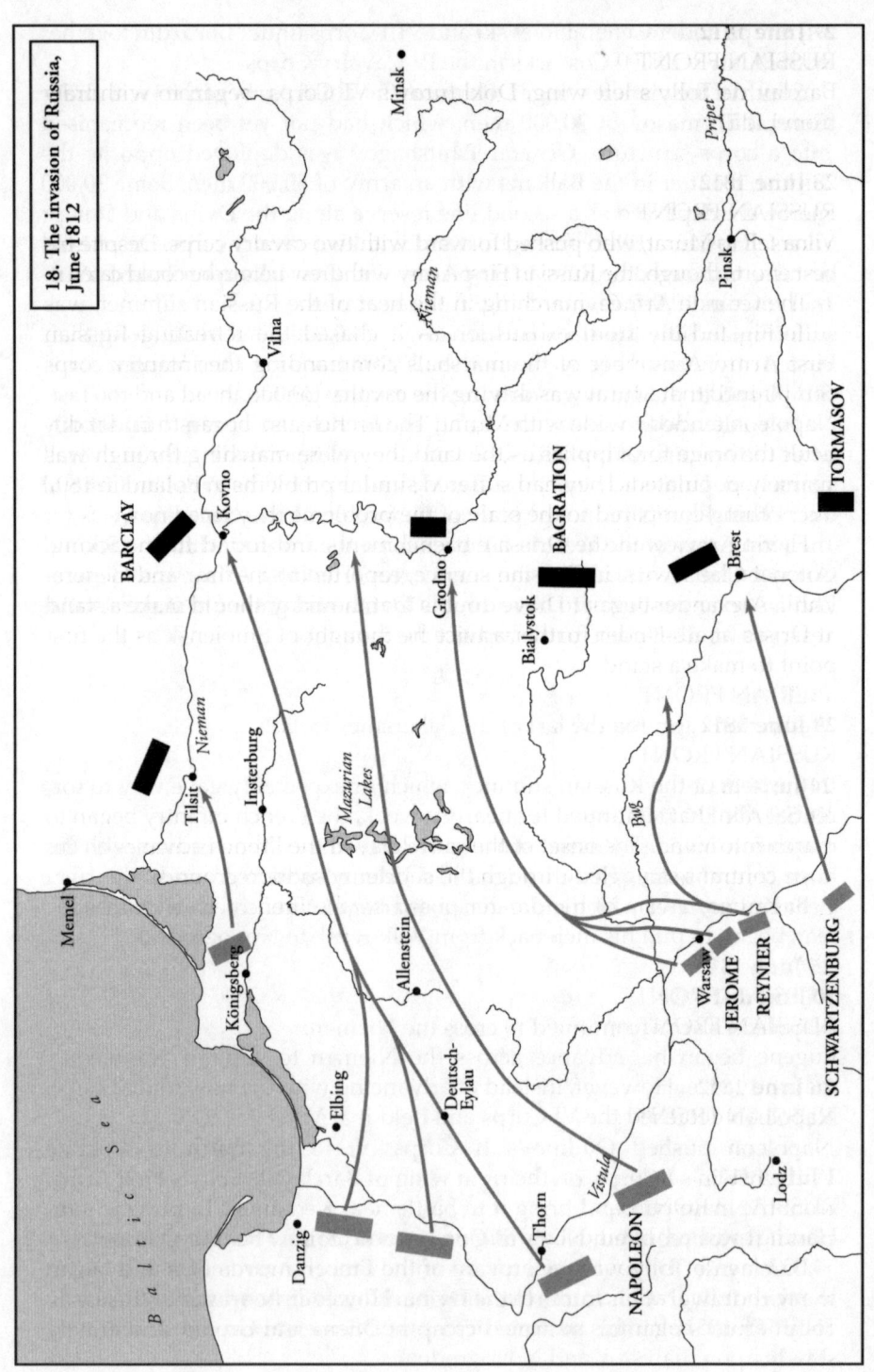

18. The invasion of Russia, June 1812

27 June 1812
RUSSIAN FRONT
Barclay de Tolly's left wing, Dokhturov's VI Corps, began to withdraw from Lida.

28 June 1812
RUSSIAN FRONT
Vilna fell to Murat, who pushed forward with two cavalry corps. Despite his best efforts though, the Russian First Army withdrew before he could catch it.

The Grande Armée, marching in the heat of the Russian summer, was suffering terribly from exhaustion as it chased the retreating Russian First Army. A number of the marshals commanding the infantry corps complained that Murat was driving the cavalry too far ahead and too fast. Napoleon tended to side with Murat. The French also began to find it difficult to forage for supplies as the land they were marching through was sparsely populated. They had suffered similar problems in Poland in 1807 but nothing compared to the scale of the problems they faced now.

Having reviewed the Drissa entrenchments and found them lacking, Colonel Clausewitz, in Russian service, reported to the Tsar and General Phull. Alexander began to have doubts that the army should make a stand at Drissa at all. Under further advice he thought of Smolensk as the first point to make a stand.

29 June 1812
RUSSIAN FRONT
In the heat of the Russian summer, which unexpectedly gave way to torrential rain that continued for nearly a week, the French infantry began to march into Vilna. The onset of the rain delayed the French advance as the huge columns struggled through the suddenly sodden ground.

Bagration, aware of the danger posed by the French advance into his rear, began to pull his men back from Volkovysk to Novogrodeck.

30 June 1812
RUSSIAN FRONT
Eugene began his advance across the Niemen to support Napoleon's main advance. However, instead of advancing with the now united force, Napoleon detached the VI Corps and held it at Vilna.

1 July 1812
RUSSIAN FRONT
Having pushed behind Bagration's Second Army, Napoleon now sent 50,000 men of Davout's I Corps on an advance towards Minsk in order to prevent Bagration from retreating in order to link up with Barclay de Tolly. Jerome began his advance across the Niemen at Grodno and moved slowly upon Bialystok and Novogrodeck.

Dokhturov, still falling back, encountered an advanced element of Davout's corps as he made for Svir. The Russians got the better of the engagement and successfully continued their withdrawal.

2 July 1812
RUSSIAN FRONT
Barclay de Tolly had withdrawn so slowly that he had managed to unite his outlying corps on the left and right with his centre. Both Wittgenstein and Dokhturov linked up with the remainder of the army.

IBERIAN FRONT
Spanish forces laid siege to Astorga.

4 July 1812
RUSSIAN FRONT
As Davout reached Tolochin, Bagration took his retreating force back towards Tschweren so that he could reach Minsk.

5 July 1812
RUSSIAN FRONT
Bagration continued to withdraw, pulling back in the direction of Bobruisk in order to avoid isolation by Davout. Jerome continued his slow advance from Grodno but, listening to the complaints of his generals about the difficulties of the march, halted his men for a few days.

6 July 1812
RUSSIAN FRONT
Bagration was prevented from reaching Minsk by Davout's advance and decided instead to fall back upon Bobruisk and from there to the Dniepr at Mogilev.

8 July 1812
RUSSIAN FRONT
Minsk fell to Davout's III Corps. Napoleon had been trying to catch Barclay de Tolly between Vilna and Minsk but the Russians managed to evade the French and continued to fall back.

Tsar Alexander inspected the Drissa entrenchment and became even more convinced of the need to withdraw farther east. General Phull's influence upon the Tsar was waning and he would shortly be dismissed. Furthermore, news of the retreat of Bagration's army undermined the Russian plan to attack the French rear, further destroying the proposed Drissa plan.

9 July 1812
RUSSIA: ARMED FORCES
Tsar Alexander appointed Barclay de Tolly to command the field armies in place of himself.

10 July 1812
RUSSIAN FRONT

Jerome had pushed forward to Novogrodeck and launched a cautious pursuit of Bagration as the Russians fell back upon Mir.

Napoleon, still around Vilna with a large part of the central army, paused the advance of all but the outlying units in order to allow the army to concentrate, it having become strung out by the advance from the frontier. Macdonald had pushed out on the northern wing with 30,000 men and was deployed around Rasianiai; Oudinot was at Solock with another 40,000. Ney was behind Oudinot with another 39,000 men while Murat was ahead of the main body at Widzy with 51,000 men. Napoleon, together with the Imperial Guard and St Cyr's corps, a force of 72,000 men, was deployed around Vilna while Davout remained in Minsk with his 50,000 men. Eugene had his 40,000 men behind the main force while Jerome was at Novogrodeck with 61,000 men of the V and VIII Corps. Reynier had been diverted to the south and was deployed around Volkovysk with 17,000 men. Schwartzenberg continued to cover the right wing with his Austrian Corps.[2]

Barclay brought his army back to Drissa and went into the armed camp. However, even as he took up his positions, Tsar Alexander was debating with his commanders whether to continue the retreat to Smolensk. Barclay's force had been reinforced and now comprised 100,000 troops while Bagration, approaching the Dniepr near Mogilev, had 45,000. Tormasov remained in his original positions around Lutsk with his 35,000 men.[3]

12 July 1812
RUSSIAN FRONT

Davout, having spent four days at Minsk, began his march east once again. He aimed to reach and cross the Dniepr at Mogilev. Eugene led his force upon Vitebsk. Jerome was attacked by Platov's Cossacks near Mir and suffered severe losses.

Napoleon, aware of the Russian concentration at Drissa, laid plans to advance with his force in order to pin the Russians down and defeat them in detail.

14 July 1812
RUSSIAN FRONT

After protracted debate Tsar Alexander abandoned the plan to fight a set-piece battle at Drissa.

15–21 July 1812
IBERIAN FRONT

Wellington, leading 47,000, attempted to outmanoeuvre Marmont's 42,000 around Salamanca. The French marched and reacted quickly and compelled Wellington to begin preparations for a retreat. Thinking the British were already in full retreat, Marmont began a premature pursuit.

16 July 1812
RUSSIAN FRONT
Barclay de Tolly drew his forces out of the Drissa camp and began a withdrawal upon Vitebsk. He left a 25,000-strong force under General Wittgenstein to cover the Dvina and marched upon Vitebsk with the remainder. Napoleon, disappointed at Jerome's lack of progress against Bagration, gave him a reprimand and informed him that he was making him subordinate to Davout. Jerome took exception to this decision and decided to quit the army, leaving for his Westphalian kingdom.

17 July 1812
RUSSIAN FRONT
Following Jerome's departure, his army was split up and distributed among the remainder of the Grande Armée. The VIII Corps was dispatched in the direction of Orsha to link up with Napoleon's main army while the V Corps continued the pursuit of Bagration. Reynier's VII Corps was to move onto the southern wing to replace Schwartzenberg's Austrian Corps, which was instructed to march to link up with Napoleon also. Schwartzenberg currently held a line from Brest Litovsk to Pinsk to protect the Pripet flank against Tormasov's forces.

As the French issued these orders Tormasov moved into action, pushing towards Kobrin with his main force while other units attacked towards Brest Litovsk.

19 July 1812
RUSSIAN FRONT
The leading Prussian units of Macdonald's corps attacked the defenders of Riga before the town. After a bitter struggle the Russians were thrown back towards the town. Macdonald led the main part of his force upon Jacobstadt.

20 July 1812
RUSSIAN FRONT
Barclay de Tolly, retreating along the line of the Dvina, detached Wittgenstein at Polotsk from his main force in order to form a protective screen covering the road north to St Petersburg. Wittgenstein remained with 25,000 men of his I Corps.

Davout reached the Dniepr at Mogilev with 20,000 men and began to establish a strong position. His aim remained to trap Bagration, who he believed would attempt to cross the Dniepr at this point.

Tormasov surprised Reynier's troops as they deployed around Brest Litovsk and inflicted more than 6,000 casualties upon the French. The main attack by Tormasov's army also struck an isolated brigade of Reynier's corps at Kobrin, involving it in fierce fighting.

21 July 1812

RUSSIAN FRONT

Bagration, with 45,000 men, reached the Dniepr at Stary Bykhov after successfully avoiding French efforts to trap him. He began to march upstream towards Mogilev in order to use the more substantial bridges there to cross the river, unaware that Davout was already there.

Reynier marched to the aid of his hard-pressed unit at Kobrin and, under Russian pressure, had to pull in his forces, drawing them back upon Slonim. Schwartzenberg still had his units around Slonim, having delayed his movement towards Napoleon's main army. He now turned his forces so as to aid Reynier's embattled corps.

IBERIAN FRONT

The French defeated a Spanish force at Castalla. Marmont's forces closed up to Salamanca as he moved to pursue Wellington.

22 July 1812

RUSSIAN FRONT

Aware that Bagration was approaching from the south, Davout took up strongly defended positions south of Mogilev.

IBERIAN FRONT

Marmont, with 49,600 men and seventy-eight cannon, was caught in an over-extended marching line near Salamanca. Wellington, with 52,000 men and sixty cannon deployed in a hidden position, launched a full-scale assault. While Picton's division stopped the French advance, the main British force hit the centre of the column. During the fighting the British General Marchant was killed. Marmont was also wounded, losing an arm, and had to hand command over to General Clausel. Clausel managed to stabilise the position and then launched a counter-attack upon the British centre. Initially the French attack made good progress but was then struck by massive British counter-fire and crumbled. Wellington then unleashed his reserves and launched his own counter-attack and would have destroyed the entire French force had the Spanish only blocked the French line of retreat.

Marmont lost suffered 7,000 casualties in the battle and also lost 7,000 men captured. Wellington lost just over 5,000.

Wellington had proved beyond any doubt that he was as good a general of the offence as he was of defence. Only a lack of co-ordination by the Spanish regular army prevented the total destruction of Marmont's force. However, the Allies had seized the initiative in Iberia for the first time, and would take the war to the French for the remainder of the year.

23 July 1812
RUSSIAN FRONT
Davout was attacked by Bagration as the latter attempted to cross the Dniepr via the Mogilev bridges. After a day of fierce fighting, during which 1,000 French and 4,000 Russian troops were killed or wounded, the Russians were compelled to abandon their march and instead erected a bridge at Stary Bykhov to effect a crossing there.

Barclay had also continued his withdrawal, reaching Vitebsk. Napoleon had detached Oudinot to pin down Wittgenstein's rearguard at Polotsk.

IBERIAN FRONT
The king's German Legion under General Bock, with 450 cavalry, attacked and defeated French infantry under General Foy at Garcia Hernandez. The German cavalry managed to break the French infantry squares and inflicted 1,400 casualties for a loss of 150 men.

24 July 1812
RUSSIAN FRONT
The Prussians of Macdonald's corps reached Riga and laid siege to the town. Macdonald now had the bulk of his corps at Riga and around a third at Jacobstadt. Farther along the Dvina, Oudinot faced Wittgenstein close to Polotsk while on the main battle front Napoleon's army was approaching Vitebsk in pursuit of Barclay de Tolly and Davout had fought Bagration at Mogilev, the latter crossing the river during the day at Stary Bykhov in order to continue his eastward retreat. Behind the main force St Cyr held a reinforcement corps at Usachi while Poniatowski and Vandamme were marching to join with the main army, having reached Berezino. On the southern wing, Schwartzenberg was deployed around Slonim while Reynier was arriving on the southern wing around Kobrin.

IBERIAN FRONT
Joseph, having decided to help Marmont, marched towards Salamanca with his Army of the Centre and was very nearly trapped by Wellington. Only a hasty withdrawal prevented the isolation and destruction of his force.

25 July 1812
RUSSIAN FRONT
Napoleon's main force approached Vitebsk as he pursued Barclay de Tolly. Murat's advance guard was involved in bitter fighting with Barclay's rear-guard to the west of the city.

Reynier had arrived on the southern wing and deployed near Chomsk and Kobrin, keeping only small outposts at Pinsk and Brest Litovsk. Rather than march immediately to join with Napoleon, Schwartzenberg deliberately delayed his movement.

26 July 1812
RUSSIAN FRONT
Oudinot captured Polotsk as he pushed forward on a wide arching attack to protect the left wing of Napoleon's army. Wittgenstein pulled his corps back upon Sebezh as Macdonald threatened his right wing from Jacobstadt.

Napoleon deployed before Vitebsk but there was further bitter fighting between Murat and the Russian rearguards. Dokhturov's corps made up the rearguard for Barclay's army and entered Vitebsk during the course of the day.

27 July 1812
RUSSIAN FRONT
Murat's advance guard pushed to the outskirts of Vitebsk after continual bitter fighting with the Russian rearguards. Three days of conflict had taken their toll on both armies. Having delayed the French long enough, Barclay de Tolly withdrew his main force of 75,000 men from the city, avoiding a major action with the French. Both Barclay and Bagration were making for Smolensk in order to unite their armies.

28 July 1812
RUSSIAN FRONT
Napoleon launched his attack at Vitebsk but Barclay de Tolly had successfully evacuated the bulk of his army, leaving behind only a small rearguard.

29 July 1812
RUSSIAN FRONT
With the Grande Armée strung out in a long column between Vitebsk and Mogilev, Napoleon halted so that the supply and artillery troops could catch up and the remainder could have a rest. As the marching units approached they took up positions between the Dvina and Dniepr rivers.

Napoleon's failure to draw the Russian field army to battle meant he was having to march deeper and deeper into Russia. As his forces penetrated farther to the east, their strength dwindled, men falling aside through disease, exhaustion and enemy rearguard actions. The Russian strategy of refusing to give battle was draining French strength far more effectively than any set piece action could have.

31 July 1812
RUSSIAN FRONT
Wittgenstein launched a surprise counter-attack from Sebezh with 20,000 men against Oudinot's corps, which had pushed forward from Polotsk. After bitter fighting the French were forced to retire towards the Dvina and Polotsk.

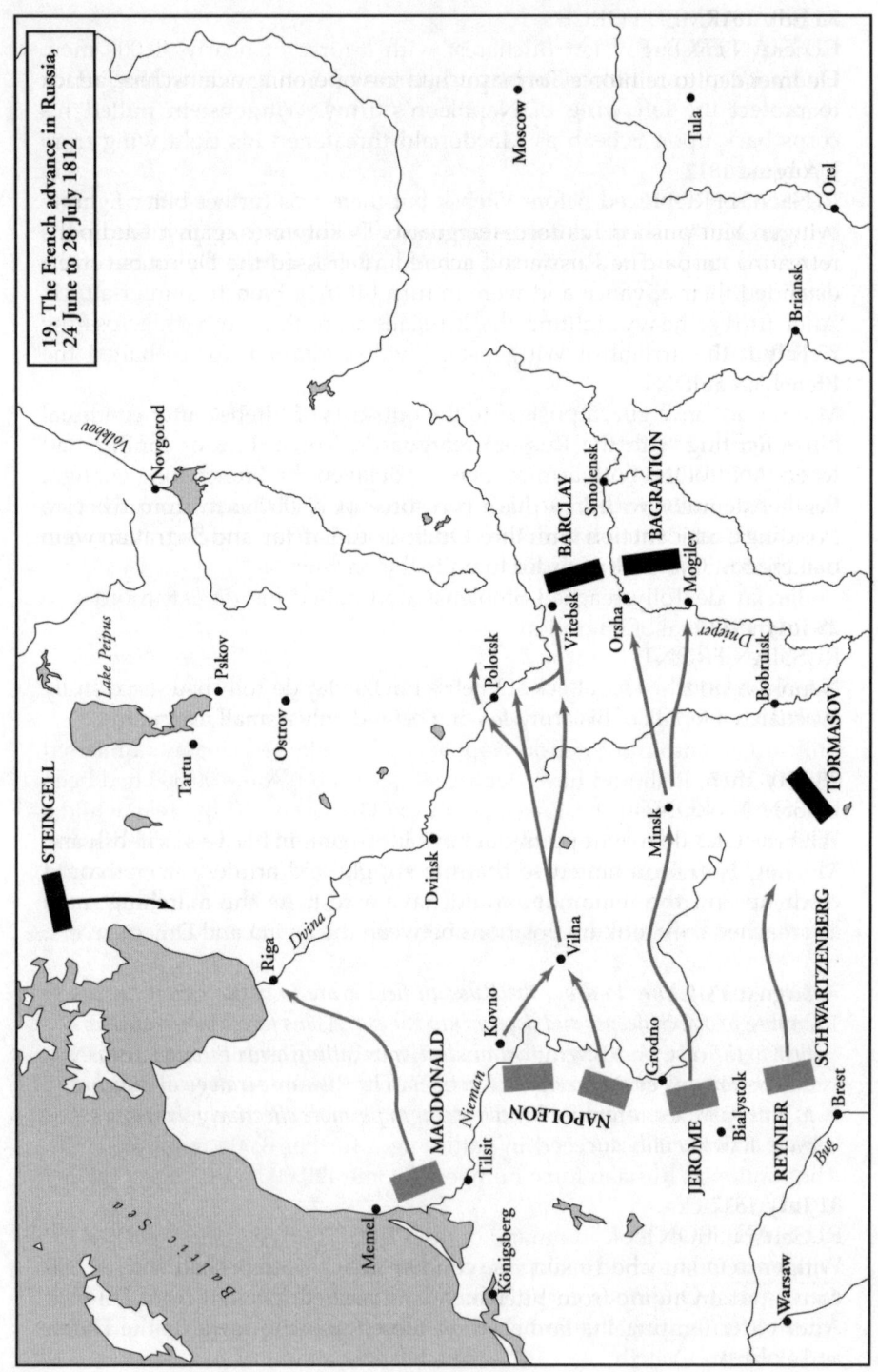

19. The French advance in Russia, 24 June to 28 July 1812

RUSSIA: ARMED FORCES
General Tshitshagov left Bucharest with a force of nearly 40,000 men. He intended to reinforce Tormasov's forces operating against the French rear.

1 August 1812
RUSSIAN FRONT
Wittgenstein pushed his forces aggressively forward against Oudinot's retreating corps. The Russians reached and crossed the Dvina but overextended their advance and were in turn hit by a French counter-attack. After further heavy fighting the Russians were thrown back across the river but the arrival of Wittgenstein with additional forces halted the French assault.

2 August 1812
RUSSIAN FRONT
Wittgenstein continued to place pressure upon Oudinot's forces before Polotsk. Under intense pressure Oudinot called for support. Napoleon detached St Cyr's corps to aid him.

Barclay de Tolly reached Smolensk and halted his retreat in order to await the arrival of Bagration.

3 August 1812
RUSSIAN FRONT
Still situated around Vitebsk, Napoleon's Grande Armée now numbered 185,000 men. It should have deployed 375,000 but some 90,000 had been detached to contain the Russians on the Dvina and in the rear while a further 100,000 had dropped out due to fatigue, battle loss and disease. The mighty French army was bleeding to death. Of the 65,000 men that the combined corps of Oudinot and St Cyr should have had at Polotsk, only 35,000 were still with the fighting units.[4]

4 August 1812
RUSSIAN FRONT
Barclay de Tolly and Bagration finally united their armies near Smolensk with the arrival of Bagration's force. Barclay assumed overall command but both armies remained individual units rather than joining as one whole. Barclay did succeed in gathering a further 8,000 reinforcements. The combined Russian force numbered some 120,000 men, plus a further 10,000 Cossacks.

General Junot took command of the VIII Corps, which had reached the Dniepr at Orsha and linked up with Davout. Napoleon had arrayed his forces out on an arc from Vitebsk, Murat and Ney being deployed near Rudnya, the Imperial Guard at Vitebsk itself, while Eugene had elements at Surazh and Velizh.

5 August 1812
RUSSIAN FRONT
St Cyr moved his corps up to support Oudinot's continued battle against Wittgenstein.

8 August 1812
RUSSIAN FRONT
Barclay de Tolly launched a counter-attack against the French deployed near Rudnya. Some 3,000 French cavalry led by General Sebastiani intercepted the 7,000-strong Cossack advance guard under General Platov near Inkovo. After a hard action the Russians defeated the French, inflicting heavy losses. Unfortunately, after this encouraging start to his offensive, Barclay de Tolly became nervous that he would draw Napoleon's entire army upon himself and therefore elected to break off the action and withdraw.

Napoleon, with 230,000 men, did indeed renew his advance, hoping to bring the Russians to battle around Smolensk. Barclay, despite his abortive counter-attack, still intended to make a stand at Smolensk, offering Napoleon the set-piece battle he desired.

General Poniatowski's V Corps marched across the Dniepr at Mogilev to form the southern wing of Napoleon's main force. To the rear the French IV Cavalry Corps marched west to attack the isolated Russian garrison of Bobruisk.

9 August 1812
RUSSIAN FRONT
Napoleon began pulling in the left flank units of his main army to bring them across the Dniepr so as to approach Smolensk from the south-west.

10 August 1812
RUSSIAN FRONT
Oudinot and St Cyr abandoned their attacks north of Polotsk and retired back to positions around the town. The Russians followed cautiously.

Napoleon continued the concentration and forward movement of the Grande Armée across the Dniepr.

IBERIAN FRONT
Under continued pressure from Wellington's army, Joseph evacuated his forces from Madrid, pulling them back upon Valencia.

11 August 1812
RUSSIAN FRONT
Barclay de Tolly decided to resume his offensive against the French around Rudnya once more.

12 August 1812
RUSSIAN FRONT
Schwartzenberg, with 18,000 men, attacked and defeated 12,000 men of Tormasov's force at Gorodechna, close to Kobrin. After a day of bitter fighting the Russians withdrew during the night.

13 August 1812
RUSSIAN FRONT
Tormasov continued to pull his forces back as Reynier and Schwartzenberg increased the pressure on his exposed positions.

IBERIAN FRONT
Wellington entered Madrid to an overwhelming welcome from the populace. The French rearguard force of 1,700 men surrendered. Wellington also captured large stocks of supplies and 180 guns. Joseph ordered Soult to bring his forces up from the south to aid him but Soult refused and stayed where he was.

14 August 1812
RUSSIAN FRONT
Napoleon had brought his army fully across the Dniepr and began a general advance upon Smolensk. After nearly two months of campaigning the French army had lost in excess of 100,000 men, mainly through sickness, leaving Napoleon with around 182,000 men to push towards Smolensk.

15 August 1812
RUSSIAN FRONT
A Russian rearguard detachment at Krasnoi was struck by Murat's cavalry and forced back after hard fighting. The French were now advancing rapidly upon Smolensk.

16 August 1812
RUSSIAN FRONT
The French caught a detachment of Bagration's army on the south bank of the Dniepr near Smolensk and launch an uninspired frontal assault.

Oudinot and St Cyr renewed their attacks against Wittgenstein. The Russians had been planning to launch an attack against the French garrison of Daugavpils but instead brought their forces back upon Polotsk.

17 August 1812
RUSSIAN FRONT
Bagration pushed additional forces into the defence of Smolensk but under intense French attack was forced to fall back into the suburbs. After a day of heavy fighting the French had penetrated deeper into the town. The battle had cost the Russians 6,000 men but the French had lost 8,500.

Oudinot and St Cyr, with 35,000 men, were struck by Wittgenstein's 28,000 Russians around Polotsk. After a day of bitter fighting Oudinot decided to retreat but was injured and compelled to hand over command to St Cyr.

18 August 1812
RUSSIAN FRONT
After another day's bitter fighting the Russians abandoned Smolensk. However, they established defensive positions on the northern bank of the Dniepr to oppose any continued French advance.

St Cyr decided against a withdrawal from Polotsk and launched a fierce counter-attack, forcing Wittgenstein back after another day of hard fighting. The two-day battle had cost the French 6,000 men killed or wounded and the Russians 5,500.

IBERIAN FRONT
Astorga fell to the Spanish. Having deliberately refused to obey Joseph's order to come to his aid, Soult decided to evacuate his forces from Andalusia and march to join him at Valencia. The decision was made more by necessity following Wellington's occupation of Madrid than through any desire to follow Joseph's orders.

19 August 1812
RUSSIAN FRONT
After remaining on the north bank of the Dniepr all day Barclay began to pull back towards nightfall. The rearguard of 40,000 men was attacked by Ney's corps of 30,000 men at Valutino but by adopting a defensive position in difficult terrain was able to avoid defeat.

After four days of hard fighting around Smolensk the French had lost almost 20,000 men to a Russian loss of 15,000. General Junot's failure to swing his corps behind the Russian army enabled Barclay to keep his line of retreat clear.

In the absence of a request for peace from Alexander, Napoleon was faced with the choice of marching his army deeper into Russia to try and engage the Russian army and inflict a knockout blow or consolidate the gains he had already made. He opted to continue the advance.

Having finally managed to bring the Russians to battle around Smolensk, Napoleon had failed to inflict the crushing defeat he so desperately needed. Using uninspired frontal tactics to break through the Russian army, he had suffered more losses than the enemy, accelerating the continued weakening of his own army.

20 August 1812
RUSSIAN FRONT
The Russian withdrawal continued with further fighting between their rearguard and the French van. Tsar Alexander dismissed Barclay de Tolly

from command of the Russian armies. He decided to appoint Marshal Kutuzov.

23 August 1812
RUSSIAN FRONT
The Russian garrison of Riga, commanded by General Lewis, attacked Macdonald's corps and inflicted heavy losses.

24 August 1812
RUSSIAN FRONT
General Lewis, having inflicted a sharp reverse on the French the previous day, drew his men back to their positions around Riga.

IBERIAN FRONT
Marshal Soult raised his siege of Cádiz and began to withdraw his forces from Andalusia.

27 August 1812
RUSSIAN FRONT
General Miloradovich brought up 15,000 reinforcements to join the main Russian army.

IBERIAN FRONT
Spanish forces stormed Seville.

FRANCE: THE MARSHALATE
General St Cyr was promoted to Marshal after his excellent performance at the Battle of Polotsk.

28 August 1812
RUSSIAN FRONT
Napoleon began the push towards Moscow. Murat again led with the cavalry, while the marching infantry struggled to keep up. By now the main French thrust consisted of just over 130,000 men with around 550 cannon.

29 August 1812
RUSSIAN FRONT
Kutuzov arrived to take command of the Russian armies west of Moscow from Barclay de Tolly. Barclay remained in command of his own force and Bagration of his, but Kutuzov had overall command. His force comprised 132,000 men and 600 cannon. He aimed to make a stand at Borodino, giving Napoleon a second chance at a major battle.

Tormasov had drawn his army back upon Lutsk and established a defensive position along the Styr river. Schwartzenberg had cautiously followed and adopted a strong line against the Russians.

September 1812
FRANCE: ARMED FORCES
In France the levy of the class of 1813 began. Napoleon called upon 137,000 men.

4 September 1812
RUSSIAN FRONT
Kutuzov reached Borodino and halted his retreat. A further 10,000 troops were sent forward to reinforce his army.

5 September 1812
RUSSIAN FRONT
The French, with 30,000 men, brought some 20,000 Russians on the left wing under attack around Schwardino. French losses were 4,000 to 6,000 Russian casualties.

Marshal Victor led his 34,000 strong IX Corps across the Niemen at Kovno to reinforce the Grande Armée. He marched for Smolensk where he would go into quarters.

6 September 1812
RUSSIAN FRONT
Kutuzov deployed his army in a strong but needlessly vulnerable position before Borodino, with his flanks exposed. The Russians had strengthened their positions with earth redoubts that had an excellent field of fire and would prove crucial to the stability of their defences.

Napoleon, ill and not up to his usual form, opted to attack the Russians frontally while Davout moved around the left flank. Davout had suggested a wide sweep to get into the Russian rear but Napoleon opted for a closer envelopment and frontal attacks. With 130,000 men and 580 cannon, the French planned to pound away at Kutuzov's force. Both sides spent the day deploying, there being little action other than by small units.

In the three weeks of fighting and advancing following the crossing of the Dniepr, the French main force had lost a further 38,000 men, many due to the fighting around Smolensk but there was still continual attrition due to sickness and fatigue.

7 September 1812
RUSSIAN FRONT
Napoleon launched his attack against Kutuzov at Borodino. Rather than press the attack against the vulnerable Russian flanks, Napoleon unleashed a series of frontal assaults against strongly defended and heavily fortified Russian positions. The Russians, committing their reserves, also launched a series of fierce counter-attacks as the battle degenerated into a bloodbath. As the French made progress in the centre the Russians moved up a concentrated force to counter-attack but this was struck by a massed

battery of French artillery and broken up. By evening the French had captured the Great Redoubt in the centre of the Russian line, compelling Kutuzov to order a retreat towards Kaluga. In this most bloody battle of the entire campaign the Russians had lost 44,000 men, including General Bagration killed, and the French 28,000, nearly fifty of their generals being killed or wounded. Napoleon could now advance upon Moscow with his remaining men and hope that Tsar Alexander would seek terms.

The French victory at Borodino had come at an immense cost, dwarfed only by the massive casualties suffered by the Russians. Bloody though the victory may have been, the last few miles on the road to Moscow now lay open to the French army. However, Tsar Alexander still refused to come to terms and so the objective of the French campaign remained unfulfilled.

10 September 1812
RUSSIAN FRONT
Miloradovich, covering the Russian retreat with his rearguard force, made a stand at Krimskoye and inflicted a sharp reverse on the French. After a day of bloody fighting a further 2,000 French troops had been killed or wounded.

14 September 1812
RUSSIAN FRONT
Kutuzov's army, now just 70,000 strong, marched into and through Moscow, abandoning it to Napoleon, whose army entered later in the day, now numbering just 95,000 men. The Russian authorities had evacuated the city, leaving the French troops free to plunder. Kutuzov marched his men east of the city, towards Ryazan.

Tshitshagov completed his march from the south and reached Lutsk where he joined forces with Tormasov. This combined Russian force numbered 65,000 men, outnumbering the 40,000 available to Reynier and Schwartzenberg.

15 September 1812
RUSSIAN FRONT
The Great Fire of Moscow began as partisans left behind by the Russians spread disorder through the deserted city. Many of the wooden buildings burned down.

Murat, with 30,000 men, moved east of Moscow in pursuit of Kutuzov's retiring army. However, unlike his earlier advances, he moved cautiously and remained at a distance from the Russians.

Faced by a sizeable Russian force along the Styr, Schwartzenberg abandoned his positions along the river and withdrew upon Brest Litovsk.

16 September 1812
RUSSIAN FRONT
Kutuzov moved south, marching his force towards Podolsk.

18 September 1812
RUSSIAN FRONT
Kutuzov reached Podolsk and halted his army. The French had pushed Murat out towards Ryazan while Poniatowski had advanced along the road towards Podolsk. Bessières deployed elements of the Imperial Guard on the road to Kaluga.

19 September 1812
IBERIAN FRONT
Wellington besieged Burgos. The defending French garrison of 2,000, detached from the Army of the North, was commanded by General Dubreton. After weeks of refusal to obey his orders, Soult finally recognised that Wellington posed the main threat to the French field armies in Spain and agreed to move his forces up from the south to aid Joseph.

20 September 1812
RUSSIAN FRONT
Kutuzov marched to Kaluga in order to pose a threat to Napoleon's lines of communication between Moscow and Smolensk. Murat, having followed the Russian line of march, approached Podolsk.

Russian reinforcements were landed in Riga from Finland, bringing the garrison up to 22,000 men.

22 September 1812
RUSSIAN FRONT
Murat deployed against Kutuzov's right flank while Poniatowski and Bessières moved to face the Russians frontally.

26 September 1812
RUSSIAN FRONT
With French pressure building up against him, Kutuzov abandoned his positions and began to fall back upon Tarutino.

The Russians launched a renewed assault out of Riga and struck General Yorck's Prussian detachment of Macdonald's corps.

27 September 1812
RUSSIAN FRONT
There was further bitter fighting around Riga as the Russians pressed their attacks.

28 September 1812
RUSSIAN FRONT
General Yorck managed to gain the upper hand in the bitter fighting around Riga and compelled the Russians to pull back into the city.

29 September 1812
RUSSIAN FRONT
Having failed to break the French hold around Riga the Russian reinforce-
ments from Finland marched inland to join Wittgenstein's detachment at
Polotsk.

2 October 1812
RUSSIAN FRONT
Kutuzov had drawn back to Tarutino and deployed into strong defensive
positions along the Nara river. During his marches around the envi-
rons of Moscow the Russians had sent up considerable reinforcements to
Kutuzov and also to Wittgenstein at Polotsk. Kutuzov's army now numbered 110,000 men while Wittgenstein numbered some 40,000. General
Winzingerode had been deployed north of Moscow to threaten the French
arc around the city.

4 October 1812
RUSSIAN FRONT
After two weeks of waiting, Napoleon wrote to Tsar Alexander to offer
him peace terms. The letter was delivered to Kutuzov and passed on to
Alexander, who, aware of the desperate state of the French army, did not
answer. Napoleon debated with his marshals over the coming weeks
whether to march north towards St Petersburg or not. His marshals were
not keen to undertake such a long march so late in the year.

9 October 1812
RUSSIAN FRONT
Schwartzenberg deployed elements of his corps before Brest Litovsk.
Tshitshagov, who had taken command of the combined Russian force in
the south, had followed and took up positions opposite the Austrians.

10 October 1812
RUSSIAN FRONT
Tshitshagov moved against Schwartzenberg, compelling the latter to pull
his men back across the Bug upon Warsaw and Bialystok. The Russians
declined to follow across the river. The Austrians still had detachments
deployed blocking the Russians at Mozyr and Bobruisk.

14 October 1812
RUSSIAN FRONT
Napoleon again wrote to Tsar Alexander to offer terms but, after negotiations between the French representative and the Russians at Kutuzov's
headquarters, was refused.

17 October 1812
RUSSIAN FRONT
Napoleon decided that the army must withdraw from Moscow and issued orders that preparations be made to pull back. Food had begun to run low during the month the French had waited in Moscow for the Russians to seek terms. With that obviously not about to happen, the army had no option but to leave the city.

18 October 1812
RUSSIAN FRONT
Napoleon, having realised that Alexander was not going to come to terms, and that his army was exposed to the approaching winter and increasing Russian army, began the retreat of French forces from Moscow. After receiving limited reinforcements during its month long stay in Moscow, Napoleon's army now numbered 103,000 men.

West of the city, Kutuzov, with 36,000 men, launched a surprise attack across the Nara river against Murat's 18,000 unprepared troops at Vinkovo. In bitter fighting Murat only just managed to extricate his force from a Russians encirclement effort but lost 3,500 men and forty cannon to a Russian loss of just 1,500.

Wittgenstein, with 40,000 men, attacked the 30,0000 French troops of St Cyr near Polotsk. The French were hard pressed and pushed back upon the town. St Cyr remained in command of both his and Oudinot's corps, Oudinot not having recovered from his wounds yet.

19 October 1812
RUSSIAN FRONT
Napoleon left Moscow. He planned to pull his men back to Smolensk, to see out the Russian winter there. Instead of retracing his steps though he aimed to move to the south-west, via Kaluga, in order to obtain fresh food and forage but more importantly to threaten Kutuzov's flank and prevent the Russians from blocking his line of march. The French army took with it a vast train of wagons loaded with the plunder of Moscow, rather than the supplies they would need to keep them going through the snow.

In a second day of heavy fighting, Wittgenstein forced the French out of Polotsk and back to the west. St Cyr, who had been wounded in the battle, aimed to cover the lines of communication with Vilna as they retired.

22 October 1812
RUSSIAN FRONT
Russian forces entered Moscow as the last units of the Grande Armée left the city. As he manoeuvred to clear his line of march, Poniatowski recaptured Vereya from Kutuzov's army. Realising Napoleon's plan to turn his position, Kutuzov moved to intercept the French by pushing units forward to Maloyaroslavets.

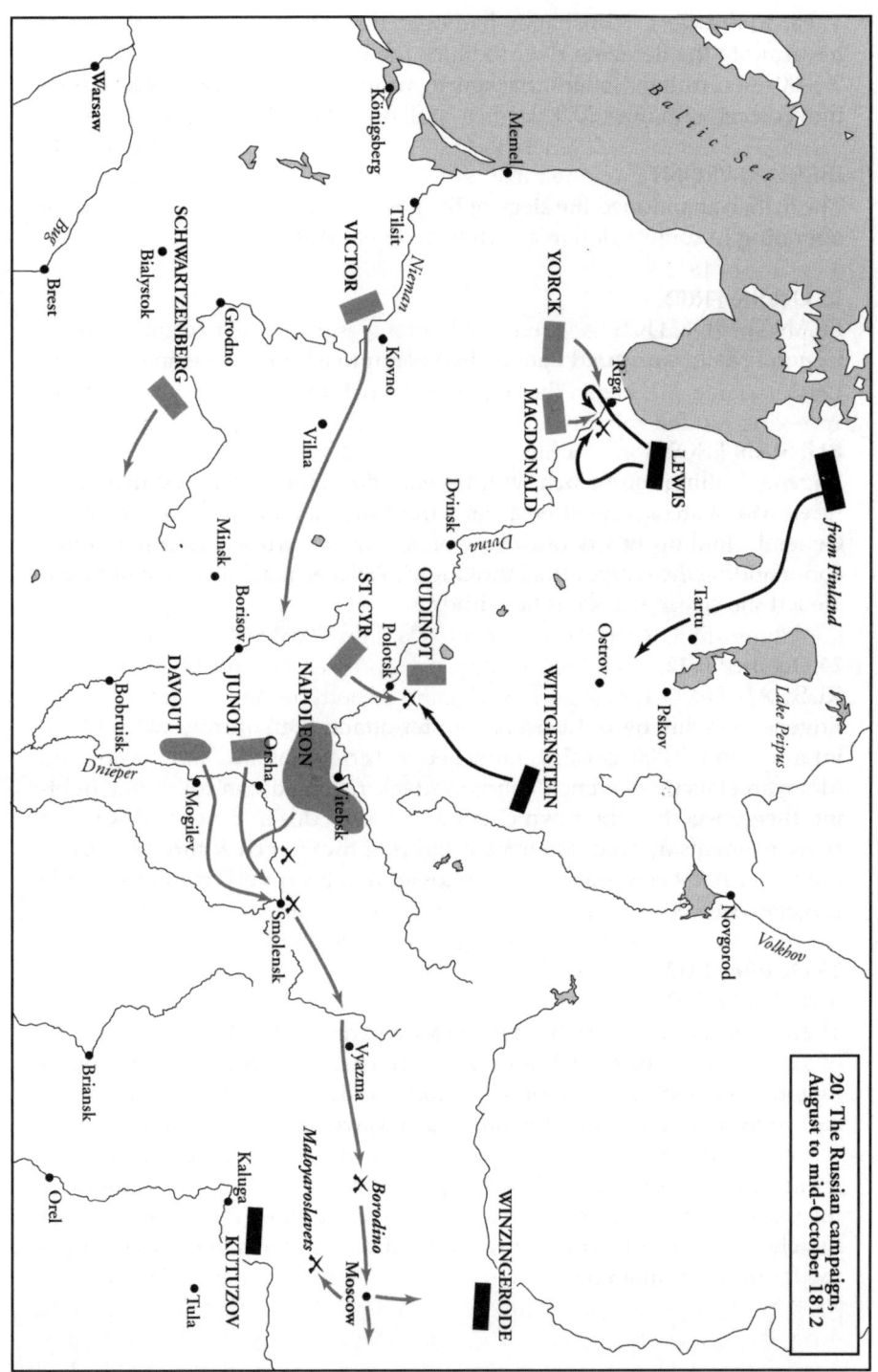

20. The Russian campaign,
August to mid-October 1812

Far to the west, Tshitshagov had been instructed to move with part of his army to the Berezina river to block the French line of retreat. Leaving 27,000 men under General Sacken to watch the Austrians, Tshitshagov moved east with over 30,000.

IBERIAN FRONT
The British abandoned the siege of Burgos. Soult, Clausel and Joseph were operating in conjunction in an effort to defeat Wellington.

23 October 1812
FRANCE: POLITICS
General Malet conspired against Napoleon in an effort to gain control of Paris.

RUSSIAN FRONT
Eugene, leading the French withdrawal with a force of 15,000 men, captured Maloyaroslavets after a hard fight against advanced elements of General Dukhturov's detachment of Kutuzov's army. General Mortier, commanding the rearguard of the Grande Armée, marched out of Moscow. He left the city in flames as he withdrew.

24 October 1812
RUSSIAN FRONT
Eugene was hit by a Russian counter-attack. Dukhturov, with 12,000 infantry and 3,000 cavalry, launched a furious attack and recaptured Maloyaroslavets. A French counter-attack regained control. Bitter fighting then ensued as the town changed hands a dozen times and Russian reinforcements arrived. After hard fighting the French secured the town but losses had been heavy. Russian losses had been 6,000 casualties while Eugene lost 5,000.

25 October 1812
RUSSIAN FRONT
There was further heavy fighting at Maloyaroslavets. Due to the severity of the action Napoleon, whose main forces had now deployed to support Eugene, decided against another assault and decided instead to turn north and resume his retreat via the previously traversed advance route.

General Platov's Cossacks launched an audacious attack against the French at Gorodnya and almost captured Napoleon. Other elements of the Cossack force continued to harass the rear of the French column as it marched, picking off stragglers and small detachments that ventured out too far from the main body.

26 October 1812
RUSSIAN FRONT
Mortier and Junot deployed to the front of the Grande Armée and launched attacks towards Smolensk. Davout commanded the rearguard, which was still at Borovsk.

27 October 1812
RUSSIAN FRONT
Kutuzov began to push his army along a parallel route to the French with the aim of reaching Vyazma. Miloradovich was to attack at Gzhatsk with a force of 25,000 men.

29 October 1812
RUSSIAN FRONT
St Cyr, retreating from Polotsk, linked up with Victor's reserve corps at Lukomlia. The combined force numbered 35,000 men and came under Victor's command.

30 October 1812
RUSSIAN FRONT
Victor determined to launch a counter-attack to drive back Wittgenstein's advancing unit. To the west, Schwartzenberg launched an attack against Sacken's force after crossing the Bug.

31 October 1812
RUSSIAN FRONT
The French retreat was progressing steadily but the army had become strung out in a column nearly seventy miles long. The advance guard had reached Vyazma while Murat was at Federovskoye and Poniatowski and Eugene were strung out near Gzhatsk. Davout still commanded the rearguard. In order to allow the army to concentrate, Napoleon ordered the advance guard to halt.

Victor marched to attack Wittgenstein but then changed his mind and abandoned the effort. Wittgenstein though took advantage of the French indecision and launched an attack himself, driving Victor back towards Senno.

IBERIAN FRONT
Wellington pulled his forces out of Madrid. The Army of Portugal had been reorganised by General Clausel and began to advance north of Madrid to threaten Wellington's lines.

1 November 1812
RUSSIAN FRONT
Miloradovich launched an attack upon the French rearguard, which had now reached Gzhatsk. To the west Schwartzenberg pushed east to

Bialystok while Reynier deployed to cover Sacken in order to protect Schwartzenberg's rear against attack.

2 November 1812
RUSSIAN FRONT
The Grande Armée resumed its retreat, having gathered its remaining 60,000 men together around Vyazma. It again became strung out in a column, but now only thirty miles long.

IBERIAN FRONT
Soult and Joseph recaptured Madrid without a fight. Wellington was pulling his army back to Ciudad Rodrigo. Joseph combined his forces around the city, gathering together a force of nearly 100,000 men.

3 November 1812
RUSSIAN FRONT
Davout's I Corps was attacked by Miloradovich's infantry and Platov's Cossacks at Vyazma. Napoleon sent forces to extricate Davout, who managed, with some difficulty, to break out to the west but at the cost of most of his men.

4 November 1812
RUSSIAN FRONT
Snow had begun to fall, slowing the French withdrawal and bringing yet more difficulties to an already difficult march. As the temperature plummeted the tin buttons on the French uniforms turned to dust, increasing the misery of his already demoralised men. To make matters worse the activities of the Cossacks intensified. French troops began to abandon their plunder and heavy equipment while deaths among the cavalry and pack horses soared.

Wittgenstein had detached a corps under General La Harpe from his main force in order to attack Vitebsk.

6 November 1812
RUSSIAN FRONT
Tshitshagov reached Slonim as his pushed forward towards Minsk and the Berezina.

7 November 1812
RUSSIAN FRONT
La Harpe launched an attack upon Vitebsk and took the town, a large portion of the French garrison surrendering to him.

8 November 1812
RUSSIAN FRONT
Kutusov reached Yelnya with his army. He had abandoned a close pursuit of the French, leaving the Cossacks to continually harass them instead.

Tshitshagov resumed his advance after a short rest at Slonim, aiming directly for Minsk.

9 November 1812
RUSSIAN FRONT
The leading elements of the Grande Armée reached Smolensk. The withdrawal had degenerated into a long column of straggling soldiers. Of the 103,000 who had marched out of Moscow, just 42,000 remained, 18,000 more having been lost in the march from Vyazma to Smolensk. An element of Baraguey d'Hilliers' division, some 2,000 men, became separated from the rest of the army and was compelled to surrender to the Russians.

10 November 1812
RUSSIAN FRONT
Schwartzenberg, moving east in pursuit of Tshitshagov, pushed on from Volkovysk towards Slonim.

12 November 1812
RUSSIAN FRONT
The French column continued to march into Smolensk but rather than winter here, Napoleon decided he must pull the army back farther to the west. The starving Grande Armée ransacked the city's depots as discipline collapsed. Discipline had become so poor that the last units of the army did not leave the city until 17 November. Napoleon attempted to strengthen his central column by calling in the flanking corps as he withdrew. In all some 5,000 men joined the retreat, bringing French strength in the centre back up to 47,000 men.

13 November 1812
RUSSIAN FRONT
Generals Junot and Poniatowski, leading the French advance guard, approached Krasnoi.

14 November 1812
RUSSIAN FRONT
Eugene led the remnants of his corps into Smolensk after covering a difficult march via Dukhovschina. Napoleon left Smolensk with part of the army. Kutuzov's advance guards reached Krasnoi and became involved in fighting with the Imperial Guard close to the town.

In an effort to prevent Wittgenstein, with 50,000 men, from linking up with the main Russian forces near the Berezina, Marshal Victor launched a fierce attack at Lubomlia and halted the Russian advance. After a bloody battle the Russians pulled back, having lost over 3,000 men to a French loss of just under 3,000. Victor then began to pull his forces back towards the Berezina to link up with the remainder of the Grande Armée.

Schwartzenberg reached Slonim. Sacken attempted to evade Reynier's efforts to block him and move in pursuit of the Austrians.

15 November 1812
RUSSIAN FRONT
On the northern wing of the front, Marshal Macdonald launched a new attack upon the Russian forces threatening his positions around Riga. The Russians were compelled to pull back across the Dvina.

Eugene marched the remnants of his corps, only 5,000 men strong, out of Smolensk, just as Ney, who constituted the rearguard, entered the town.

The Imperial Guard attacked Miloradovich as he deployed close to Krasnoi. After bitter fighting the French managed to push their way into the town.

To the west the French garrison of Minsk launched a sortie against the approaching advance guard of General Tshitshagov's force. After a brisk battle the French were repulsed. As this battle was being fought Sacken attacked Reynier at Volkovysk and inflicted heavy losses upon the French. Schwartzenberg left a garrison of 6,000 men in Slonim and marched west once more to relieve the pressure on Reynier.

IBERIAN FRONT
Wellington, with 65,000 men, made a stand at Salamanca. Soult, with 80,000, did not attack so the British continued their withdrawal towards the Portuguese frontier.

16 November 1812
RUSSIAN FRONT
Davout pulled his corps out of Smolensk. Marshal Ney put his troops to work destroying all of the store houses in the town before he too pulled out.

Eugene's weak corps encountered Miloradovich blocking his march to Krasnoi. Despite being outnumbered the French attempted to force their way through the Russian line. After a hard fight Eugene abandoned his attempt and instead marched around the Russian force.

Elements of Tshitshagov's army entered Minsk and forced the 4,000-strong French garrison out of the town. The French retired upon Borisov. Sacken attacked Reynier again but was himself attacked from the rear by Schwartzenberg. After a confused battle Sacken managed to extricate his force and pull back upon Brest Litovsk.

17 November 1812
RUSSIAN FRONT
Marshal Ney pulled his troops out of Smolensk as he once again formed the rearguard of the Grande Armée. He left the store houses in the city ablaze.

Following Eugene's difficulty in retreating through Krasnoi, and with Ney and Davout still east of the town, Napoleon launched an assault upon Kutuzov with the 16,000 men of his Imperial Guard and smashed his way through after a hard fight. Despite this, Davout still came under heavy attack by Miloradovich but managed to escape. While Napoleon held open the escape route for Davout, Junot and Poniatowski pushed ahead towards Orsha. Ney had yet to reach Krasnoi and remained in extreme danger.

Sacken pulled back towards Brest Litovsk, pursued by Reynier. Schwartzenberg now moved his force towards Kobrin.

18 November 1812
RUSSIAN FRONT

Ney's rearguard corps, around 6,000 strong and still marching west to Krasnoi, was prevented from reaching Krasnoi itself by Miloradovich's blocking force. Unable to break through after two costly attacks, he attempted to march around the Russian flank. Under cover of the freezing night, he marched his remaining men to the west. All but 1,000 of his 6,000 men had been lost and they had had to leave behind all of their wagons and supplies they could not carry. Total French losses during the days of fighting around Krasnyi exceeded 25,000 men and 230 cannon.

19 November 1812
RUSSIAN FRONT

Marshal Ney, retreating on foot in the midst of his men, was joined by Eugene who, with 4,000 men, helped Ney fight off almost continuous Cossack attacks. The retreating column, which had set out from Smolensk some 45,000 strong, had largely reached Orsha but now numbered no more than 20,000 men. There were many more thousands of stragglers strung out behind those units that retained some semblance of fighting order.

20 November 1812
RUSSIAN FRONT

The Grande Armée successfully crossed the Dniepr at Orsha and pushed on towards Minsk. Between this city and the French lay the Berezina river, which Napoleon planned to cross at Borisov. Having failed to establish a blocking position on the Dniepr, the Russians aimed to trap and destroy the French force on the Berezina.

Sacken marched towards the Berezina at Borisov in order to threaten the French retreat. He attacked a French detachment forward of the town and inflicted heavy losses, capturing the bridge over the river in the course of the action.

22 November 1812
RUSSIAN FRONT

General Tshitshagov, having already captured Minsk, moved to capture the remaining bridges across the Berezina, severing the French line of retreat. He deployed his advance guard close to Borisov, supporting Sacken.

23 November 1812
RUSSIAN FRONT
Napoleon, aware that his line of retreat across the Berezina had been cut by the Russian capture of Borisov, sent Oudinot's corps, which had pulled back from the north to join the main column, forward to attack and draw off Tshitshagov. In a fierce battle the French recaptured Borisov but the vital bridge across the Berezina had been destroyed by the retreating Russians.

24 November 1812
RUSSIAN FRONT
Oudinot elected Studianka, seven miles north of Borisov, as the best crossing point for the Grande Armée and set the engineers to constructing three bridges across the river. Unfortunately the French had no bridging equipment so all of this day and the next was spent in the preparation of materials with which to erect the bridge. In order to divert Russian attention from the main French effort, a sizeable detachment of troops was sent south of Borisov.

While the French closed up to the Berezina, Kutuzov led his forces across the Dniepr at Kopys. Wittgenstein continued to press down from the north.

25 November 1812
RUSSIAN FRONT
Oudinot was steadily reinforced as Napoleon and the main body of the Grande Armée closed up to the Berezina near Borisov. Unfortunately for the French the river was not frozen, making its bridging that much more difficult. In order to ensure that the bridges they did build were sufficiently strong, General Elbe, commanding the bridging effort, decided to build two rather than three crossings. One bridge was built to carry the infantry forces, the other to carry the logistic train across.

Schwartzenberg deployed at Kobrin but was ordered by Napoleon to move his force up to Minsk.

26 November 1812
RUSSIAN FRONT
The long columns of retreating French troops, some 30,000 men still in fighting condition and another 60,000 camp followers and stragglers, began to cluster in the Borisov area as French engineers completed the bridges over the Berezina. By a supreme effort the French engineers built their bridges and Oudinot led the advance guard across.

Tshitshagov, taken in by the French diversionary efforts, mistakenly believed Napoleon would try to cross south of Borisov in order to link up with Schwartzenberg and therefore moved his men south, away from the area into which the Grande Armée was just arriving. Finding the Russians on the west bank considerably weakened, Oudinot had no difficulty in forcing them back and establishing a strong bridgehead. Ney then crossed to the west bank to take up positions while Victor's and Davout's corps, together with the Old Guard, took up positions before crossing the following day.

27 November 1812
RUSSIAN FRONT

Bitter fighting raged around the French perimeter on the east and west banks of the Berezina. The French pushed cavalry and artillery forces across the river to stabilise the west bank bridgehead. During the night the bridges had suffered two collapses and a further one during the afternoon. By a heroic effort the French engineers repaired them, allowing the French to continue to evacuate their force from the east bank. Victor protected the rear and late in the day came under attack from Wittgenstein's advance guard. Leaving behind a rearguard of 4,000 men at Borisov, Victor marched with the remainder upon Studianka. Wittgenstein's attack overran the rearguard and killed or captured the entire force.

Schwartzenberg began his march from Kobrin to Minsk. Reynier also received orders from Napoleon to move his force upon Minsk.

28 November 1812
RUSSIAN FRONT

During the morning Davout, Eugene and the Old Guard crossed the Berezina bridges to the west bank. Seeing these forces retire the mob of disorganised troops still on the east bank flooded the bridges, compelling Napoleon to force a passage with his own entourage.

After a day of bitter fighting against Wittgenstein, Victor disengaged the remnants of his corps and, in the winter darkness, pulled back across the river. With the overwhelming weight of the French army now on the west bank, Tshitshagov was pushed back and the line of withdrawal opened fully.

29 November 1812
RUSSIAN FRONT

Seeing the Russians closing in upon the Berezina bridges, General Elbe ordered his men to burn the crossing, stranding thousands on the east bank. Having saved the cadre of his army from destruction on the Berezina, Napoleon ordered the retreat to continue to Vilna. Kutuzov's main force now lagged far behind, its advance guard, led by General Miloradovich, reaching Borisov during the day. Napoleon had managed to save the remaining fighting units of the Grande Armée to fight another day. However, for those left behind there followed a terrible massacre as the Cossacks and Russian troops fell upon the trapped French soldiers and camp followers. French losses exceeded 25,000 soldiers killed or wounded and around 30,000 camp followers killed, nearly two thirds dying as they tried to cross the river after the bridges had been partially destroyed. Russian losses were around 10,000 men.

The escape of the French army across the Berezina had inflicted further crippling losses upon the French, but enabled the core of the army to continue its march to the west. Such were the scale of the losses that the Grande Armée was no longer an effective fighting force, having been reduced to no more than a ragged band of desperate troops.

1 December 1812
RUSSIAN FRONT
Reynier began his march from the area of Brest Litovsk towards Minsk.

4 December 1812
RUSSIAN FRONT
The Grande Armée reached Smorgoni, just 9,000 strong, as it continued its march towards Vilna.

5 December 1812
RUSSIAN FRONT
Napoleon left the Grande Armée at Smorgoni and rode for Paris in order to raise a new army and secure his position following Malet's attempt to seize power (he had declared Napoleon dead in Russia and attempted to overthrow the government).

The remaining men continued to withdraw under the command of Marshal Murat but the bulk of the army was reduced to a ragged band of stragglers, covered by Marshal Ney's rearguard. The Russians had given up their pursuit as the winter weather closed in even further, bitter cold being more of an enemy to the French troops now than the Russian Cossacks.

8 December 1812
RUSSIAN FRONT
The remnants of the Grande Armée, no more than 4,500 in fighting order with thousand more stragglers following, reached Vilna and ransacked the supply depots. Murat hurried to continue the retreat, leaving behind any soldiers who could not keep up. The French now made for Kovno. Some outlying units had joined up with the central column, bringing its numbers back up to 17,000 men.

10 December 1812
RUSSIAN FRONT
Marshal Macdonald received orders to make preparations to withdraw his corps from the Dvina.

11 December 1812
RUSSIAN FRONT
The French reached Kovno but it took another two days for the rearguard to reach the town. Their numbers had reduced again to around 4,000 fighting troops. Tshitshagov reached Vilna.

13 December 1812
RUSSIAN FRONT
Platov's Cossacks reached Kovno and hastened the French on towards East Prussia. Miloradovich reached Vilna.

14 December 1812
RUSSIAN FRONT
Schwartzenberg, uninformed as to the deterioration of the French army, but realising himself that they must have withdrawn from the Berezina upon Prussia, decamped from Slonim and began a march towards Bialystok.

The rearguard of the once Grande Armée, led by the ragged and dishevelled Marshal Ney, crossed the Niemen into East Prussia.

18 December 1812
RUSSIAN FRONT
Marshal Macdonald, until now scarcely informed of the scale of the defeat in the centre, was instructed to raise the siege of Riga and pull back to the Prussian frontier. Tshitshagov had already reached the Niemen.

19 December 1812
RUSSIAN FRONT
The remnants of the Grande Armée reached Konigsberg. Macdonald began his withdrawal. He split his force into two groups, an advance guard and rearguard (composed largely of Prussian troops under General Yorck) and marched towards Tilsit.

FRANCE: POLITICS
Napoleon reached Paris and began to secure his authority once again. He issued a bulletin announcing that the defeat in Russia was due to the bad weather but that he was alive and well.

IBERIAN FRONT
Napoleon ordered Joseph to establish his headquarters at Valladolid. Joseph was advised that his mission now was to protect the roads into France against any Allied advance. Despite Napoleon's order, Joseph remained in Madrid. Napoleon also drew off some of Joseph's troops to rebuild his armies but there were still around 200,000 troops in the Iberian Peninsula.

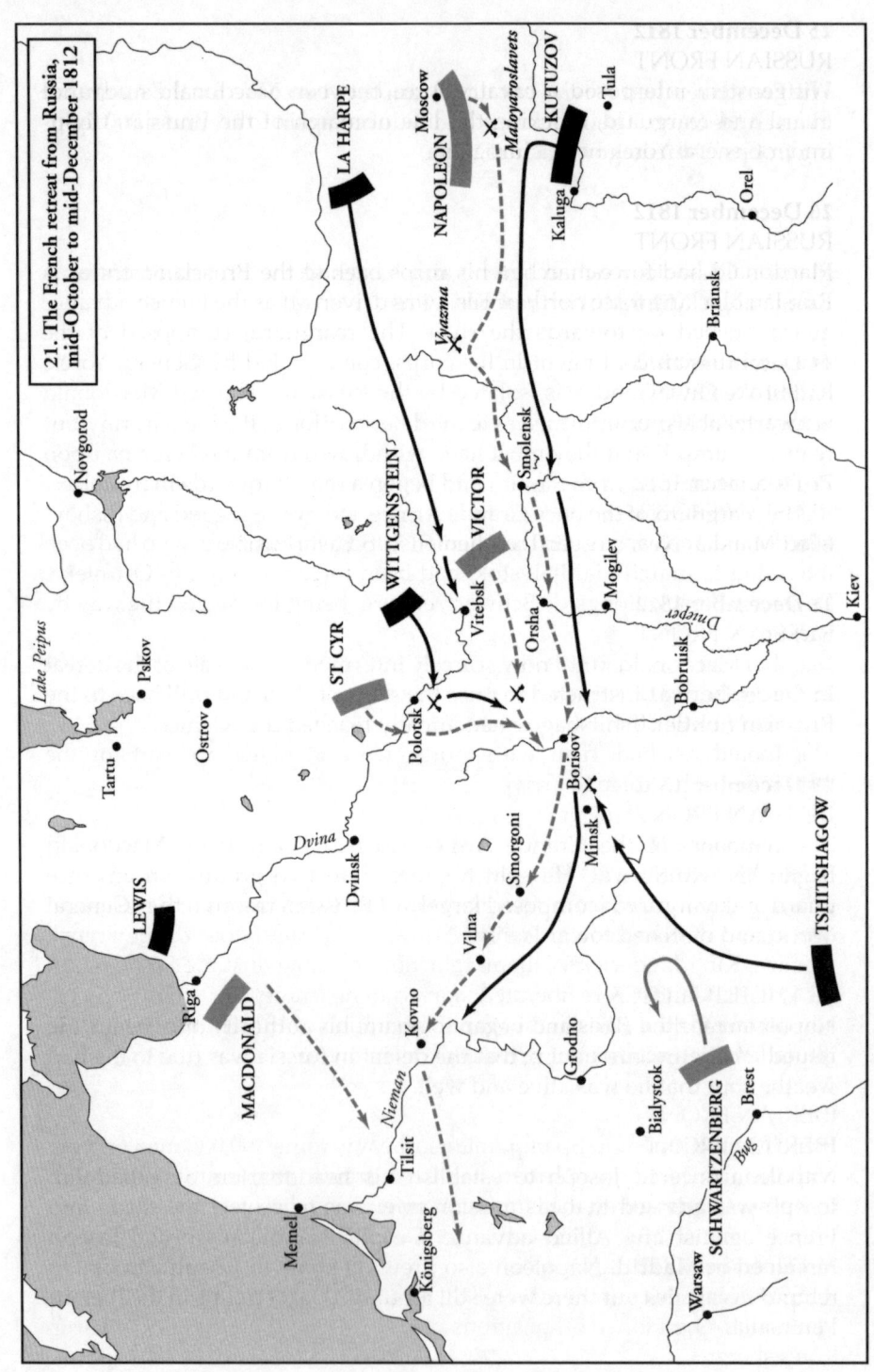

21. The French retreat from Russia, mid-October to mid-December 1812

Novgorod

Lake Peipus

Pskov

Ostrov

Tartu

Dvinsk

Dvina

LEWIS

Riga

MACDONALD

Nieman

Memel

Königsberg

Tilsit

Kovno

Grodno

Vilna

Smorgoni

Polotsk

ST CYR

WITTGENSTEIN

Vitebsk

VICTOR

Smolensk

Orsha

Mogilev

Dniester

Borisov

Minsk

Bobruisk

Kiev

TSHITSHAGOW

Bialystok

Brest

Bug

Warsaw

SCHWARTZENBERG

LA HARPE

Moscow

NAPOLEON

Vyazma

Maloyaroslavets

KUTUZOV

Kaluga

Tula

Orel

Briansk

284

25 December 1812
RUSSIAN FRONT
Wittgenstein interposed a cavalry force between Macdonald's advance guard and rearguard, blocking the line of march of the Prussian troops under General Yorck near Tauroggen.

26 December 1812
RUSSIAN FRONT
Macdonald had force-marched his corps back to the Prussian frontier. A Russian blocking force north of Tilsit was driven off as the French advance guard pushed on towards the river. The rearguard, composed of the mainly Prussian contingent in his corps, commanded by General Yorck, had broken away and was isolated by the Russians. This left Macdonald with just 7,000 men.

27 December 1812
RUSSIAN FRONT
Macdonald's advance guard reached Tilsit. Schwartzenberg, who had been intending to march via Bialystok, had been forced to retire to Ostroleka. Reynier fell back alongside Schwartzenberg, being harried all the way by Sacken.

28 December 1812
RUSSIAN FRONT
Macdonald reached Tilsit with more men and halted to wait for the remainder of his force to arrive.

30 December 1812
RUSSIAN FRONT
The Convention of Tauroggen between the Russians and the Prussian contingent of Napoleon's Grande Armée took Prussia out of the French alliance. King Frederick William, reluctant to act against the French until his Prussian lands were liberated, agreed to neutrality but would eventually declare for the allies in the War of Liberation of 1813. Publicly, the king refuted Yorck's actions but privately was in favour.

IBERIAN FRONT
French commitment to Spain remained heavy, some 200,000 men serving with the armies. Large numbers had been drawn off prior to the invasion of Russia to strengthen the Grande Armée, men who were now lost.

31 December 1812
RUSSIAN FRONT
Macdonald abandoned his positions around Tilsit and pulled back towards Konigsberg.

The campaign in Russia had cost the French and their allies upwards of 550,000 men killed, wounded, missing or captured, 175,000 horses lost and 1,200 cannon. Individual unit losses had been crippling. Davout's 72,000-strong I Corps had been reduced to just 2,300 men, the Guard to just 500 men fit for action and a further 800 sick. Of Napoleon's central army, which had pushed into Russia with 150,000 men in June, barely 6,500 were left.

Russian losses were around 250,000 men plus a further 50,000 Cossack cavalry. For the Russians this was a serious casualty return but for the French it was nothing short of disastrous. The crème of the French army, together with the very best of their allies, had been lost. More importantly though, the French defeat sent a message around Europe that the French were on the run, that Napoleon could be decisively defeated.

Notes

1. Clausewitz, *The Campaign of 1812 in Russia*, p. 12
2. Ibid, p. 52
3. Ibid.
4. Ibid, p. 60

CHAPTER IX

The War of Liberation

The disaster in Russia had virtually wiped out French strength in the east. Only the severity of the winter weather prevented the Russians from surging west but the French defeat galvanised resistance throughout the empire. 1813 would prove to be a decisive year, one during which the French capability to field fresh armies out of nothing was stunningly demonstrated, but also during which the Allies finally began to act in unison against Napoleon and his forces. As the main focus of the war remained fixed on the eastern front of the empire, the cancerous struggle that was the Peninsular War continued to drain French strength.

* 1813 *

1 January 1813
POLISH FRONT
Informed of Yorck's defection, Murat decided to continue the French retreat and ordered the remnants of the Grande Armée west across the Vistula.

3 January 1813
POLISH FRONT
Macdonald reached Konigsberg and linked up with Heudelet's division. Murat was already in the process of evacuating his forces from the city. Wittgenstein continued to pursue Macdonald's retreating force.

4 January 1813
POLISH FRONT
The French pulled the last of their units, Macdonald's corps and Heudelet's division, out of Konigsberg and began their withdrawal. The Austrian contingent had split away from the main component on the southern wing, under General Reynier and rather than pulling back upon Kalisch with the French, fell back upon Krakow. Negotiations between Schwartzenberg and his Russian counterpart, General Miloradovich, kept the two forces aware

287

of each other's movements. General Poniatowski, commanding the 9,000 strong Polish contingent of the Grande Armée, had retreated alongside the Austrians and would find himself isolated from the French in Galicia.

8 January 1813
POLISH FRONT

Yorck's Prussian corps, acting in conjunction with the Russians although officially they were neutral, occupied Konigsberg.

11 January 1813
FRANCE: ARMED FORCES

The Cohorts of the National Guards, raised during March 1812, were transferred into the regular field army. They comprised twenty-two regiments.

To augment the reformation of the French army after the disaster in Russia, Napoleon demanded the mobilisation of the classes of 1809 to 1812, a total of 100,000 men.[1]

12 January 1813
POLISH FRONT

Russian forces reached the Niemen river in strength and began to cross.

13 January 1813
POLISH FRONT

The Russian right wing, a force of 30,000 men under the command of General Wittgenstein, reached the Vistula river. Tshitshagov was marching upon Thorn with his force of 20,000 men while Kutuzov pushed his 30,000 towards Plock.

16 January 1813
POLISH FRONT

Wittgenstein detached 20,000 men from his unit to besiege the French garrison left behind in Danzig. General Rapp commanded the French troops inside the city.

To the west, the remnants of the Grande Armée, some 12,000 men, reached Posen.

17 January 1813
POLISH FRONT

Eugene de Beauharnais took command of the remnants of the French forces at Posen. Murat left the army and headed for Naples, with the remnants of his Neapolitan detachment, as quickly as he could.

Prussian forces under General Bulow began to raise reinforcements, officially to reinforce the French army, but in actual fact in order to fight against them once Frederick William declared for the Allies.

22 January 1813
GERMAN FRONT
King Frederick William of Prussia left Berlin for Breslau. He aimed to throw off his alliance with France, but wanted to settle his affairs with the Allies first.

24 January 1813
INTERNATIONAL POLITICS
Metternich, representing Austria, informed Napoleon that Austria was withdrawing from its alliance with France and was adopting a position of armed neutrality.

25 January 1813
GERMAN FRONT
The French had brought up 18,000 men from Italy to Germany. They deployed around Berlin and were formed as the XI Corps under St Cyr.

28 January 1813
POLISH FRONT
Tshitshagov's Russians reached Thorn as they continued their steady advance westwards.

30 January 1813
AUSTRIA: ARMED FORCES
Schwartzenberg took his corps out of the French army and continued his retreat into Galicia.

February 1813
FRANCE: ARMED FORCES
Napoleon made another demand for more troops to be mobilised. He took the unprecedented step of calling up classes ahead of their time, the 150,000 men of the class of 1814 being called upon. To reinforce the field armies, a further 8,000 naval marines were drafted into the army.[2]

Eugene gathered up as many troops as he could in Germany and formed a new army. The remnants of the Grande Armée of Russia was dispersed to form the garrisons of Stettin, Kustrin, Spandau and Glogau.

RUSSIA: ARMED FORCES
The Russian forces in Poland numbered just over 110,000 men, 70,000 being infantry and 30,000 cavalry.[3] As the advance of their main armies was slow they formed a number of free corps and sent these ahead to disrupt the French. They surged forward through Pomerania and eventually reached the Oder.

3 February 1813
PRUSSIA: ARMED FORCES
The Prussians began the enlistment of reserves and volunteer jaegers to

expand their army, which currently comprised 56,000 men with 236 cannon. The volunteer jaegers were men between the ages of 17 and 24 who armed and equipped themselves at their own expense, or at the expense of their communities.

5 February 1813
RUSSIA: ARMED FORCES
The Russians began the formation of a reserve army at Bialystok in order to reinforce the field army. Men were brought in and trained before being sent forward to reinforce or replace losses in the campaigning regiments.

7 February 1813
POLISH FRONT
Warsaw fell to Miloradovich's advancing Russians. Eugene had assembled around 15,000 survivors from Russia and the garrisons in East Prussia and Poland and deployed them around Posen and in a screen covering the line of the Vistula.

8 February 1813
POLISH FRONT
Tshitshagov reached Bromberg while Kutuzov reached Plock. Reynier's VII Corps was falling back before Kutuzov's advance and now turned to fall back upon Glogau.

9 February 1813
PRUSSIA: ARMED FORCES
King Frederick William issued a decree calling for the creation of a 'Landwehr'. The cost of equipping and clothing these soldiers would fall upon themselves and their communities. The decree was not enacted until March.

10 February 1813
POLISH FRONT
The Russians attacked Eugene's outlying forces along the Vistula.

11 February 1813
POLISH FRONT
Fighting continued around Posen as the Russians brought up additional troops.

12 February 1813
POLISH FRONT
Eugene ordered his forces to abandon the defence line along the Vistula. Garrisons were left behind to hold Thorn and Modlin. A new line would be established on the Oder.

15 February 1813
GERMAN FRONT
The French began to form their Corps of Observation on the Elbe around Magdeburg. It was commanded by General Lauriston and would later be renamed the V Corps.

16 February 1813
GERMAN FRONT
Russian free corps Cossacks crossed the Oder at Kustrin and harassed the French troops close to Berlin.

18 February 1813
GERMAN FRONT
Having abandoned Poland, Eugene reached Frankfurt on the Oder river. He linked up with St Cyr's XI Corps which had moved forward of Berlin, bringing his total force to around 30,000 men. Augereau remained in Berlin with another 6,000 men while there were a further 3,000 garrisoning Spandau. The V Corps was deployed at Magdeburg but was still in the process of formation. In order to secure the line of the Oder Eugene placed a garrison of 9,000 men in Stettin, 4,000 in Kustrin and 4,000 in Glogau.

Following the French through Poland, Wittgenstein was in Pomerania with 19,000 men while Kutuzov had reached Kalisch with 40,000. Sacken had 20,000 in the south, masking the movement of the Austrians towards Galicia.[4]

19 February 1813
GERMAN FRONT
The French VII Corps reached Glogau. Reynier's force had been reduced to just 9,000 men.

20 February 1813
GERMAN FRONT
Cossacks, operating behind Eugene's rear, broke into Berlin but then quickly fell back to the Oder.

22 February 1813
GERMAN FRONT
Eugene began to pull the French forces back from the Oder line, leaving behind garrisons to disrupt the Allied advance. Stettin, Kustrin, Glogau and Spandau were retained as strongholds and a force of 4,000 was left behind at Frankfurt. He intended to construct a defence line on the Elbe river. Had he concentrated his forces midway between the Oder and Berlin, Eugene could have maintained his positions but advice from Augereau convinced him to pull his men back.

28 February 1813
INTERNATIONAL POLITICS
The Convention of Kalisch established a secret Russo–Prussian alliance. King Frederick William III of Prussia dropped his neutrality and joined the Allies.

March 1813
INTERNATIONAL POLITICS
Metternich took Austria out of the French sphere and moved towards the Allies as Napoleon's position in Germany crumbled.

FRANCE: ARMED FORCES
The French began to form their 1st and 2nd Corps of Observation on the Rhine. Marshal Ney commanded the 1st Corps, which was deployed around Mayence, while Marshal Marmont commanded the 2nd Corps, also close to Mayence. These units would later go on to form the new III and IV Corps of Napoleon's reconstituted army in Germany. The Corps of Observation of Italy was formed under General Bertrand. It would later be split in two to form the IV Corps under Bertrand and XII Corps under Oudinot. Also under formation in Germany were the new I, II and VII Corps.

ALLIED PLANNING
Believing the French to be extremely weak in Germany, the Allies adopted a plan to march on a wide front to the Elbe. There they would concentrate the bulk of their armies on their left wing in order to keep the lines of communication to Austria open. Wittgenstein would hold the right wing with 19,000 Russian troops and 30,000 Prussians. He aimed to cross the Oder between Stettin and Kustrin. Blücher was to push forward from Silesia with 27,000 Prussian and 14,000 Russian troops towards Dresden on the left wing, with Kutuzov bringing a further 30,000 Russians behind. This left the Allied armies widely separated and vulnerable to counter-attack.

1 March 1813
GERMAN FRONT
Wittgenstein crossed the Oder near Kustrin. Eugene pulled his forces back to the west of Berlin.

3 March 1813
INTERNATIONAL POLITICS
Sweden, now led by Crown Prince Bernadotte, formerly Napoleon's marshal, agreed an alliance with Britain and gave a promise to enter the coalition against France. Swedish forces, approximately 50,000 strong, would shortly be shipped to Stralsund to join the Allied armies.

4 March 1813
GERMAN FRONT
Wittgenstein had sent a light force of 7,000 cavalry and 5,000 infantry ahead of his main force. They entered Berlin later in the day. Eugene now pulled his force, 30,000 strong and easily capable of tackling the weak Allied force, back upon Wittenberg. The detachment he had left behind at Frankfurt launched a break out attempt and marched to join up with the main force as it withdrew.

10 March 1813
GERMAN FRONT
Allied forces reached the Elbe near Torgau. Eugene had now brought his army back across the river, having deployed the XI Corps, with 18,000 men, at Wittenberg, while Davout was on the right with 17,000 men between Dresden and Torgau. Torgau was held by a Saxon detachment of 6,000 men under the command of General Thielmann. On the left, Eugene deployed Lauriston's V Corps with 35,000 men, grouping them around Magdeburg. He established the French headquarters at Leipzig while in the rear Marshal Victor was organising a reinforcement of 12,000 men along the Saale river.[5]

Having dispersed his army widely along the Elbe, Eugene received instructions to concentrate his forces around Magdeburg.

11 March 1813
FRANCE: MILITARY PLANNING
Napoleon informed Eugene of his plan of campaign in Germany once he had formed a new army for deployment along the Main river. The primary objective of the campaign was to be the relief of Danzig. The armies of the Main and Elbe were to converge upon Stettin before moving through Pomerania to Danzig. In order to divert Allied attentions from his main objective, he would use a smaller force to hold Allied attention around Dresden.

12 March 1813
GERMAN FRONT
French forces withdrew from Hamburg and pulled back upon Bremen.

16 March 1813
INTERNATIONAL POLITICS
Prussia declared war on France.

IBERIAN FRONT
Repeating his order of late 1812, Napoleon demanded that Joseph remove himself and his forces to Valladolid. Joseph relented but did not march all of his forces north, leaving a sizeable contingent to secure Madrid for his supporters.

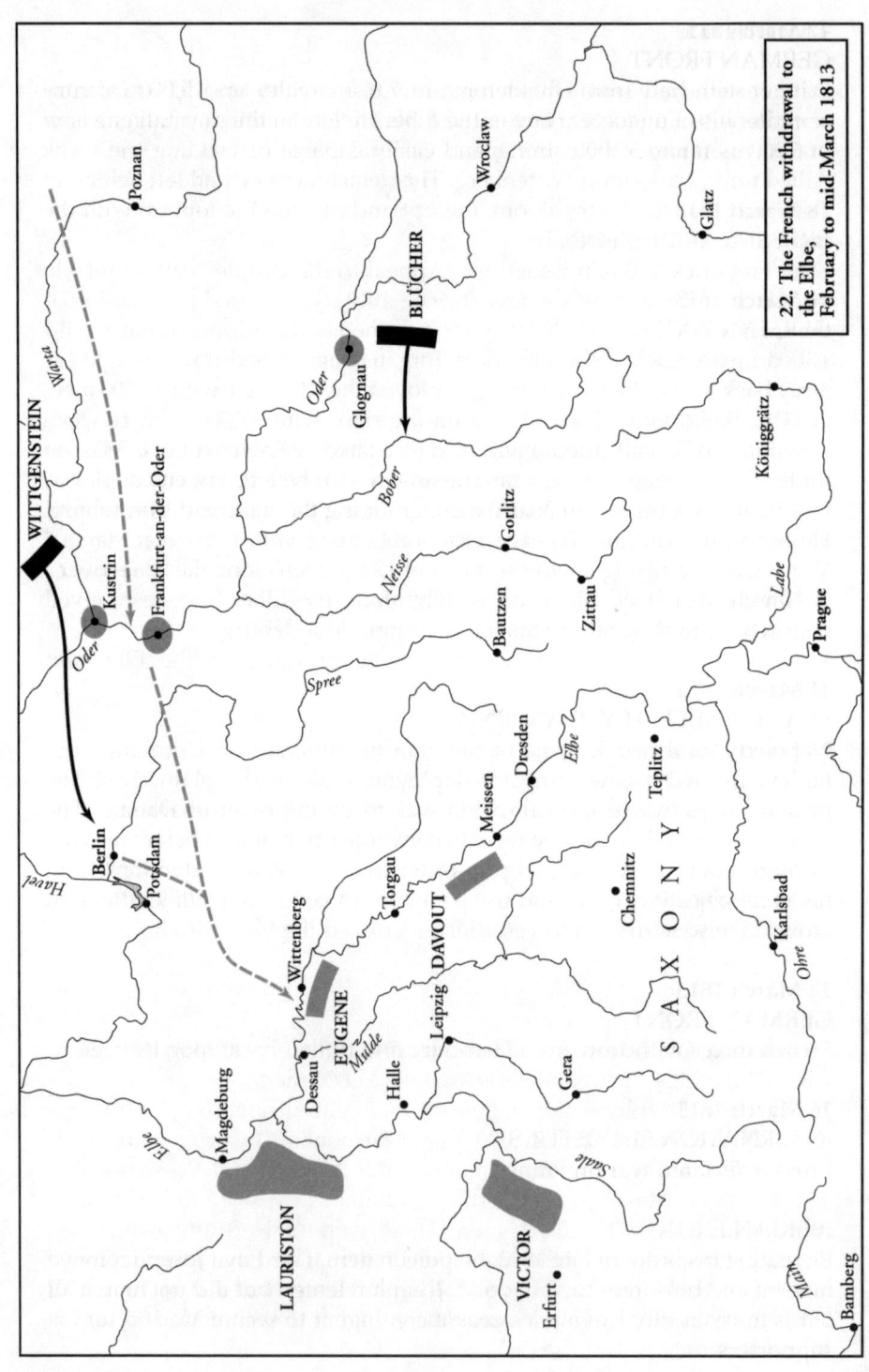

22. The French withdrawal to the Elbe, February to mid-March 1813

17 March 1813
GERMAN FRONT
Davout withdrew from Dresden in order to march to Magdeburg to concentrate with Eugene's army on the Elbe. He left behind a small garrison of 6,000 men under the command of General Durutte.

18 March 1813
PRUSSIA: ARMED FORCES
King Frederick William issued his 'Appeal to the People', calling for the populace to rise against the French. The military activated the creation of the *Landwehr*, a force of 100,000 poorly trained and equipped infantry and 11,000 cavalry.

GERMAN FRONT
A popular rising in Hamburg, recently evacuated by French troops, declared for the Allied cause. Prussian and Russian troops entered the city.

A 12,000-strong Swedish army under Prince Bernadotte began to land at Stralsund to aid the Allied armies.

20 March 1813
GERMAN FRONT
Wittgenstein sent forces forward from Berlin towards the Elbe and Magdeburg.

25 March 1813
GERMAN FRONT
General Durutte withdrew from Dresden as the Allies approached.

27 March 1813
GERMAN FRONT
Dresden fell to Prussian forces. Blücher crossed the Elbe with his army.

31 March 1813
GERMAN FRONT
Eugene had concentrated 50,000 men and 4,000 cavalry at Magdeburg and covered the Elbe upstream with Davout's 11,000 men.

On the Main river front the French had concentrated Ney's III Corps around Schweinfurt, with 40,000 men, Marmont's VI Corps, with 25,000 men, at Hanau, the Imperial Guard under Mortier and Bessières with 16,000 men at Mayence and Bertrand's Italian Corps of Observation en route from Italy with 40,000 men. There were still a number of allied German troops in the field with the French. The Bavarians deployed a force of 8,000 men at Bayreuth, Baden-Hesse had a detachment of 8,000 at Wurzburg while Wurttemberg had a detachment of 7,000 at Mergentheim.

FRANCE: MILITARY PLANNING

Having realised that his forces were insufficient for a drive to relieve Danzig, Napoleon amended his campaign plan to concentrate on the destruction of the Allied forces on the Elbe line and ensure the safety of Saxony. His army was ordered to concentrate upon Erfurt towards the end of April.

2 April 1813
GERMAN FRONT
The Allies defeated a force of 2,000 French reinforcements at Luneberg.

3 April 1813
FRANCE: ARMED FORCES
Napoleon made further demands for troops for the army. Since the defeat in Russia he had called on more than 600,000 men to rebuild the armies.

3–5 April 1813
GERMAN FRONT
Wittgenstein launched a series of attacks against Eugene's forces forward of Magdeburg, fighting a number of bloody actions around Mockern. Eugene decided to pull his forces back from the Elbe and establish a line on the Saale.

10 April 1813
GERMAN FRONT
Wittgenstein led his Russian force across the Elbe. Blücher reached Leipzig with his Prussians.

12 April 1813
GERMAN FRONT
The French continued to concentrate their forces in Germany. There were three main forces, the Army of the Elbe under Eugene with 65,000 men, now deployed along the Saale, III Corps and VI Corps together with the Imperial Guard marching upon Erfurt with a total of 110,000 men and the Corps of Observation of Italy en route with its 40,000 men. Davout had a further 18,000 men deployed along the lower Elbe.

13 April 1813
IBERIAN FRONT
The French were defeated at Castalla.

15 April 1813
GERMAN FRONT
Napoleon left Paris in the early hours of the morning to join his newly assembled army on the Main in Germany. He planned to link up with Eugene along the Saale and Elbe rivers. The new force was inexperienced and woefully short of experienced NCOs and officers.

16 April 1813
GERMAN FRONT
General Miloradovich began to cross the Elbe at Dresden with his Russian troops.

17 April 1813
GERMAN FRONT
Napoleon reached Mayence and paused for a week to collect together additional forces. He also reorganised his forces in the field, redesignating the various corps of observation as new numbered corps.

18 April 1813
POLISH FRONT
Thorn fell to Barclay de Tolly's Russians. He would shortly march west with his 13,000 men to join the main Allied army.

19 April 1813
GERMAN FRONT
Miloradovich linked up with Blücher's Prussians at Altenburg.

20 April 1813
GERMAN FRONT
The French army destined for service in Germany with Napoleon numbered 210,000 infantry, 175,000 of them being French soldiers and the remainder Allies.[6]

21 April 1813
GERMAN FRONT
Spandau fell to the Russians.

PRUSSIA: ARMED FORCES
Frederick William announced the creation of the *Landsturm*, a militia organisation aimed at providing resistance to the French occupation forces.

24 April 1813
GERMAN FRONT
Napoleon left Mayence for the Army of the Main. Tsar Alexander and King Frederick William of Prussia reached Dresden.

25 April 1813
GERMAN FRONT
Napoleon, having reached Erfurt, completed the reorganisation of his forces in Germany. His Army of the Main now comprised 140,000 men split between Ney's III Corps at Weimar, Marmont's VI Corps near Gotha, Bertrand's IV Corps at Coburg and Oudinot's XII Corps together

with elements of the Imperial Guard at Anspach and Nuremburg. The army was now directed to advance upon Naumburg.

Eugene's Army of the Elbe comprised Macdonald's XI Corps, Lauriston's V Corps and further elements of the Imperial Guards, a combined force of 62,000 men. It was ordered to push forward to Halle.

The deployment of the new French armies throughout Germany was a considerable achievement considering the dire straits they found themselves in at the beginning of the year. However, while Napoleon had managed to create a numerically significant force, it lacked combat experience and the marching ability of the French armies of previous campaigns. Only by stripping forces from the armies in Spain was a core of experience created in the German armies.

26 April 1813
GERMAN FRONT
The Allies continued their slow and deliberate advance west. Wittgenstein had Bulow's detachment on his northern wing near Rosslau while Yorck was close to Halle. Blücher deployed his main force on the roads to Leipzig. Wittgenstein's intention was to concentrate upon Leipzig so that he could catch any French offensive movement in a battle near Lutzen.

27 April 1813
GERMAN FRONT
Wittgenstein began to concentrate his forces around Leipzig. Blücher and Miloradovich were at Chemnitz and Zwickau.

ALLIED COMMAND
Followed a marked decline in the health of the Allied commander, Marshal Kutuzov, Tsar Alexander appointed General Wittgenstein commander in chief of the 'combined army of allied powers'. Unfortunately, Alexander only made Wittgenstein directly responsible for the forces under Generals Blücher and Winzingerode. The other Russian commanders, Generals Tormasov and Miloradovich, received their orders directly from the Tsar, leaving Wittgenstein with little knowledge of the movement of the other armies.

28 April 1813
GERMAN FRONT
There was inconclusive fighting at Halle as Lauriston's corps attacked Kleist's Prussians. The French were repulsed.

ALLIED COMMAND
Marshal Kutuzov died after a long illness.

29 April 1813
GERMAN FRONT

Advancing French troops drove General Yorck's detachment out of Merseburg. His reverse compelled Kleist to pull his force out of Halle later in the day. Wittgenstein pushed his forces forward to positions around Lutzen but his cavalry screen encountered the leading elements of Marshal Ney's corps and suffered a minor reverse.

30 April 1813
GERMAN FRONT

Napoleon led his Army of the Main, with 133,000 infantry, 7,500 cavalry and 370 cannon concentrated, towards Leipzig. The inexperience of his troops, and shortage of cavalry for reconnaissance, meant he did not learn of Wittgenstein's concentration (of 88,000 men, including 24,000 cavalry and 550 cannon) around Lutzen.

Eugene had pushed the Army of the Elbe forward and now stood with his forces on the right bank of the Saale.

1 May 1813
GERMAN FRONT

Winzingerode, leading the Allied advance guard, launched a surprise attack upon Napoleon's advance forces, striking the III Corps commanded by Marshal Ney, and Marshal Bessières' Guard Cavalry, near Lutzen. Ney successfully drove off the Russian cavalry that struck his force but Bessières was killed in the fighting.

The fighting alerted Napoleon to the concentration of Allied forces and he correctly deduced that they were likely to try and attack his forces around Lutzen in greater strength.

ALLIED DEPLOYMENT

Swedish forces began to deploy in strength in Pomerania to join the armies fighting the French.

INTERNATIONAL POLITICS

Austria, represented by the wily Metternich, negotiated between the French and Allies while beginning the secret mobilisation of their forces.

2 May 1813
GERMAN FRONT

Napoleon pushed his troops forward upon Leipzig in an effort to launch a turning attack against the Allied forces. Lauriston's advancing V Corps ran into Kleist's corps of Prussians at Lindenau. After a brisk battle the Allies pulled back, abandoning Leipzig to the French.

While the fighting flared around Leipzig, Wittgenstein, with 73,000 men, launched his main attack around Lutzen. The attack struck the

45,000 unprepared men of Ney's III Corps. Fighting raged back and forth as the attacks and counter-attacks were launched by both armies. Through sheer determination, and the support of the Guard, the French managed to stabilise their positions.

Napoleon, realising the danger, immediately ordered Ney to hold his positions while the VI moved to support his right and the IV Corps launched a strike against the Allied left wing. Simultaneously, the XI Corps was to attack the Allied right wing.

French strength increased to 110,000 men throughout a day of furious action. Towards nightfall Napoleon ordered a final fierce counter-attack, supported by a massed battery of eighty cannon and the Imperial Guard, and drove in the Allied flanks. Wittgenstein managed to extricate his forces, largely through the inexperience and exhaustion of the French troops, and pulled back upon Dresden. Losses had been very heavy, the French losing 18,000 men and the Allies 12,000.

As the battle raged around Lutzen, General Bulow led his Prussian corps against the 6,000-strong French garrison of Halle. After a brief battle the French were compelled to withdraw.

3 May 1813
GERMAN FRONT
Napoleon issued orders for the pursuit of the defeated Allies. Unfortunately, the French troops were still fatigued after their battle of the previous day and progress was limited.

4 May 1813
GERMAN FRONT
The French pushed their forces upon Dresden and Torgau in an effort to catch the retreating Allies. Ney took his III Corps together with elements of the VII Corps and Victor's and Sebastiani's newly created provisional corps from Leipzig towards Torgau and Wittenberg. He had a combined force of 60,000 infantry, 4,000 cavalry and 130 cannon.[7]

Napoleon led the IV Corps on his right, XI Corps in the centre and V Corps on the left, comprising 120,000 infantry, 11,000 cavalry and 380 cannon, towards Dresden. There was little contact with the Allies.

ALLIED COMMAND
The Allies could not decide where to make a stand against the advancing French. The Prussians were keen to cover the approaches to Berlin while the Russians preferred to cover the lines of communication to Warsaw via Gorlitz. A long series of councils followed.

5 May 1813
GERMAN FRONT
The French advance continued. Ney reached Wittenberg while elements

of Eugene's XI Corps encountered Prussian troops close to Colditz and drove them back. It was clear to the French by now that the Allies were indeed falling back upon Dresden, their withdrawal being covered by Miloradovich's skilful rearguard actions.

7 May 1813
GERMAN FRONT
The Russians fell back across the Elbe at Dresden while the Prussians crossed at Meissen. Elements of Reynier's VI Corps reached Torgau but found that the 9,000-strong Saxon garrison, commanded by General Thielmann, refused them entry. The King of Saxony had attempted to assert his neutrality in preparation for a movement over to the Allies.

8 May 1813
GERMAN FRONT
Napoleon captured Dresden with the XI Corps while the V Corps moved up to Meissen. Ney was ordered, with more than 50,000 men, to march around the Allied wing to take them by surprise.

INTERNATIONAL POLITICS
Napoleon delivered a stern warning to the King of Saxony that unless he ordered Thielmann to join forces with Reynier he would be considered an enemy.

ALLIED COMMAND
Wittgenstein issued orders for the defence of the Elbe, the Russians to hold at Meissen and the Prussians to their north.

9 May 1813
GERMAN FRONT
Napoleon crossed the Elbe to the south of Dresden, the bridge across the river in the town having been destroyed in March and not fully repaired. Miloradovich's Russians attempted to prevent the French effecting a crossing but a battery of sixty cannon ensured French success. The failure of his efforts to hold the Elbe convinced Wittgenstein that the Allies forces should retire to the north to cover Berlin.

INTERNATIONAL POLITICS
The King of Saxony meekly joined the French cause, ordering Thielmann to ally his forces with the French. Thielmann followed his orders but then joined the Allies.

10 May 1813
GERMAN FRONT
French engineers worked to repair the Dresden bridge so that the bulk of

the army could cross the Elbe. Wittgenstein pulled his forces back in an effort to establish a line in order to protect Berlin.

11 May 1813
GERMAN FRONT
Ney, with the III Corps, V Corps and VII Corps, crossed the Elbe at Torgau with 45,000 men. Following their orders, the Saxon garrison of Torgau surrendered the city to the French.

The engineers completed the repair of the Dresden bridge and enabled Napoleon to push 70,000 men across the river.

12 May 1813
GERMAN FRONT
Wittgenstein, concerned by the continued advance of the French past Dresden, ordered his 110,000-strong force to fall back beyond Bautzen, crossing the Spree near the town. Miloradovich covered the withdrawal once again and fought a delaying action against Macdonald's XI Corps at Schmiedefeld. Bulow had been detached from the main Allied force to cover the direct approaches to Berlin.

15 May 1813
GERMAN FRONT
Napoleon had brought up additional forces to reinforce his main army. Ney's separate command now numbered 84,000 men, 30,000 with his own III Corps, 27,000 with Lauriston's V Corps, 9,000 with Reynier's VII Corps and 13,000 with Victor's II Corps. He had nearly 5,000 cavalry. Napoleon commanded the main force with 119,000 men. This comprised Bertrand's IV Corps with 25,000 men, Marmont's VI Corps with 22,000 men, Macdonald's XI Corps with 17,000 men, Oudinot's XII Corps with 24,000, the Imperial Guard with 19,000 men and 4,000 cavalry and the regular cavalry, numbering 8,000 troops.[8] The Army of the Elbe was now disbanded. Eugene left to take command of French forces in Italy.

Miloradovich again turned to fight a delaying action against Macdonald as the latter attempted to cross the Spree. The French now became fully aware of the Allied concentration at Bautzen.

INTERNATIONAL POLITICS
Metternich dispatched envoys to the Allies and to Napoleon in order to reach a negotiated settlement. Stadion went to the Allied camp and Bubna to the French.

16 May 1813
GERMAN FRONT
Napoleon was convinced that the Allies planned to make a stand at Bautzen and issued orders for the XI, VI and IV Corps to take up positions

close to Bautzen, the XI being on the right wing, the IV protecting the left and the VI Corps in the centre. Ney began to advance on Spremberg with the III, II and VII Corps while Lauriston's V Corps moved upon Hoyerswerda. Napoleon had meant for Ney to advance alone with his III Corps while Victor led the II and VII Corps towards Berlin.

17 May 1813
GERMAN FRONT
Ney realised his error and ordered Victor, with 25,000 men, to push on towards Berlin. However, in the meantime Napoleon had changed his mind and ordered Ney to reunite his force and push once more upon Bautzen.

IBERIAN FRONT
Joseph Bonaparte, acting under instructions from Napoleon, ordered the withdrawal of his remaining forces from Madrid. He began to pull back to the line of the Ebro.

INTERNATIONAL POLITICS
Napoleon sent Cauliancourt to try to negotiate a settlement with Tsar Alexander directly rather than through the other Allied powers. The Allies refused to let the French emissary cross their lines.

18 May 1813
GERMAN FRONT
Forward elements of the French V Corps reached Hoyerswerda as Ney concentrated his forces. Napoleon also continued his advance, aiming to unite his two armies on 19 or 20 May.

The Allies were aware, through captured French dispatches, that Napoleon intended to attack them at Bautzen. Wittgenstein therefore proposed a counter-attack aimed at isolating Lauriston's corps as it advanced. Barclay de Tolly was to attack with 24,000 Prussian and Russian troops.

19 May 1813
GERMAN FRONT
Napoleon deployed his main force in front of Wittgenstein at Bautzen. Barclay de Tolly launched his force across the Spree in an effort to attack the French left wing as it deployed close to the river. In heavy fighting around Wartha the French lost 2,800 men to an Allied loss of 2,000 but the French managed to overcome the Allied thrust, compelling them to pull back across the Spree.

Wittgenstein had been ordered to make a stand by Tsar Alexander and King Frederick William. He deployed his army in strongly fortified positions back from the Spree river, on a seven-mile front. The river itself was covered by a weaker advance guard as it could be easily crossed by the French. Napoleon aimed to pin the Allied force frontally while Ney marched into their rear to turn their northern wing. The Allied force comprised 64,300

Russian troops and 32,000 Prussians, the whole including a total of 23,000 cavalry and 620 cannon. Miloradovich's Russians formed the advance guard at Bautzen (some 14,600 men) while the main line comprised the Russians to the north and Prussians to the south. Napoleon faced the Allies with a force of 115,000 men and 450 cannon.

20 May 1813
GERMAN FRONT

At Bautzen, Napoleon took the offensive, striking the Allies in order to tie them down long enough for Ney to strike their northern wing and push into the rear. Napoleon's aim was to drive the Allies back upon the Austrian frontier, just a few miles off their southern wing though his orders to Ney did not make the intention clear. Tsar Alexander, having the most influence at Allied headquarters, believed the French would attack the southern wing in an effort to drive them back to the north-east and accordingly deployed stronger forces on this wing.

Marmont's VI Corps and Macdonald's XI Corps opened the French attack to the north and south of Bautzen, followed shortly after by Oudinot's XII Corps to their south. Macdonald managed to secure a crossing of the Spree south of Bautzen while Marmont pushed elements of his corps into the town itself from the north. Under intense pressure Miloradovich pulled his advance guard back upon the main force. This French activity against the centre and southern wing of the Allied force convinced Alexander that the French would indeed attempt to roll up their army from the south, and he therefore brought additional forces over from the northern wing. Soult and Bertrand had been involved in fighting on the French left and succeeded in crossing the Spree.

21 May 1813
GERMAN FRONT

Napoleon renewed the attack at Bautzen, Oudinot, with 15,000 men, attacking the Allied left wing. Believing this to be the start of the main French attack against his southern wing, Alexander reinforced Miloradovich and ordered a counter-attack. With 20,000 men the Allies pushed the French back after hard fighting. Oudinot managed to stabilise his position around midday. In the centre of the line Macdonald attempted to pin the Allies down under heavy cannon fire while waiting for Ney to arrive with his 85,000 men against the Allied right.

Ney had launched his attack at dawn and quickly pushed across the Spree. Lauriston's V Corps became involved in sporadic fighting with Lanskoi's Russian cavalry before Ney brought up his advance guard to strike Barclay de Tolly. Both French groups then pushed Barclay back upon the main force but Ney delayed his advance as Napoleon had specified he reach into the Allied flank at 11am and he had arrived early. Rather than pushing his attack he waited and then when he did attack he pushed against the heights of Klein Bautzen rather than against the Allied rear. Throughout the afternoon though Ney built up the pressure upon the Allied right wing. Tsar Alexander then realised the real danger to the Allied army, despite having been warned of it earlier by Wittgenstein, and ordered a retreat. As they withdrew, Napoleon threw in the Imperial Guard but they were unable to prevent the Allies from extricating their force intact. During the two days of hard fighting the French lost 22,000 men and the Allies 11,000, and Napoleon had failed again to inflict a decisive defeat on the Allies.

22 May 1813
GERMAN FRONT

The French moved forward to pursue the retreating Allies. Reynier's VII Corps, with Latour-Maubourg's I Cavalry Corps in support, led the push towards Reichenbach, with Marmont's VI Corps and the Imperial Guard behind. The Allies left behind their rearguard under Eugene of Wurttemberg at Reichenbach to delay the pursuit as they pulled their main body back upon Gorlitz. The French attacked Eugene's front and right flank. With his position threatened Eugene abandoned his position and fell back to a new position before Gorlitz. Some 14,000 French troops were engaged against 16,000 Russians. French losses were 1,900 casualties to 1,100 Russian. Among the French killed was Marshal Duroc.

Oudinot was to remain around Bautzen in order to gather reinforcements before moving upon Berlin.

INTERNATIONAL POLITICS

The Allies opened negotiations with the French via the Austrian emissary, Count Stadion. They would find Napoleon willing to seek a settlement.

23 May 1813
GERMAN FRONT

The Allies pulled back from Gorlitz and split into two columns. One column retreated upon Bunzlau and the other upon Lauban. Lauriston pursued the Allies towards Bunzlau and was involved in further fighting with the Allied rearguard.

Davout, leading his corps on a northward sweep, laid siege to Hamburg.

IBERIAN FRONT

Wellington advanced into Spain. He had been appointed commander of all the Allied forces in Spain, a force of some 52,500 British soldiers, 29,000 Portuguese and 46,000 Spanish. The French in Iberia numbered 200,000.

24 May 1813
GERMAN FRONT

The French continued to pursue the Allies but were held up once again by dogged rearguard actions. The Allied army now numbered just 80,000 men and was becoming demoralised by their continued retreat.

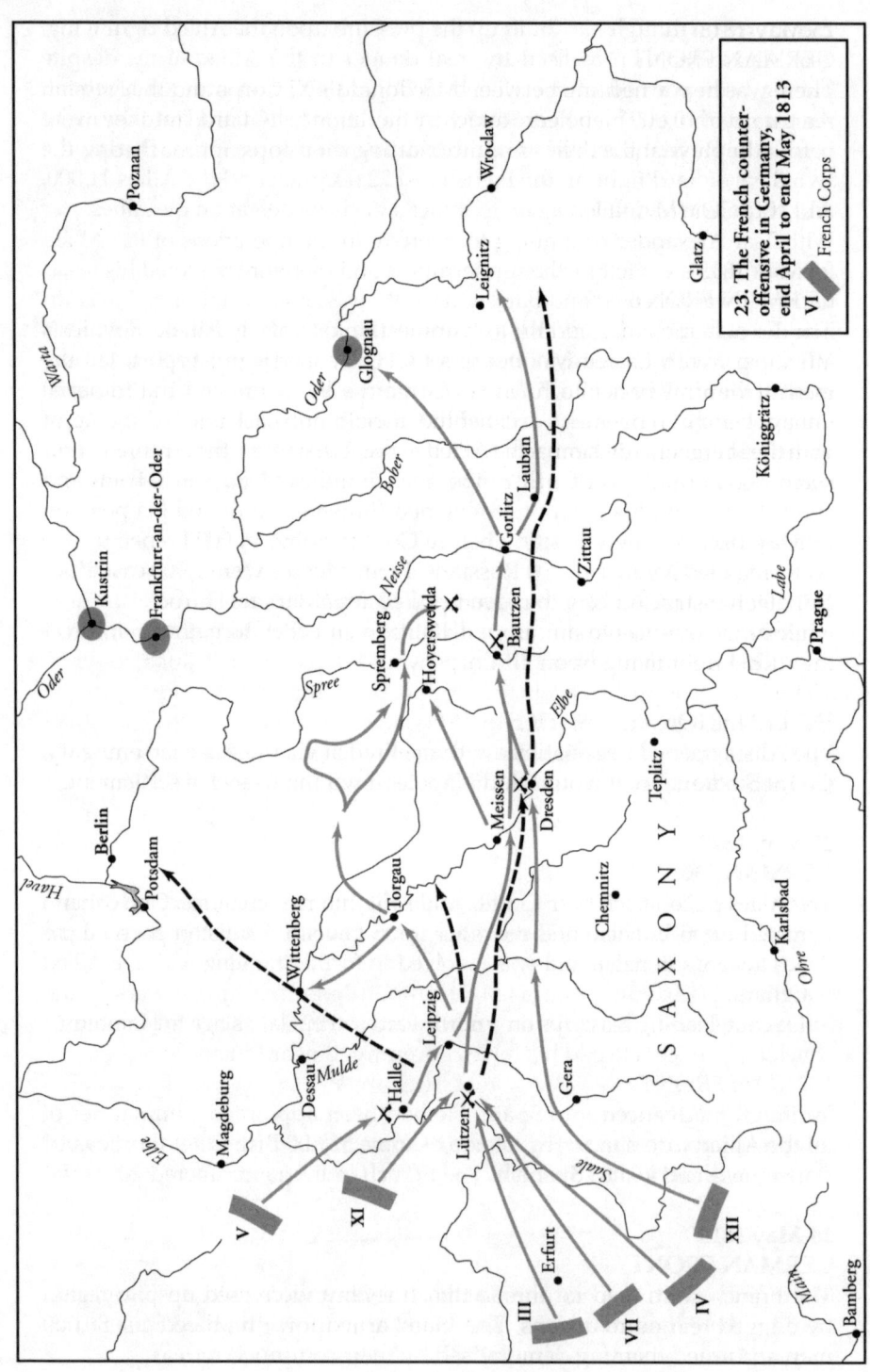

23. The French counter-offensive in Germany, end April to end May 1813

VI ▬ French Corps

25 May 1813
GERMAN FRONT
There was heavy fighting between Macdonald's XI Corps and the Russian rearguard of 10,000 men near Stekicht. The action lasted until into the night before the Russians retired as additional French troops approached.

ALLIED COMMAND
With Tsar Alexander continuing to interfere in the operations of the Allied force, Wittgenstein felt further undermined and therefore tendered his resignation. It was accepted and Barclay de Tolly was quickly appointed as commander of the Prussian and Russian armies. Unfortunately for Alexander, his intentions were the same as Wittgenstein's. He planned to pull the Russian element of the army back into Poland to reorganise and reinforce. The Prussians, unhappy at this movement, decided they would pull back into Silesia. Faced with the imminent division of the Allied army, Alexander intervened and brokered a compromise action, by proposing a withdrawal upon Schweidnitz.

26 May 1813
GERMAN FRONT
Napoleon instructed Ney to move upon Hainau with the V and VII Corps while Marmont was to link up with Macdonald and Bertrand to strike at the Allies' right flank. Ney's III Corps would deploy before Bunzlau while Victor's II Corps pushed north to Sprottau. Elements of the V Corps captured Hainau but were then attacked by Prussian cavalry and suffered more than 1,000 casualties. The main Allied forces retired across the Katzback river. As the French advance threatened, the Allies raised their siege of Glogau.

27 May 1813
GERMAN FRONT
Sprottau fell to Victor's II Corps while the main French force advanced around Leignitz. The Allies retired upon Schweidnitz. Victor then began to advance upon Sagan.

Oudinot had commenced his advance upon Berlin, reaching Hoyerswerda. Bulow remained before Berlin with a force of 30,000 men and moved to attack the French. He had his force concentrated near Lukau.

IBERIAN FRONT
Joseph Bonaparte evacuated his forces from Madrid for the last time, and began a withdrawal to the Ebro.

28 May 1813
GERMAN FRONT
Marmont's corps reached the Katzbach river and crossed despite resistance by the Allied rearguard. The main Allied force reached Striegau as they continued their withdrawal.

Bulow attacked Oudinot at Hoyerswerda but was repulsed with heavy losses. Oudinot failed to press his advantage and, rather than pushing towards Luckau, remained inactive.

29 May 1813
GERMAN FRONT
The Allies reached Schweidnitz but decided to continue their withdrawal rather than stand. The French armies remained largely stationary as they drew their forces together.

30 May 1813
GERMAN FRONT
Allied forces under General Walmoden evacuated Hamburg. Walmoden had been expecting support from Bernadotte's Swedish troops but that did not prove forthcoming, forcing him to abandon the city in the light of Davout's advance.

31 May 1813
GERMAN FRONT
Some 30,000 French and Danish troops of the XIII Corps recaptured Hamburg. Napoleon placed Davout in command of the forces in the city.

The French approached Breslau as they continued their advance in Silesia.

1 June 1813
GERMAN FRONT
Lübeck fell to Davout's forces.

PRUSSIA: ARMED FORCES
Prussian mobilisation since the beginning of the year had successfully brought the strength of the regular army to 150,000 men while the *Landwehr* had 120,000.

2 June 1813
GERMAN FRONT
Barclay de Tolly continued to pull the Allied forces back upon the Oder at Brieg.

IBERIAN FRONT
The British launched an attack upon Tarragona using amphibious forces.

INTERNATIONAL POLITICS
Napoleon and the Allied powers came close to agreeing an armistice so Napoleon ordered the suspension of the advance in Silesia.

4 June 1813
INTERNATIONAL POLITICS
After mediation by Metternich, the Armistice of Pleischwitz was proposed and accepted by the Allies, bringing a temporary ceasefire in hostilities between France and the Allied Powers. The armistice was to last for seven weeks unless an extension was agreed. Napoleon used the lull to train his inexperienced troops while the Allies continued the concentration of their considerable forces.

IBERIAN FRONT
Wellington's advance into Spain had taken Joseph by surprise. Joseph had allowed his forces to become dispersed. Of the 100,000 men he had concentrated, 50,000 of them were with him around Valladolid while the remainder were spread out widely on the roads to France. Not keeping a close watch on the British, despite being advised to do so by Napoleon, he was surprised when the Allies appeared on the Douro river, against his northern flank with a force of close to 100,000 men.

5 June 1813
GERMAN FRONT
Not informed yet that an armistice had been agreed, General Voronzov, the Allied commander of Magdeburg, advanced with a force of 5,000 men with the aim of attacking the French in Leipzig.

5–9 June 1813
IBERIAN FRONT
Joseph began to pull his forces back along the Douro towards France. Wellington, advancing parallel to the French line of retreat, repeatedly threatened their northern wing, preventing the French forces from establishing an effective defensive position.

6 June 1813
GERMAN FRONT
Also unaware that an armistice had been agreed, Oudinot attack Bulow at Luckau but was repulsed with a loss of 2,000 men. The French were compelled to retreat.

7 June 1813
GERMAN FRONT
Voronzov reached Leipzig and attacked the raw French recruits he found there. The Russian force was on the verge of capturing the place when they were advised that the armistice had come into force.

9 June 1813
GERMAN FRONT
Bulow moved to attack Oudinot but received news of the armistice and abandoned his plan.

10 June 1813
FRENCH COMMAND
Napoleon established his headquarters in Dresden and began making plans should the campaign with the Allies be renewed. He began the establishment of strong positions along the line of the Elbe. Davout was to anchor the extreme left wing at Hamburg with a force of 40,000 men while the main armies deployed between Magdeburg and Dresden.

10–12 June 1813
IBERIAN FRONT
Wellington laid siege to, and quickly captured, Burgos.

14 June 1813
AUSTRIA: DEPLOYMENT
Metternich authorised the full mobilisation of the Austrian army as he began to turn against the French but also looked to protect Austrian interests against the Prussians and Russians.

15 June 1813
IBERIAN FRONT
British forces marched into the valley of the Ebro, near the village of Arenas. Joseph Bonaparte occupied extended positions north of the Ebro to Vittoria, having been forced by British manoeuvring to abandon the Ebro line. He deployed 63,000 men with 150 cannon of the combined Armies of the Centre, Portugal and South.

INTERNATIONAL POLITICS
By the Treaty of Reichenbach the British, Russians and Prussians agreed not to negotiate a separate peace with France.

18 June 1813
IBERIAN FRONT
The British reached San Milan as Wellington advanced towards Vittoria. In an effort to push the French force back towards the Franco-Spanish border Wellington had detached 40,000 men under General Graham to threaten the French flank.

In other operations, the forces landed at Tarragona were evacuated.

21 June 1813
IBERIAN FRONT
Wellington, with 70,000 men, attacked the badly deployed French at Vittoria. Jourdan led the French defence, deploying the Army of the South on the left wing, the Army of the Centre in its rightful place and the Army of Portugal on the right. In heavy fighting his centre buckled and flanks caved in. Despite a ferocious defence the French were compelled to withdraw. Joseph lost 8,400 men and 143 cannon to a British loss-of 5,000 men. Wellington also captured the French treasury and a large quantity of supplies. The British then were unable to immediately continue their push towards the French border due to their soldiers' looting of the treasures. The broken French forces pulled back on Pamplona.

22 June 1813
IBERIAN FRONT
British forces laid siege to Pamplona.

24 June 1813
INTERNATIONAL POLITICS
Austria was urged to join the coalition with Britain, Prussia, Russia and Sweden. Metternich had been attempting a negotiated settlement so that France was maintained as a balance against the Prussians and Russians. Austrian diplomacy throughout this period was based upon the premise that the status quo be maintained, rather than upon the elimination of Napoleon.

26 June 1813
INTERNATIONAL POLITICS
Metternich presented the Austrian sponsored peace terms to Napoleon at a meeting in Dresden, fully expecting that he would reject them. The proposed terms demanded that France hand over Illyria to Austria, pull out of the German states, restore Prussian territories and dissolve the Grand Duchy of Warsaw. Napoleon offered to restore Illyria to Austria in return for her neutrality but rejected the rest.

27 June 1813
INTERNATIONAL POLITICS
In another meeting of the Allies at Reichenbach, Austria agreed to join the coalition if Napoleon rejected the terms proposed on 26 June.

IBERIAN FRONT
The British laid siege to San Sebastian.

28 June 1813
IBERIAN FRONT
Joseph Bonaparte left Spain, reaching St Jean de Luz in France.

1 July 1813
IBERIAN FRONT
Joseph collected the various garrisons from northern Spain into a new Army of Spain. His force numbered 79,000 men and 140 cannon and deployed along the Spanish frontier.

5 July 1813
IBERIAN FRONT
With the French forces in the south of Spain still active, Spanish forces were forced out of Valencia.

9 July 1813
ALLIED COMMAND
Tsar Alexander, King Frederick William of Prussia and Bernadotte of Sweden met at Trachenberg near Breslau to discuss Allied plans after the expiry of the armistice.

10 July 1813
ALLIED COMMAND
The Allies continued their discussions at Trachenberg.

11 July 1813
ALLIED COMMAND
The Allies agreed a strategy against the French should hostilities be resumed at the end of the armistice period. After three days of talks the Allies decided that they should concentrate their efforts against the main French grouping of armies while their units on the flanks should attack the French lines of communication. To undertake this task the bulk of the Allied armies would deploy in Bohemia, therefore Blücher would transfer 100,000 men from his Army of Silesia to join the Austrians in Bohemia. Bernadotte was to cover Davout with around 20,000 men while moving with 70,000 upon Leipzig, there to link up with the remainder of the Army of Bohemia. However, if Napoleon moved against Bernadotte then the Austrians would attack his rear. The main objective of the campaign was the defeat of the enemy field army but a crucial part of the plan was the avoidance of battle with Napoleon but aggressive action against his marshals.

12 July 1813
FRANCE: POLITICS
Napoleon ordered Joseph into retirement. Marshal Soult took over command of his forces.

13 July 1813
INTERNATIONAL POLITICS
In a meeting of the Allies at Trachenberg the Prussian and Russians forced Bernadotte to agree to send his army against the French rather than invade Denmark.

19 July 1813
INTERNATIONAL POLITICS
The Convention of Reichenbach extended the ceasefire in Germany. Metternich for Austria and Napoleon for France met once again but each was stalling for time in order to mobilise or rebuild his armies. Napoleon in due course refused to accept the terms proposed on 26 June and determined to continue the war. However, he did agree to a further conference in an effort to gain more time.

25 July 1813
IBERIAN FRONT
Wellington launched an abortive attack upon San Sebastian. The well-entrenched garrison was able to repulse each Allied attack. As his attacks got underway, Wellington learned of Soult's offensive through the Pyrenees. Soult pushed his forces through the passes at Roncesvalles and Maya.

26 July 1813
IBERIAN FRONT
Soult had concentrated 60,000 men at the passes of Maya and Roncesvalles on Wellington's right wing. He began his attack from Sorauren with 30,000 of his men, in an effort to relieve Pamplona. Wellington had expected him to try and relieve San Sebastian first. Bitter fighting erupted as the 16,000 men on the British wing attempted to fend off the French assaults. In order to concentrate his army, Wellington raised the siege of San Sebastian.

27 July 1813
IBERIAN FRONT
Bitter fighting continued as Soult pressed his attacks through the Pyrenees passes.

28 July 1813
IBERIAN FRONT
There was extremely bloody fighting as Wellington, now with 24,000 men, organised his defences and repulsed more French attacks at Sorauren. The nature of the terrain meant the French were trying to break through by sheer brute force. This day of fighting cost the French 4,000 casualties to a British loss of 2,600.

29 July 1813
IBERIAN FRONT
The bloody fight for the Pyrenees passes continued but the French assaults were being turned back each time.

30 July 1813
IBERIAN FRONT
Soult began the difficult task of disengaging his army from the Pyrenees passes but had to fight his way out. The French suffered a further defeat near Sorauren, losing another 3,500 men.

31 July 1813
IBERIAN FRONT
The French withdrawal continued, sustaining heavy losses

1 August 1813
IBERIAN FRONT
Wellington had defeated Soult's effort to break through to Pamplona. Wellington continued his attacks and drove the French back. French losses were in excess of 13,000 men while the British lost 7,000.

7 August 1813
ALLIES: ARMED FORCES
The Russians began moving their army through Poland to deploy with the Prussian and Austrian field armies. This movement was a breach of the terms of the armistice but the Allies had already decided they were going to renew the conflict rather than extend its term again.

10 August 1813
INTERNATIONAL POLITICS
Further negotiations between Napoleon and Metternich failed to reach agreement, despite Metternich reducing the Austrian claims. It was clear Napoleon would not accept any compromise, so the Austrians determined to enter the war. The Allies thereby duly renounced the armistice agreement and made preparations to renew the war. According to the original terms, six days' clear notice had to be given before the commencement of hostilities.

12 August 1813
GERMAN FRONT
Austria, now openly part of the coalition, declared war on France. Metternich had conducted the mobilisation of the Austrian army over the last two months.

Napoleon was faced with three Allied armies in Germany. These were the Austrian Army of Bohemia under General Karl Schwarzenberg, the Prussian Army of Silesia under General Blücher with 195,000 men and 376 cannon and the Prusso-Swedish Army of the North under Bernadotte with 110,000 men. Schwartzenberg was the overall commander of the Allied armies. Blücher had 30,000 of his men detached from the main army to cover the French forces besieged in Kustrin, Stettin, Danzig and Glogau. The Russians contributed a force of 296,000 men to the Allied cause.

Schwartzenberg's plan, named the Trachenberg Plan, was to attack Napoleon's generals whenever possible but to avoid battle with Napoleon himself. Total Allied field forces comprised 512,000 troops with a further 143,000 in reserve and 112,000 garrisoning fortresses.

AUSTRIA: ARMED FORCES
Schwartzenberg commanded the main Austrian contingent, deployed in Bohemia with 130,000 men, while there were 30,000 along the Inn river against the Bavarians and 36,000 in Upper Austria. There were also an additional 27,000 deployed on garrison duties and a further 37,000 to protect the Italian frontiers. The mobilisation continued throughout the remainder of the month.

SWEDEN: ARMED FORCES
For commitment against the French in Germany, Prince Bernadotte deployed a force of 27,000.

FRANCE: MILITARY COMMAND
Napoleon estimated that the Austrians could deploy no more than 100,000 men against his forces in Germany. He believed the Allies still held their main force in Silesia with a strength of no more than 200,000 men. Napoleon's own forces numbered 450,000 men in the field, no reserves to speak of and 77,000 men held down in garrisons on the Oder, Elbe and Vistula.

Napoleon's plan was for the main army, arrayed between Gorlitz and Bautzen, to await the Allied attack before launching a counter-strike that would destroy their armies in Silesia. This force comprised the Imperial Guard in reserve at Gorlitz, Vandamme's I Corps at Bautzen, Victor's II Corps also held in reserve at Gorlitz, Ney's III Corps on the Katzbach river, Lauriston's V Corps, also along the Katzbach, Marmont's VI Corps on the Bober river, behind those forces deployed on the Katzbach, together with Macdonald's XI Corps, Poniatowski's VIII Corps deployed on the right wing around Zittau and St Cyr's XIV Corps at Dresden. Latour-Maubourg's I Cavalry Corps was in reserve at Gorlitz, Sebastiani's II Cavalry Corps supporting Ney and Lauriston along the Katzbach, Kellermann's IV Cavalry Corps at Bautzen and L'Heritier's V Cavalry Corps at Dresden, a total strength of 300,000 men, including 48,000 cavalry and with just over 1,000 cannon.

The second major French force was to the north. Oudinot, deployed around Baruth with Bertrand's IV Corps, Reynier's VII Corps and his own XII Corps together with Arrighi's III Cavalry Corps, was to advance upon Berlin and from there to Stettin. Oudinot's force comprised 75,000 troops, including 8,000 cavalry and 210 cannon. Davout had the 35,000 French and Danish troops, including 2,000 cavalry and 100 cannon, of his XIII Corps around Hamburg and was also to push upon Berlin. There were smaller forces between these two groups, giving the whole of the Berlin offensive force a strength of 120,000 men.

15 August 1813
GERMAN FRONT
Blücher began offensive action is Silesia, invading the neutral zone around Breslau and overrunning French outposts. The armistice had been due to expire on 17 August following the Allied denunciation of the 10th.

IBERIAN FRONT
Marshal Suchet pulled his forces out of Tarragona.

16 August 1813
GERMAN FRONT
Napoleon received information that the Russians had moved their forces forward from Poland and were deploying in Bohemia and Silesia. He believed the Prussians were advancing upon Bunzlau with no more than 50,000 men and that the Austrians and Russians in Bohemia would press upon Dresden. Therefore, he aimed to attack Blücher first before moving upon the remaider of the Allied armies. With this in mind, Napoleon instructed Macdonald and Lauriston, with around 60,000 men, to hold the Prussians up at Lowenberg while Ney with a further 80,000 held between Bunzlau and Hainau. The Guard was to deploy at Lauban. Napoleon would then march with the main body upon Blücher. Unfortunately for the French, Blücher actually had closer to 90,000 men, significantly outnumbering the force Napoleon intended to contain him with.

BALKAN FRONT
Austria launched an invasion of the French Illyrian provinces.

18 August 1813
GERMAN FRONT
Oudinot began his advance upon Berlin from Baruth, pushing forward towards Luckenwalde. To the south the Russians began to deploy into Bohemia as the Austrians began their advance across the Elbe.

20 August 1813
GERMAN FRONT
Blücher reached the Bober river near Lowenberg. Ney's II Corps, Lauriston's V Corps and Macdonald's XI Corps were already deployed to oppose his crossing and Marmont's VI Corps together with the Imperial Guard were marching to their reinforcement. Napoleon issued orders for an attack the following day.

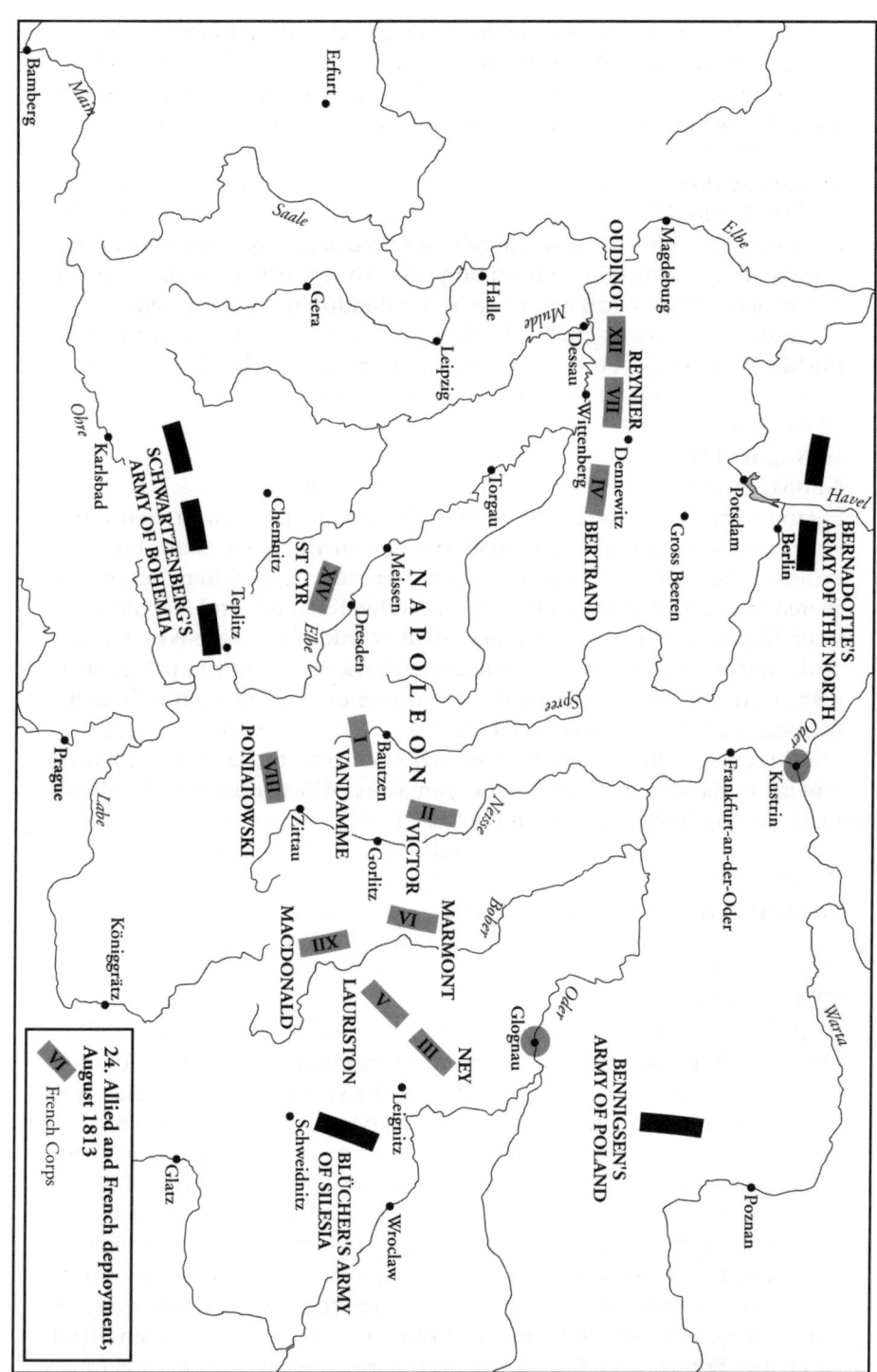

Bamberg

Erfurt

Main

Saale

Gera

Halle

Leipzig

Magdeburg

Dessau

Mulde

Wittenberg

Dennewitz

Torgau

OUDINOT XII REYNIER

VII

IV BERTRAND

Gross Beeren

Potsdam

Elbe

Havel

Berlin

BERNADOTTE'S
ARMY OF THE NORTH

Obre

Karlsbad

SCHWARTZENBERG'S
ARMY OF BOHEMIA

Chemnitz

Teplitz

ST CYR XIV

Meissen

Dresden

N A P O L E O N

Elbe

Spree

Frankfurt-an-der-Oder

Oder

Kustrin

Prague

Labe

PONIATOWSKI VIII

Zittau

VANDAMME I

Bautzen

Gorlitz

VICTOR II

Neisse

MARMONT VI

Bober

Warta

Königgrätz

MACDONALD IIX

LAURISTON V

III NEY

Glognau

Oder

BENNIGSEN'S
ARMY OF POLAND

Poznan

Glatz

BLÜCHER'S ARMY
OF SILESIA

Schweidnitz

Leignitz

Wroclaw

24. Allied and French deployment,
August 1813

VI French Corps

Oudinot reached Luckenwalde as he continued his advance. He now began to turn north to reach Berlin.

21 August 1813
GERMAN FRONT
Lowenberg fell to the French after limited fighting as Napoleon launched his attack upon the Prussian army. In line with Allied policy, Blücher immediately began to retire so as not to enter into an action with Napoleon. Napoleon, not realising their strategy, believed it was a weakness of the Allied leadership which had caused the abandonment of their advance.

Oudinot's forces captured Trebbin and drew close to Zossen as they pushed back the Allied outposts on the approaches to Berlin.

22 August 1813
GERMAN FRONT
Napoleon continued the advance against the retreating Prussians, crossing the Katzbach through the course of the day. As the advance progressed Napoleon was advised of the Austrian march towards Dresden and determined to bring his main force back to support St Cyr. Macdonald was therefore left in command of the forces on the Katzbach and Napoleon left with Ney. Unfortunately, Napoleon had intended to leave Ney's troops with Macdonald but Ney misunderstood the order and marched them off to Bunzlau. This left Macdonald with minor elements of the III Corps, together with the V Corps and XI Corps.

Wittgenstein encountered the French XIV Corps forces near Hellendorf and drove its advance guards back after a day of heavy fighting. The Allies were driving their forces upon Dresden.

IBERIAN FRONT
Wellington reinvested San Sebastian.

23 August 1813
GERMAN FRONT
Oudinot continued his advance as the Allies fell back slowly before him. Oudinot's XII Corps was on the left wing, Reynier's VII Corps in the centre heading for Grossbeeren, and Bertrand's IV Corps on the right faced by Tauenzein's 13,000 men. Bertrand attacked during the morning but was held up by fierce Prussian cannon fire. Reynier meanwhile had marched upon Grossbeeren and attacked the Prussian garrison, part of Bulow's main force. Quickly taking the town, the French then stopped for the remainder of the afternoon, believing the Prussians had been driven off. However, Bulow was marching against Reynier and late in the afternoon launched a counter-attack. An artillery duel opened the battle, with the Prussian infantry suffering severe losses. However, the Prussian attack threw the French back from Grossbeeren. Reynier then pulled his forces

back and re-established his units. French losses were around 3,000 men to a Prussian loss of around 1,000. However, Oudinot decided to abandon his advance upon Berlin

Napoleon soon appointed Ney to command the army in place of Oudinot. Oudinot remained to command his corps, but there was bad feeling between him and Ney and a subsequent lack of co-operation.

Wittgenstein continued to push on towards Drsden, driving elements of the XIV Corps back to within two miles of the town. French cavalry covered the approaches to Leipzig.

24 August 1813
GERMAN FRONT

There was intermittent skirmishing around Dresden as the Allies built up their forces around the town. Napoleon reached Bautzen as he marched to catch the Allies as they attacked Dresden. St Cyr had 15,000 French and 5,000 Westphalian troops to secure Dresden.

Blücher realised that Napoleon had departed from the Katzbach sector and began to make preparations to attack Macdonald.

25 August 1813
GERMAN FRONT

Schwartzenberg, bringing up a force of 160,000 men, unleashed a minor attack upon St Cyr's 20,000 in Dresden. St Cyr, hastily fortifying his positions, sent a message to Napoleon that the Austrian main force was before him. Napoleon increased the pace of his march to aid St Cyr. The Allies, unaware of Napoleon's approach, could not decide whether to launch a full-scale assault or not, which resulted in the execution of a minor action only against St Cyr's heavily outnumbered force. Tsar Alexander and Wittgenstein were keen to launch an immediate attack but Schwartzenberg stalled on the grounds of waiting for his remaining Austrian units to arrive.

Blücher began a series of probing attacks against Macdonald's outposts on the Katzbach. His troops confirmed his suspicions and so he ordered a general attack for 26 August. Macdonald meanwhile was making his own plans to attack Blücher. He deployed 12,000 men on his right wing to guard against a Prussian advance while 22,000 were to push towards Jauer and a further 67,000, on the left wing, were to outflank the Prussians at Jauer.

26 August 1813
GERMAN FRONT

Blücher, with 110,000 men in total, struck Macdonald along the Katzbach. Confused fighting followed as each army attempted to deploy for its proposed attacks, hampered by a downpour of rain, which prevented the muskets from firing in many cases. Macdonald launched a vigorous attack with 40,000 of his men against the Prussian right. Badly co-ordinated, the French attack broke down and Blücher began his own counter-attack, striking the

27,000 troops in the French centre with 55,000 men. In bitter hand-to-hand fighting Macdonald did well to disengage his army but at a price. The French lost 20,000 men and 100 cannon to a Prussian loss of almost 10,000 men.

Schwartzenberg had decided to launch his main attack upon Dresden but rather than attack at first light delayed until later in the morning. The attack was to be made by five columns of troops, Wittgenstein with 10,000 Russians on the right wing, 35,000 Prussians launched a diversionary attack to the left, Colleredo, with 15,000 Austrians was to attack in the centre, Chasteler with 10,000 near the left wing and Bianchi, with 35,000 Austrians, on the extreme left. The attack was to start on the right before the main assault went in on the left late in the day.

The Allied attack duly began on the right wing and made only slow progress against the French defences. The Prussians and Russians were involved in heavy fighting and were only able to advance after three hours of bitter resistance by the French. The Austrians unleashed their attack in the centre an hour after the Prussians and Russians and drove the French front back. Despite fierce counter-fire with their entrenched cannon the French were unable to stop the Austrians. However, around noon a lull descended on the battlefield as the Allies regrouped for their main attack later in the afternoon.

Napoleon arrived in Dresden at around 10am, ahead of his army, which was marching to reinforce St Cyr. The main French army, a further 50,000 men, began to arrive around 2pm.

Following the lull in the fighting the Allies had been debating their progress and were undecided as to whether to continue the battle. Tsar Alexander advocated withdrawing due to the suspicion of the approach of Napoleon but Frederick William of Prussia wished to continue the assault. After a long debate it was decided to cancel the attack but Schwartzenberg failed to pass out the new order and the Allied offensive was resumed at 4pm.

The Russians and Prussians resumed their attacks on the right and made only limited progress against stiff French resistance. A French counter-attack succeeded in driving the Allied forces back. The main Allied attack was then unleashed by the forces in the centre and on the left wing. Amid fierce French cannon fire the Austrians stalled but unfortunately for the French they ran out of ammunition, enabling the Austrians to overrun the guns. As the advance gained ground both in the centre and on the left, the French committed their reserves. After an hour of bloody fighting Napoleon had managed to bring his strength up to 70,000 but was faced by 150,000 Allies. He issued orders for a counter-attack at 6pm, which rippled along the length of the line. After heavy fighting the French regained all of the ground they had lost during the day and inflicted heavy losses upon the Allied force.

Vandamme, with nearly 40,000 men operating against the flank and rear of the main Allied force attacking Dresden, defeated Eugene of Wurttemburg at Pirna.

French forces continued to arrive at Dresden throughout the night, bringing their strength up to 120,000 men. The Allies remained with nearly 160,000 men and a further 20,000 marching to reinforce them. Unfortunately the Allied commanders spent the night in indecision, with confidence lost following their failure to drive the French out of Dresden.

27 August 1813
GERMAN FRONT

Having debated through the night the Allied commanders agreed to make a stand at Dresden but not to renew their attack. Napoleon meanwhile had reinforced his army and planned to resume his attack of the preceding afternoon, crushing the Allied wings while holding steady in the centre.

On the right wing Napoleon deployed 12,000 cavalry and 23,000 infantry under Murat against 22,000 Allied infantry and 2,000 cavalry. In the centre of the line the Allies had 100,000 men against 41,000 French troops contained in the VI and XIV Corps, commanded by Marmont and St Cyr. On the left the French had another 10,000 cavalry and 40,000 men under Mortier and Ney against 24,000 Allied troops.

The French attack, in pouring rain, was opened by Mortier and Ney on the left wing. Steady progress was made against the heavily outnumbered Allies. The Russian troops on this wing put up a stiff resistance but were compelled to fall back after repulsing a number of French assaults. In the centre the French launched attacks aimed at pinning down the Allies while their wings were crushed. Murat and Victor opened their attacks and also steadily drove back the Austrian troops opposite them. Bitter fighting raged on both wings throughout the morning. The rain helped the French as it prevented the Allies from establishing a clear picture of their troop movements and strength of their forces.

As the Allied wings began to collapse, and their centre crumbled, Schwartzenberg ordered a general withdrawal. Allied losses in two days of furious fighting were 38,000 men and forty cannon guns. Among the Allied dead was the former French general Moreau, killed while in service with the Tsar of Russia. The French had lost 10,000 men.

Following the battle the Allied commanders held another of many councils of war, debating whether to renew the battle the following day or retire. Frederick William of Prussia called for a renewed assault but Schwartzenberg elected to withdraw during the night, his main reason being lack of provisions for his men.

General Vandamme, one of Napoleon's more able subordinates, realised that he could cut the Austrian lines of communication, and launched a rapid march towards Bohemia with his corps of 37,000 men. Napoleon, suffering from one of his periods of lethargy, failed to react and left Vandamme without any assistance.

Macdonald had pulled his forces back across the Katzbach following his defeat of the previous day. Blücher launched a vigorous pursuit and harried the French back to Lowenberg. The retreat then continued to Bunzlau.

28 August 1813
GERMAN FRONT
Napoleon, not believing the Allies would retire, continued to stand at Dresden as Schwartzenberg disengaged. Realising later in the morning that the Allies had indeed pulled back, the French began their pursuit. However, Napoleon had been informed of Oudinot's and Macdonald's defeats and had to keep a watch on his own rear against an Allied advance from the north.

Vandamme pushed forward against Eugene of Wurttemberg's retreating force. In heavy fighting the Allied units were scattered and suffered severe losses.

29 August 1813
GERMAN FRONT
Vandamme pressed his advance against General Ostermann and Eugene of Wurttemberg. Heavy fighting erupted near Kulm as the Allies made a stand against the French advance. Vandamme soon found himself in difficulties as the Allies rapidly built up their forces against him. He was shortly attacked by 20,000 Russians under Ostermann. The French fought a skilful defensive action but desperately needed support. Vandamme believed St Cyr or Mortier was advancing to his support but they had not received orders to aid him. Napoleon intentionally left Vandamme to his own devices. After a day of bitter fighting, both forces had suffered around 6,000 casualties.

30 August 1813
GERMAN FRONT
Kleist arrived with 10,000 Prussian troops in Vandamme's rear while another 20,000 Allied soldiers arrived to reinforce Ostermann. Realising support was not going to arrive, Vandamme began to fight his way out of the Allied encirclement around Kulm. In bitter fighting fewer than 14,000 French troops managed to escape while 4,000 had been killed and a further 13,000 men captured. The survivors were scattered. Vandamme was among those captured. His tenacious defence though had cost the Allied force around 5,000 casualties.

FRANCE: COMMAND
Napoleon decided upon the next phase of his campaign against the Allies. After discounting a march upon Prague, which would have left the remainder of his line overextended and vulnerable to Allied attack, he decided upon a general advance upon Berlin. This movement would draw the Allies away from Bohemia, the Prussians in defence of their capital, and the Russian forces away to cover their lines of communication into Poland.

31 August 1813
IBERIAN FRONT
Wellington stormed San Sebastian. The French garrison, commanded by General Rey, retained control of the citadel but negotiated a surrender.

British losses during the assault were around 4,500 men killed or wounded to a French loss of 2,000.

Soult was defeated at San Marcial by Spanish troops.

AUSTRIA: ARMED FORCES
The Austrian mobilisation had reached its peak, some 480,000 Austrian troops now being under arms, of whom 300,000 were committed to the war against Napoleon.

2 September 1813
GERMAN FRONT
Napoleon issued orders for Ney to advance from Wittenberg upon Baruth, while he moved his own forces upon Luckau. Ney would then push directly upon Berlin and drive back the Allied Army of the North.

3 September 1813
GERMAN FRONT
Macdonald, still being pressed by Blücher around Bautzen, called for reinforcement by Napoleon. The latter therefore abandoned his march to Luckau to support Ney's advance on Berlin and moved instead to support Macdonald. Napoleon immediately attacked and drove in Blücher's advance guard at Hochkirch.

Ney arrived to take command of the 58,000 men Oudinot had along the Elbe. The force was deployed around Wittenberg, the IV Corps on the right, XII Corps in the centre and VII Corps on the left.

4 September 1813
GERMAN FRONT
Napoleon continued to advance against Blücher, but the Prussian commander realised he was facing the French Emperor and in accordance with the Trachenberg plan began to pull back upon Gorlitz to avoid battle. Napoleon though realised the Allied plan and broke off the pursuit, aware that the Allies were trying to draw him away from his base at Dresden.

Ney began the advance upon Berlin, pushing the XII Corps forward. Bernadotte's forces were widely scattered and fell back to concentrate as the French advanced.

5 September 1813
GERMAN FRONT
Napoleon returned his army to Reichenbach and Bautzen. Ney pushed the XII and IV Corps towards Juterbog and the VII Corps upon Baruth. Bernadotte intended to mask the French approach while manoeuvring against the left flank and rear.

St Cyr's XIV Corps came under attack by the Army of Bohemia as the Allies resumed their advance upon Dresden. Schwartzenberg was moving with

60,000 troops upon Zittau in order to threaten Macdonald's right wing, which was facing Blücher, while the bulk of the Allied army pushed against St Cyr.

6 September 1813
GERMAN FRONT

Ney continued his advance upon Berlin but Bertrand's IV Corps ran into Tauenzien's Prussians at Dennewitz. The French attacked immediately and drove in the Prussian wings. Tauenzien then committed his small cavalry reserve and repelled the French thrust. Meanwhile, Bulow moved up additional forces against the French left flank and launched a counter-attack. After bitter fighting the Prussians were repulsed. The Prussians renewed their attacks during the afternoon and forced Bertrand to fall back with severe losses. However, Reynier's VII Corps then arrived to support Bertrand and they successfully halted the retreat and began to force the Prussians back. Yet again the Prussians renewed their attack and recaptured Dennewitz. Oudinot was late in marching to the battle and only arrived mid-afternoon. Bulow managed to hold off the French attacks while Bernadotte brought up additional Russian and Swedish troops to support the Prussians. Fortunately for the Allies, Ney personally launched an ill-conceived attack against their right wing. The Allies were able to repel the French and again resumed their attacks, pushing the French back all across their line. A disordered retreat ensued as Ney's force was scattered. The VII and XII Corps fell back upon Torgau while Ney and Bertrand's IV Corps withdrew towards Dahme.

Napoleon had ordered his forces to push up to Hoyerswerda to support Ney. However, he shortly received news of the advance of the Austrian Army of Bohemia upon Dresden and again abandoned this movement. Macdonald was again left to follow Blücher. St Cyr was compelled to give ground in the face of the Allied advance.

7 September 1813
GERMAN FRONT

Reynier's VII Corps and Oudinot's XII pulled back to Torgau. Ney was back at Dahme with Bertrand and aimed to reunite his army by bringing the whole back together at Torgau. However, as he commenced his march the Allies attacked and took more than 3,000 prisoners.

Two days of fighting around Dennewitz and during the subsequent French retreat had cost the Allies some 7,000 killed and wounded. However, Ney had lost more than fifty cannon, 13,500 prisoners and 9,000 killed or wounded.

St Cyr halted his withdrawal before Dresden and awaited the arrival of Napoleon, whose units began to arrive throughout the day.

Blücher received orders to march with 50,000 men to Bohemia in order to link up with the remainder of the Allied army. A force of 50,000 would be left to face Macdonald. The Russian forces under General Bennigsen, currently approaching from Poland, were also ordered up to the Elbe sector to threaten Dresden and Torgau.

IBERIAN FRONT
The 42nd Highlanders landed at Passages to reinforce Wellington around San Sebastian and blockade Pamplona. The French there were greatly reinforced by Marshal Soult.

8 September 1813
GERMAN FRONT
St Cyr's outposts were driven in by the Allies as their advance upon Dresden continued. However, with the arrival of reinforcements the French counter-attacked and regained the lost ground.

Ney concentrated the remains of his army at Torgau and crossed the Elbe to the west bank in order to complete the restructuring of his somewhat disorganised force. While Ney undertook these activities, Bulow moved to besiege Wittenberg.

9 September 1813
GERMAN FRONT
Napoleon and St Cyr began to advance against the Allied flank and rear but, realising what the French were up to, the Allies began to pull back. By evening the French had reached Furstenwalde. Having again realised they were facing Napoleon, the Allied commanders refused to offer battle.

10 September 1813
GERMAN FRONT
Napoleon continued his advance but declined a plan by St Cyr to attack the separated Allied columns as they retired.

12 September 1813
GERMAN FRONT
Thielmann took a detachment of cavalry ahead of the main Allied forces to operate against the French lines of communication. His force reached Weissenfels, where they attacked the French and captured 1,000 prisoners.

At his own suggestion, Blücher's direction of march was changed from a march to Bohemia to an advance upon the Elbe to threaten Dresden and Torgau. Bennigsen was now to advance to join the main Allied force in Bohemia. Blücher would link up with Bernadotte's Army of the North.

13 September 1813
IBERIAN FRONT
Suchet defeated an Anglo-Spanish force at Ordal.

14 September 1813
IBERIAN FRONT
Suchet defeated the Anglo-Spanish at Villafranca.

15 September 1813
GERMAN FRONT
Allied forces laid siege to Magdeburg. Napoleon and St Cyr continued their steady advance against the Allies, pushing forward towards Breitenau and Teplitz.

In an effort to turn the French front on the Elbe, Bernadotte began the construction of bridges near Wittenberg.

16 September 1813
GERMAN FRONT
The French were defeated by the Allies at Gohrde.

17 September 1813
GERMAN FRONT
A force of 35,000 Prussian and Russian troops defeated 25,000 French at Teplitz. The French advance had stalled, largely due to Napoleon's lethargy. He had returned to Pirna and awaited an improvement in the weather before moving his forces.

18 September 1813
GERMAN FRONT
Merseburg fell to Thielmann.

19 September 1813
GERMAN FRONT
The French XII Corps was disbanded and its elements were handed over to VII Corps and for rear area guard duties. Oudinot was placed in command of two divisions of the Young Guard.

21 September 1813
GERMAN FRONT
Napoleon issued orders that reorganised his forces slightly. St Cyr was to take command of the co-ordination of the XIV, I and V Corps, a force of around 50,000 men, to protect the Elbe front against an Allied advance from Bohemia. Victor was to deploy his corps at Chemnitz, Marmont was to protect Freiberg and Macdonald, now with just his own XI Corps left under command, was to pull back upon Dresden. Ney was to hold the Elbe line from Torgau to Magdeburg with the IV, VII and III Corps.

Ney received reports that Bernadotte was preparing to cross the Elbe in force near Wittenberg and therefore began the movement of his army to oppose this move.

22 September 1813
GERMAN FRONT
The Allied commanders decided upon a new plan of advance. Rather than

operating against Dresden, they would push towards Chemnitz and then upon Leipzig.

23 September 1813
GERMAN FRONT
Elements of the French III and XI Corps, with Napoleon present with them, pushed Blücher's advance guard back upon Bautzen. It was at this point that news arrived of the Allied building of a bridge across the Elbe in Ney's sector. Napoleon therefore determined to abandon the lands east of the Elbe and concentrate his forces at Dresden, Meissen and Torgau.

24 September 1813
GERMAN FRONT
The French began to pull their forces back behind the Elbe in line with Napoleon's orders on 23 September.

Ney deployed near Wartenburg in order to oppose Bernadotte's crossing of the Elbe near Wittenberg. Bernadotte abandoned his advance and pulled his men back across the river.

INTERNATIONAL POLITICS
With the war in Germany dragging on and the Allies making steady, if slow, progress, the German states of the Confederation of the Rhine began to grow discontented.

25 September 1813
GERMAN FRONT
The French continued their redeployment. The XI Corps was back to Weissig, V Corps and the Imperial Guards were deployed around Dresden, III and VI Corps and I Cavalry Corps were at Meissen, VIII Corps was moving to operate against the Allied free corps in the French rear, XIV Corps and I Corps south of Dresden, II Corps at Freiberg and Ney's group, IV and VII Corps, at Wartenburg. Augereau was marching to reinforce the field army with his IX Corps, which was currently near Jena. Davout remained in Hamburg with his XIII Corps.

26 September 1813
IBERIAN FRONT
The British moved forward to the bridge of Janca.

28 September 1813
GERMAN FRONT
Thielmann, who had linked up with the Cossack free corps, attacked Lefebvre-Desnoettes' cavalry at Altenburg and inflicted a sharp defeat.

Another Allied Cossack force, some 2,500 strong, had marched deep into the French rear and attacked Cassel in Westphalia. The French garrison was compelled to surrender.

30 September 1813
GERMAN FRONT
The Allies continued their advance across their front. Bernadotte's 76,000-strong Army of the North was around Herzberg, with Bulow at Wartenburg, Blücher, with 64,000 men, was near Bautzen and Schwartzenberg was continuing his advance upon Chemnitz.

ITALIAN FRONT
French forces, led by Eugene, in northern Italy began to establish a defence line on the Isonzo river, abandoning the Illyrian provinces.

1 October 1813
GERMAN FRONT
Blücher reached Wartenburg to link up with the Army of the North.

2 October 1813
GERMAN FRONT
Bertrand deployed at Wartenburg to oppose the Prussian crossing of the Elbe. Napoleon directed Murat to concentrate the II, V and VIII Corps, together with the V Cavalry Corps, against the 200,000 men of the Army of Bohemia, who were advancing upon Leipzig.

3 October 1813
GERMAN FRONT
Blücher launched his attack across the Elbe at Wartenburg in order to establish a secure bridgehead for operations on the west bank. After a day of fighting Bertrand's 13,000 men were driven back, with the loss of around 2,500 killed, wounded and captured to a Prussian loss of around 1,500.

4 October 1813
GERMAN FRONT
Blücher completed the crossing of the Elbe with his army at Wartenburg. Bernadotte was also now across in force. The Army of the North left a contingent to lay siege to Torgau and Wittenberg. Ney abandoned his positions on the Elbe and pulled back upon the Mulde river. Chemnitz fell to elements of the Army of Bohemia but the French V Corps recaptured the town only to be forced out once again.

5 October 1813
GERMAN FRONT
Napoleon directed Marmont to take the III Corps and VI Corps to Torgau

before marching to link up with Ney, whose command these forces would then be subordinated to. Auguereau was instructed to reinforce the garrison of Leipzig with his IX Corps.

6 October 1813
GERMAN FRONT
Napoleon issued orders for his new plan, which aimed to defeat Blücher and Schwartzenberg along the Elbe before Schwartzenberg could reach Leipzig. He would then bring his force back in order to attack and defeat the Austrians.

7 October 1813
IBERIAN FRONT
Wellington crossed the Bidassoa and invaded France. A French force, under Taupin, was defeated by Wellington at Vera. Soult fought a series of delaying actions as Wellington advanced. The French main army in the south was down to just 50,000 men, Napoleon having drawn off sizeable contingents for his forces in Germany.

8 October 1813
GERMAN FRONT
Bavaria withdrew from the Confederation of the Rhine and joined the Allies in the war against the French.

The Allies closed upon Dresden as the French pulled in the defences to the city limits.

9 October 1813
GERMAN FRONT
Napoleon, with 140,000 men, began to move in order to attack Blücher, who was at Duben with 60,000 troops, marching towards Halle. Bernadotte was near Dessau with another 40,000.

10 October 1813
GERMAN FRONT
Blücher pulled back before Napoleon's advance, drawing him away from the approach of the Army of Bohemia towards Leipzig. Reynier relieved the garrison of Witttenberg as the Allies were driven off.

Bennigsen launched a light attack against Dresden but rather than storm the city left a force of 20,000 to mask it. He then continued with his main force of 30,000 towards Colditz and then Leipzig. Murat fell back before the approaching Russians.

Napoleon was suffering from considerable indecision as to the best course of action, whether to continue to concentrate against the Allied Army of the North, or move south to support Murat against the approaching Army of Bohemia.

11 October 1813
GERMAN FRONT
Napoleon continued to be troubled by indecision. He could not decide between tackling Blücher and Bernadotte, masking them or moving south to confront the Army of Bohemia.

Murat brought his forces, the V, II and VIII Corps, together around Leibertwolkwitz to guard against the continued Allied advance upon Leipzig. Napoleon determined to send him reinforcements.

12 October 1813
GERMAN FRONT
Blücher reached Halle. Murat, with a force of 32,000 infantry and 8,000 cavalry, encountered and defeated Schwartzenberg's advance guards at Colditz. Augereau arrived at Leipzig. The concentration for the forthcoming battle of the nations had begun.

13 October 1813
GERMAN FRONT
Napoleon finally decided upon the concentration of his forces at Leipzig.

14 October 1813
GERMAN FRONT
Murat was attacked by the Allied advance guard at Liebertwolkwitz. With 60,000 infantry and 6,000 cavalry the Allies should have repulsed and defeated the French force. A series of fierce cavalry charges by both sides met with mixed results as each army threw in more and more reserves. After a full day of fighting both armies broke off the battle, the French having lost 1,500 casualties and 1,000 captured while the Allies lost 2,500 men and around 500 captured.

ITALIAN FRONT
Eugene abandoned his defence line on the Isonzo and began to fall back to the line of the Adige.

15 October 1813
GERMAN FRONT
The Allied and French army began to converge around Leipzig. Napoleon aimed to launch an attack against what he believed was the flank of the Army of Bohemia but was actually the rapidly approaching Army of Silesia.

16 October 1813
GERMAN FRONT
After considerable disagreement from the other Allied generals, which caused him to alter his plan, Schwartzenberg issued orders for operations against the French around Leipzig. Blücher was to attack from north of

Leipzig with 54,000 men and 310 cannon while Gyulai attacked Lindenau with 19,000 men and sixty cannon, Meerveldt's 30,000 Austrians were to attack between the Pleisse and Elster rivers, while Wittgenstein, Kleist and Klenau were to strike from south of Leipzig with a combined force of 97,000 men and 460 cannon.

Around Leipzig and against this force Napoleon had 191,000 men and nearly 700 cannon, 138,000 being south of the town, 3,000 at Lindenau and a further 50,000, under Marmont, north of the town. Marmont had been ordered by Napoleon to move to the southern perimeter, despite the obvious presence of Blücher's forces.

The Allies began their attack from the south, aiming at Wachau but, moving forward in five columns, their attack lacked force and was brought to a halt as French reinforcements, in the form of Augereau's corps, were committed. During heavy fighting Wachau changed hands a number of times before finally being secured by the French. Bloody fighting also raged in Liebertwolkwitz, where Macdonald deployed to reinforce the French line. The Austrian attack between the Elster and Pleisse rivers also stalled before fierce artillery fire by Bertrand's IV Corps. Numerous French counter-attacks compelled the Allies to abandon their offensive efforts in this sector. While the fighting raged at Wachau and between the rivers, the Allied detachment under Gyulai attacked Arrighi in Lindenau. After a difficult advance the Austrians attacked the town but were repulsed by fierce French artillery fire. Elements of Bertrand's IV Corps reinforced Arrighi and drove the Austrians off around midday.

North of Leipzig, Blücher began his attack just as Marmont was starting his march to the south. Quickly gaining ground, Blücher pushed Yorck's men on towards Mockern, where Marmont had halted his movement south in order to face Blücher's attack. Initial Allied attacks upon the town were repulsed before they managed to break through. There then followed fierce fighting back and forth through the streets as each force attacked and counter-attacked. The fighting around Mockern was particularly bloody and raged unabated until late into the afternoon. The town eventually fell to the Prussians after a ferocious struggle and Marmont was compelled to pull his force back farther. Total Prussian losses were around 14,000 killed or wounded to more than 10,000 French casualties. Marmont's defeat north of Leipzig ensured that the French could not use this route to break out.

With the Allied attacks to the south of Leipzig during the morning were either repulsed or bogged down, the French went onto the offensive themselves. Pulling in additional forces from the northern wing to support his southern one, Napoleon aimed to drive the Allies off the field. The French attack pushed Wittgenstein's forces back to their start lines but the late redeployment of Marmont and Souham from the northern wing delayed the development of the French movement. Despite this, the French pressed on and continued to push the Allies back. However, exhaustion brought the advance to a halt and a renewed advance by the Austrians near the

Pleisse threatened their rear. This movement was halted by the arrival of Souham and the capture of the Austrian commander, General Meerveldt.

The battle wound down by dusk with a lack of real progress by either side. A day of furious fighting had seen the lines surge back and forth but neither army had managed to inflict a knock out blow.

17 October 1813
GERMAN FRONT

The Allies launch half-hearted attacks against the French clustered around Leipzig as they used most of the day to concentrate their forces and bring up reinforcements. Blücher continued to bring up additional elements of his army to face the French left wing. Schwartzenberg planned to renew the offensive the following day with attacks all around the French perimeter.

Napoleon had 157,000 men around the city, Bertrand's corps having been withdrawn to help protect the lines of communication to the west. The Emperor was determined to fight a stubborn defensive action around his perimeter, which he intended to draw in to better concentrate his force in order to fight off the increasingly strong Allied assaults.

Bremen fell to a detachment of Allied troops led by General Tettenborn.

18 October 1813
GERMAN FRONT

During the night of the 17th/18th, the French pulled their forces back into tighter positions around Leipzig. The right wing, commanded by Murat, comprised the corps of Poniatowski, Augereau and Victor together with elements of the Guard, while Macdonald's central group, comprised his own corps and that of Lauriston. The left wing was commanded by Ney, who had available Reynier's corps, Marmont's and Souham's. At Lindenau, deployed to protect the lines of communication to the west, Mortier held further elements of the Guards. Napoleon now had 195,000 men and more than 700 cannons clustered north, east and south of the city but was beginning to run low on ammunition.

Allied strength at Leipzig had increased to 295,000 men and 1,460 cannons following the arrival of additional forces on 17 October. In an effort to stall the Allies Napoleon had sent the captured General Meerveldt back to the Allied commanders bearing proposed terms, but the Allies were determined to press on and drive the French back to the Rhine.

The Allies duly attacked in six columns around the French perimeter, driving those elements of the French force which had not already retired back to their new positions. Bennigsen's attack upon the French left started well but was hampered by the failure of Bernadotte to arrive on his right. While fighting continued some Saxon and Westphalian elements of Ney's force began to change sides. Bernadotte began to deploy during the afternoon, enabling the Allies to complete their ring to the north, east and south.

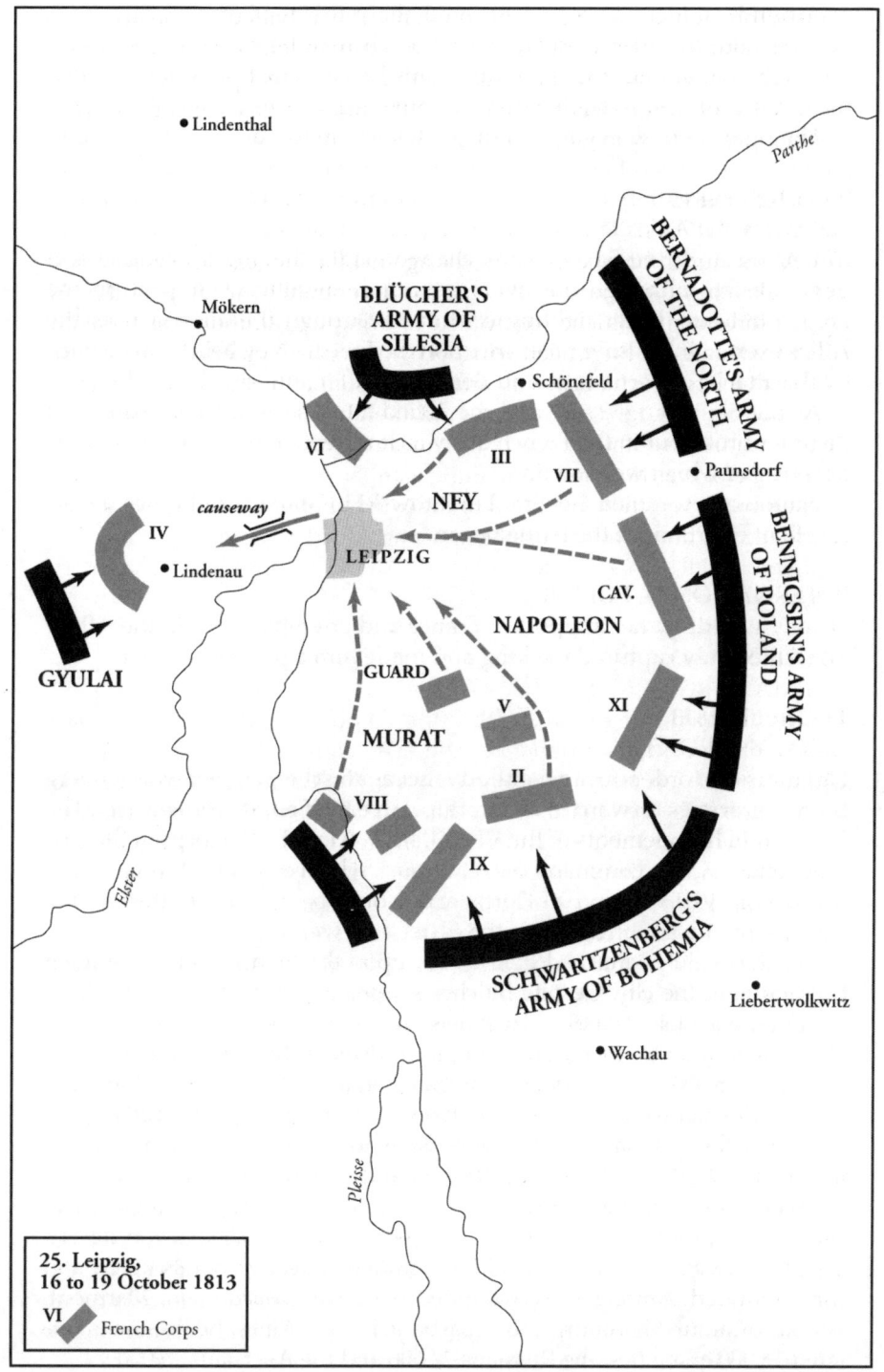

Lindenthal

Parthe

Mökern

BLÜCHER'S
ARMY OF
SILESIA

BERNADOTTE'S ARMY
OF THE NORTH

Schönefeld

VI

III

VII

Paunsdorf

NEY

causeway

BENNIGSEN'S ARMY
OF POLAND

IV

Lindenau

LEIPZIG

CAV.

NAPOLEON

GYULAI

GUARD

V

XI

MURAT

II

VIII

IX

Elster

SCHWARTZENBERG'S
ARMY OF BOHEMIA

Liebertwolkwitz

Wachau

Pleisse

**25. Leipzig,
16 to 19 October 1813**

VI   French Corps

Around midday Napoleon ordered the retirement of his army from Leipzig and, in order to protect the French rear, Bertrand attacked and defeated Gyulai at Lindenau. Napoleon's line of retreat was, for the time being, assured and a steady stream of men began to march west.

The fighting now began to swing back and forth, as Poniatowski and Augereau launched fierce attacks on the left. Victor was also involved in bitter fighting with Barclay de Tolly's column near Probstheida. A furious battle saw the Allies fail to take the village. As the fighting spread closer to Leipzig itself the Saxon corps changed sides, having a negative and demoralising, although not overwhelmingly significant, impact on the French defence. Bitter fighting continued through the afternoon as the Allies exerted increasing pressure upon the French, Ney being forced back by the attacks of Bernadotte and Bennigsen after suffering heavy losses.

As the night progressed, and the Allied attacks ceased, confusion and disorder broke out in the French army as it retreated through Leipzig, the outskirts of which were on fire.

Napoleon promoted General Poniatowski to Marshal of France for his excellent efforts since the battle began.

INTERNATIONAL POLITICS
Saxony withdrew her support of France and attempted to join the Allies. The Allies duly captured the king and made him a prisoner of war.

19 October 1813
GERMAN FRONT
Having issued orders for a general advance against Leipzig, Schwartzenberg threw his armies forward in an effort to drive the French from the city. The French still had elements of the VII, VI, III, V, XI and VIII Corps in the city. Macdonald was to command the rearguard, which comprised some 30,000 men of the VII, VIII and XI Corps and would be evacuated after a final stand, blowing the bridge over the Elster as it went.

The Allies duly launched their attack upon the French and drove them back through the city. Despite Blücher's repeated efforts to sever his lines of communication, Napoleon managed to extricate the bulk of his army. Unfortunately for the rearguard though, the Elster bridge was destroyed early, stranding 15,000 French troops. Marshals Poniatowski and Macdonald and General Reynier were stranded with their men. The two marshals attempted to swim to the west bank but Poniatowski, who had been injured in the fighting, died in the attempt. Generals Reynier and Lauriston were captured.

French losses during the four days of bitter fighting in and around Leipzig exceeded 38,000 killed or wounded, 30,000 captured, 5,000 Saxon deserters plus 325 guns. French casualties included sixteen generals killed and fifty wounded. Among those wounded were Ney, Macdonald, Marmont, Souham, Latour-Maubourg and Sebastiani. For the Allies the Prussians suffered 16,000 casualties, the Russians 22,600 and the Austrians 15,000.

Napoleon issued orders to St Cyr, instructing him to abandon Dresden while the forces on the Rhine front were placed on alert.

Napoleon's defeat at Leipzig ended for good his efforts to retain control over Germany. Over the coming weeks the French army would fall back upon the Rhine, France's German allies falling away as her troops left. However, Napoleon left behind him a number of garrisons in key cities, still believing that his defeat was purely temporary. These troops would be sorely missed in the critical campaigns of 1814.

20 October 1813
GERMAN FRONT
As the French continued their retreat, crossing the Salle successfully at Weissenfels, the Allied pursuit stalled. Blücher was tied down reordering his army after the battle, drawing in outlying units, while Schwartzenberg began a leisurely advance, leaving the Bavarians under Wrede to strike ahead.

21 October 1813
GERMAN FRONT
Elements of Gyulai's force encountered the French rearguard on the Saale at Kosen. After bitter fighting the Allies secured a crossing. In a day of fighting the Allies lost 1,000 men and the French nearly 1,700.

22 October 1813
GERMAN FRONT
As the French retreated there was a minor action at Eckartsberga, where a force of 2,500 French troops was attacked by 8,000 Austrian soldiers.

23 October 1813
GERMAN FRONT
The French army had fallen back upon Erfurt, now numbering some 90,000 demoralised men.

26 October 1813
GERMAN FRONT
There was a sharp action near Eisenach as 13,000 French troops forced their way past a blocking force comprising 5,600 Prussians of Yorck's corps. The French lost 2,600 men during the fighting, the Prussians just 500.

28 October 1813
GERMAN FRONT
General Wrede, with a force of Austrian and Bavarian troops, moved against the retreating French near Hanau. Wrede believed he was acting against a minor part of the French army, rather than the whole force.

30 October 1813
GERMAN FRONT
Wrede, with a combined Austrian and Bavarian army, 30,000 strong with fifty cannon, attempted to cut Napoleon's line of retreat at Hanau. Fighting broke out along the Kinzig river as the French advance guards encountered the Allied force. Unfortunately for the Allies, Wrede had split his units between both sides of the river and deployed close to a thick wood, preventing him from observing the French approach. Napoleon approached with 17,000 men during the afternoon and drove those elements of Wrede's force before him back across the river.

Torgau fell after a second siege.

IBERIAN FRONT
Pamplona fell to the British.

31 October 1813
GERMAN FRONT
In the early hours of the morning the French occupied Hanau. Napoleon, having concentrated 60,000 men, launched a stunning attack with a massed battery of fifty cannon and cavalry troops against Wrede's left. Marshal Macdonald led the initial assault and was quickly reinforced by the arrival of Marshal Mortier. Wrede launched a vain attack aimed at regaining the bridge over the river but was driven off. Casualties were heavy, Wrede losing 10,000 men to a French loss of 6,000 men. Napoleon's line of retreat was clear once more and he continued his march upon Frankfurt.

2 November 1813
GERMAN FRONT
Hesse-Cassel and Wurttemburg left the largely defunct Confederation of the Rhine and joined the Allies.

5 November 1813
GERMAN FRONT
The French concentrated their army around Mainz. The Allies had given up any efforts at a close pursuit following their defeat at Hanau.

ITALIAN FRONT
Austrian forces laid siege to Venice. It held out until the end of hostilities.

6 November 1813
GERMAN FRONT
Napoleon cut his way through Germany and reached the Rhine with 70,000 men. The retreat had cost him a further 10,000 casualties. Some 40,000 French troops were still on the east bank of the Rhine, trying to

catch up with the retreating main force while Napoleon had intentionally left around 100,000 men to garrison various German cities.

8 November 1813
INTERNATIONAL POLITICS
The Allies, coerced by Metternich and following a meeting of their leaders at Frankfurt, offered Napoleon peace terms on the basis that France would be confined to borders on the Alps and the Rhine. Napoleon would have to rescind any claims to Spain, Italy and Holland and give up his territories in Germany, Illyria and the Grand Duchy of Warsaw. Belgium and the Rhineland would remain in the French sphere.

Sweden and Austria were keen to end the war on this basis but the British wanted to see it through to its end while the Prussians and Russians urged the removal of Napoleon from power. Metternich was concerned that the Russians would come to an agreement with Prussia over the dismemberment of Poland and the settlement of territories in Germany.

FRANCE: ARMED FORCES
Over the next two months Napoleon made strenuous efforts to raise a new army, stripping France bare of any spare soldiers. Some 950,000 were called up, the class of 1815 being called early. Furthermore, the National Guard was reorganised, its manpower being absorbed into fighting units.

9 November 1813
IBERIAN FRONT
British and Portuguese forces under Hope defeated Soult at St Jean de Luz on the Nive river.

ITALIAN FRONT
Eugene defeated an Austrian force at Ala.

10 November 1813
IBERIAN FRONT
Wellington, with 45,000 men, defeated Soult, with 18,000, at Petite La Rhune in France, moving up to the passage of the Bidassoa and of the Nivelle. Soult was compelled to fall back, having lost 4,500 men to a British loss of 5,300.

11 November 1813
GERMAN FRONT
The French garrison of Dresden surrendered to the Allies.

12 November 1813
NETHERLANDS FRONT
The Allied corps of Bulow and Winzingerode entered the Kingdom of

Holland in strength. The French had pulled their forces back to Utrecht, abandoning areas of Holland that the Allies had not yet reached.

13 November 1813
ITALIAN FRONT
Eugene continued his skilful defence of northern Italy, defeating the Austrians at Caldiero.

16 November 1813
NETHERLANDS FRONT
Popular revolts broke out in the French evacuated areas of Holland. The people called for the restoration of the Prince of Orange.

1 December 1813
INTERNATIONAL POLITICS
Napoleon had delayed so long that the Allies, including Metternich, had seen exactly what he was doing (rebuilding his armies) and withdrew their peace offer. The Allies declared they would fight on until all non-French people had been freed from Napoleonic rule.

5 December 1813
INTERNATIONAL POLITICS
Despite the Allied announcement that they had withdrawn their offer of peace, Napoleon declared that he accepted the Frankfurt terms, provided they allowed him to evacuate his garrisons on the Vistula and Oder and add them to his field army. Unsurprisingly, the Allies refused his offer.

DANISH FRONT
Bernadotte, with an army of 40,000 men, launched the Allied invasion of Denmark.

6 December 1813
NETHERLANDS FRONT
The British began to land forces in Holland.

9 December 1813
IBERIAN FRONT
Soult attacked Wellington's forces along the Nive at Bayonne. The British resisted the French advance.

10–12 December 1813
IBERIAN FRONT
In three more days of bitter fighting Wellington defeated Soult near Bayonne.

11 December 1813
INTERNATIONAL POLITICS
By the Treaty of Valencay Napoleon and Ferdinand VII agreed to the withdrawal of French forces from Spain. The treaty was rejected by the Spanish Council of the Regency.

13 December 1813
IBERIAN FRONT
Soult attacked Hill's division of Wellington's army in force at St Pierre. Wellington had preempted Soult's move though by reinforcing Hill with the 6th Division. Soult suffered a defeat but the British victory was costly.

21 December 1813
GERMAN FRONT
Allied forces closed up to the Rhine at Mannheim and Coblenz. Elements of Schwartzenberg's Army of Bohemia began to cross to the west bank.

FRANCE: ARMED FORCES
Napoleon had 70,000 men stretched out along the eastern frontier and an army of 40,000 held in a central reserve to defeat the Allied armies as they advanced. Victor was deployed on the Upper Rhine, between Hunningen and Landau, with a force of 10,000 men while Marmont had 13,000 between the latter and Coblenz. Sebastiani had a smaller force of 4,500 men between Coblenz and the Lippe river. Holding the left wing was Marshal Macdonald with 11,500 men between the Lippe and Nijmegen. General Maison commanded the hard pressed 15,000 strong garrison of Holland. General Morand held a strong blocking force of 15,000 men at Mayence. On the extreme southern wing, Augereau was building a new army around Lyon, but it currently held just 1,500 men. Around Metz, Ney and Mortier were concentrating further reserves.[9]

22 December 1813
GERMAN FRONT
Bavarian forces laid siege to Hunningen, turning Victor's flank.

24 December 1813
GERMAN FRONT
The Allies laid siege to Hamburg with an army of 120,000 men, trapping Davout's corps of 30,000 men. During the months of fighting in Germany Davout had strengthened the city defences, carefully siting his 350 cannon. He had also made extensive material preparations to resist the siege and had ordered the populace to stockpile a year's worth of food or leave the city. He expelled 25,000 civilians in order to ensure enough supplies for his men.

25 December 1813
SWISS FRONT
A revolt broke out in the Helvetian Republic against French rule. Schwartzenberg sent a force of 12,000 men under the command of General Bubna into Switzerland to secure Austrian communications and help the rebels.

29 December 1813
GERMAN FRONT
The Allies began to cross the Rhine in force.

30 December 1813
GERMAN FRONT
General Rapp surrendered Danzig to the Russians after a long siege.

1813 had proved a disastrous year for the French Empire. A revitalised army, committed to the defence of Germany had been comprehensively defeated and forced to flee to the Rhine to avoid total annihilation. Despite this, with the French so obviously defeated, the Allies still remained divided as to their course of action. It was this division that would enable Napoleon to carry the fight on into 1814, a year which would finally bring to an end ten years of continual conflict in Europe.

Notes

1. F Loraine Petre, *Napoleon's Last Campaign in Germany, 1813*, p. 11
2. Ibid, p. 12
3. Ibid, p. 26
4. Ibid, p. 35
5. Ibid, p. 39
6. ibid, p. 15
7. Ibid, p. 92
8. Ibid, p. 101
9. Ibid, p. 13

CHAPTER X

The Defeat of France

After years spent dominating continental Europe, Napoleon found himself defending the very borders of France itself. Once again faced with the difficult task of building a new army out of the wreckage that remained, he set about his task with the determination of old. 1814 would prove to be a year of staggering achievement, as the exhausted forces of France battled the overwhelming armies of the Allied powers, powers which had finally recognised that only the total defeat of Napoleon would bring peace to Europe.

* 1814 *

FRANCE: ARMED FORCES

French forces were widely spread following their retreat from Germany. Napoleon remained committed to campaigns in Spain, Italy and the long eastern border of France. To disrupt the Allied advance, and provide a number of bases for a subsequent counter-offensive, the French had left nearly 100,000 men tied down in garrisons throughout Germany, the largest contingent of 30,000 being with Davout at Hamburg. Along the Rhine front Napoleon had 118,000 men, stretched out between Antwerp and Lyon. The French again attempted to block the Allied invasion routes by planting substantial garrisons throughout Holland, Belgium and their eastern borders. General Maison commanded the 15,000-strong French garrison in the Netherlands.

In Iberia, French commitment remained high, Soult fielding a force of 60,000 men on the western Pyrenees front while Suchet had a further 37,000 in Catalonia. They faced a united Anglo-Portuguese and Spanish army against the Atlantic coast and Spanish insurgents in Catalonia. Napoleon had stripped Soult of nearly 15,000 men and Suchet of 10,000 in an effort to form an experienced cadre for the new recruits, which made up the bulk of his army.

Facing renewed Austrian efforts to dominate northern Italy, Eugene de Beauharnais had 50,000 French and Italian troops. In southern Italy, Murat commanded his Neapolitan forces.

In the year since January 1813 the French had called up 1,000,000 men for service with the army. Of this number 90% were called at the end of 1813 to reconstitute the shattered armies on the eastern borders. Of the more than 900,000 called up, barely 130,000 reported for duty.

The army was not only short of infantry, it was critically weak in artillery and cavalry. The French Navy, thanks to Napoleon's continued efforts to establish a fleet strong enough to challenge the British, now numbered seventy-nine ships of the line with another thirty-nine under construction.

ALLIES: ARMED FORCES
After numerous councils of war during the final weeks of 1813, the Allies had opted for an invasion of France on two main axes.

Schwartzenberg, commanding the Austro-Russian Army of Bohemia, with some 210,000 men (including Prince Colloredo's I Corps, Gyulai's III Corps, Wurttemberg's IV Corps, Wrede's V Corps and Wittgenstein's VI Corps) was to cross the Rhine around Basel and push towards the source of the Meuse, Marne and Seine. Blücher, with the 75,000-strong Prusso-Russian Army of Silesia, was to cross the Rhine between Mayence and Coblenz. His task was to hold the French centre so that Schwartzenberg could operate against their flank.

On the extreme northern wing the Allied Army of the North was to secure control of Holland and continue the siege of Hamburg. The corps of Bulow and Winzingerode were to operate against the French forces in the Low Countries while Bernadotte, aided by Bennigsen's Russians, secured Denmark and Hamburg.

To the south, in Italy, another Austrian force under General Bellegarde, around 50,000 strong, was to tie down Eugene to prevent him sending reinforcements to Napoleon.

In the Iberian Peninsula Wellington continued to attack the French, directing his forces against Soult while the Spanish tied down Suchet.

1 January 1814
INVASION OF FRANCE
Blücher completed the crossing of the Rhine with his Army of Silesia while Schwartzenberg entered France via Switzerland.

6 January 1814
NETHERLANDS FRONT
General Winzingerode crossed the Rhine as his forces continued to push steadily forward in Holland.

11 January 1814
INTERNATIONAL POLITICS
Murat signed a separate peace with the Allies. In order to keep his Neapolitan throne he renounced his claims to Sicily. Napoleon realised that the hand behind Murat's betrayal was his sister's, Murat's wife Caroline.

14 January 1814
INTERNATIONAL POLITICS
Denmark, occupied by Swedish troops, made peace with the Allies and left the French sphere.

18–20 January 1814
IBERIAN FRONT
Marshal Suchet pulled back from Barcelona but left a garrison to hold the city. The Spanish moved forward and laid siege to the now isolated force.

INTERNATIONAL POLITICS
Viscount Castlereagh, British foreign minister, met with Metternich to agree a policy for the structure of a post-Napoleonic Europe. Metternich advised Schwartzenberg to break off military operations until the talks were complete. The British proposed that Holland and Belgium be united into a single kingdom under the Prince of Orange and that Spain and Portugal revert to their former monarchs. If the Austrians agreed to these terms, the British would support Austrian claims on Italy and their proposals for the settlement of territories in central Europe. Both powers were keen that France remain a major power in order to ensure that the balance of power in Europe remained stable. The destruction of France was very definitely not an objective, even the ousting of Napoleon was not a requirement, just that he either be contained or the Bourbons be restored to power. Therefore the war would continue in order to defeat France and to achieve these objectives.

22 January 1814
INVASION OF FRANCE
Blücher led his Army of Silesia forward and crossed the Meuse river.

24 January 1814
ITALIAN FRONT
Murat marched into Rome at the head of his Neapolitan army. He claimed to be fighting for Italian unity.

25 January 1814
INVASION OF FRANCE
Allied forces drove Victor's II Corps out of St Dizier.

26 January 1814
INVASION OF FRANCE
Napoleon arrived from Paris to take command of his armies. As he took command Victor was falling back from St Dizier with his 14,000 men while Marmont's VI Corps was near Vitry with 12,000 men. Ney had brought his Young Guard divisions, 14,500 strong, up to Chalons and Vitry. Deployed neat St Menehould were the detachments of Sebastiani and Macdonald,

each with around 5,000 men. Mortier had another 20,000 men at Troyes, pursued at leisure by Schwartzenberg.[1]

27 January 1814
INVASION OF FRANCE
Napoleon ordered his army forward, to join battle with Blücher. He pushed forward towards Brienne along roads turned to mud by melting winter snows. Victor had turned his force about and now forced the Allies back out of St Dizier.

28 January 1814
INVASION OF FRANCE
Blücher reached Brienne, having failed to recognise the recapture of St Dizier as the opening of a French attack. Olsufiew's and Sacken's corps led the Prussian advance into and through Brienne.

Bar-le-Duc fell to Yorck's corps of Blücher's army as Marmont fell back.

ITALIAN FRONT
Having switched sides in an effort to protect his own position, Murat led a Neapolitan invasion of the Kingdom of Italy.

29 January 1814
INVASION OF FRANCE
Napoleon, with 36,000 men, attacked Blücher's 25,000 at Brienne. Blücher's force was spread out as it marched upon Paris. Napoleon threw Grouchy in first in a frontal attack to pin down the Prussian force, followed by Ney and Victor as they launched a fierce attack that secured Brienne, Blücher narrowly escaping capture as the French advanced. The Allies then launched a fierce counter-attack, Sacken's corps fighting its way back into Brienne during the night. By midnight the town had changed hands again.

With his flanks threatened by Napoleon's advance, Blücher pulled his men back to regroup, having lost 3,000 men to a French loss of 3,500. Though victorious on the field, Napoleon had failed to defeat Blücher in detail.

Marmont took up strong positions near Joinville and delayed the advance of Yorck's corps, which had linked up with Wrede's force.

30 January 1814
INVASION OF FRANCE
Blücher began to call in his outlying units in order to overwhelm Napoleon's much smaller force, which sat inactive around Brienne. Realising that the Prussian force would soon significantly outnumber his own, Napoleon made preparations to pull back.

St Dizier fell to Yorck's troops as the French pulled out of the town once more.

31 January 1814
INVASION OF FRANCE
Blücher made plans to attack Napoleon. He had assembled 53,000 men from his own army and units drawn in from the Army of Bohemia. There were also the 26,000 men under Wrede and 34,000 under Barclay de Tolly marching to reinforce the Prussians.

1 February 1814
INVASION OF FRANCE
Blücher, having pulled together a force of 85,000 men and 200 cannon, launched a vigorous attack against Napoleon's 45,000 men and 130 cannon deployed around La Rothière, near Brienne. Prevented from conducting his withdrawal, Napoleon was forced to fight a defensive battle. In heavy fighting the French managed to hold off the Prussian attacks until nightfall. He was able to avoid total annihilation by a timely withdrawal during the night but had suffered a heavy defeat, losing 6,000 men and sixty cannon to an Allied loss of 8,000. Blücher continued his push towards Paris along the Marne while Schwartzenberg approached via the Seine.

ITALIAN FRONT
Eugene withdrew his forces from the Adige to the Mincio.

2 February 1814
INVASION OF FRANCE
Napoleon ordered a withdrawal upon Troyes. The Allied pursuit was delayed by a few hours, enabling the bulk of the French forces to disengage unhindered. Wrede pushed his corps forward after Marmont but soon fell behind.

ALLIED COMMAND
After a conference of the Allied commanders, Schwartzenberg issued orders for the armies to separate and follow different axes of advance. Blücher was to push towards Chalons, uniting the corps of Yorck, Kleist, Kapzewitch and Langeron as he advanced. From there he was to then push upon Meaux. Schwartzenberg would continue his advance upon Troyes. Between the two armies, Wittgenstein and Seslawin were to form a connecting screen of cavalry troops.[2]

3 February 1814
INVASION OF FRANCE
The Allied invasion stalled in indecision. As Napoleon withdrew, guessing correctly the Allied intention to split their armies, all Allied knowledge of his movements dried up. Retreating through the course of the day, the French reached Troyes.

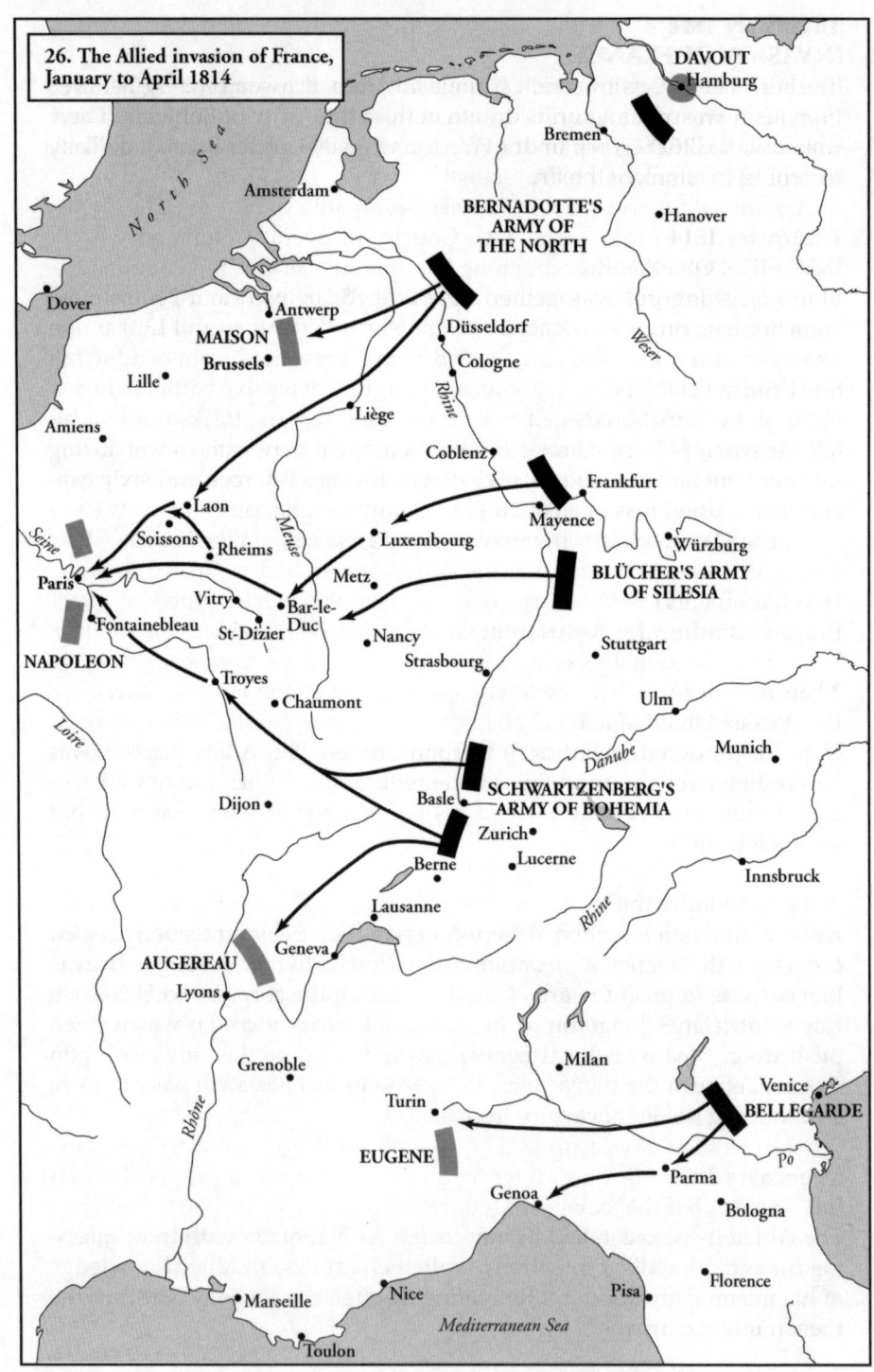

26. The Allied invasion of France,
January to April 1814

North Sea

DAVOUT
Hamburg

Bremen

Amsterdam

Hanover

BERNADOTTE'S
ARMY OF
THE NORTH

Dover

Antwerp

Weser

MAISON

Düsseldorf

Brussels

Cologne

Lille

Rhine

Liège

Amiens

Coblenz

Frankfurt

Laon

Mayence

Würzburg

Luxembourg

BLÜCHER'S ARMY
OF SILESIA

Seine

Soissons

Rheims

Meuse

Metz

Paris

Vitry

Bar-le-
Duc

Nancy

St-Dizier

Stuttgart

Fontainebleau

Strasbourg

NAPOLEON

Troyes

Ulm

Chaumont

Danube

Munich

Loire

SCHWARTZENBERG'S
ARMY OF BOHEMIA

Dijon

Basle

Zurich

Innsbruck

Berne

Lucerne

Lausanne

Rhine

Geneva

AUGEREAU

Lyons

Grenoble

Milan

Venice

Turin

BELLEGARDE

EUGENE

Parma

Po

Genoa

Bologna

Marseille

Nice

Pisa

Florence

Mediterranean Sea

Toulon

4 February 1814
INVASION OF FRANCE
The Allies began a slow and cautious advance. Schwartzenberg believed Napoleon was manoeuvring to attack his lines of communication and, unknown to Blücher, began drawing forces away from the Army of Silesia to protect his flank and rear.

Assembled around Troyes, Napoleon reorganised his army. His cavalry was formed into four corps with Gouchy in overall command while a new VII Corps was raised among the infantry, under the command of Oudinot. This corps was created out of newly arrived troops transferred from Soult's army.

5 February 1814
INVASION OF FRANCE
The Austrian I Corps reached Bar-sur-Seine while the main army continued its leftward movement, away from Blücher's forces. Selaswin was ordered to bring his cavalry across to cover the Austrian right.

Macdonald, with 10,000 men and pursued by General Yorck, abandoned Chalons. Realising that the Allied armies had neglected to maintain the junction between their forces, Napoleon determined to attack Blücher. Blücher decided to unite his main force with Yorck in an effort to destroy Macdonald's retreating unit, pushing his advance forward to Château Thierry. Schwartzenberg's movement to the left had convinced the Prussian that Napoleon had been drawn away from his own army. As yet, Blücher was unaware that his connection with the Army of Bohemia had been broken by Selaswin's movement.

6 February 1814
INVASION OF FRANCE
Leaving behind Mortier to cover Troyes and stop the enemy observing his movement, Napoleon began to pull his forces back in order to redeploy them against Blücher. To prevent any march by the Army of Bohemia to join with the Army of Silesia, Napoleon left Oudinot's VII and Victor's II Corps to watch Schwartzenberg, a total force of around 40,000 men.

7 February 1814
INVASION OF FRANCE
Schwartzenberg closed up to Troyes with his main force and prepared to launch an assault upon the town. Just before he had arrived Mortier had evacuated the town to follow Napoleon. Instead of pursuing, Schwartzenberg ordered his army to rest, and was carefully watched by Oudinot and Victor.

Napoleon marched towards Blücher with Marmont, Ney and Mortier, the latter bringing up the rear.

INTERNATIONAL POLITICS
Despite the continuation of fighting, the Allies offered Caulaincourt, French foreign minister, peace terms to be forwarded to Napoleon. They proposed peace on the basis of France's 1789 borders. The offer was not unanimous though, Tsar Alexander opposing it. Cauliancourt accepted the offer and went to Napoleon for confirmation.

8 February 1814
INVASION OF FRANCE
With Prussian strength building against him, Macdonald had pulled back to Château Thierry. Sacken's corps of Blücher's army was close to Montmirail. Blücher had allowed his army to become overextended as it advanced, being unaware of Napoleon's continuing movement against him.

ITALIAN FRONT
As the Austrians moved up to the Mincio in pursuit of the withdrawing French forces, they suffered a sharp defeat.

9 February 1814
GERMAN FRONT
The Allies, with around 60,000 Russian troops around Hamburg commanded by General Bennigsen, launched a fierce attack upon the city defences. Davout, with his XIII Corps, led a skilful defence and repelled each Allied assault with heavy losses. Holding the walls with the bulk of his force, the French commander also kept a sizeable reserve of men and cannon to rush to any threatened area of the defence line. The Russians were repulsed with heavy losses.

INVASION OF FRANCE
Marmont and Ney closed upon Sezanne. Macdonald continued to draw the Prussians upon him, crossing the Marne after a brief skirmish with Sacken's advance cavalry units.

10 February 1814
INVASION OF FRANCE
Napoleon, with Marmont and Ney forward of a total force of 30,000 available, struck at Blücher's strung out army and defeated Olssufiev's 5,000 Russian troops, deployed close to Champaubert. Rather than withdraw as he should, Olssufiev made a stand and was virtually wiped out, 4,000 of his men being lost. Olssufiev was captured. French losses were fewer than 600 casualties.

After a delay of three days, Schwartzenberg renewed his advance from Troyes. Victor and Oudinot retreated before the Austrian offensive.

11 February 1814
INVASION OF FRANCE

Napoleon, having pushed west with 20,000 men, struck at Sacken's corps of Blücher's army, situated close to Montmirail. The French opened the attack with just 10,000 men but reinforcements quickly brought this up to 20,000. Sacken, with 18,000 men, was defeated and pushed back before Yorck's 20,000 men, held up by a small detachment of Napoleon's main force, could come to his aid. The Prussians suffered around 3,400 casualties to Napoleon's 2,000.

Schwartzenberg continued his advance along the Seine, elements of Wurttemberg's corps crossing at Montereau.

12 February 1814
INVASION OF FRANCE

Napoleon, having been reinforced by the arrival of Mortier to around 30,000 men, attacked and defeated the united but retreating corps of Yorck and Sacken, a total force of around 30,000 men. They were pulling back upon Château Thierry in order to fall back across the Marne river. Ney launched the main French attack, which broke the Allied position. Only the commitment of their artillery reserve prevented the collapse of the Allied positions. The Allies had lost a further 3,000 men for a French loss of just 600.

Victor made a rearguard stand against Schwartzenberg's advance at Nogent. Wittgenstein and Wrede led their corps across the Seine. Schwartzenberg now learned of Olsufiev's defeat.

13 February 1814
INVASION OF FRANCE

Napoleon spent the day regrouping his forces around Château Thierry. He aimed to turn on Schwartzenberg. Blücher had held fast after the defeat at Champaubert and launched an attack against Marmont. Because of this threat, Napoleon decided to issue another blow against Blücher before beginning his movement against Schwartzenberg.

14 February 1814
INVASION OF FRANCE

Napoleon had deployed Marmont with 11,000 men around Vauchamps to guard his positions at Château Thierry. Blücher sent forward Kleist's corps with 21,000 men to push along the road to Montmirail but he ran into Marmont. In a brisk battle the Prussians were badly mauled, their cavalry suffering heavy losses. Napoleon marched to reinforce Marmont but on his approach the Prussians withdrew. He then attempted to cut Blücher's retreat by pushing Grouchy's cavalry forward, but the soaked ground slowed the French advance. After losing 3,200 men in the fighting to a French loss of just 600 men, in a disorganised withdrawal the Prussians also lost large quantities of supplies. Blücher now pulled his forces back, north of the Marne.

Soissons fell to Winzingerode's corps of the Army of Bohemia. The Austrians immediately vacated the town and marched upon Reims.

IBERIAN FRONT
The French garrison of Lerida surrendered.

15 February 1814
INVASION OF FRANCE
Having delayed Blücher for the time being, Napoleon began to redeploy in order to halt the Army of Bohemia's advance along the Seine towards Paris. The inexperienced French troops began a sixty-mile forced march, to be completed in two days.

Napoleon, in an effort to threaten Schwartzenberg's deep lines of communication, ordered Augereau, whose army at Lyon was now 27,000 strong, to attack towards Chalon-sur-Saône.

16 February 1814
INVASION OF FRANCE
The French marched towards the Austrian army, losing stragglers as they went. The young and inexperienced French troops were not used to the rigours of a typical Napoleonic campaign. Schwartzenberg, wanting to avoid contact with Napoleon, issued orders for his forces to begin a limited withdrawal.

IBERIAN FRONT
The French garrison of Monzon surrendered.

17 February 1814
INVASION OF FRANCE
Grouchy and Gerard, with 18,000 men, launched a fierce attack against the Allies and defeated Wrede's advance guard of 4,300 troops at Valjouan. Unfortunately the French were unable to fully concentrate for an assault on Montereau, enabling the Austrians to continue their planned withdrawal. Allied losses were 3,100 killed or wounded while the French lost just 600 men.

GERMAN FRONT
Bennigsen again launched a serious assault upon Hamburg. Davout once more used his central reserve to repel the Allied attacks.

18 February 1814
INVASION OF FRANCE
A full-scale assault by 30,000 French troops upon Montereau, opened by the fire of a massed battery and followed up by a fierce infantry assault, carried the town. In heavy fighting Schwartzenberg lost 6,000 of his 15,000 men and Napoleon 2,500. The Austrians now fully disengaged, pulling back forty miles upon Troyes.

While Napoleon had been tackling Schwartzenberg, Blücher had regrouped and, with 85,000 men, recommenced his march towards Paris.

IBERIAN FRONT
The French garrison of Mequinenza surrendered.

20 February 1814
INVASION OF FRANCE
Schwartzenberg ordered Blücher, currently deployed around Arcis-sur-Aube, to support Wittgenstein's movements as the Army of Bohemia withdrew.

21 February 1814
INVASION OF FRANCE
Augereau had launched half-hearted attacks from Lyon towards Chalon-sur-Saône and Besançon. Napoleon urged him to take more decisive action. Augereau's movements were enough to convince Schwartzenberg to detach additional troops to Dijon to protect his lines of communication.

22 February 1814
INTERNATIONAL POLITICS
The Treaty of Troyes was agreed between Austria, Russia and Prussia on the prosecution of the war on France. Following their series of defeats against Napoleon during the first few weeks of the campaign, the Allied powers again offered Napoleon the opportunity to agree terms on the basis of the 1792 borders. Incredibly, Napoleon rejected the offer, believing he could overcome the Allied armies, despite the fact that France was very obviously exhausted.

25–27 February 1814
IBERIAN FRONT
Wellington defeated Soult at Orthez. Soult lost 4,000 men to a British loss of 2,000 and was forced to fall back upon Toulouse.

26 February 1814
INVASION OF FRANCE
With the Army of Bohemia slowly falling back, Blücher advanced towards Paris, pushing Marmont back before him. Napoleon ordered Oudinot to follow the Austrian retreat upon Bar-sur-Aube. Macdonald was to push towards Chatillon. Napoleon himself was again about to change the axis of operation to attack Blücher.

French deployment against the main Allied forces now consisted of Macdonald with 16,000 men and Oudinot with 27,000 against Schwartzenberg. Marmont and Mortier, deployed near Meaux with 10,000 men, were to operate against Blücher's front. Napoleon, with 35,000 troops, marched into Blücher's rear.[3]

27 February 1814
INVASION OF FRANCE

Realising Napoleon had left his front, Schwartzenberg sent forward the corps of Wittgenstein and Wrede, a force of 26,000, to attack Oudinot. Due to badly placed deployment, Oudinot was only able to bring 18,000 of his men together. While Wrede held the French frontally near Bar-sur-Aube, Wittgenstein attacked their left. Oudinot suffered a severe defeat, losing 3,500 men, and began a retreat towards Troyes. His failure meant Macdonald was also compelled to abandon his positions and conduct an ordered withdrawal upon Troyes.

Blücher had penetrated to La Ferté-sous-Jouarre, just twenty-five miles from Paris. With Blücher so close to Paris, Napoleon rushed north to prevent the capture of the capital.

IBERIAN FRONT

Wellington laid siege to Bayonne.

ITALIAN FRONT

The French defeated an Austrian force at Parma.

GERMAN FRONT

Bennigsen launched a third major assault upon Hamburg during the night. Using flares to light up the attackers, Davout inflicted heavy losses with concentrated cannon fire. Bennigsen was again forced to abandon his assault and now determined to settle down for a prolonged siege.

28 February 1814
INVASION OF FRANCE

Meaux surrendered to Sacken's corps. Marmont launched a rapid counter-attack and drove Sacken's Russian troops back. Blücher meanwhile drew the bulk of his army up to the Marne, unaware that Napoleon was marching against him.

1 March 1814
INVASION OF FRANCE

Having received a communication that Napoleon was operating against him, and not sure of his whereabouts, Blücher decided to pull his forces back behind the Marne. Napoleon approached Blücher's force later that day, just as the last of the Prussian troops evacuated their positions and pulled down the bridges across the river at La Ferté-sous-Jouarre. Due to his lack of bridging equipment, he was unable to follow.

While the main part of the Army of Silesia withdrew, Kleist pushed his corps forward towards Meaux.

INTERNATIONAL POLITICS
To prevent Napoleon's continued efforts to separate the Allies, the leaders of the continental Allies met at Chaumont, agreeing to fight until Napoleon was defeated and not to agree a separate peace.

2 March 1814
INVASION OF FRANCE
Having abandoned the line of the Marne, Blücher began a withdrawal upon Soissons. He expected Winzingerode's and Bulow's corps to link up with him there but was out of touch with them at present.

3 March 1814
INVASION OF FRANCE
Winzingerode, retreating to link up with Blücher, attacked the French garrison of Soissons but was repulsed. Luckily for the Prussians, Soissons surrendered later in the day, the French garrison evacuating the town.

4 March 1814
INVASION OF FRANCE
Blücher had drawn elements of his army back before Soissons and from there continued to fall back upon Fismes. He linked up with Winzingerode, bringing his force up to 70,000 men. Napoleon was attempting to pursue with a smaller force in two parts. He believed Blücher was marching upon Laon.

As Oudinot and Macdonald continued their slow withdrawal, Troyes fell to Schwartzenberg's army. The French were losing many men to desertion and sickness but despite their failing strength Schwartzenberg decided to halt his advance for a week.

5 March 1814
INVASION OF FRANCE
Reims was secured by French troops. Marmont and Mortier launched an attack upon Soissons but were repulsed. Napoleon issued orders for the garrisons of Metz and Mezières to march west into Blücher's rear.

6 March 1814
INVASION OF FRANCE
Napoleon pushed his forces forward towards Laon. Strong resistance was encountered around Craonne. Blücher now understood Napoleon's plan and began turning his own forces so as to fall on the French with his superior numbers.

7 March 1814
INVASION OF FRANCE
Napoleon, with around 45,000 men, forced Blücher's 85,000 back across the Aube to Craonne. While Napoleon attempted to pin the Prussians frontally,

Ney attacked to envelop the flank. Unfortunately the plan misfired, with Blücher aware of his intentions and being heavily outnumbered, Ney attacked too early and suffered severe losses. After a day of bitter fighting, in which the Allied army was driven slowly back by repeated French attacks, Blücher disengaged in good order and began a controlled withdrawal to Laon. Both armies lost around 5,000 men.

ITALIAN FRONT
Murat's advance drove the French out of Para.

8 March 1814
INVASION OF FRANCE
Bernadotte transferred two of his corps to Blücher, giving the Prussian a force of 100,000 men. Napoleon continued to pursue but did not know of the enemy's increase in strength. Napoleon moved against Blücher with 40,000 men while Marmont's 10,000-strong VI Corps was sent around the Prussian left. Blücher deployed Bulow with 17,000 men before Laon while Winzingerode was on the right with 25,000. Holding the left wing were Yorck's and Kleist's corps with a total of 24,000 men. Held in reserve were the corps of Langeron and Sacken, a group of 36,000 men. Fighting broke out during the afternoon as the French closed up to the town and the Allied positions.

NETHERLANDS FRONT
The British began a strong attack against the French forces in Bergen-op-Zoom.

ITALIAN FRONT
British forces led by Lord Bentinck landed at Leghorn.

9 March 1814
INTERNATIONAL POLITICS
The Treaty of Chaumont was concluded. The British, Russians, Austrians and Prussians agree to pursue the war against Napoleon to the very end.

INVASION OF FRANCE
Napoleon attacked Blücher at Laon but his plan to envelop the left flank again failed as Marmont moved late. Swinging around on the flank, Marmont was in contact with the Prussians throughout the afternoon but at dusk he left the field for a comfortable night's sleep. His men failed to post a guard when they settled down for the evening and were therefore taken entirely by surprise by a Prussian cavalry attack. In considerable disorder, the French fled the field and only late in the night was the French force reorganised. However, Marmont had lost 3,500 men and forty-five of his fifty-five guns.

Napoleon's frontal attack had also became bogged down in bitter fighting and failed to drive in the Prussian flanks.

NETHERLANDS FRONT
After heavy casualties the British abandoned their attack on Bergen-op-Zoom.

10 March 1814
INVASION OF FRANCE
Not aware of the scale of Marmont's defeat during the night, Napoleon resumed his attacks at Laon. However, when news of Marmont's disaster came through, a furious Napoleon was forced to redeploy his own forces so as to threaten the Prussian right. However, the Prussians fought the French to a standstill and compelled Napoleon to begin organising a withdrawal. Only the illness of Blücher, who had had to give command over to Gneisenau, prevented Napoleon being totally defeated.

After two days of bloody fighting the French had lost 6,500 men to an Allied loss of just 1,000. Napoleon began to pull his force back upon Soissons. He ordered Marmont and Mortier to move towards Paris to protect the city from Allied attack.

Impatient at Schwartzenberg's delay, Tsar Alexander pressed for a renewal of the advance upon Paris.

11 March 1814
INVASION OF FRANCE
Napoleon, his army down to 24,000 men, was back to the north of Soissons after its defeat at Laon. Marmont was pulling back upon Fismes with the remnants of his force, just 6,000 strong.[4]

12 March 1814
INVASION OF FRANCE
The corps of St Priest, advancing ahead of the main Prussian force towards Chalons, captured Reims. Napoleon, determined to retake the town and inflict a quick defeat on the Army of Silesia, ordered the garrison of Strasbourg to march west to join the main army. The garrisons currently along the Meuse and Moselle were ordered to march to Marmont's aid.

Schwartzenberg, still under pressure from Tsar Alexander to move, began a limited reconnaissance from Troyes.

IBERIAN FRONT
Bordeaux rose against Napoleon, declaring for Louis XVIII. However, the civil authorities only made their move when they were sure that Wellington's army was about to enter the city.

13 March 1814
INVASION OF FRANCE
Napoleon launched a fierce counter-attack with 10,000 men against the 14,000 Prussian troops at Reims. St Priest's corps was hard pressed by the overwhelming French assault, and after a hard fight, fell back. The attack

upon Reims cost the French 700 men. Prussian losses exceeded 6,000 men, including St Priest who was killed in the fighting.

14 March 1814
INVASION OF FRANCE
The remnants of the corps of St Priest retreated to Berry-au-Bac. Napoleon aimed to march south to cut Schwartzenberg's lines of communication and compel him to abandon his advance on Paris. First though he spent a few days reorganising his forces and pulling in units to reinforce his army.

Confident after Napoleon's defeat at Laon, Schwartzenberg launched an attack against Macdonald's weak forces and drove them back across the Seine.

ITALIAN FRONT
Eugene negotiated an armistice in Italy with the Allied powers.

15 March 1814
INVASION OF FRANCE
The Army of Bohemia advanced once more, driving back Macdonald before it.

16 March 1814
INVASION OF FRANCE
Marshal Ney secured Chalons. After reorganising his army, Napoleon began his march towards Arcis-sur-Aube, with 24,000 men, against Schwartzenberg's rear. He left Marmont and Mortier, with a force of 21,000 men, to guard against any renewed attack by Blücher.

Schwartzenberg's forces continued their advance, having pushed Macdonald back to Provins and Montereau. However, news arrived of St Priest's defeat at Reims so the Austrian advance was suspended in order to regroup around Troyes and Arcis-sur-Aube.

17 March 1814
INVASION OF FRANCE
Blücher defeated Marmont at Fismes. Schwartzenberg concentrated his forces around Troyes and Arcis. Napoleon, marching towards the Army of Bohemia, reached Epernay.

IBERIAN FRONT
Bordeaux fell to Wellington's army.

18 March 1814
INVASION OF FRANCE
Schwartzenberg had a change of heart and decided to send his V Corps out to Fère-Champenoise, while other units were in dispersed positions around Arcis-sur-Aube and Troyes. The Austrian commander mistakenly

believed that Napoleon was marching against Blücher once more.

Blücher pressed his advance against Marmont, forcing the French out of Berry-au-Bac. Mortier remained at Reims.

19 March 1814
INVASION OF FRANCE
Schwartzenberg began to move his V and VI Corps north of Arcis-sur-Aube. He was receiving reports that Napoleon was marching upon his positions. Orders were immediately issued for Wrede to pull his forces back from Arcis while the III Corps, IV Corps and VI Corps were to fall back upon Troyes.[5] Napoleon's advance, and the subsequent Austrian withdrawal, had freed the pressure on Macdonald, who was now to advance to catch Wrede between himself and Napoleon.

20 March 1814
INVASION OF FRANCE
Napoleon, with 20,000 men, attacked Wrede's retreating force of 43,000 men at Arcis-sur-Aube. The French drove the Austrians out of the town after a day of bloody fighting. French losses were 2,000 men to an Allied loss of around 1,800.

Marmont began to fall back upon Fismes, Mortier marching from Reims to join with him. Marmont's orders from Napoleon were to protect the approaches to Paris against the Army of Silesia.

21 March 1814
INVASION OF FRANCE
Schwartzenberg, having pulling in his units overnight to give him a strength of 74,000 men, and realising the weakness of the French, repelled the attack of Napoleon's 28,000 and launched a strong counter-attack. Due to Schwartzenberg's slow attack Napoleon, realising the danger, managed to pull most of his forces back, leaving Oudinot to conduct a skilled rearguard action. Schwartzenberg's pursuit was cut short when Oudinot successfully destroyed the bridge over the Aube. French losses were 3,000 men while the Austrians lost 4,000.

Realising that his army was not strong enough to defeat the Allies in a set-piece battle, Napoleon now marched east towards St Dizier to threaten the Allied lines of communication.

Marmont and Mortier reached Château Thierry while elements of Blücher's army began to attack Soissons as well as pursuing the retreating French.

FRANCE: POLITICS
Napoleon ordered the National Guard and citizens of Paris mobilised against Allied attack. Marshal Marmont and Marshal Mortier were to take command. Joseph was installed as Lieutenant General to the Emperor and head of the civil authorities in Paris.

22 March 1814
INVASION OF FRANCE
Macdonald continued to fight a rearguard action at Arcis-sur-Aube. Confusion reigned in the headquarters of the Army of Bohemia as Schwartzenberg could not decide whether to follow Napoleon or continue the advance upon Paris. Napoleon had reached Vitry but an assault failed to take the town so Marshal Ney was left with a covering force while the main body continued their move upon St Dizier.

23 March 1814
INVASION OF FRANCE
Macdonald managed to cross the Marne despite being under continuous attack by Wrede. He was attempting to march to link up with Napoleon, who had reached St Dizier. Napoleon meanwhile had decided to attack Bar-sur-Aube and made preparations for a new march.

The Allies captured a French despatch rider and learned of Napoleon's plans to threaten their lines of communication. However, he was so far in their rear that it was unlikely they would catch him before he could raise fresh forces from his garrisons. The very fact though that he was so far advanced meant that he had placed the Allies between himself and Paris.

24 March 1814
INVASION OF FRANCE
With more intelligence coming in on the state of the French forces and of the ferment building in Paris, Tsar Alexander decided to study all the information available. He realised that Paris was for the taking and that Napoleon should just be masked with minor forces rather than pursued with the main. Conferring with his generals first, he then met King Frederick William of Prussia and Schwartzenberg. The King of Prussia agreed with Alexander, leaving Schwartzenberg with no option than to accept the king's change of plan. He therefore ordered his Army of Bohemia to converge upon La Fére-Champenoise while detaching Winzingerode to watch Napoleon. Orders were sent to Blücher to capture Soissons before moving upon Meaux. Both armies were to join up on 28 March prior to the general advance on Paris. Blücher left Bulow to lay siege to Soissons and then moved with his army.

IBERIAN FRONT
Ferdinand VII returned to Spain, having been released by the French.

25 March 1814
INVASION OF FRANCE
Schwartzenberg launched an overwhelming attack upon the heavily outnumbered corps of Marmont and Mortier at La Fère-Champenoise. The French, attacked throughout the day and forced steadily back, suffered a serious defeat, losing 2,000 killed or wounded and a further 4,000

captured of a total force of 19,000 available.

A second French force of 4,000 men commanded by Pacthod, marching towards Marmont, was also attacked by the Austrian and Russian forces and, forced into defensive squares, was almost destroyed. Allied losses in both actions were no more than 2,000 men.

Napoleon captured Chaumont but became increasingly concerned at the lack of Allied progress against him. Due to Schwartzenberg's usually hesitant approach, he did not consider yet that the Allies were moving upon Paris.

26 March 1814
INVASION OF FRANCE
Napoleon's army reached Vassy and he began to realise that the Allied screen facing him was nothing more than that. Forcing a crossing of the Marne, Napoleon broke Winzingerode's line with his cavalry and inflicted heavy losses as he attempted to pull back upon Bar-le-Duc. The Russian force lost 1,500 men in the brief battle. From captured Russian troops he began to learn that the Allies were marching with their main forces upon Paris.

Under intense Allied pressure Marmont and Mortier pulled their force back to Sezanne but were blocked by advance elements of the Army of Silesia. They then turned towards Provins.

27 March 1814
INVASION OF FRANCE
Napoleon realised his plan to draw the Allies east to protect their lines of communication had not worked, but had in fact placed him too far away from Paris to be able to get back quickly enough to stop the Allies attacking the city. He issued orders to begin a forced march towards the capital by way of Bar-sur-Aube, Troyes and Fontainebleau.

Marmont and Mortier continued their withdrawal upon Paris.

28 March 1814
INVASION OF FRANCE
Schwartzenberg united his army with Blücher's at Meaux and began their march on Paris. Napoleon began a forced march west with his 36,000 men to try and catch the Allies before Paris fell. He and his army were only just setting out from St Dizier.

INTERNATIONAL POLITICS
Realising the desperation of the situation, Napoleon sent Cauliancourt back to the Allies in an effort to reopen negotiations.

29 March 1814
INVASION OF FRANCE
With the enemy at the gates of Paris, Joseph sent Empress Marie-Louise and Napoleon's son to Rambouillet to prevent their capture. Napoleon's

troops reached Troyes after a difficult forced march.

Marmont and Mortier reached Paris ahead of the Allied spearheads. Altogether, a force of 107,000 Allied troops were closing upon the city. Marmont had just 12,000 men and Mortier 11,000. General Moncey commanded the garrison of Paris, a force of 19,000 National Guards.

30 March 1814
INVASION OF FRANCE
General Moncey made a stand at Clichy with his National Guards but was pushed back into Paris. Mortier then vainly attempted to stop the Allied advance at Montmartre while Marmont was driven back from the Belleville Heights. After a day of heavy fighting Marmont opened negotiations with the Allies.

Napoleon, realising he was needed more in Paris than with his army, went on ahead of his advance.

31 March 1814
INVASION OF FRANCE
Marmont negotiated a truce with the Allies, enabling them to enter Paris. In two days of bitter fighting before the capital the French had lost 4,000 men to an Allied loss of 8,000. Marmont's truce left Mortier with no option but to surrender his own force. Joseph Bonaparte fled before the Allied approach.

Napoleon, travelling as quickly as his small guard could go, reached Fontainebleau. He was informed that Marie-Louise and his son had been sent out of the city and that fighting was raging around the capital.

1 April 1814
INVASION OF FRANCE
Learning of Marmont's cessation of hostilities, Napoleon abandoned his rush towards Paris.

INTERNATIONAL POLITICS
The Allies announced they would no longer negotiate with Napoleon or members of his family. They would only recognise the authority of the French Senate. Talleyrand was active in undermining Napoleon's position.

2 April 1814
INVASION OF FRANCE
Napoleon attempted to assemble his forces for an attack aimed at recapturing the capital. He began to meet resistance from the marshals.

INTERNATIONAL POLITICS
Prompted and prodded by Talleyrand, the French Senate voted that Napoleon be deposed of power and invited Louis XVIII to return to claim the throne.

3 April 1814
INVASION OF FRANCE
Talleyrand established a provisional government in Paris. Napoleon began to realise that all was lost but still would not give up the fight.

4 April 1814
INVASION OF FRANCE
Marshals Ney, Berthier, Macdonald, Oudinot and Lefebvre argued with Napoleon to abdicate and end the war. Ney led the argument against continuing military action, informing Napoleon that they, and their troops, would not follow him anymore

INTERNATIONAL POLITICS
Under continued pressure from the marshals, Napoleon agreed to abdicate in favour of his son. The Allies rejected this.

5 April 1814
INVASION OF FRANCE
Having already agreed a truce and ceased hostilities, Marmont surrendered his 11,000 men to the Allies. Napoleon finally accepted that his efforts to continue the fight were in vain and that he needed to come to terms with the Allies.

6 April 1814
INTERNATIONAL POLITICS
Napoleon accepted that he must abdicate unconditionally and surrender to the Allies.

Essentially, the Napoleonic Wars were at an end. Having fought a sometimes brilliant campaign throughout eastern France, Napoleon had been unable to halt the overwhelming strength of the Allied armies. Once Paris fell, and his marshals advocated surrender, even Napoleon knew that the fight was at an end. More than a decade of absolute power had ended in defeat and abdication, and the loss of all that Napoleon had fought for, a dynastic succession for his son.

10 April 1814
IBERIAN FRONT
Wellington, with 50,000 men, attacked Soult's 42,000 well entrenched troops in Toulouse. Wellington delivered his attack from three points. General Hill was to launch a diversionary assault against the western suburbs of the city while Picton attacked from the north. Beresford was to conduct the main assault against the heights overlooking the city to the east in an effort to compel the French to withdraw their forces.

Beresford's first two attacks failed amid fierce French fire. Freire, with Spanish troops, attempted to attack the northern face of Mont Rave, but was routed. The Spanish then abandoned the field in panic. Beresford pushed forward for two miles along a marshy strip of road, past the heavily defended flank of Mont Rave. He reached the southern extremity of the ridge and proceeded to assault the hill. Soult, recognising this as the weakest point in his line, brought up two divisions to provide reinforcement. The French launched a vigorous counter-attack to crush Beresford's extended line but were smashed by disciplined British fire. The French cannon on the hill were overrun and Wellington was able to bring guns to bear upon the city. With his positions thus threatened, Soult was compelled to organise a withdrawal. During the ferocious struggle Wellington had lost 6,700 men but Soult lost 4,000.

11 April 1814
IBERIAN FRONT
Soult evacuated Toulouse as his army withdrew into the interior.

INTERNATIONAL POLITICS
The Treaty of Fontainebleau confirmed the unconditional surrender of France and the abdication of Napoleon. The Allies granted Napoleon the kingdom of Elba, with a guard of 600 men and an income of two million francs a year, to live out his retirement.

12 April 1814
IBERIAN FRONT
Soult surrendered his army to the British when he learned of Napoleon's surrender.

ITALIAN FRONT
Murat continued his attacks against the French in northern Italy, defeating them at Borgo San Donnino.

13 April 1814
FRANCE: POLITICS
During the night Napoleon attempted suicide by taking the vial of poison he carried. He had carried it since his close shave with the Cossacks during the invasion of Russia and, possibly due to its age, it failed to work.

14 April 1814
IBERIAN FRONT
General Thouvenot, commanding the Bayonne garrison, led 5,000 men on a break-out attempt. Despite what appeared to be initial successes, the British rushed up reinforcements and threw the French back into the town. British forces under Hope defeat the French under Thouvenot at Bayonne as they tried to break out. British and French losses were about equal, some 900 men being lost by each force.

15 April 1814
ITALIAN FRONT
There was a minor skirmish between Murat's Neapolitan troops and Eugene's forces in Italy. Murat had been manoeuvring in an effort to avoid making contact with Eugene, despite having declared for the Allies in January.

16 April 1814
ITALIAN FRONT
Informed of Napoleon's abdication, Eugene agreed an armistice with the Austrians.

17 April 1814
ITALIAN FRONT
Eugene surrendered his army to the Austrians.

18 April 1814
ITALIAN FRONT
Genoa surrendered to the British and Sicilians.

20 April 1814
INTERNATIONAL POLITICS
Napoleon set out on his journey to Elba. He reviewed his Old Guard at Fontainebleau before leaving.

25 April 1814
GERMAN FRONT
The Allies informed Davout, still holding out in Hamburg, of Napoleon's abdication. He was unwilling to accept their information and waited for confirmation from France.

26 April 1814
ITALIAN FRONT
Eugene Beauharnais abdicated his position as Viceroy of Italy. He went into exile in Bavaria, being married to the daughter of the King of Bavaria.

27 April 1814
INVASION OF FRANCE
Bayonne surrendered to the British.

30 April 1814
GERMAN FRONT
Having received news from Paris, Davout finally accepted Napoleon's defeat and agreed to surrender Hamburg to the Allies. However, negotiations over the surrender would last through most of May.

3 May 1814
INTERNATIONAL POLITICS
Louis XVIII, brother of the deposed and long deceased Louis XVI, entered Paris.

4 May 1814
INTERNATIONAL POLITICS
Napoleon landed on Elba.

27 May 1814
GERMAN FRONT
Davout marched his men out of Hamburg and back towards France, in possession of their arms and with full military honours. The siege had cost the French 11,000 men lost, mainly due to disease.

Nearly two months after the fall of Napoleon's regime the last of his troops surrendered to the Allies, bringing peace to Europe. What now remained was for the Allies to agree how they should establish a stable and peaceful Europe without the threat of Napoleon to galvanise them into action.

30 May 1814
INTERNATIONAL POLITICS
The First Treaty of Paris between France and the Allied Powers led to the restoration of the Bourbon monarchy on France's 1792 borders.

1 November 1814
INTERNATIONAL POLITICS
The Congress of Vienna opened. Its aim was to settle European affairs following the overthrow of Napoleon's France. Napoleon's bid for power in 1815 interrupted it.

The peace which settled upon Europe was merely temporary. In less than a year Napoleon would set foot on the continent once more, plunging Europe into a final round of bloody conflict.

Notes

1. F Loraine Petre, *Napoleon at Bay*, pp. 17–18
2. Ibid, p. 43
3. Ibid, p. 101
4. Ibid, p. 147
5. Ibid, p. 161

CHAPTER XI

The Hundred Days

After just a few months on Elba, Napoleon felt unable to resist the urge to meddle in the affairs of France. Undertaking an audacious escape from his island prison, he would once more draw men to his cause, turning whole armies sent against him from protectors of their king to loyal soldiers of the emperor. The last bloody chapter of the Napoleonic Wars had begun.

* 1815 *

26 February 1815
THE HUNDRED DAYS CAMPAIGN
Napoleon escaped from Elba with his battalion of 1,000 men and headed for mainland France.

1 March 1815
THE HUNDRED DAYS CAMPAIGN
Napoleon landed at Fréjus, near Cannes, and launched his bid to regain control of France. He began to march upon Paris with his bodyguard.

7 March 1815
THE HUNDRED DAYS CAMPAIGN
General Marchand, sent by the authorities to apprehend Napoleon, deployed his men at Grenoble to oppose Napoleon and his bodyguard. Napoleon marched forward and challenged the men of the 5th Line to kill their emperor. Almost to a man Marchand's force deserted to Napoleon's cause. Marchand fled.

13 March 1815
THE HUNDRED DAYS CAMPAIGN
The Allies, still meeting at the Congress of Vienna, declared Napoleon an international outlaw and enemy of humanity. Marshal Ney was sent south with the task of apprehending Napoleon, defeating his growing army if necessary. Ney promised King Louis XVIII that he would bring Napoleon back to Paris in an iron cage.

15 March 1815
THE HUNDRED DAYS CAMPAIGN
Marshal Ney, sent by Louis XVIII to stop Napoleon, and having promised to bring him to Paris in an iron cage, encountered him at Auxerre. He and his men joined the emperor's march.

19 March 1815
THE HUNDRED DAYS CAMPAIGN
Napoleon reached Fontainbleau. Louis XVIII fled Paris.

ITALIAN FRONT
Muray, King of Naples, attacked Austrians in northern Italy with his army of 40,000 men. He hoped to gain favour with Napoleon.

20 March 1815
THE HUNDRED DAYS CAMPAIGN
Napoleon returned to Paris to the delight of a large part of the population. He declared that he wished only for peace and continued the institution of the Senate and Chamber of Deputies but realised that the Allies were determined to remove him from power.

25 March 1815
ALLIED PLANNING
The Seventh Coalition was formed. The Allies agreed to depose Napoleon and not to make any separate peace. England hurried her best troops to the Netherlands, where a mixed army under Wellington was assembling. The four major powers, Britain, Russia, Prussia and Austria, each promised to field 150,000 men against Napoleon.

FRANCE: ARMED FORCES
Napoleon began a hasty programme to raise and train as many regiments as possible. Only six marshals had responded to his call, Brune, Davout, Mortier, Ney, Soult and Suchet. Napoleon promoted the cavalry commander, General Grouchy, to marshal. Berthier had gone into exile following the accession of the Bourbons to the throne of France so Napoleon appointed Soult his chief of staff, a role he was unaccustomed to.

Napoleon deployed his forces around the nation's borders to protect against Allied invasion while keeping a major part of the army together at Paris to launch an offensive strike.

At Paris there was the Paris Corps, 20,000 men under Marshal Louis Davout, Minister of War and Governor of Paris, while along the Atlantic coast there was the Army of the West with 10,000 men under General Lamarque, on the Rhine at Strasbourg, General Rapp had the 23,000 men of the V Corps of the Army of the North, formed as the Army of the Rhine. In the Jura Mountains there was an observation detachment of 8,400 men commanded by General Lecourbe and in the Alps Marshal Suchet's 23,500 men of the Army of the Alps. Marshal Brune commanded the small 5,500-strong, Army of the Var while there were two armies of the Pyrenees, the Army of the Western Pyrenees with 6,800 men under General Clausel and the Army of the Eastern Pyrenees with 7,600 men under General Decaen. In all Napoleon had mobilised 188,000 men for the field with another 100,000 in garrisons and 300,000 in training camps.

By far the strongest force was the Army of the North, located around Paris, which Napoleon commanded and would personally lead into Belgium. It had some 124,000 men and 350 cannon, deployed between d'Erlon's I Corps, Reille's II Corps, Vandamme's III Corps, Gerard's IV Corps, Lobau's VI Corps, Pajol's I Cavalry Corps, Exelmans' II Cavalry Corps, Kellermann's III Cavalry Corps and Milhaud's IV Cavalry Corps.[1]

ALLIES: ARMED FORCES
In Luxembourg the Prussians deployed the Army of Northern Germany under General Kleist von Nollendorf with 26,000, men, while the Russian armies in central Europe still numbered 200,000 men under the command of Generals Witzingerode (40,000 men) and Barclay de Tolly (with the main body of 167,000 men). On the Upper Rhine, from Mannheim to Basel, the Austrians deployed their I, II, III and IV Corps, a total force of 210,000 men under the command of Schwartzenberg. In Switzerland there was the 37,000-strong Army of Switzerland commanded by General Bachmann while in northern Italy the Austrians deployed their 75,000-strong Army of Upper Italy under General Frimont. In the Netherlands the Allies began to concentrate a British and a Prussian army.

31 March 1815
ITALIAN FRONT
Murat, still ruling his Kingdom of Naples, declared war on Austria in support of Napoleon. Napoleon ignored his offer of support and left Murat to his own devices.

4 April 1815
ITALIAN FRONT
Murat, with 36,000 men, defeated the Austrians outside Modena and captured the town.

NETHERLANDS FRONT
British forces reached Brussels as they deployed forward to the French frontier.

1 May 1815
ITALIAN FRONT
Murat attacked the Austrians at Tolentino but was unable to secure a victory.

2 May 1815
ITALIAN FRONT
The Austrians, with 10,000 men under Bianchi defeated Murat's poorly trained army of Neapolitans at Tolentino. Murat lost 1,700 men killed or wounded and a further 2,400 captured to an Austrian loss of fewer than 800.

19 May 1815
ITALIAN FRONT
Murat fled to France as his army collapsed. He aimed to offer his services to Napoleon.

1 June 1815
THE HUNDRED DAYS CAMPAIGN
Allied forces began to concentrate along the French border. Wellington had assembled 95,000 men and 200 cannon in Belgium, about 30,000 of whom were British, 16,000 Dutch, 15,000 Hanoverian and the remainder from various German states. The British-led army deployed the I Corps under the inexperienced and impetuous Prince of Orange, II Corps under General Hill, a cavalry corps under General Paget and a strong reserve of around 25,000 men under Wellington's personal command.

Blücher had his 124,000 man and 300 cannon-strong Army of the Lower Rhine marching to meet the mixed British force. The Prussian force was deployed in four corps, with the I Corps thrown forward as an advance guard to protect Charleroi.

Napoleon planned to take the offensive, striking into Belgium to defeat the Allies one by one before they could unite.

3 June 1815
ALLIED PLANNING
Blücher and Wellington met to agree their strategy against a possible French attack. It was agreed that in the event of a move against them by Napoleon, Wellington would march his army to join the Prussians

9 June 1815
INTERNATIONAL POLITICS
The Congress of Vienna drew to a conclusion. France had been allowed to keep some of the territories annexed since 1792, mainly thanks to the excellent negotiating skill of Talleyrand. Northern Italy was partitioned between Austria and Piedmont-Sardinia while a Swiss Confederation was formed. In place of the now defunct Confederation of the Rhine a new German Confederation was created. The Austrians failed in their efforts to resurrect the Holy Roman Empire. Poland suffered following her alliance with France, being partitioned between Prussia and Russia.

11 June 1815

THE HUNDRED DAYS CAMPAIGN

Napoleon began his march from Paris. He left the able Davout in charge of the Paris garrison and had appointed Soult as his chief of staff. The flighty Ney and unreliable Grouchy had been appointed corps commanders while Murat's offer of a field command had been refused. Davout, possibly his most able marshal, was left in command of Paris, a grave mistake.

14 June 1815

THE HUNDRED DAYS CAMPAIGN

Napoleon concentrated his force on a fifteen-mile front before Charleroi. Blücher's corps near Charleroi reported the French build up, prompting the Prussian commander to begin moving his other three corps forward to Ligny. A high ranking French deserter confirmed with Blücher that Napoleon planned to launch an invasion of the Netherlands from around Charleroi.

15 June 1815

THE HUNDRED DAYS CAMPAIGN

Napoleon, having quickly concentrated in force before Charleroi, invaded the Netherlands on a six-mile front. Charleroi was quickly captured. Blücher, forewarned, reacted swiftly to Napoleon's move, assembling three of his corps, some 84,000 men, near Sombreffe. Wellington began to concentrate fifteen miles west of the city, believing wrongly that Napoleon intended to cut his lines of communication with the Channel ports. By doing so he was failing to act in accordance with the agreed plan to concentrate upon the Prussian army and inadvertently left the junction of the two armies, at Quatre Bras, very weakly held.

Ney was given command of the I and II Corps on the left wing while Grouchy was to lead the III and IV Corps on the right. Ney was ordered to seize the intersection at Quatre Bras while Grouchy was to push towards Sombreffe. Napoleon pushed up in the centre with the VI Corps, the cavalry reserves and the Imperial Guard.

16 June 1815

THE HUNDRED DAYS CAMPAIGN

Just after noon, having wasted the morning in inaction through his own tardiness and Soult's poor staffwork, Ney launched an attack at Quatre Bras with the II Corps but intended to use the I Corps to roll up the Allied position. Unaware that Napoleon had ordered the I Corps to join his forces, Ney ordered it back towards him. The end result was that d'Erlon's corps fought in neither battle. Ney conducted a poorly devised attack with 24,000 men. In bitter fighting he was held up by the 8,000 men of the heavily outnumbered Nassau Brigade until British reinforcements arrived in the early afternoon. Wellington, realising during the early hours of the morning that he had been outwitted by Napoleon, ordered his army to march east to join up with the Prussians, and in doing so was able to quickly concentrate 32,000 men at Quatre Bras. Ney personally led a series of charges against the Allied line, losing sight of the fact that as army commander he should have retained an independent eye. Enmeshed in the thick of the fighting, Ney was unable to effectively co-ordinate the actions of his forces. The fighting continued until nightfall, by which time Wellington was still in control of Quatre Bras.

Napoleon, with the 57,000 men of the III and IV Corps, attacked Blücher's 81,000 near Ligny. While he held the Prussians frontally, he ordered Ney to strike their flank to wipe out Blücher's army. Unfortunately Ney was unable to manage this, having been held up at Quatre Bras. Napoleon then ordered d'Erlon to strike at the Prussian wing only to find that Ney had ordered him back to aid him at Quatre Bras. Without the option of a flank attack, Napoleon unleashed a series of costly frontal attacks during the afternoon. By evening the Prussian centre had been broken. Blücher led a cavalry counter-attack to restore the situation but was thrown from his horse and ridden over during the charge. Like Ney, Blücher had lost touch with his army command. In the absence of their general, Gneisenau, army chief of staff took command and began to pull the Prussian forces back upon Wavre. Blücher was found by his troops and, wounded, was taken from the field. Prussian losses at Ligny were 15,000 men and twenty cannon while the French lost 11,000 men.

17 June 1815
THE HUNDRED DAYS CAMPAIGN
Napoleon, having delayed overnight, sent Grouchy with 33,000 men to pursue the retreating Prussians. Despite the Prussian head start, Grouchy moved slowly. Napoleon himself moved with the bulk of the army to join Ney in a renewed attack upon Wellington's force at Quatre Bras. With an assurance from the Prussians that they would send two corps to support his army, Wellington began a limited withdrawal along the Brussels road, taking up strong positions on Mont St Jean. Ney delayed any further attacks upon Wellington's forces during the morning, allowing the British to disengage and conduct an ordered withdrawal. Napoleon's arrival in the afternoon prompted Ney into action but by then it was too late

18 June 1815
THE HUNDRED DAYS CAMPAIGN
Wellington had deployed his army of 67,000 infantry, 12,000 cavalry and 200 cannon in a strong defensive position on the ridge of Mont St Jean, using his much practised reverse slope tactic to hide his true strength from the French. The bulk of the Prince of Orange's 31,000 strong I Corps and General Hill's 27,000-strong II Corps were hidden from view. Uxbridge had his 12,000-strong cavalry corps behind the main line while General Picton held in reserve some 23,000 men of his corps. Wellington protected the approaches by heavily fortifying the farmsteads to his front. The first

British defence line rested on the Château du Hougomont on the right wing, and Le Haye Saint, a walled farm, on the left. Concerned to cover a line of retreat to the Channel coast, Wellington had placed a force of more than 15,000 men at Hale, eight miles to the west of his main body.

Napoleon, with 74,000 men, planned to attack Wellington frontally in order to break the British centre. The II Corps was deployed on the French left wing and was tasked with taking Hougomont to divert British attention from the main attack by the I Corps on the centre and right. The main attack by d'Erlon's I Corps was supported by a massed battery of eighty cannon. Concentrated cavalry formations protected the French flanks. In a second line Napoleon placed the VI Corps while the Imperial Guard was held in reserve. Ney was give battlefield command, despite his less than brilliant actions during the campaigns of 1813 and at Quatre Bras just two days before.

Planning to attack early, Napoleon was forced to delay the assault to allow the ground to dry, it having rained heavily overnight. Grouchy continued to follow the recovered Blücher but was unaware that the Prussians had rallied and were now marching west to join Wellington.

Napoleon attacked at noon, sending units forward against Hougomont. Rather than drawing British units away from the centre the tenacious British defence drew in more and more French units. After an hour the main French attack began. Four columns of infantry marched towards Le Haye Saint but were mauled by British counter-fire. The British cavalry then charged forward but pushed too far and were attacked by French cavalry, suffering heavy losses.

While the I Corps conducted its attack, Napoleon was made aware of the Prussian advance from the east, against his right wing. While Grouchy continued his slow pursuit of the Prussian rearguard at Wavre, Blücher had force marched his main body towards Wellington.

In an effort to defeat Wellington before Blücher could arrive, Napoleon ordered an all-out assault on Le Haye Saint but Ney, mistaking a British reorganisation of the line for a full-scale withdrawal, launched a massive, totally unsupported cavalry attack. The British deployed into squares and repulsed each French assault, inflicting heavy losses. Ney renewed his attack upon Le Haye Saint with massed infantry and after very hard fighting managed to capture the farm. Requesting reinforcements to exploit his advantage, Napoleon could not supply anything. With the VI Corps in the second line, Napoleon had had to pull it around on to his right wing to build a protected flank against the approach of the Prussians. Heavy fighting developed against the Prussian advance guards at Plancenoit, and as more came forward the town was taken. With just the Young and Old Guard left in reserve, Napoleon threw the Young Guards into a counterattack, recapturing Plancenoit. However, the Prussians now had the I, IV and II Corps present against the French right wing and in a fierce assault carried Plancenoit again. Napoleon then threw in part of the Old Guard and captured Plancenoit once more.

Assailed on both his front and right wing, Napoleon committed the remainder of the Old Guard against Wellington. In a furious musketry barrage the British repulsed the Guards, which broke and heralded the collapse of the entire French position. With the VI Corps forming a desperate rearguard, the French army streamed back towards Charleroi, discipline broken. The Allied armies now began to attack along the entire length of the line and by 9pm had joined up at La Belle Alliance.

Napoleon, with a small bodyguard, joined the rout towards Charleroi. In one of the bloodiest battles of the Napoleonic age, the Allies had halted Napoleon's gamble for good. French losses had been very heavy at 25,000 killed or wounded and 7,000 captured while the British lost 15,000 men and the Prussians 7,000.

At Wavre, Grouchy learned of Napoleon's defeat and began to withdraw.

19 June 1815
THE HUNDRED DAYS CAMPAIGN
Napoleon left Charleroi for Paris, intending to raise another army. The Allies began their invasion of France, forces moving forward between Sedan and Basel.

20 June 1815
THE HUNDRED DAYS CAMPAIGN
Mezières, Montmédy and Strasbourg were besieged by the Allies.

Back in Paris, the civil authorities denied Napoleon authorisation to raise fresh troops. Davout and Lucien Bonaparte urged Napoleon to install himself as dictator but he declined. Davout, who had left Paris following the defeat at Waterloo, was gathering a new army in the Loire valley to fight the Allied advance upon Paris.

21 June 1815
THE HUNDRED DAYS CAMPAIGN
Returning to Paris ahead of the slower Allies, Napoleon realised his intention to raise new forces was impossible without precipitating a civil war throughout France. An ultimatum by the Chamber of Deputies, led by Joseph Fouché and the Marquis de Lafayette, demanded that he either resign or be deposed. Marshal Davout moved his army forward in an effort to delay the Allies but was unable to hold back the massive strength of the Allied forces.

22 June 1815
THE HUNDRED DAYS CAMPAIGN
Napoleon abdicated for a second time. The Chamber of Deputies proposed to elect a Council of Regency in favour of Napoleon's son. Fouché and Lafayette pressed for the return of Louis XVIII.

27 June 1815
THE HUNDRED DAYS CAMPAIGN
The French defeated a Prussian force at Senlis while a French force was defeated at Villers-Cotterets. Davout, fighting a skilful delaying action against the Allied armies west of Paris, learned of Napoleon's abdication and resigned his command in disgust.

28 June 1815
THE HUNDRED DAYS CAMPAIGN
Austrian troops captured Montbéliard while the French were defeated at Soissons.

29 June 1815
THE HUNDRED DAYS CAMPAIGN
French forces were defeated at La Souffel as the Allies began their encirclement of Paris. Napoleon left the city to avoid capture.

3 July 1815
THE HUNDRED DAYS CAMPAIGN
Allied forces completed the encirclement of Paris. To avoid bloodshed, the Convention of St Cloud was signed, which allowed the French forces in Paris to withdraw. The French Provisional Government finally recognised Louis XVIII. Napoleon reached Rochefort, where Joseph had a ship ready to take him to America. He refused to leave aboard it.

7 July 1815
THE HUNDRED DAYS CAMPAIGN
The Allies and Louis XVIII entered Paris.

9 July 1815
THE HUNDRED DAYS CAMPAIGN
Piedmontese forces, having invaded France, captured Grenoble.

11 July 1815
THE HUNDRED DAYS CAMPAIGN
Lyon fell to Austrian forces.

15 July 1815
THE HUNDRED DAYS CAMPAIGN
Napoleon, realising there would be no escape, surrendered to the British at Rochefort. He boarded HMS *Bellerophon*, which set sail for Plymouth.

Napoleon's fall from power was now complete. Never again would he be able to loose his unbridled ambition upon the people and nations of Europe.

24 July 1815
THE HUNDRED DAYS CAMPAIGN
Strasbourg surrendered to the Allies.

2 August 1815
THE HUNDRED DAYS CAMPAIGN
The Allies declared Napoleon a prisoner of war. Britain was given responsibility for finding a secure place for him to be imprisoned. They selected St Helena.

7 August 1815
THE HUNDRED DAYS CAMPAIGN
Napoleon, having been transferred aboard HMS *Northumberland*, sailed to St Helena.

26 August 1815
THE HUNDRED DAYS CAMPAIGN
The French troops in Huningen, having held out against the Allies since 1813, finally surrendered.

1 September 1815
THE HUNDRED DAYS CAMPAIGN
Mezières surrendered to the Allies.

13 September 1815
THE HUNDRED DAYS CAMPAIGN
Montmédy surrendered to the Allies as French resistance finally came to an end.

13 October 1815
Murat was tried and shot by the Allies.

17 October 1815
Napoleon landed on St Helena.

22 October 1815
Wellington was appointed commander in chief of the Allied armies in occupation of France.

20 November 1815
The Second Treaty of Paris finally ended hostilities between the Allies and France and reduced France's borders to those of 1790. The Quadruple Alliance between Britain, Austria, Prussia and Russia ensured the terms of the treaty would be enforced.

7 December 1815
Ney was executed following a lengthy trial.

5 May 1821
Napoleon died on St Helena.

The Revolutionary and Napoleonic Wars encompassed a quarter century of European history, and included some of the most spectacular campaigns in military history. From the citizen armies of the revolutionary period, to the professional organisation honed and used by Napoleon to devastating effect, the French had forced the often defeated armies of her enemies to adapt to their methods. Military organisation had developed to new levels, command and control had proved decisive.

However, it was the sheer brilliance of Napoleon, his overwhelming personal ambition and desire for power, which had kept the French at war with their neighbours for so long. Only by realising that they could only undermine Napoleon by defeating his generals, and acting in co-operation with each other, had the Allies proved victorious.

Note

1. Haythornthwaite, *Napoleon's Military Machine*, p. 189

Bibliography

Arnold, J R, *Crisis on the Danube*, London, 1990

Best, G (ed.), *The Permanent Revolution: The French Revolution and its Legacy, 1789–1989*, London,1989

Bertaud, J, *The Army of the French Revolution: from Citizen Soldiers to Instrument of Power*, Princeton NJ, 1988

Blanning, T C W, *The French Revolutionary Wars, 1787–1802*, London 1996

Cauliancourt, A de, *With Napoleon in Russia*, New York, 1935

Chandler, D G, *The Campaigns of Napoleon*, London, 1967

Clausewitz, C von, *The Campaign of 1812 in Russia*, 1995

Collins, I, *Napoleon, First Consul and Emperor of the French*, London, 1986

Connelly, O, *The French Revolution & Napoleonic Era*, 2000

Duffy, C, *Austerlitz 1805*, London 1977

Dupuy, R E & Dupuy, T N, *Encyclopedia of Military History*, London,1993

Elting, J R, *Swords Around the Throne: Napoleon's Grande Armée*, London 1988

Emsley, C, *The Longman Companion to Napoleonic Europe*, London, 1993

Esdaile, C J, *The Wars of Napoleon*, 1995

Gates, D, *The Spanish Ulcer*, London 1986

Haythornthwaite, P J, *Napoleon's Military Machine*, London, 1988

_____*Wellington's Military Machine*, London, 1989

_____*The Napoleonic Wars Source Book*, London, 1990

Jones, R B, *Napoleon, Man & Myth*, London, 1977

Koch, H W, *History of Warfare*, London, 1987

Lawford, J P, *Napoleon: The Last Campaigns 1813–1815*, New York 1977

Mahan, A T, *The Influence of Seapower upon the French Revolution and Empire,1793–1812*, London, 1892

Maude, F N, *The Ulm Campaign, 1805*, London, 1912

_____*The Jena Campaign, 1806*, London, 1909

Oliver, M & Partridge, R, *Napoleonic Army Handbook: The French Army and her Allies*, London, 2002

Partridge, R & Oliver, M, *Napoleonic Army Handbook: The British Army and her Allies*, London, 1999

Petre, F Loraine, *Napoleon's Campaign in Poland 1806–1807*, London, 1989

_____*Napoleon & the Archduke Charles*, London, 1991

_____*Napoleon's Conquest of Prussia 1806*, London, 1993

_____*Napoleon at Bay 1814*, London, 1994

_____*Napoleon's Last Campaign in Germany 1813*, London, 1974

Rothenberg, G E, *The Napoleonic Wars*, London, 2001

_____*The Art of War in the Age of Napoleon*, London, 1977

Index